Praise for *UML 2 and the Unified Pro*

"OMG's UML 2 standard defines UML very systematically anu uioroughly, but lacks how to actually apply UML 2 in a real-world project. That is where *UML 2 and the Unified Process, Second Edition,* comes in. The book manages to convey the practical use of UML 2 in clear and understandable terms with many examples and guidelines. Even for people not working with the Unified Process, the book is still of great use. *UML 2 and the Unified Process, Second Edition,* is a must-read for every UML 2 beginner and a helpful guide and reference for the experienced practitioner."

> —Roland Leibundgut, Technical Director, Zühlke Engineering Ltd.

"The authors provide great detail on the constructs of the UML and how they support the Unified Process. This book is a good starting point for organizations and individuals who are adopting UP and need to understand how to provide visualization of the different aspects needed to satisfy it."

> —Eric Naiburg
> Market Manager, Desktop Products
> IBM Rational Software

"Many books today cover either UML or the Unified Process (UP), but not both. Arlow and Neustadt have filled this void with a book that is a perfect blend of UML and the UP. The authors provide a wealth of experience invaluable to novice modelers and seasoned OO analysts and designers. The logical organization based on the UP workflows and the unique presentation style of using activity diagrams to provide book and chapter overviews make reading less demanding. Both practitioners and students will certainly keep this book within close reach all the time."

> —Ishan De Silva
> Software Engineer
> Millennium Information Technologies, Sri Lanka

"If you are looking for a cookbook, read something else. This book will make you think! It explains all the syntactic elements of UML, but more importantly it gives practical advice on how and when to use—or not to use—UML. You will learn to think about the role that modeling plays in the development process. This knowledge enables you to decide for yourself how and when to use UML to gain the optimal situation for your project. *UML 2 and the Unified Process, Second Edition,* will prepare you for successfully using UML."

> —Jos Warmer
> Ordina System Integration & Development, The Netherlands

"The authors have crafted a book that brings two important topics, UML and the Unified Process, together in one volume. *UML 2 and the Unified Process* is an excellent reference for UML 2. It tells you what UML can do and how to apply it to the analysis and design disciplines of the Unified Process. This book belongs on every professional's bookshelf."

> —Gary Pollice
> Professor of Practice, Computer Science
> Worcester Polytechnic Institute

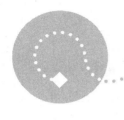

UML 2 and
the Unified Process,
Second Edition

The Addison-Wesley Object Technology Series

Grady Booch, Ivar Jacobson, and James Rumbaugh, Series Editors
For more information, check out the series web site at www.awprofessional.com/otseries.

The Component Software Series

Clemens Szyperski, Series Editor
For more information, check out the series web site at www.awprofessional.com/csseries.

JIM ARLOW AND ILA NEUSTADT

UML 2 and the Unified Process, Second Edition

Practical Object-Oriented Analysis and Design

✦Addison-Wesley

Upper Saddle River, NJ • Boston• Indianapolis • San Francisco
New York • Toronto • Montreal • London • Munich • Paris • Madrid
Capetown • Sydney • Tokyo • Singapore • Mexico City

The publisher offers excellent discounts on this book when ordered in quantity for bulk purchases or special sales, which may include electronic versions and/or custom covers and content particular to your business, training goals, marketing focus, and branding interests. For more information, please contact:

U.S. Corporate and Government Sales
(800) 382-3419
corpsales@pearsontechgroup.com

For sales outside the U.S., please contact:

International Sales
international@pearsoned.com

Visit us on the Web: www.awprofessional.com

Library of Congress Cataloging-in-Publication Data

Arlow, Jim, 1960-
    UML 2 and the unified process : practical object-oriented analysis and design / Jim Arlow, Ila Neustadt.—
    2nd ed.
         p.   cm.
    Includes bibliographical references and index.
    ISBN 0-321-32127-8 (pbk. : alk. paper)
      1. Object-oriented methods (Computer science)   2. Computer software--Development.   3. UML (Computer science)   I. Neustadt, Ila.   II. Title.

QA76.9.O35A74 2005
005.1'1—dc22

2005004126

ISBN   0-321-32127-8

Text printed in the United States on recycled paper at Courier in Westford, Massachusetts.

Tenth printing, October 2014

To our parents

Contents

Acknowledgments

We would like to thank Fabrizio Ferrandina, Wolfgang Emmerich, and our friends at Zühlke Engineering for encouraging us to create the UML training course that led to this book. Special thanks to Roland Leibundgut of Zühlke for his comments on the use case chapters and to Jos Warmer and Tom Van-Court for their insightful comments on the OCL chapter. Thanks are also due to our other technical reviewers, Glen Ford, Birger Møller-Pedersen, Rob Pettit, Gary Pollice, Ishan De Silva, and Fred Waskiewicz. Thanks to Sue and David Epstein for essential nontechnical support throughout the course of the project. Thanks to Andy Pols for sharing his thoughts on use cases and software engineering with us. Thanks to Lara Wysong, Mary Lou Nohr, and Kim Arney Mulcahy at Addison-Wesley for their great work on the text, and to our editor, Mary O'Brien. Thanks to the Neustadt family for their patience and to Al Toms for light relief. And thanks to our cats, Homer, Paddy, and Meg, for the many hours they spent sleeping on the various drafts of the manuscript, thereby imbuing it with that "quality without a name".

Finally, we must acknowledge the "Three Amigos"—Grady Booch, Jim Rumbaugh, and Ivar Jacobson—for their fine work on UML and UP that this book is all about.

Preface

About this book

The aim of this book is to take you through the process of object-oriented (OO) analysis and design using the Unified Modeling Language (UML) and the Unified Process (UP).

UML provides the visual modeling language for OO modeling, and UP provides the software engineering process framework that tells you how to perform OO analysis and design.

There is a lot to UP, and in this book we present only those aspects directly pertinent to the work of the OO analyst/designer. For details on the other aspects of UP, you should refer to [Rumbaugh 1] and the other UP books in the bibliography.

In this book we show you enough UML and associated analysis and design techniques so that you can apply modeling effectively on a real project. According to Stephen J Mellor [Mellor 1], there are three approaches to UML modeling.

- UML as a sketch – this is an informal approach to UML where diagrams are sketched out to help visualize a software system. It's a bit like sketching an idea for something on the back of a napkin. The sketches have little value beyond their initial use, are not maintained, and are finally discarded. You typically use whiteboards or drawing tools such as Visio and PowerPoint (www.microsoft.com) to create the informal sketches.

- UML as a blueprint – this is a more formal and precise approach whereby UML is used to specify a software system in detail. This is like a set of architect's plans or a blueprint for a machine. The UML model is actively maintained and becomes an important deliverable of the project. This approach demands the use of a real modeling tool such as Rational Rose (www.rational.com) or MagicDraw UML (www.magicdraw.com).

- UML as executable – using Model Driven Architecture (MDA), UML models may be used as a programming language. You add enough detail to UML models so that the system can be compiled from the model. This is the most formal and precise use of UML, and, in our view, it is the future of software development. In this approach, you need an MDA-enabled UML tool such as ArcStyler (www.arcstyler.com). MDA is beyond the scope of this book, although we discuss it briefly in Section 1.4.

Our focus in this book is on UML as a blueprint. The techniques you learn will also apply to using UML as an executable. Having learned UML as a blueprint, you will naturally be able to use UML as a sketch should you need to.

We have tried to make our presentation of UML and UP as straightforward and accessible as possible.

Conventions

To help you navigate through the book we have provided each chapter with a roadmap in the form of a UML activity diagram. These diagrams indicate reading activities and the order in which sections might be read. We cover activity diagrams in detail in Chapter 14, but Figure 1 should be sufficient to let you understand the roadmaps.

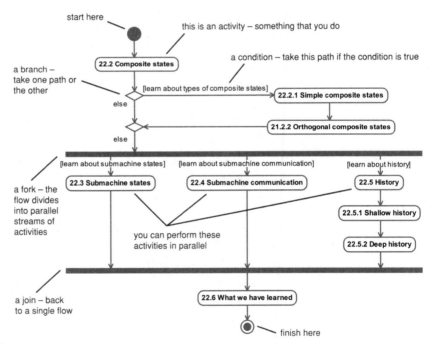

Figure 1

Most of the diagrams in this book are UML diagrams. The annotations, in blue, are not part of UML syntax.

We have provided notes in the margin to highlight important information. We have used the UML note icon for this. An example is shown in the margin.

Notes indicate important information.

We have used different fonts throughout the book:

This font is for UML modeling elements.
This font is for code.

Who should read this book

We can think of several possible readers for this book.

- You are an analyst/designer who needs to learn how to perform OO analysis and design.
- You are an analyst/designer who needs to learn how to perform OO analysis and design within the framework of the Unified Process.
- You are a student taking a UML course at a university.
- You are a software engineer who needs a UML reference.
- You are a software engineer taking a UML training course, and this is your course book.

Clear View Training provides a four-day UML training course based on this book. This course is given throughout Europe by our partners, Zühlke Engineering (www.zuhlke.com), and is available for licensing. If you are an academic institution using this book as your course book, you can use our training course for free. See www.clearviewtraining.com for more on commercial and academic licensing.

How to read this book

So many books, so little time to read them all! With this in mind we have designed this book so that you can read it in several different ways (as well as cover to cover) according to your needs.

Fast track

Choose Fast Track if you just want an overview of the whole book or a particular chapter. This is also the "management summary".

- Choose a chapter.
- Read the chapter roadmap so that you know where you're going.
- Go through the chapter looking at the figures and reading the margin notes.

- Read the "What we have learned" section.
- Go back to any section that takes your interest and read it.

Fast Track is a quick and efficient way to read this book. You may be pleasantly surprised at how much you can pick up! Note that Fast Track works best if you can first formulate a clear idea of the information you want to obtain. For example "I want to understand how to do use case modeling."

Reference

If you need to know a particular part of UML or learn a particular technique, we have provided a detailed index and table of contents that should help you locate the information you need quickly and efficiently. The text is carefully cross-referenced to help you to do this.

Revision

There are two strategies for revision with this text.

- If you need to refresh your knowledge of UML as quickly and efficiently as possible, read the outline summaries of each chapter in the "What we have learned" section. When you don't understand something, go back and read the appropriate section.
- If you have more time, you can also browse through each chapter studying the diagrams and reading the margin notes.

Dipping

If you have a few minutes to spare, you might pick up the book and open it at random. We have tried to ensure that there is something interesting on every page. Even if you already know UML quite well, you may still discover new things to learn.

Book roadmap

Figure 2 shows a roadmap for this book. We have indicated where chapters may be read in any order and where there are advanced techniques that you may choose to skip on first reading.

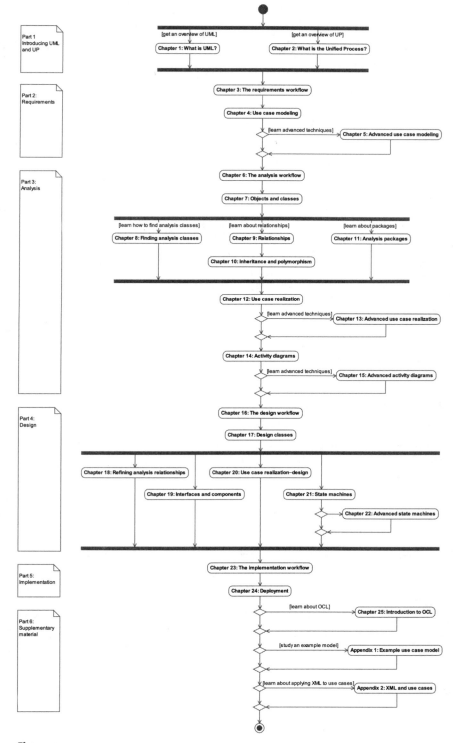

Figure 2

part **1**

Introducing
UML and UP

chapter 1
What is UML?

1.1 Chapter roadmap

This chapter provides a brief overview of the history and high-level structure of the UML. We mention many topics that will be expanded in later chapters.

Beginners should start by learning about UML history and principles. If you have experience in UML, or are satisfied that you already know enough about UML history, you can skip straight to Section 1.7 and the discussion of UML structure. There are three main strands to this discussion, which may be read in any order. You can find out about UML building blocks (1.8), UML common mechanisms (1.9), and architecture and UML (1.10).

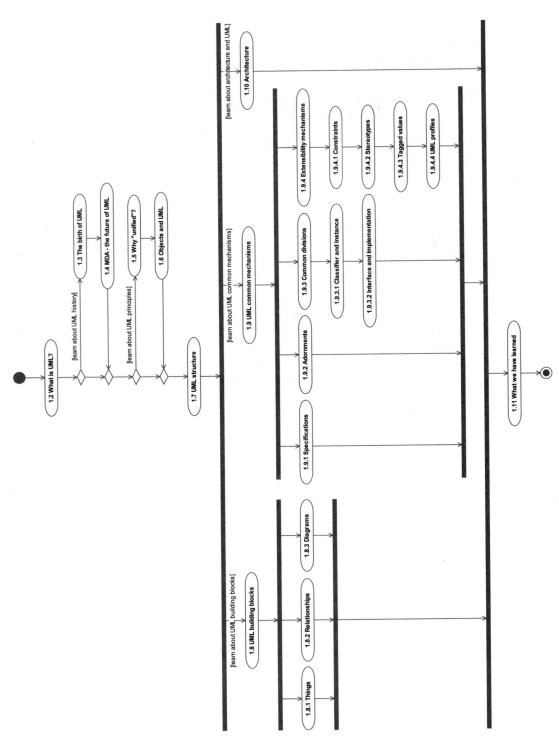

Figure 1.1

1.2   What is UML?

The Unified Modeling Language (UML) is a general-purpose visual modeling language for systems. Although UML is most often associated with modeling OO software systems, it has a much wider application than this due to its inbuilt extensibility mechanisms.

UML was designed to incorporate current best practice in modeling techniques and software engineering. As such, it is explicitly designed to be implemented by UML modeling tools. This is in recognition of the fact that large, modern software systems generally require tool support. UML diagrams are human-readable and yet are easily rendered by computers.

It is important to realize that UML does *not* give us any kind of modeling methodology. Naturally, some aspects of methodology are implied by the elements that comprise a UML model, but UML itself just provides a visual syntax that we can use to construct models.

> UML is not a methodology – it is a universal visual modeling language. UP is a methodology.

The Unified Process (UP) *is* a methodology—it tells us the workers, activities, and artifacts that we need to utilize, perform, or create in order to model a software system.

UML is *not* tied to any specific methodology or life cycle, and indeed it is capable of being used with all existing methodologies. UP uses UML as its underlying visual modeling syntax and you can therefore think of UP as being the *preferred* method for UML, as it is the best adapted to it, but UML itself can (and does) provide the visual modeling support for other methods. For a specific example of a mature methodology that also uses UML as its visual syntax, see the OPEN (Object-oriented Process, Environment, and Notation) method at www.open.org.au.

The goal of UML and UP has always been to support and encapsulate best practice in software engineering based on the experience of the last decade. To do this UML and UP *unify* previous attempts at visual modeling languages and software engineering processes into a best-of-breed solution.

1.3   The birth of UML

Prior to 1994, the OO methods world was a bit of a mess. There were several competing visual modeling languages and methodologies all with their strengths and weaknesses and all with their supporters and detractors. In terms of visual modeling languages (summarized in Figure 1.2), the clear leaders were Booch (the Booch Method) and Rumbaugh (Object Modeling Technique or OMT), who between them had over half the market. On the methodologies side, Jacobson had by far the strongest case as although many

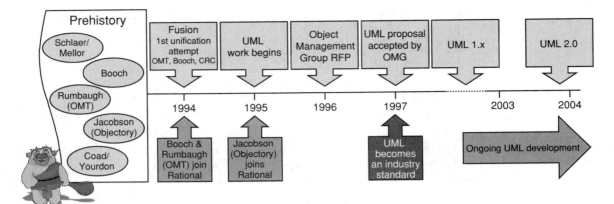

Figure 1.2

authors claimed to have a "method", all that many of them actually had was a visual modeling syntax and a collection of more or less useful aphorisms and guidelines.

> UML is the open, industry-standard visual modeling language approved by the OMG.

There was a very early attempt at unification in 1994 with Coleman's fusion method. However, although laudable, this attempt did not involve the original authors of the constituent methods (Booch, Jacobson, and Rumbaugh) and was also quite late to market with a book explaining the approach. Fusion was rapidly overtaken by the course of events when, in 1994, Booch and Rumbaugh joined Rational Corporation to work on UML. This worried a lot of us at the time, as it gave Rational over half the methods market. However, these fears have proved to be entirely unfounded and UML has since become an open industry standard.

In 1996, the Object Management Group (OMG) produced a request-for-proposal (RFP) for an OO visual modeling language, and UML was submitted. In 1997, OMG accepted the UML and the first open, industry-standard OO visual modeling language was born. Since then, all of the competing methods have faded away and UML stands unchallenged as the industry standard OO modeling language.

In 2000, UML 1.4 introduced a significant extension to UML by the addition of action semantics. These describe the behavior of a set of primitive actions that may be implemented by specific action languages. Action semantics plus an action language allow the detailed specification of the behavioral elements of UML models (such as class operations) *directly* in the UML model. This was a very significant development as it made the UML specification computationally complete and thus it became possible to make UML models executable. For an example of a UML implementation that has an action semantics-compliant action language, see xUML from Kennedy Carter (www.kc.com).

As we update this book to its second edition, it is 2005 and the UML 2.0 specification has been finalized. UML is now a very mature modeling language. It has been almost seven years since its initial release, and it has proven its value in thousands of software development projects worldwide.

UML 2 introduces quite a lot of new visual syntax. Some of this replaces (and clarifies) existing 1.x syntax, and some of it is completely new and represents new semantics added to the language. UML has always provided many options about how a particular model element may be displayed, and not all of these will be supported by every modeling tool. We try to use the most common syntactic variants consistently throughout this book, and highlight other variants where we feel that they serve a useful purpose in common modeling situations. Some syntactic options are quite specialized and so we mention them only in passing, if at all.

Although UML 2 makes many syntactic changes to UML compared to UML 1.x, the good news is that the fundamental principles remain more or less the same. Modelers who are accustomed to using previous versions of UML should experience an easy transition to UML 2. In fact, the deepest changes introduced in UML 2 have been to the UML metamodel and will not be encountered directly by most modelers. The UML metamodel is a model of the UML language that is itself expressed in a subset of UML. It precisely defines the syntax and semantics of all of the UML modeling elements that you will encounter in this book. These changes to the UML metamodel have largely been about improving the precision and consistency of the UML specification.

In one of his books, Grady Booch says "If you have a good idea then it's mine!" In a way this summarizes the UML philosophy—it takes the best of that which has gone before and integrates and builds on it. This is reuse in its broadest sense, and the UML incorporates many of the best ideas from the "prehistoric" methods while rejecting some of their more idiosyncratic extremes.

1.4 MDA – the future of UML

The future of UML may be defined by a recent OMG initiative called Model Driven Architecture (MDA). Although this isn't an MDA book, we will give a very brief overview of MDA in this section. You can find more information on the OMG's MDA website (www.omg.org/mda) and in *MDA Explained* [Kleppe 1] and *Model Driven Architecture* [Frankel 1].

MDA defines a vision for how software can be developed based on models. The essence of this vision is that models drive the production of the executable software architecture. To some extent this happens today, but

MDA mandates a degree of automation of this process that is, as yet, rarely achieved.

In MDA, software is produced through a series of model transformations aided by an MDA modeling tool. An abstract computer-independent model (CIM) is used as a basis for a platform-independent model (PIM). The PIM is transformed into a platform-specific model (PSM) that is transformed into code.

The MDA notion of model is quite general, and code is considered to be just a very concrete kind of model. Figure 1.3 illustrates the MDA model transformation chain.

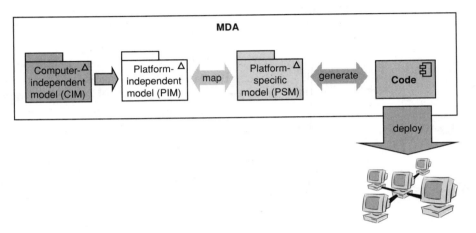

Figure 1.3

The CIM is a model at a very high level of abstraction that captures key requirements of the system and the vocabulary of the problem domain in a way that is *independent* of computers. It is really a model of that part of the business that you are going to automate. Creation of this model is optional, and if you choose to create it, you use it as a basis for producing the PIM.

The PIM is a model that expresses the business semantics of the software system independently of any underlying platform (such as EJB, .NET, and so on). The PIM is generally at roughly the same level of abstraction as the analysis model that we will talk about later in this book, but it is more complete. This is necessarily so, as it has to provide a sufficiently complete basis to be transformed into a PSM from which code can be generated. A point worth noting is that the term "platform independent" means very little unless you define the platform or platforms from which you wish to be independent! Different MDA tools support different levels of platform independence.

The PIM is adorned with platform-specific information to create the PSM. Source code is generated from the PSM against the target platform.

In principle, 100% of the source code and ancillary artifacts such as documentation, test harnesses, build files, and deployment descriptors can be generated from a sufficiently complete PSM. If this is to happen, the UML model must be made *computationally complete*—in other words, the semantics of all operations must be specified in an action language.

As we mentioned earlier, some MDA tools already provide an action language. For example, the iUML tool from Kennedy Carter (www.kc.com) provides Action Specification Language (ASL) that complies with UML 2 action semantics. This action language is at a higher level of abstraction than languages such as Java and C++, and you can use it to create computationally complete UML models.

Other MDA tools, such as ArcStyler (www.io-software.com), allow generation of between 70% and 90% of the code and other artifacts, but operation bodies still have to be completed in the target language (e.g., Java).

In the MDA vision, source code, such as Java and C# code, is just the "machine code" resulting from the compilation of UML models. This code is generated as needed directly from the PSM. As such, code has an intrinsically lower value in MDA development than UML models. MDA shifts UML models from their current role as precursors to manually created source code into the primary mechanism of code production.

As we go to press, more and more modeling tool vendors are adding MDA capabilities to their products. You should check out the OMG MDA website for the latest details. There are also some very promising open source MDA initiatives, for example, the Eclipse Modeling Framework (www.eclipse.org/emf) and AndroMDA (www.andromda.org).

In this section we have limited ourselves to the "big picture" of MDA. There is much more to the MDA specification than we have mentioned here, and we encourage you to check out the references we mentioned at the beginning of this section for more information.

1.5   Why "unified"?

UML unification is not just historical in scope; UML attempts (and largely succeeds) in being unified across several different domains.

- Development life cycle – UML provides visual syntax for modeling right through the software development life cycle from requirements engineering to implementation.

- Application domains – UML has been used to model everything from hard real-time embedded systems to management decision support systems.

- Implementation languages and platforms – UML is language neutral and platform neutral. Naturally, it has excellent support for pure OO languages (Smalltalk, Java, C#, etc.), but it is also effective for hybrid OO languages such as C++ and object-based languages such as Visual Basic. It has even been used to model for non-OO languages such as C.
- Development processes – although UP and its variants are probably the preferred development processes for OO systems, UML can (and does) support many other software engineering processes.
- Its own internal concepts – UML valiantly tries to be consistent and uniform in its application of a small set of internal concepts. It doesn't (as yet) always succeed, but it is still a big improvement on prior attempts.

1.6   Objects and UML

UML models the world as systems of interacting objects. An object is a cohesive cluster of data and function.

The basic premise of UML is that we can model software and other systems as *collections of interacting objects*. This is clearly a great fit with OO software systems and languages, but it also works very well for business processes and other applications.

There are two aspects to a UML model.

- Static structure – this describes what types of objects are important for modeling the system and how they are related.
- Dynamic behavior – this describes the life cycles of these objects and how they interact with each other to deliver the required system functionality.

These two aspects of the UML model go hand-in-glove, and one is not truly complete without the other.

We look at objects (and classes) in full detail in Chapter 7. Until we get there, just think of an object as being a cohesive cluster of data and behavior. In other words, objects contain information and can perform functions.

1.7   UML structure

You can begin to understand how UML works as a visual language by looking at its structure. This is illustrated in Figure 1.4 (as you will see later, this is a valid UML diagram). This structure consists of

- building blocks – these are the basic UML modeling elements, relationships, and diagrams;
- common mechanisms – common UML ways of achieving specific goals;
- architecture – the UML view of system architecture.

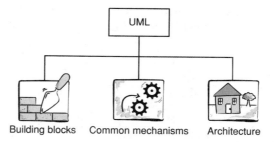

Figure 1.4

Understanding the structure of UML gives us a useful organizing principle for the rest of the information presented in this book. It also highlights that UML is, itself, a designed and architected system. In fact, UML has been modeled and designed using UML! This design is the UML metamodel.

1.8 UML building blocks

According to *The Unified Modeling Language User Guide* [Booch 2], UML is composed of just three building blocks (see Figure 1.5).

- Things – these are the modeling elements themselves.
- Relationships – these tie things together. Relationships specify how two or more things are semantically related.
- Diagrams – these are *views* into UML models. They show collections of things that "tell a story" about the software system and are our way of visualizing *what* the system will do (analysis-level diagrams) or *how* it will do it (design-level diagrams).

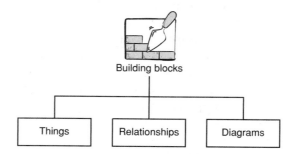

Figure 1.5

We'll look at the different types of building blocks in a little more detail in the next three sections.

1.8.1 Things

UML things may be partitioned into

"Things" are the nouns of a UML model.

- structural things – the nouns of a UML model, such as class, interface, collaboration, use case, active class, component, node;
- behavioral things – the verbs of a UML model, such as interactions, activities, state machines;
- grouping things – the package, which is used to group semantically related modeling elements into cohesive units;
- annotational things – the note, which may be appended to the model to capture ad hoc information, very much like a yellow sticky note.

We'll look at these things, and how they are usefully applied in UML modeling, in Part 2 onwards.

1.8.2 Relationships

Relationships allow you to show on a model how two or more things relate to each other. Thinking of families, and the relationships between all of the people in a family, gives you a pretty good idea of the role relationships play in UML models—they allow you to capture meaningful (semantic) connections between things. For example, UML relationships that apply to the structural and grouping things in a model are summarized in Table 1.1.

Understanding the exact semantics of the different types of relationship is a very important part of UML modeling, but we will defer a detailed exploration of these semantics until later sections of the book.

1.8.3 Diagrams

In all UML modeling tools, when you create a new thing or new relationship, it is added to the model. The model is the repository of all the things and relationships that you have created to help describe the required behavior of the software system you are trying to design.

Diagrams are only views into the model.

Diagrams are *windows* or *views* into the model. The diagram is *not* the model itself! This is actually a very important distinction, as a thing or relationship may be deleted from a diagram, or even from all diagrams, but may still exist in the model. In fact, it will stay in the model until explicitly deleted from it. A common error of novice UML modelers is to delete things from diagrams but leave them in the model.

Table 1.1

Type of relationship	UML syntax source target	Brief semantics	Section
Dependency	- - - - - - - - - ->	The source element depends on the target element and may be affected by changes to it	9.5
Association	———————	The description of a set of links between objects	9.4
Aggregation	◇———————	The target element is a part of the source element	18.4
Composition	◆———————	A strong (more constrained) form of aggregation	18.5
Containment	⊕———————	The source element contains the target element	11.4
Generalization	——————▷	The source element is a specialization of the more general target element and may be substituted for it	10.2
Realization	- - - - - - - - -▷	The source element guarantees to carry out the contract specified by the target element	12.3

There are thirteen different types of UML diagrams, and these are listed in Figure 1.6. In the figure, each box represents a type of diagram. When the text in the box is in italics, it represents an abstract category of diagram types. So, for example, there are six different types of StructureDiagram. Normal text indicates a concrete diagram that you could actually create. Shaded boxes indicate concrete diagram types that are new in UML 2.

We can usefully divide this set of diagrams into those that model the static structure of the system (the static model) and those that model the dynamic structure of the system (the dynamic model). The static model captures the things and the structural relationships between things; the dynamic model captures how things interact to generate the required behavior of the software system. We'll look at both the static and dynamic models from Part 2 onwards.

There is no specific order in which UML diagrams are created, although you typically start with a use case diagram to define the system scope. In fact, you often work on several diagrams in parallel, refining each one as you

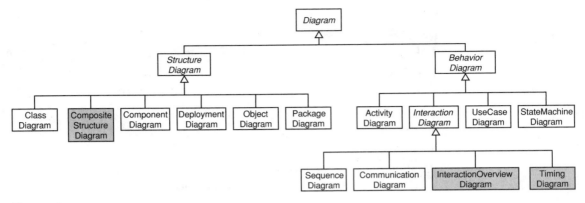

Figure 1.6

uncover more and more information and detail about the software system you are designing. Thus, the diagrams are both a view of the model and the primary mechanism for entering information into the model.

UML 2 introduces a new syntax for diagrams that is illustrated in Figure 1.7. Each diagram may have a frame, a heading area, and a contents area. The heading area is an irregular pentagon that contains the diagram's kind (optional), name, and parameters (optional).

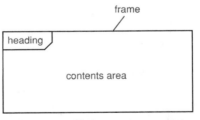

heading syntax: <kind> <name> <parameters>
N.B. <kind> and <parameters> are optional

Figure 1.7

The <kind> specifies what type of diagram it is and should normally be one of the concrete diagram types listed in Figure 1.6. The UML specification states that <kind> may abbreviated but does not provide a list of standard abbreviations. You rarely need to specify <kind> explicitly because it is usually clear from the visual syntax.

The <name> should describe the semantics of the diagram (e.g., CourseRegistration), and the <parameters> supply information needed by model elements in the diagram. You'll see examples of using <parameters> later in this book.

Optionally, a diagram may have an implied frame. This is where the frame is implied by a diagram area in the modeling tool. You can see an example of an implied frame in Figure 1.8.

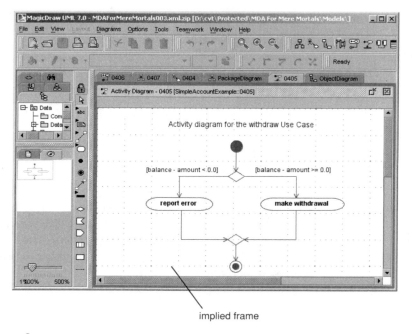

implied frame

Figure 1.8

1.9   UML common mechanisms

UML has four common mechanisms that apply consistently throughout the language. They describe four strategies for approaching object modeling, which are applied repeatedly in different contexts throughout UML. Once again, we see that UML has a simple and elegant structure (Figure 1.9).

1.9.1   Specifications

UML models have at least two dimensions: a graphical dimension that allows you to visualize the model using diagrams and icons, and a textual dimension that consists of the specifications of the various modeling elements. Specifications are textual descriptions of the semantics of an element.

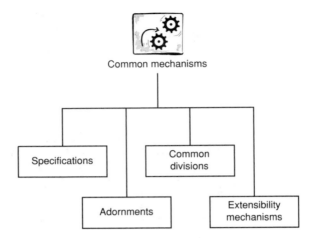

Common mechanisms

Figure 1.9

For example, we may visually represent a class, such as a BankAccount class, as a box with various compartments (Figure 1.10), but this representation doesn't really tell us anything about the business semantics of that class. The semantics behind modeling elements are captured in their specifications, and without these specifications you can only guess what a modeling element actually represents.

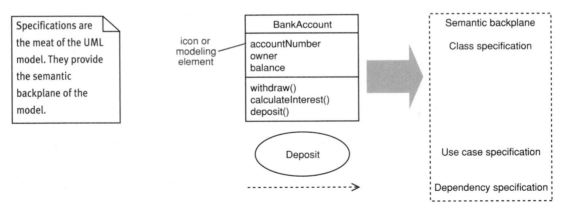

Specifications are the meat of the UML model. They provide the semantic backplane of the model.

Figure 1.10

Diagrams present views into the backplane.

The set of specifications is the real "meat" of the model, and forms the *semantic backplane* that holds the model together and gives it meaning. The various diagrams are just views or visual projections of that backplane.

This semantic backplane is typically maintained using a UML modeling tool that provides ways to enter, view, and modify specifications for each modeling element.

UML allows a great deal of flexibility in constructing models. In particular, models may be

- elided – some elements are present in the backplane, but hidden in any particular diagram in order to simplify the view;
- incomplete – some elements of the model may be missing entirely;
- inconsistent – the model may contain contradictions.

The fact that the completeness and consistency constraints are relaxed is important, as you will see that models evolve over time and undergo many changes. However, the drive is always toward *consistent models* that are *sufficiently complete* to allow construction of a software system.

It is common practice in UML modeling to start with a largely graphical model, which allows you to visualize the system, and then to add more and more semantics to the backplane as the model evolves. However, for a model to be considered in any way useful or complete, the model semantics *must* be present in the backplane. If not, you don't have a model, just a meaningless collection of boxes and blobs connected by lines! In fact, a common modeling error made by novices might be called "death by diagrams": the model is overdiagrammed but underspecified.

1.9.2 Adornments

A nice feature of UML is that every modeling element has a simple symbol to which you may add a number of adornments that make visible aspects of the element's specification. Using this mechanism you can tailor the amount of visible information on a diagram to your specific needs.

We adorn model elements on UML diagrams to highlight important details.

You can start by constructing a high-level diagram by using just the basic symbols with perhaps one or two adornments. You can then refine the diagram over time by adding more and more adornments until the diagram is sufficiently detailed for your purposes.

It is important to remember that any UML diagram is only a view of the model, and so you should only show those adornments that highlight important features of the model and that increase the overall clarity and readability of the diagram. There is generally no need to show everything on a diagram—it is more important that the diagram is clear, illustrates exactly the points you want it to make, and is easy to read.

Figure 1.11 shows that the minimal icon for a class is a box with the class name in it. However, you can expose various features of the underlying model as adornments to extend this minimal view. The text in gray indicates optional possible adornments.

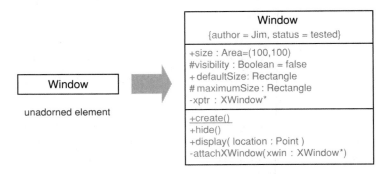

Figure 1.11

1.9.3 Common divisions

Common divisions describe particular ways of thinking about the world. There are two common divisions in UML: classifier/instance and interface/ implementation.

1.9.3.1 *Classifier and instance*

UML considers that we might have the abstract notion of a type of thing (such as a bank account) and then specific, concrete instances of that abstraction (such as "my bank account" or "your bank account"). The abstract notion of a type of thing is a classifier, and the specific, concrete things themselves are instances. This is a very important concept that is actually quite easy to grasp. Classifiers and instances surround us. Just think of this UML book—we might say that the abstract idea of the book is "UML 2 and the Unified Process" and that there are many instances of this book, such as the one you are reading right now. We will see that this notion of classifier/ instance is a key concept that permeates UML.

In UML an instance usually has the same icon as the corresponding classifier, but for instances the name on the icon is underlined. At first, this can be quite a subtle visual distinction to grasp.

UML 2 provides a rich taxonomy of thirty-three classifiers. Some of the more common classifiers are listed in Table 1.2. We'll look at all of these (and others) in detail in later sections.

> Classifier – an abstract notion, e.g., a type of bank account. Instance – a concrete thing, e.g., your bank account or my bank account.

Table 1.2

Classifier	Semantics	Section
Actor	A role played by an outside user of the system to whom the system delivers some value	4.3.2
Class	A description of a set of objects that share the same features	7.4
Component	A modular and replaceable part of a system that encapsulates its contents	19.8
Interface	A collection of operations that are used to specify a service offered by a class or component	19.3
Node	A physical, runtime element that represents a computational resource, for example, a PC	24.4
Signal	An asynchronous message passed between objects	15.6
Use case	A description of a sequence of actions that a system performs to yield value to a user	4.3.3

1.9.3.2   *Interface and implementation*

Interface, e.g., the buttons on the front of your VCR. Implementation, e.g., the mechanism inside your VCR.

The principle here is to separate *what* something does (its interface) from *how* it does it (its implementation). For example, when you drive a car you are interacting with a very simple and well-defined interface. This interface is implemented in different ways by many different physical cars.

An interface defines a contract (which has much in common with a legal contract) that specific implementations guarantee to adhere to. This separation of what something promises to do from the actual implementation of that promise is an important UML concept. We discuss this in detail in Chapter 17.

Concrete examples of interfaces and implementations are everywhere. For example, the buttons on the front of a video recorder provide a (relatively) simple interface to what is actually a very complex mechanism. The interface shields us from this complexity by hiding it from us.

1.9.4   Extensibility mechanisms

UML is an extensible modeling language.

The designers of UML realized that it was simply not possible to design a completely universal modeling language that would satisfy everyone's needs present and future, so UML incorporates three simple extensibility mechanisms that we summarize in Table 1.3.

We'll look at these three extensibility mechanisms in more detail in the next three sections.

Table 1.3

UML extensibility mechanisms	
Constraints	These extend the semantics of an element by allowing us to add new rules
Stereotypes	These allow us to define a new UML modeling element based on an existing one – we define the semantics of the stereotype ourselves
	Stereotypes add new elements to the UML metamodel
Tagged values	These provide a way of extending an element's specification by allowing us to add new, ad hoc information to it

1.9.4.1   Constraints

Constraints allow you to add new rules to modeling elements.

A constraint is simply a text string in braces ({}) that specifies some condition or rule about the modeling element that *must* be maintained as true. In other words, it constrains some feature of the element in some way. You'll come across examples of constraints throughout the book.

UML defines a constraint language called OCL (Object Constraint Language) as a standard extension. We provide an introduction to OCL in Chapter 25.

1.9.4.2   Stereotypes

Stereotypes allow you to define new modeling elements

The UML Reference Manual [Rumbaugh 1] states, "A stereotype represents a variation of an existing model element with the same form (such as attributes and relationships) but with a modified intent."

Stereotypes allow you to introduce new modeling elements based on *existing* elements. You can do this by appending the stereotype name in guillemets («...») to the new element. Each model element can have zero to many stereotypes.

Each stereotype may define a set of tagged values and constraints that apply to the stereotyped element. You can also associate an icon, color, or texture with the stereotype. Typically, use of color and texture should be avoided in UML models as some readers (the color-blind for example) may have trouble interpreting the diagrams, and diagrams often have to be printed in black and white anyway. However, it is common practice to associate a new icon with a stereotype. This allows you to extend the UML graphical notation in a controlled manner.

Because stereotypes introduce *new* modeling elements with different intent, you have to define the semantics of these new elements somewhere.

How do you do this? Well, if the modeling tool doesn't provide inbuilt support for documenting stereotypes, most modelers just put a note in the model, or insert a reference to an external document in which the stereotypes are defined. At present, modeling tool support for stereotypes is rather patchy—most tools support stereotypes to some degree, but not all tools provide facilities for capturing stereotype semantics.

You can model stereotypes themselves by using the class element (Chapter 7) with the special predefined UML stereotype «stereotype». This creates a metamodel of your system of stereotypes. It is a metamodel because it is a model of a modeling element and is on a completely different level of abstraction from the usual UML system or business models. Because this is a metamodel, you must *never* merge it with your normal models—you must always keep it as a separate model. Creating a new model just for the stereotypes is only really worth doing when there are a lot of stereotypes. This is very rare, so most modelers tend to document stereotypes with a note or an external document.

There is a lot of flexibility in how stereotypes can be displayed. However, most modelers just use the stereotype name in « » or the icon. The other variants don't tend to be used that much and the modeling tool often limits what you can do. Some examples are shown in Figure 1.12. (N.B. The stars are *not* part of UML syntax—they just highlight the most useful display options.)

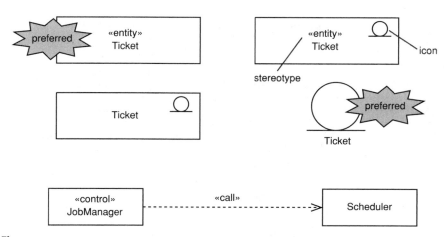

Figure 1.12

Notice that you can stereotype relationships as well as classes. You'll see many uses for this throughout the book.

1.9.4.3   Tagged values

> Tagged values allow you to add your own properties to model elements.

In UML, a property is any value attached to a model element. Most elements have large numbers of predefined properties. Some of these are displayable on diagrams, and others are just part of the semantic backplane of the model.

UML allows you to add your own properties to modeling elements by using tagged values. A tagged value is a very simple idea—it is just a keyword that can have a value attached. The syntax for tagged values is shown here: { tag1 = value1, tag2 = value2, ..., tagN = valueN }. This is a comma-delimited list of tag/value pairs separated by an equal sign. The list of tags is enclosed in curly brackets.

Some tags are just extra information applied to a model element, such as {author = Jim Arlow}. However, other tags indicate properties of new modeling elements defined by a stereotype. You should not apply these tags directly to model elements; rather, you should associate them with the stereotype itself. Then, when the stereotype is applied to a model element, it also gets the tags associated with that stereotype.

1.9.4.4   UML profiles

> A UML profile defines a set of stereotypes, tags, and constraints that customizes UML for a specific purpose.

A UML profile is a collection of stereotypes, tagged values, and constraints. You use a UML profile to customize UML for a specific purpose.

UML profiles allow you to customize UML so that you can apply it effectively in many different domains. Profiles allow you to use stereotypes, tags, and constraints in a consistent and well-defined manner. For example, if you want to use UML to model a .NET application, then you could use the UML profile for .NET that is summarized in Table 1.4.

Table 1.4

Stereotype	Tags	Constraints	Extends	Semantics
«NETComponent»	None	None	Component	Represents a component in the .NET framework
«NETProperty»	None	None	Property	Represents a property of a component
«NETAssembly»	None	None	Package	A .NET runtime packaging for components
«MSI»	None	None	Artifact	A component self-installer file
«DLL»	None	None	Artifact	A portable executable of type DLL
«EXE»	None	None	Artifact	A portable executable of type EXE

This profile is one of the example UML profiles in the UML 2.0 specification [UML2S], and it defines new UML modeling elements that are adapted for modeling .NET applications.

Each stereotype in a profile extends one of the UML metamodel elements (e.g., a Class or an Association) to create a new, customized element. The stereotype can define new tags and constraints that were not part of the original element.

1.10 Architecture

The UML Reference Manual [Rumbaugh 1] defines system architecture as "The organizational structure of a system, including its decomposition into parts, their connectivity, interaction, mechanisms and the guiding principles that inform the design of a system." The IEEE defines system architecture as "The highest-level concept of a system in its environment."

> You can capture the strategic aspects of a system in a "4+1 view" of architecture: logical view, process view, implementation view, deployment view, and use case view.

Architecture is all about capturing the strategic aspects of the high-level structure of a system. There are many ways of looking at architecture, but a very common way is the "4+1 View" described by Philippe Kruchten [Kruchten 2]. The essential aspects of system architecture are captured in four different views of the system: the logical view, the process view, the implementation view, and the deployment view. These are all integrated by a fifth view, the use case view. Each of these views addresses different aspects of the software architecture as is indicated in Figure 1.13.

Let's look at each of these views in turn.

- Logical view – captures the vocabulary of the problem domain as a set of classes and objects. The emphasis is on showing how the objects and classes that compose a system implement the required system behavior.

- Process view – models the executable threads and processes in a system as active classes (classes that have their own thread of control). It is really a process-oriented variation on the logical view and contains all the same artifacts.

- Implementation view – models the files and components that make up the physical code base of the system. It is also about illustrating dependencies between components and about configuration management of sets of components to define a version of the system.

- Deployment view – models the physical deployment of artifacts onto a set of physical, computational nodes such as computers and peripherals. It allows you to model the distribution of artifacts across the nodes of a distributed system.

- Use case view – captures the basic requirements for the system as a set of use cases (see Chapter 4). These use cases provide the basis for the construction of the other views.

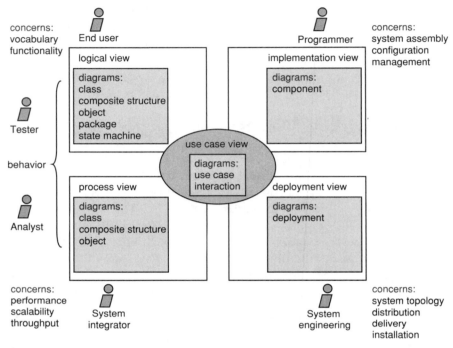

Figure 1.13   Adapted from Figure 5.1 [Kruchten 1] with permission from Addison-Wesley

As you will see in the rest of this book, UML provides excellent support for each of the 4+1 views and UP is a requirements-driven approach that fits the 4+1 model very well.

Once you have created your 4+1 views, you have explored all of the key aspects of the system architecture with UML models. If you follow the iterative UP life cycle, this 4+1 architecture is not created in one go, but evolves over time. The process of UML modeling within the framework of the UP is a process of stepwise refinement towards a 4+1 architecture that captures *just enough* information about the system to allow it to be built.

1.11   What we have learned

This chapter has provided an introduction to UML history, structure, concepts, and key features. You have learned the following.

- The Unified Modeling Language (UML) is an open, extensible, industry standard visual modeling language approved by the Object Management Group.

- UML is not a methodology.
- The Unified Process (UP), or a variant, is the type of methodology that best complements UML.
- Object modeling regards the world as systems of interacting objects. Objects contain information and may perform functions. UML models have:
  - static structure – what types of object are important and how they are related;
  - dynamic behavior – how objects collaborate together to perform the functions of the system.
- UML is composed of three building blocks:
  - things:
    - structural things are the nouns of a UML model;
    - behavioral things are the verbs of a UML model;
    - there is only one grouping thing, the package – this is used to group semantically related things;
    - there is only one annotational thing, the note – this is just like a yellow sticky note;
  - relationships link things together;
  - diagrams show interesting views of the model.
- UML has four common mechanisms:
  - specifications – textual descriptions of the features and semantics of model elements – the meat of the model;
  - adornments – items of information exposed on a modeling element in a diagram to illustrate a point;
  - common divisions:
    - classifier and instance:
      - classifier – the abstract notion of a type of thing, e.g., a bank account;
      - instance – a specific instance of a type of thing, e.g., my bank account;
    - interface and implementation:
      - interface – a contract that specifies the behavior of a thing;
      - implementation – the specific details of how the thing works;
  - extensibility mechanisms:
    - constraints allow us to add new rules to modeling elements;
    - stereotypes introduce new modeling elements based on old ones;
    - tagged values allow us to add new properties to model elements – a tagged value is a keyword with an associated value.
    - A UML profile is a collection of constraints, stereotypes, and tagged values – it allows you to customize UML for a specific purpose.

- UML is based on a 4+1 view of system architecture:
  - logical view – system functionality and vocabulary;
  - process view – system performance, scalability, and throughput;
  - implementation view – system assembly and configuration management;
  - deployment view – system topology, distribution, delivery, and installation;
  - these are united by the use case view, which describes stakeholder requirements.

chapter **2**

What is the Unified Process?

2.1	**Chapter roadmap**

This chapter gives a concise overview of the Unified Process (UP). Beginners should start by learning about UP history. If you already know this, then you may choose to skip ahead to Section 2.4, a discussion of UP and the Rational Unified Process (RUP), or to Section 2.5, which discusses how you can apply UP on your project.

Our interest in UP, as far as this book is concerned, is to provide a process framework within which the techniques of OO analysis and design can be presented. You will find a complete discussion of UP in [Jacobson 1] and excellent discussions of the related RUP in [Kroll 1], [Kruchten 2], and also in [Ambler 1], [Ambler 2], and [Ambler 3].

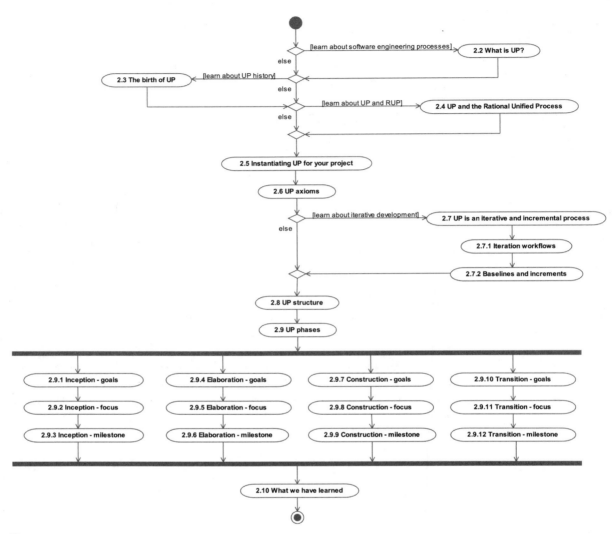

Figure 2.1

2.2   What is UP?

A software engineering process (SEP), also known as a software development process, defines the *who*, *what*, *when*, and *how* of developing software. As illustrated in Figure 2.2, a SEP is the process in which we turn user requirements into software.

The Unified Software Development Process (USDP) is a SEP from the authors of the UML. It is commonly referred to as the Unified Process or UP [Jacobson 1]. We use the term UP throughout this book.

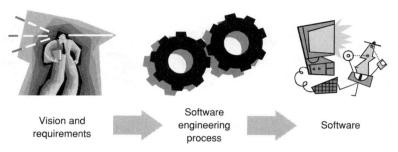

Vision and requirements → Software engineering process → Software

Figure 2.2

The UML project was meant to provide both a visual language *and* a software engineering process. What we know today as UML is the visual language part of the project—UP is the process part. However, it's worth pointing out that whereas the UML has been standardized by the OMG, the UP has not. There is therefore still no *standard* SEP to complement UML.

> A software engineering process describes how requirements are turned into software.

UP is based on process work conducted at Ericsson (the Ericsson approach, 1967), at Rational (the Rational Objectory Process, 1996 to 1997) and other sources of best practice. As such, it is a pragmatic and tested method for developing software that incorporates best practice from its predecessors.

2.3   The birth of UP

When we look at the history of UP, depicted in Figure 2.3, it is fair to say that its development is intimately tied to the career of one man, Ivar Jacobson. In fact, Jacobson is often thought of as being the father of UP. This is not to minimize the work of all of the other individuals (especially Booch) who have contributed to the development of UP; rather, it is to emphasize Jacobson's pivotal contribution.

> SEP work that was to develop into the UP began in 1967 at Ericsson.

UP goes back to 1967 and the Ericsson approach, which took the radical step of modeling a complex system as a set of interconnected blocks. Small blocks were interconnected to form larger blocks building up to a complete system. The basis of this approach was "divide and conquer" and it was the forerunner of what is known today as component-based development.

Although a complete system might be incomprehensible to any individual who approaches it as a monolith, when broken down into smaller blocks it can be made sense of by understanding the services each block offers (the interface to the component in modern terminology) and how these blocks fit together. In the language of UML, large blocks are called subsystems, and each subsystem is implemented in terms of smaller blocks called components.

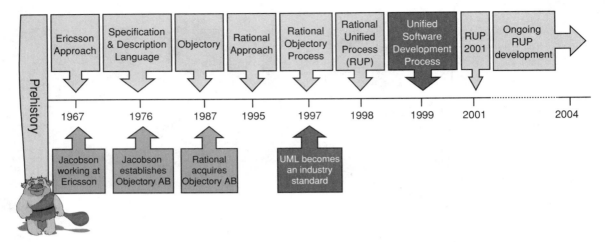

Figure 2.3

Another Ericsson innovation was a way of identifying these blocks by creating "traffic cases" that described how the system was to be used. These traffic cases have evolved over time and are now called use cases in UML. The result of this process was an architecture representation that described all the blocks and how they fitted together. This was the forerunner of the UML static model.

As well as the requirements view (the traffic cases) and the static view (the architecture description), Ericsson had a dynamic view that described how all the blocks communicated with each other over time. This consisted of sequence, communication, and state machine diagrams, all of which are still found in UML, albeit in a much-refined form.

The next major development in OO software engineering was in 1980 with the release of the Specification and Description Language (SDL) from the international standards body CCITT. SDL was one of the first object-based visual modeling languages, and in 1992 it was extended to become object-oriented with classes and inheritance. This language was designed to capture the behavior of telecommunications systems. Systems were modeled as a set of blocks that communicated by sending signals to each other. SDL-92 was the first widely accepted object modeling standard and it is still used today.

In 1987, Jacobson founded Objectory AB in Stockholm. This company developed and sold a software engineering process, based on the Ericsson Approach, called Objectory (*Object Factory*). The Objectory SEP consisted of a set of documentation, a rather idiosyncratic tool, and some probably much needed consultancy from Objectory AB.

Perhaps the most important innovation during this time was that the Objectory SEP was viewed as a system in its own right. The workflows of the process (requirements, analysis, design, implementation, and test) were expressed in a set of diagrams. In other words, the Objectory process was modeled and developed just like a software system. This paved the way for the future development of the process. Objectory, like UP, was also a process framework and needed vigorous customization before it could be applied to any specific project. The Objectory process product came with some templates for various types of software development project, but it almost invariably needed to be heavily customized further. Jacobson recognized that all software development projects are different, and so a "one size fits all" SEP was not really feasible or desirable.

When Rational acquired Objectory AB in 1995, Jacobson went to work unifying the Objectory process with the large amount of process-related work that had already been done at Rational. A 4+1 view of architecture based around four distinct views (logical, process, physical, and development) plus a unifying use case view was developed. This still forms the basis of the UP approach to system architecture. In addition, iterative development was formalized into a sequence of phases (Inception, Elaboration, Construction, and Transition) that combined the discipline of the waterfall life cycle with the dynamic responsiveness of iterative and incremental development. The main participants in this work were Walker Royce, Rich Reitmann, Grady Booch (inventor of the Booch method), and Philippe Kruchten. In particular, Booch's experience and strong ideas on architecture were incorporated into the Rational Approach (see [Booch 1] for an excellent discussion of his ideas).

The Rational Objectory Process (ROP) was the result of the unification of Objectory with Rational's process work. In particular, ROP improved areas where Objectory was weak—requirements other than use cases, implementation, test, project management, deployment, configuration management, and development environment. Risk was introduced as a driver for ROP, and architecture was defined and formalized as an "architecture description" deliverable. During this period Booch, Jacobson, and Rumbaugh were developing UML at Rational. This became the language in which ROP models, and ROP itself, were expressed.

From 1997 onward, Rational acquired many more companies bringing in expertise in requirements capture, configuration management, testing, and so on. This led to the release of the Rational Unified Process (RUP) in 1998. Since then, there have been many releases of RUP, each one consistently better than the previous. See www.rational.com and [Kruchten 1] for more details.

In 1999, we saw the publication of an important book, the *Unified Software Development Process* [Jacobson 1], which describes the Unified Process.

UP is a mature, open SEP from the authors of UML.

Whereas RUP is a Rational process product, UP is an open SEP from the authors of UML. Not surprisingly, UP and RUP are closely related. We have chosen to use UP rather than RUP in this book as it is an open SEP, accessible to all, and is not tied to any specific product or vendor.

2.4   UP and the Rational Unified Process

RUP is a commercial product that extends UP.

The Rational Unified Process (RUP) is a commercial version of UP from IBM, who took over Rational Corporation in 2003. It supplies all of the standards, tools, and other necessities that are not included in UP and that you would otherwise have to provide for yourself. It also comes with a rich, web-based environment that includes complete process documentation and "tool mentors" for each of the tools.

UP and RUP are much more similar than they are different.

Back in 1999 RUP was pretty much a straight implementation of UP. However, RUP has moved on a lot since then and now extends UP in many important ways. Nowadays, we should view UP as the open, general case and RUP as a specific commercial subclass that both extends and overrides UP features. But RUP and UP still remain much more similar than different. The main differences are those of completeness and detail rather than semantic or ideological differences. The basic workflows of OO analysis and design are sufficiently similar that a description from the UP perspective will be just as useful for RUP users. By choosing to use UP in this book, we make the text suitable for the majority of OO analysts and designers who are not using RUP, and also for the significant and growing minority who are.

Both UP and RUP model the *who*, *when*, and *what* of the software development process, but they do so slightly differently. The latest version of RUP has some terminological and syntactic differences to UP, although semantics of the process elements remain essentially the same.

Figure 2.4 shows how the RUP process icons map to the UP icons we use in this book. Notice that there is a «trace» relationship between the RUP icon and the original UP icon. In UML a «trace» relationship is a special type of dependency between model elements that indicates that the element at the beginning of the «trace» relationship is a historical development of the element pointed to by the arrow. This describes the relationship between UP and RUP model elements perfectly.

To model the "who" of the SEP, UP introduces the concept of the worker. This describes a role played by an individual or team within the project. Each worker may be realized by many individuals or teams, and each individual or team may perform as many different workers. In RUP workers are actually called "roles", but the semantics remain the same.

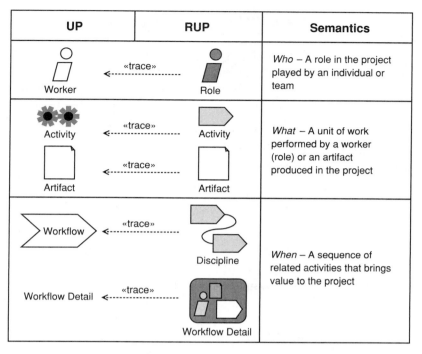

UP	RUP	Semantics
Worker	«trace» Role	*Who* – A role in the project played by an individual or team
Activity «trace» Artifact «trace»	Activity Artifact	*What* – A unit of work performed by a worker (role) or an artifact produced in the project
Workflow «trace» Workflow Detail «trace»	Discipline Workflow Detail	*When* – A sequence of related activities that brings value to the project

Figure 2.4

UP models the "what" as activities and artifacts. Activities are tasks that will be performed by individuals or teams in the project. These individuals or teams will always *adopt specific roles* when they perform certain activities and so, for any activity, UP (and RUP) can tell us the workers (roles) that participate in that activity. Activities may be broken down into finer levels of detail as needed. Artifacts are things that are inputs and outputs to the project— they may be source code, executable programs, standards, documentation, and so on. They can have many different icons depending on what they are, and in Figure 2.4 we show them with a generic document icon.

UP models the "when" as workflows. These are sequences of related activities that are performed by workers. In RUP, high-level workflows, such as Requirements or Test, are given a special name, *disciplines*. Workflows may be broken down into one or more workflow details that describe the activities, roles, and artifacts involved in the workflow. These workflow details are only referred to by name in UP but have been given their own icon in RUP.

2.5   Instantiating UP for your project

UP is a generic software development process that has to be instantiated for an organization and then for each particular project. This recognizes that all software projects tend to be different, and that a "one size fits all" approach to SEP just doesn't work. The instantiation process involves defining and incorporating

UP and RUP must be instantiated for each project.

- in-house standards;
- document templates;
- tools – compilers, configuration management tools, and so on;
- databases – bug tracking, project tracking, and so on;
- life cycle modifications – for example, more sophisticated quality control measures for safety-critical systems.

Details of this customization process are outside the scope of this book but are described in [Rumbaugh 1].

Even though RUP is much more complete than UP, it must still be customized and instantiated in a similar way. However, the amount of work that needs to be done is much less than starting from raw UP. In fact, with *any* software engineering process you can generally expect to invest a certain amount of time and money in instantiation, and you may need to budget for some consultancy from the SEP vendor to help with this.

2.6   UP axioms

UP has three basic axioms. It is

- requirements and risk driven;
- architecture-centric;
- iterative and incremental.

We look at use cases in great depth in Chapter 4, but for now let's just say that they are a way of capturing requirements, so we could accurately say that UP is requirements driven.

UP is a modern SEP that is driven by user requirements and risk.

Risk is the other UP driver because if you don't actively attack risks they will actively attack you! Anyone who has worked in a software development project will no doubt agree with this sentiment, and UP addresses this by predicating software construction on the analysis of risk. However, this is really a job for the project manager and architect, and so we don't cover it in any detail in this book.

The UP approach to developing software systems is to develop and evolve a robust system architecture. Architecture describes the strategic aspects of how the system is broken down into components and how those components interact and are deployed on hardware. Clearly, a quality system architecture will lead to a quality system, rather than just an ad hoc collection of source code that has been hacked together with little forethought.

Finally, UP is iterative and incremental. The iterative aspect of UP means that we break the project into small subprojects (the iterations) that deliver system functionality in chunks, or increments, leading to a fully functional system. In other words, we build software by a process of stepwise refinement to our final goal. This is a very different approach to software construction compared to the old waterfall life cycle of analysis, design, and build that occur in a more or less strict sequence. In fact, we return to key UP workflows, such as analysis, several times throughout the course of the project.

2.7 UP is an iterative and incremental process

| UP aims to build a robust system architecture incrementally. |

To understand UP, we need to understand iterations. The idea is fundamentally very simple—history shows that, generally speaking, human beings find small problems easier to solve than large problems. We therefore break a large software development project down into a number of smaller "mini projects", which are easier to manage and to complete successfully. Each of these "mini projects" is an iteration. The key point is that each iteration contains *all* of the elements of a normal software development project:

- planning
- analysis and design
- construction
- integration and test
- an internal or external release

Each iteration generates a baseline that comprises a *partially complete* version of the final system and any associated project documentation. Baselines build on each other over successive iterations until the final finished system is achieved.

The difference between two consecutive baselines is known as an increment. This is why UP is known as an iterative and incremental life cycle.

As you will see in Section 2.8, iterations are grouped into phases. Phases provide the macrostructure of UP.

2.7.1   Iteration workflows

> UP has five core
> workflows.

In each iteration, five core workflows specify what needs to be done and what skills are needed to do it. As well as the five core workflows there will be other workflows such as planning, assessment, and anything else specific to that particular iteration. However, these are not covered in UP.

The five core workflows are

- requirements – capturing what the system should do;
- analysis – refining and structuring the requirements;
- design – realizing the requirements in system architecture;
- implementation – building the software;
- test – verifying that the implementation works as desired.

Some possible workflows for an iteration are illustrated in Figure 2.5. We look at the requirements, analysis, design, and implementation workflows in more detail later in the book (the test workflow is out of scope).

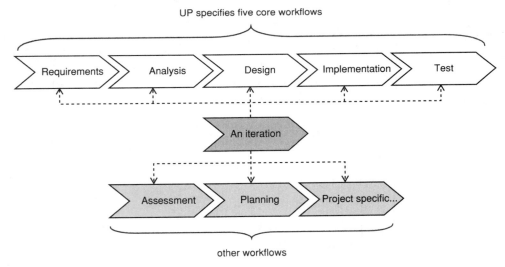

Figure 2.5

Although each iteration may contain all of the five core workflows, the emphasis on a particular workflow depends on where the iteration occurs in the project life cycle.

Breaking the project down into a series of iterations allows a flexible approach to project planning. The simplest approach is just a time-ordered sequence of iterations, where each leads to the next. However, it is often possible to schedule iterations in parallel. This implies an understanding of the dependencies between the artifacts of each iteration and requires an approach to software development predicated on architecture and modeling. The benefit of parallel iterations is better time-to-market and perhaps better utilization of the team, but careful planning is essential.

2.7.2 Baselines and increments

Every UP iteration generates a baseline. This is an internal (or external) release of the set of reviewed and approved artifacts generated by that iteration. Each baseline

- provides an agreed basis for further review and development;
- can be changed *only* through formal procedures of configuration and change management.

Increments, however, are just the *difference* between one baseline and the next. They constitute a step toward the final, delivered system.

2.8 UP structure

UP has four phases, each of which ends with a major milestone.

Figure 2.6 shows the structure of UP. The project life cycle is divided into four phases—Inception, Elaboration, Construction, and Transition—each of which ends with a major milestone. Within each phase we can have one or more iterations, and in each iteration we execute the five core workflows and any extra workflows. The exact number of iterations per phase depends on the size of the project, but each iteration should last no more than two to three months. The example is typical for a project that lasts about 18 months and is of medium size.

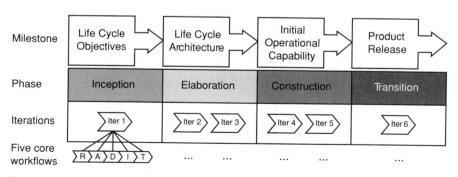

Figure 2.6

As can be seen from Figure 2.6, UP consists of a sequence of four phases, each of which terminates with a major milestone:

- Inception – Life Cycle Objectives;
- Elaboration – Life Cycle Architecture;
- Construction – Initial Operational Capability;
- Transition – Product Release.

As the project shifts through the phases of the UP, so the amount of work that is done in each of the five core workflows changes.

Figure 2.7 is really the key to understanding how UP works. Along the top, we have the phases. Down the left-hand side, we have the five core workflows. Along the bottom, we have some iterations. The curves show the relative amount of work done in each of the five core workflows as the project progresses through the phases.

> The amount of work done in each core workflow varies according to the phase.

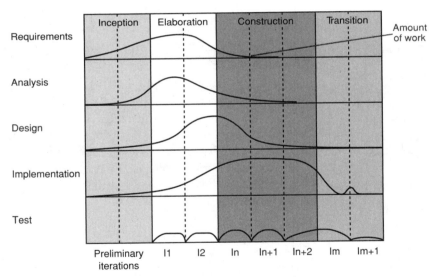

Figure 2.7 Adapted from Figure 1.5 [Jacobson 1] with permission from Addison-Wesley

As Figure 2.7 shows, in the Inception phase most of the work is done in requirements and analysis. In Elaboration the emphasis shifts to requirements, analysis, and some design. In Construction the emphasis is clearly on design and implementation. Finally, in Transition the emphasis is on implementation and test.

> UP is a goal-based process rather than a deliverable-based process.

One of the great features of UP is that it is a goal-based process rather than a deliverable-based process. Each phase ends with a milestone that consists of a set of conditions of satisfaction, and these conditions may involve the creation of a particular deliverable, or not, depending on the specific needs of your project.

In the rest of this chapter, we give a brief overview of each of the UP phases.

2.9   UP phases

Every phase has a goal, a focus of activity with one or more core workflows emphasized, and a milestone. This will be our framework for investigating the phases.

2.9.1   Inception – goals

The goal of Inception is to "get the project off the ground". Inception involves

> Inception is about initiating the project.

- establishing feasibility – this may involve some technical prototyping to validate technology decisions or proof of concept prototyping to validate business requirements;

- creating a business case to demonstrate that the project will deliver quantifiable business benefit;

- capturing essential requirements to help scope the system;

- identifying critical risks.

The primary workers in this phase are the project manager and system architect.

2.9.2   Inception – focus

The primary emphasis in Inception is on requirements and analysis workflows. However, some design and implementation might also be done if it is decided to build a technical, or proof-of-concept, prototype. The test workflow is not generally applicable to this phase, as the only software artifacts are prototypes that will be thrown away.

2.9.3   Inception – milestone: Life Cycle Objectives

While many SEPs focus on the creation of key artifacts, UP adopts a different approach that is goal-oriented. Each milestone sets certain goals that *must* be achieved before the milestone can be considered to have been reached. Some of these goals might be the production of certain artifacts and some might not.

The milestone for Inception is the Life Cycle Objectives. The conditions that must be met for this milestone to be attained are given in Table 2.1. We also suggest a set of deliverables that you may need to create to realize these conditions. However, please remember that you only create a deliverable when it adds true value to your project.

> You only create a deliverable when it adds true value to your project.

Table 2.1

Conditions of satisfaction	Deliverable
The stakeholders have agreed on the project objectives	A vision document that states the project's main requirements, features, and constraints
System scope has been defined and agreed on with the stakeholders	An initial use case model (only about 10% to 20% complete)
Key requirements have been captured and agreed on with the stakeholders	A project glossary
Cost and schedule estimates have been agreed on with the stakeholders	An initial project plan
A business case has been raised by the project manager	A business case
The project manager has performed a risk assessment	A risk assessment document or database
Feasibility has been confirmed through technical studies and/or prototyping	One or more throwaway prototypes
An architecture has been outlined	An initial architecture document

2.9.4   Elaboration – goals

The goals of Elaboration may be summarized as follows:

- create an executable architectural baseline;
- refine the risk assessment;
- define quality attributes (defect discovery rates, acceptable defect densities, and so on);

- capture use cases to 80% of the functional requirements (you'll see exactly what this involves in Chapters 3 and 4);
- create a detailed plan for the construction phase;
- formulate a bid that includes resources, time, equipment, staff, and cost.

> Elaboration is about creating a partial but working version of the system – an executable architectural baseline.

The main goal of Elaboration is to create an executable architectural baseline. This is a real, executable system that is built according to the specified architecture. It is *not* a prototype (which is throwaway), but rather the "first cut" of the desired system. This initial executable architectural baseline will be added to as the project progresses and will evolve into the final delivered system during the Construction and Transition phases. Because future phases are predicated on the results of Elaboration, this is perhaps the most critical phase. In fact, this book focuses very much on the Elaboration activities.

2.9.5   Elaboration – focus

In the Elaboration phase, the focus in each of the core workflows is as follows:

- requirements – refine system scope and requirements;
- analysis – establish what to build;
- design – create a stable architecture;
- implementation – build the architectural baseline;
- test – test the architectural baseline.

The focus in Elaboration is clearly on the requirements, analysis, and design workflows, with implementation becoming very important at the end of the phase when the executable architectural baseline is being produced.

2.9.6   Elaboration – milestone: Life Cycle Architecture

The milestone is the Life Cycle Architecture. The conditions of satisfaction for this milestone are summarized in Table 2.2.

2.9.7   Construction – goals

> Construction evolves the executable architectural baseline into a complete, working system.

The goal of Construction is to complete all requirements, analysis, and design and to evolve the architectural baseline generated in Elaboration into the final system. A key issue in Construction is *maintaining the integrity of the system architecture*. It is quite common once delivery pressure is on and coding begins in earnest for corners to be cut, leading to a corruption of the

Table 2.2

Conditions of satisfaction	Deliverable
A resilient, robust executable architectural baseline has been created	The executable architectural baseline
The executable architectural baseline demonstrates that important risks have been identified and resolved	UML static model UML dynamic model UML use case model
The vision of the product has stabilized	Vision document
The risk assessment has been revised	Updated risk assessment
The business case has been revised and agreed with the stakeholders	Updated business case
A project plan has been created in sufficient detail to enable a realistic bid to be formulated for time, money, and resources in the next phases The stakeholders agree to the project plan	Updated project plan
The business case has been verified against the project plan	Business case
Agreement is reached with the stakeholders to continue the project	Sign-off document

architectural vision and a final system with low-quality and high-maintenance costs. Clearly, this outcome should be avoided.

2.9.8   Construction – focus

The emphasis in this phase is on the implementation workflow. Just enough work is done in the other workflows to complete requirements capture, analysis, and design. Testing also becomes more important—as each new increment builds on the last, both unit and integration tests are now needed. We can summarize the kind of work undertaken in each workflow as follows:

● requirements – uncover any requirements that had been missed;
● analysis – finish the analysis model;
● design – finish the design model;
● implementation – build the Initial Operational Capability;
● test – test the Initial Operational Capability.

2.9.9   Construction – milestone: Initial Operational Capability

In essence, this milestone is very simple—the software system is finished ready for beta testing at the user site. The conditions of satisfaction for this milestone are given in Table 2.3.

Table 2.3

Conditions of satisfaction	Deliverable
The software product is sufficiently stable and of sufficient quality to be deployed in the user community	The software product The UML model Test suite
The stakeholders have agreed and are ready for the transition of the software to their environment	User manuals Description of this release
The actual expenditures vs. the planned expenditures are acceptable	Project plan

2.9.10   Transition – goals

The Transition phase starts when beta testing is completed and the system is finally deployed. This involves fixing any defects found in the beta test and preparing for rollout of the software to all the user sites. We can summarize the goals of this phase as follows:

> Transition is about deploying the completed system into the user community.

- correct defects;
- prepare the user sites for the new software;
- tailor the software to operate at the user sites;
- modify the software if unforeseen problems arise;
- create user manuals and other documentation;
- provide user consultancy;
- conduct a post-project review.

2.9.11   Transition – focus

The emphasis is on the implementation and test workflows. Sufficient design is done to correct any design errors found in beta testing. Hopefully, by this point in the project life cycle, there should be very little work being done in the requirements and analysis workflows. If this is not the case, then the project is in trouble.

- Requirements – not applicable.
- Analysis – not applicable.
- Design – modify the design if problems emerge in beta testing.
- Implementation – tailor the software for the user site and correct problems uncovered in beta testing.
- Test – beta testing and acceptance testing at the user site.

2.9.12 Transition – milestone: Product Release

This is the final milestone: beta testing, acceptance testing, and defect repair are finished and the product is released and accepted into the user community. The conditions of satisfaction for this milestone are given in Table 2.4.

Table 2.4

Conditions of satisfaction	Deliverable
Beta testing is completed, necessary changes have been made, and the users agree that the system has been successfully deployed	The software product
The user community is actively using the product	
Product support strategies have been agreed on with the users and implemented	User support plan Updated user manuals

2.10 What we have learned

- A software engineering process (SEP) turns user requirements into software by specifying *who* does *what, when*.
- The Unified Process (UP) has been in development since 1967. It is a mature, open SEP from the authors of UML.
- Rational Unified Process (RUP) is a commercial extension of UP. It is entirely compatible with UP but is more complete and detailed.
- UP (and RUP) must be instantiated for any specific project by adding in-house standards, etc.
- UP is a modern SEP that is:
  — risk and use case (requirements) driven;
  — architecture centric;
  — iterative and incremental.
- UP software is built in iterations:
  — each iteration is like a "mini project" that delivers a part of the system;
  — iterations build on each other to create the final system.
- Every iteration has five core workflows:
  — requirements – capturing what the system should do;
  — analysis – refining and structuring the requirements;
  — design – realizing the requirements in system architecture (how the system does it);

— implementation – building the software;
— test – verifying that the implementation works as desired.

● UP has four phases, each of which ends with a major milestone:
— Inception – getting the project off the ground: Life Cycle Objectives;
— Elaboration – evolving the system architecture: Life Cycle Architecture;
— Construction – building the software: Initial Operational Capability;
— Transition – deploying the software into the user environment: Product Release.

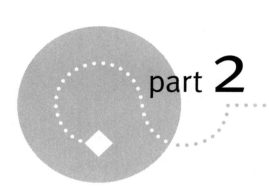

part **2**

Requirements

chapter 3

The requirements workflow

3.1 Chapter roadmap

This chapter is all about understanding system requirements. We discuss the details of the UP requirements workflow and introduce the notion of requirements. We also present a UP extension for dealing with requirements *without* using UML use cases.

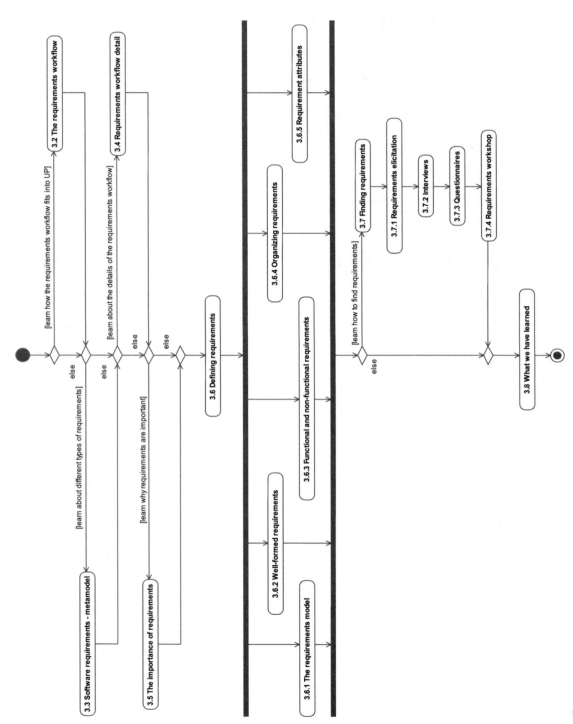

Figure 3.1

3.2   The requirements workflow

As shown in Figure 3.2, most of the work in the requirements workflow occurs throughout the Inception and Elaboration phases right at the beginning of the project life cycle. This is hardly surprising, as you can't progress beyond Elaboration until you know roughly what you are going to build!

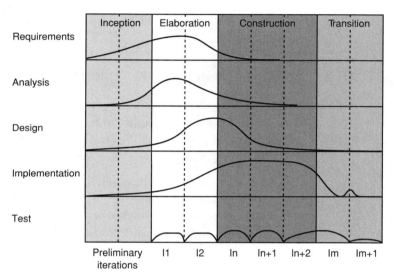

Figure 3.2   Adapted from Figure 1.5 [Jacobson 1] with permission from Addison-Wesley

Before you can even begin to work on OO analysis and design, you have to have some idea of what you are trying to achieve, and this is the purpose of the requirements workflow. From the point of view of the OO analyst/designer, the purpose is to discover and reach agreement on what the system should do, expressed in the language of the users of the system. Creating a high-level specification for what the system should do is part of *requirements engineering*.

For any given system, there may be many different stakeholders: many types of user, maintenance engineers, support staff, salespeople, managers, and so on. Requirements engineering is about eliciting and prioritizing the requirements these stakeholders have for the system. It is a process of negotiation as there are often conflicting requirements that must be balanced. For example, one group might want to add many users, which may result in unrealistic traffic on the existing database and communications infrastructure. This is a common conflict at the moment as more and more companies open up parts of their system to a huge user base via the Internet.

> Most requirements work is done at the beginning of the project in the Inception and Elaboration phases.

Some UML books (and indeed training courses) state that the UML notion of use cases is the only way to capture requirements, but this assertion doesn't really stand up to close examination. Use cases can only really capture functional requirements, which are statements about *what the system will do*. However, there is another set of non-functional requirements that are statements about *constraints on the system* (performance, reliability, and the like), which are not really suitable for capture by use cases. We therefore present in this book a robust requirements engineering approach by which we illustrate powerful and complementary ways to capture *both* sets of requirements.

3.3   Software requirements – metamodel

Figure 3.3 shows the metamodel for our approach to requirements engineering in this book. It contains quite a lot of UML syntax that we have not covered yet. Don't worry! We cover these things in depth later on. For now, the following is all you need to know.

● The icons that look like folders are UML packages. They are the UML grouping mechanism and contain groups of UML modeling elements. In effect, they act very much like real folders in a filing system in that they are used to organize and group related things. When the package has a

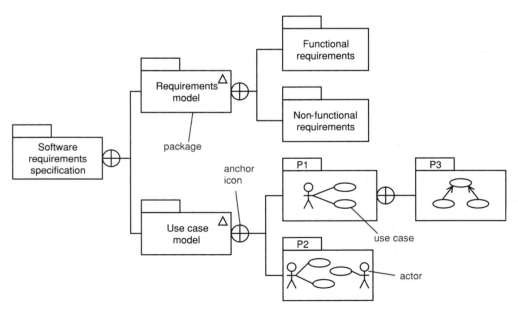

Figure 3.3

small triangle in its upper right-hand corner, this indicates that the package contains a model.

- The anchor icon indicates that the thing at the circle end *contains* the thing at the other end of the line.

Our metamodel shows that the Software requirements specification (SRS) contains a Requirements model and a Use case model. These two models are different, yet complementary, ways to capture system requirements.

You can see that the Requirements model contains Functional requirements (requirements specifying what the system should do) and Non-functional requirements (requirements expressing non-functional constraints on the system).

The Use case model contains many use case packages (we only show three here) that contain use cases (specifications of system functionality), actors (external roles that interact directly with the system), and relationships.

The SRS is really the very beginning of the software construction process. It is generally the initial input to OO analysis and design.

We cover requirements in detail in the rest of this chapter, and use cases and actors in the next.

3.4   Requirements workflow detail

Figure 3.4 shows the specific tasks for the UP requirements workflow. A diagram such as this is known as a workflow detail as it details the component tasks of a specific workflow.

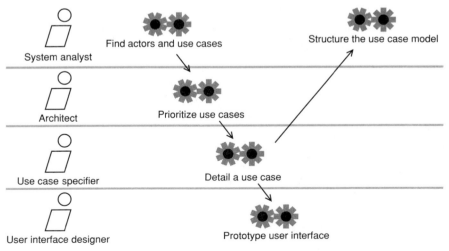

Figure 3.4 Reproduced from Figure 7.10 [Jacobson 1] with permission from Addison-Wesley

A workflow detail shows us the workers and activities involved in a particular workflow.

UP workflow details are modeled as workers (the icons on the left-hand side) and activities (the icons that look like cogs). UP variants such as RUP may use different icons, but the semantics are the same (see Section 2.4 for a brief discussion of the relationship between UP and RUP). The arrows are relationships that show the normal flow of work from one task to the next. However, it is worth bearing in mind that this is only an approximation of the workflow in the "average" case and might not be a particularly exact representation of what happens in practice. In the real world, you can expect some tasks to be done in a different order or in parallel according to circumstances.

Because this is an analysis and design book, we focus only on the tasks important to OO analysts and designers. In this case, we are interested in the following tasks.

- Find actors and use cases.

- Detail a use case.

- Structure the use case model.

The other tasks in the requirements workflow are not that relevant to us as analyst/designers. Prioritize use cases is primarily an architecture and project planning activity, and Prototype user interface is a programming activity. If you need to, you can learn more about these activities in [Jacobson 1].

We extend the UP requirements workflow to deal with requirements expressed in structured English.

In Figure 3.4 you can see that the standard UP workflow focuses on use cases to the exclusion of any other requirements elicitation techniques. This is fine as far as it goes, but, as we have said, it doesn't really address the non-functional aspect of requirements particularly well. In order to deal with requirements rigorously, we make a simple extension to the UP requirements workflow to add the following new tasks.

- Find functional requirements.

- Find non-functional requirements.

- Prioritize requirements.

- Trace requirements to use cases.

We have also introduced a new worker, the requirements engineer. The new tasks and workers are shown in Figure 3.5.

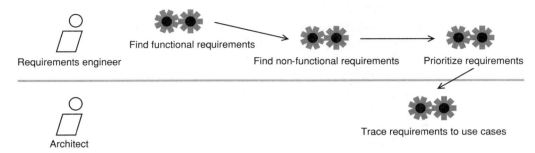

Figure 3.5

3.5   The importance of requirements

Requirements engineering is a term used to describe the activities involved in eliciting, documenting, and maintaining a set of requirements for a software system. It is about discovering what the stakeholders need the system to do for them.

According to [Standish 1], incomplete requirements and lack of user involvement were the two top reasons cited for project failure. Both of these issues are failures in requirements engineering.

As the final software system is predicated on a set of requirements, effective requirements engineering is a critical success factor in software development projects.

3.6   Defining requirements

We can define a requirement as "a specification of what should be implemented". There are basically two types of requirements:

- functional requirements – what behavior the system should offer;
- non-functional requirements – a specific property or constraint on the system.

Requirements
tell us what we should
build, not how we
should build it.

Requirements are (or at least should be) the basis of all systems. They are essentially a statement of what the system should do. In principle, requirements should *only* be a statement of *what* the system should do, and not *how* it should do it. This is an important distinction. We can specify *what* a system should do and what behavior a system should exhibit without necessarily saying anything about *how* this functionality may be actually realized.

While it is certainly attractive in theory to separate the "what" from the "how", in practice a set of requirements will tend to be a mix of "what" and "how". This is partly because it is often easier to write and understand an implementation description, rather than an abstract statement of the problem, and partly because there may be implementation constraints that predetermine the "how" of the system.

Despite the fact that system behavior and, ultimately, end-user satisfaction is predicated on requirements engineering, many companies still don't recognize this as an important discipline. As we have seen, the primary reason that software projects fail is due to problems in requirements.

3.6.1   The requirements model

Many companies still have no formal notion of requirements or of a requirements model. Software is specified in one or more informal "requirements documents" that are often written in natural language, and come in all shapes and sizes, and in varying degrees of usefulness. For *any* requirements document, in whatever form, the key questions are "how useful is it to me?" and "does it help me to understand what the system should do or not?" Unfortunately, many of these informal documents are of only limited usefulness.

UP has a formal approach to requirements based on a use case model, and we extend that here with a requirements model based on traditional ideas of functional and non-functional requirements. This extension is in direct accordance with the more sophisticated approach to requirements engineering in RUP. Our requirements metamodel (Figure 3.3) shows that the SRS consists of a use case model *and* a requirements model.

The use case model is usually created in a UML modeling tool such as Rational Rose. We discuss use cases in detail in Chapter 4 and Chapter 5.

The requirements model may be created in text or in special requirements engineering tools such as RequisitePro (www.ibm.com) or DOORS (www.telelogic.com). We recommend that you use requirements engineering tools if possible! We look at how to write well-formed requirements in the next few sections.

3.6.2   Well-formed requirements

UML does not provide any recommendations on writing traditional requirements. In fact UML deals with requirements entirely by the mechanism of use cases, which we examine later. However, many modelers (us included) believe that use cases are not enough and that we still need traditional requirements and requirements management tools.

We recommend a very simple format for stating requirements (see Figure 3.6). Each requirement has a unique identifier (usually a number), a keyword (shall) and a statement of function. The advantage of adopting a uniform structure is that requirements management tools such as DOORS can parse requirements more easily.

> Use simple "shall" statements to capture requirements.

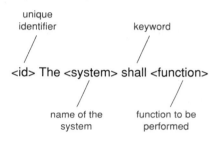

Figure 3.6

3.6.3 Functional and non-functional requirements

It is useful to divide requirements into functional and non-functional requirements. There are many other ways of categorizing requirements, but we will keep things as simple as possible and work initially with these two categories.

A functional requirement is a statement of what the system should do— it is a statement of system function. For example, if you were collecting requirements for an automated teller machine (ATM), you might identify the following functional requirements.

> Functional requirement – what the system should do.

1. The ATM system shall check the validity of the inserted ATM card.
2. The ATM system shall validate the PIN number entered by the customer.
3. The ATM system shall dispense no more than $250 against any ATM card in any 24-hour period.

A non-functional requirement is a constraint placed on the system. For your ATM system, there may be the following non-functional requirements.

> Non-functional requirement – a constraint on the system.

1. The ATM system shall be written in C++.
2. The ATM system shall communicate with the bank by using 256-bit encryption.
3. The ATM system shall validate an ATM card in three seconds or less.
4. The ATM system shall validate a PIN in three seconds or less.

You can see that non-functional requirements specify, or constrain, how the system will be implemented.

3.6.4   Organizing requirements

If you are using a requirements management tool, you will be able to organize your requirements into a *taxonomy*. This is a hierarchy of requirement types that you can use to categorize your requirements. The main reason for using requirement types is that they can organize a large, unstructured sea of requirements into smaller, more manageable domains. This should help you work with the requirements more effectively.

The basic split into functional and non-functional requirements that we describe above is a very simple taxonomy, but you could, for example, further categorize your requirements by extending this taxonomy as shown in Figure 3.7.

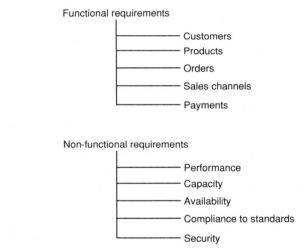

Figure 3.7

The specific requirement types you choose depends on the type of software you are building. This is especially true for functional requirements. For non-functional requirements, the set of requirement types shown in Figure 3.7 is fairly standard and provides a good starting point.

Organizing requirements by type is a useful approach if you have a lot of requirements (more than a hundred or so) to deal with. It is *especially* useful if you are using a requirements engineering tool as this will let you query the requirements model by requirement type to extract useful information.

In principle, your hierarchy of requirement types can be as deep as you like. In practice, about two or three levels seems to be about right unless you are working on a very complex system.

3.6.5   Requirement attributes

Each requirement may have a set of attributes that captures extra information (metadata) about the requirement.

Each requirement attribute has a descriptive name and a value. For example, a requirement may have an attribute called dueDate that has as its value the date the requirement must be delivered. The requirement might also have a source attribute that has as its value a description of where the requirement originated. The precise set of attributes you choose to use depends on the nature and needs of your project and may vary by requirement type.

Perhaps the most common requirement attribute is priority. The value of this attribute is the priority of the requirement relative to all the other requirements. A common scheme for assigning priority is the set of MoSCoW criteria described in Table 3.5.

Table 3.5

Priority attribute values	Semantics
Must have	Mandatory requirements that are fundamental to the system
Should have	Important requirements that may be omitted
Could have	Requirements that are truly optional (realize if there is time)
Want to have	Requirements that can wait for later releases of the system

When MoSCoW is used, each requirement has a Priority attribute that can take one of the values M, S, C, or W. Requirements engineering tools generally let you query the requirements model by attribute value so that you could, for example, generate a list of all top-priority (Must have) requirements. This is very useful!

The virtue of MoSCoW is its simplicity. However, it does confuse two different attributes of a requirement: its importance and its precedence. The importance of a requirement, once set, tends to remain relatively stable. However, the precedence of a requirement—when it will be realized with respect to other requirements—can change during the course of the project for reasons unrelated to importance. For example, the availability of resources, or dependencies on other requirements.

RUP defines a more complete set of requirement attributes that separates importance (Benefit) and precedence (TargetRelease). The RUP attributes are summarized in Table 3.6.

Whether you use MoSCoW, RUP, or some other set of requirement attributes depends on your particular project. The key point when defining a set of attributes is to keep it as simple as you can. Choose only those attributes that deliver benefit to your project. If an attribute doesn't deliver benefit, don't use it.

> Keep requirement attributes to the minimum that benefits your project.

Table 3.6

Attribute	Semantics
Status	This can have one of the following values: Proposed – requirements that are still under discussion and have not been agreed Approved – requirements that have been approved for implementation Rejected – requirements that have been rejected for implementation Incorporated – requirements that have been implemented in a particular release
Benefit	This can have one of the following values: Critical – the requirement *must* be implemented; otherwise, the system will not be acceptable to the stakeholders Important – the requirement might be omitted, but this would adversely affect the usability of the system and stakeholder satisfaction Useful – the requirement might be omitted with no significant impact on the acceptability of the system
Effort	An estimate of the time and resources needed to implement the feature measured in person days or some other unit such as function points (www.ifpug.org)
Risk	The risk involved in adding this feature – High, Medium, or Low
Stability	An estimate of the probability the requirement will change in some way – High, Medium, or Low
TargetRelease	The product version in which the requirement should be implemented

3.7   Finding requirements

Requirements come from the context of the system you are trying to model. This context includes

- direct users of the system;
- other stakeholders (e.g., managers, maintainers, installers);
- other systems with which the system interacts;
- hardware devices with which the system interacts;
- legal and regulatory constraints;
- technical constraints;
- business goals.

Requirements engineering generally starts with a vision document that outlines what the system is going to do, and what benefits it will deliver to a set of stakeholders. The idea of this document is to capture the essential goals of the system from the stakeholders' point of view. The vision document is produced by system analysts during the Inception phase of the UP.

After the vision document, requirements engineering begins in earnest. We will look at some techniques for requirements elicitation in the next few sections.

3.7.1   Requirements elicitation – the map is not the territory

The three filters of deletion, distortion, and generalization shape natural language.

Whenever you work with people to capture the requirements for a software system, you are trying to elicit from them an accurate picture, or map, of their model of the world. According to Noam Chomsky, in his 1975 book *Syntactic Structures* [Chomsky 1] on transformational grammar, this map is created by the three processes of deletion, distortion, and generalization. This is entirely necessary, as we just don't have the cognitive equipment to capture every nuance and detail of the world in an infinitely detailed mental map, so we have to be selective. We make our selection from the vast array of possible information by applying these three filters:

- deletion – information is filtered out;
- distortion – information is modified by the related mechanisms creation and hallucination;
- generalization – information is abstracted into rules, beliefs, and principles about truth and falsehood.

These filters shape natural language. It is important to know about them when you are carrying out detailed requirements capture and analysis, as you may need to actively identify and challenge them to recover information.

Below are some examples from a library management system. For each there is a challenge to the filter and a possible response to that challenge.

- Example: "They use the system to borrow books" – deletion.
    - Challenge: Who specifically uses the system to borrow books?
    - Response: Library members, other libraries, and librarians.

- Example: "Borrowers can't borrow another book until all overdue books have been returned" – distortion.
    - Challenge: Are there any circumstances under which someone could borrow a new book before all overdue books had been returned?
    - Response: Actually, there are two circumstances under which a borrower's right to borrow books may be restored. First, all overdue books are returned; second, any overdue book that has not been returned has been paid for.

- Example: "Everyone must have a ticket to borrow books" – generalization.
    - Challenge: Is there any user of the system who might not need to have a ticket?
    - Response: Some users of the system, such as other libraries, may not need a ticket or may have a special type of ticket with different terms and conditions.

The last two cases are particularly interesting as examples of a common language pattern: the universal quantifier. Universal quantifiers are words such as

- all;
- everyone;
- always;
- never;
- nobody;
- none.

Whenever you encounter a universal quantifier, you may have found a deletion, a distortion, or a generalization. They often indicate that you have reached the limits, or bounds, of someone's mental map. As such, when doing analysis it is often a good idea to challenge universal quantifiers. We almost wrote "it is *always* a good idea to challenge universal quantifiers", but then we challenged ourselves!

3.7.2   Interviews

Interviewing stakeholders is the most direct way of gathering requirements. Usually, you are better off having one-on-one interviews where possible. The essential points are noted below.

- Don't hallucinate a solution – you may *think* you have a very good idea of what the stakeholders need, but you must set this preconception aside during the interview. This is the only way you will ever find out what they really need.

- Ask context-free questions – these are questions that don't presuppose any particular answer and encourage the interviewee to talk about the problem. For example, "Who uses the system?" is context-free and encourages discussion, whereas "Do you use the system?" implies a yes/no answer and closes discussion down.

- Listen – this is the only way you will find out what stakeholders want, so give them the time to talk. Allow them to talk around a question and explore it in their own way. If you are looking for specific answers to questions, you may well have hallucinated a solution and be asking closed questions predicated on that hallucination.

- Don't mind-read – in fact, we all mind-read to some extent. Mind-reading is hallucinating that you know what someone feels, wants, or is thinking, based on what you would feel, want, or think in a similar situation. This is an important human skill because it is the basis of empathy. However, it can get in your way when you are trying to elicit requirements as you may end up with what *you* require rather than what the *stakeholder* requires.

- Have patience!

The interview context can have a big impact on the quality of the information you receive. Personally, we prefer informal contexts, such as a coffee bar, as they allow both interviewer and interviewee to relax and open up.

The best way to capture information during an interview is pen and paper! Typing things into a laptop is distracting to both parties and can feel quite intimidating to the interviewee. We like to use mind maps as a flexible, nonthreatening, and graphically rich way of collecting information. You can find out more about these at www.mind-map.com.

After an interview, you analyze the information and construct some candidate requirements.

3.7.3   Questionnaires

Questionnaires are no substitute for interviews.

If you decide to use questionnaires *without* doing any interviews, you may find yourself in an impossible situation where you must decide on a list of questions before you know the right questions to ask.

Questionnaires can be a useful supplement to interviews. They are very good at getting answers to specific, closed questions. You may uncover key questions from interviews and incorporate these into a questionnaire that you can then distribute to a wider audience. This can help you to validate your understanding of the requirements.

3.7.4   Requirements workshop

This is one of the most efficient ways of capturing requirements. You get the key stakeholders to participate in a workshop to identify key requirements.

The workshop should focus on brainstorming. This is a powerful technique for capturing information.

The participants in the meeting should be a facilitator, a requirements engineer, and the key stakeholders and domain experts. The procedure is as follows.

1. Explain that this is a true brainstorm.
    1.1. All ideas are accepted as good ideas.
    1.2. Ideas are recorded but *not* debated – never argue about something, just write it down and then move on. Everything will be analyzed later.

2. Ask the team members to name their key requirements for the system.
    2.1. Write each requirement on a sticky note.
    2.2. Stick the note on a wall or whiteboard.

3. You may then choose to iterate over the identified requirements and note additional attributes against each one (see Section 3.6.5).

After the meeting, analyze the results and turn them into requirements as we discussed earlier in this chapter. Circulate the results for comment.

Requirements engineering is an iterative process where you uncover requirements as you refine your understanding of the needs of the stakeholders. You may need to hold several workshops over time as your understanding deepens.

You can find lots more information about running workshops and requirements engineering in general in [Leffingwell 1] and [Alexander 1].

3.8   What we have learned

This chapter has presented the UP requirements workflow and a general discussion of software requirements. You have learned the following.

- Most of the work in the requirements workflow occurs in the Inception and Elaboration phases of the UP project life cycle.

- Our requirements metamodel (Figure 3.3) shows that there are two ways of capturing requirements – as functional and non-functional requirements and as use cases and actors.

- The UP requirements workflow detail contains the following activities that are of interest to us as OO analysts and designers:
  — Find actors and use cases;
  — Detail a use case;
  — Structure the use case model.

- We extend the standard UP requirements workflow with:
  — actor: Requirements engineer;
  — activity: Find functional requirements;
  — activity: Find non-functional requirements;
  — activity: Prioritize requirements;
  — activity: Trace requirements to use cases.

- Most project failures are due to problems with requirements engineering.

- There are two types of requirements:
  — functional requirements – what behavior the system should offer;
  — non-functional requirements – a specific property or constraint on the system.

- Well-formed requirements should be expressed in simple structured English using shall statements, so that they can be easily parsed by requirements engineering tools.
  — <id> The <system> shall <function>

- The requirements model contains the functional and non-functional requirements for a system. This may be:
  — a document;
  — a database in a requirements management tool.

- Requirements may be organized into a taxonomy – a hierarchy of requirement types that categorizes the requirements.

- Requirements may have attributes – extra information (metadata) associated with each requirement:
  - for example, priority – MoSCoW (Must have, Should have, Could have, Want to have)
  - for example, RUP attributes (Status, Benefit, Effort, Risk, Stability, TargetRelease)
  - Keep attribute requirements to the minimum that benefits your project.

- The map is not the territory. Natural language contains:
  - deletions – information is filtered out;
  - distortions – information is modified;
  - generalizations – information is abstracted into rules, beliefs, and principles about truth and falsehood.

- Universal quantifiers ("all", "every", for example) can indicate the boundary of someone's mental map of their world – you should challenge them.

- Techniques for finding requirements:
  - interviews;
  - questionnaires;
  - workshops.

chapter 4
Use case modeling

4.1   Chapter roadmap

In this chapter, we discuss the basics of use case modeling, which is another form of requirements engineering. We take you through the process of use case modeling as defined by UP. We concentrate on specific techniques and strategies that the OO analyst/designer can use to perform use case modeling effectively. To focus on these techniques, we keep the use cases in this section as simple as possible. There is a complete (and more complex) worked example on our website at www.umlandtheunifiedprocess.com.

UML does not specify any formal structure for the use case specification. This is problematic, as different modelers adopt different standards. To help with this, we have adopted a simple and effective standard in this chapter and in our worked example. To help you to apply our approach, our website provides open source XML (eXtensible Markup Language) schema for use cases and actors that you are free to use in your projects. These templates are based on industry best practice and provide a simple, yet effective, standard for capturing use case specifications.

Our website also includes a very simple XSL (eXtensible Stylesheet Language) stylesheet that transforms XML use case documents into HTML for display in a browser. This stylesheet is a useful example that can easily be customized to incorporate branding or other document standards for different organizations. A detailed discussion of XML is beyond the scope of this book, and you may need to refer to XML texts such as [Pitts 1] and [Kay 1] to use these documents effectively.

As well as open source schema and stylesheets, we are working on a more flexible approach called SUMR (Simple Use case Markup Restructured—pronounced "summer"). It is a simple, open source structured text markup language for use cases and actors. We provide sample SUMR schema, parsers, and XML and HTML generators on our website. See Section 2.2 for more details.

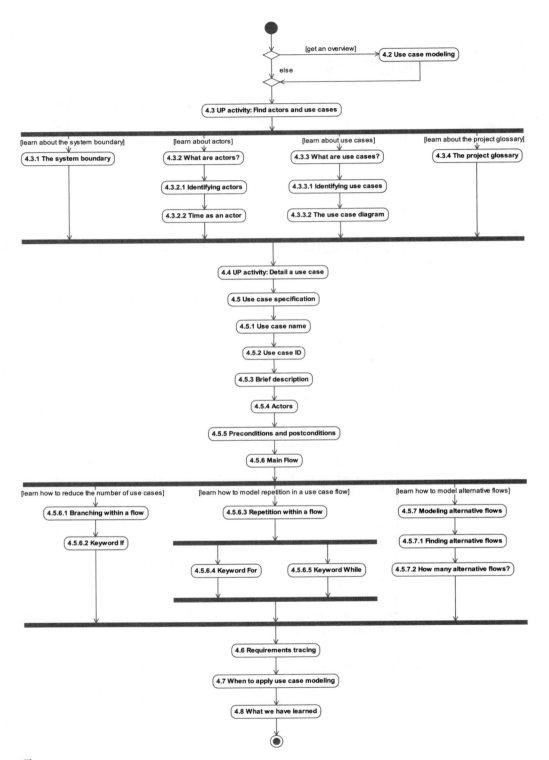

Figure 4.1

4.2 Use case modeling

Use case modeling is a form of requirements engineering. In Section 3.6, you saw how to create a requirements model comprising functional and non-functional requirements in what we might call the "traditional" way. Use case modeling is a different and complementary way of eliciting and documenting requirements. Use case modeling typically proceeds as follows.

- Find a candidate system boundary.
- Find the actors.
- Find the use cases:
  — specify the use case;
  — identify key alternative flows.
- Iterate until use cases, actors, and system boundary are stable.

You generally begin with some initial estimate of where the system boundary lies, to help you scope the modeling activity. The actions are then performed iteratively and often in parallel.

The output of these activities is the use case model. There are four components of this model.

Use cases are a way of capturing requirements.

- System boundary – a box drawn around the use cases to denote the edge or boundary of the system being modeled. This is known as the *subject* in UML 2.
- Actors – roles played by people or things that use the system.
- Use cases – things that the actors can do with the system.
- Relationships – meaningful relationships between actors and use cases.

The use case model provides a prime source for objects and classes. It is the primary input to class modeling.

4.3 UP activity: Find actors and use cases

Use case modeling involves finding actors and use cases.

In this section, we focus on the activity Find actors and use cases from the requirements workflow (see Section 3.4). This is shown in Figure 4.2. We go on in Section 4.4 to look at the activity Detail a use case.

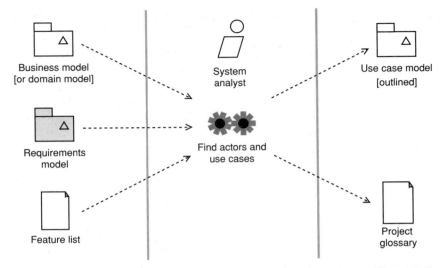

Figure 4.2 Adapted from Figure 7.11 [Jacobson 1] with permission from Addison-Wesley

It's worth looking at the inputs to Find actors and use cases.

- Business model – you may, or may not, have a business model available that relates to the system you are modeling. If you do, this is an excellent source of requirements.

- Requirements model – we described creation of this model in Chapter 3. These requirements provide useful input to the use case modeling process. In particular, the functional requirements will suggest use cases and actors. The non-functional requirements will suggest things you may need to keep in mind when constructing the use case model.

- Feature list – this is a set of candidate requirements that might take the form of a vision document or similar.

In Jacobson's original work, the requirements model (grayed in Figure 4.2 to show it is modified from the original figure) was replaced by supplementary requirements. This document consisted of requirements (usually non-functional) that didn't relate to any particular use case. The supplementary requirements document was primarily a catch-all for non-functional requirements that cut across use cases. In our more robust approach to requirements engineering it has been subsumed by, and is a subset of, the requirements model.

4.3.1   The subject (system boundary)

The subject
separates the system
from the rest of the
world.

The first thing you need to do when you are thinking about building a system is to decide where the boundaries of the system are. In other words, you need to define what is *part* of your system (inside the system boundary) and what is *external* to your system (outside the system boundary). This sounds obvious, but we have come across many projects where severe problems arose from an uncertain system boundary. The positioning of the system boundary typically has an enormous impact on the functional (and sometimes non-functional) requirements, and you have already seen that incomplete and ill-specified requirements can be the primary reason that projects fail. In UML 2, the system boundary is referred to as the *subject*, and this is the term we will use from now on.

The subject is defined by who or what uses the system (i.e., the actors) and what specific benefits the system offers to those actors (i.e., the use cases).

The subject is drawn as a box, labeled with the name of the system, with the actors drawn *outside* the boundary and the use cases *inside*. You will start use case modeling with only a tentative idea of where the subject actually lies. As you find the actors and use cases, the subject becomes more and more sharply defined.

4.3.2   What are actors?

Actors are roles
adopted by things that
interact directly with
the system.

An actor specifies a role that some external entity adopts when interacting with your system *directly*. It may represent a user role, or a role played by another system or piece of hardware, that touches the boundary of your system.

In UML 2, actors may also represent other subjects, giving you a way to link different use case models.

A role is like a hat
that something wears
in a particular context.

To understand actors, it's important to understand the concept of roles. Think of a role as being like a hat a thing wears in a particular context. Things may have many roles simultaneously and over time. This means that a given role may be played by many different things simultaneously and over time.

For example, if we have identified the Customer actor for our system, the real people Jim, Ila, Wolfgang, Roland, and many others may all play that role. These people may also play other roles. For example, Roland might also administer the system (the SystemAdministrator actor) as well as using it as a Customer.

The most fundamental mistake that beginners make in use case modeling is to confuse a role that something plays in the context of the system with the thing itself. Always ask yourself, "what *role* does this thing play with respect to the system?" This way, you can find common behavior among many different things and thereby simplify your use case model.

Actors are represented in UML as shown in Figure 4.3. They can be shown as a class icon stereotyped «actor» or as the "stick man" actor icon. Both forms of the actor notation are valid, but many modelers prefer to use the "stick man" form to represent roles that are likely to be played by people, and the class icon form to represent roles likely to be played by other systems.

Figure 4.3

> Actors are external to the system.

It is important to realize that actors are always *external* to the system. For example, if you are using an e-commerce system such as an online bookstore to buy a book, then you are external to that system. However, it is interesting to note that although actors themselves are always external to the system, systems often maintain some internal representation of one or more actors. For example, the online bookstore would maintain a customer details object for most customers that contains their name, address, and other information. This is an internal system representation of the external Customer actor. Now, it's important to be crystal clear about this difference—the Customer actor is *external* to the system, but the system might maintain a CustomerDetails class, which is an *internal* representation of individuals who play the role of Customer actor.

4.3.2.1   *Identifying actors*

To identify the actors, you need to consider who or what uses the system, and what roles they play in their interactions with the system. You can arrive at the roles that people and things play in relation to a system by considering cases of specific people and things and then generalizing. Asking the following questions will help you identify actors.

> To find actors ask: "Who or what uses or interacts with the system?"

- Who or what uses the system?
- What roles do they play in the interaction?
- Who installs the system?
- Who or what starts and shuts down the system?

- Who maintains the system?
- What other systems interact with this system?
- Who or what gets and provides information to the system?
- Does anything happen at a fixed time?

In terms of modeling actors, remember the following points.

- Actors are always external to the system—they are therefore outside your control.
- Actors interact *directly* with the system—this is how they help define the subject.
- Actors represent roles that people and things play in relation to the system, not specific people or specific things.
- One person or thing may play many roles in relation to the system simultaneously or over time. For example, if you were writing as well as delivering training courses, from the perspective of a course-planning system you would play two roles—Trainer and CourseAuthor.
- Each actor needs a short name that makes sense from the business perspective.
- Each actor must have a short description (one or two lines) that describes what this actor is from a business perspective.
- Like classes, actors may have compartments that show attributes of the actor and events that the actor may receive. Typically these compartments are not used that much and are rarely shown on use case diagrams. We won't consider them any further.

4.3.2.2 *Time as an actor*

When you need to model things that happen to your system at a specific point in time but which *don't* seem to be triggered by any actor, you can introduce an actor called Time as illustrated in Figure 4.4. An example of this would be an automatic system backup that runs every evening.

Time

Figure 4.4

4.3.3   What are use cases?

The UML Reference Manual [Rumbaugh 1] defines a use case as "A specification of sequences of actions, including variant sequences and error sequences, that a system, subsystem or class can perform by interacting with outside actors."

A use case is something an actor wants the system to do. It is a "case of use" of the system by a specific actor:

> A use case describes behavior that the system exhibits to benefit one or more actors.

- use cases are *always* started by an actor;
- use cases are *always* written from the point of view of the actors.

We usually think of use cases at the system level but, as the definition states, we may also apply use cases to describe "cases of use" of a subsystem (part of a system) or even an individual class. Use cases can also be very effective in business process modeling, although we don't address that aspect in this book.

The UML icon for use cases is shown in Figure 4.5. The name of the use case may be written inside or underneath the oval.

Figure 4.5

4.3.3.1   *Identifying use cases*

> To find use cases ask "How does each actor use the system?" and "What does the system do for each actor?"

The best way of identifying use cases is to start with the list of actors, and then consider how each actor is going to use the system. Using this strategy you can obtain a list of candidate use cases. Each use case must be given a short, descriptive name that is a verb phrase—after all, the use case is *doing* something!

As you identify use cases, you may also find some new actors. This is OK. Sometimes you have to consider system functionality very carefully before you find all the actors, or all the *right* actors.

Use case modeling is iterative and proceeds via a process of stepwise refinement. You begin with just a name for a use case and fill in the details later. These details consist of an initial short description that is refined into a complete specification. Here is a helpful list of questions that you can ask when trying to identify use cases.

- What functions will a specific actor want from the system?
- Does the system store and retrieve information? If so, which actors trigger this behavior?
- What happens when the system changes state (e.g., system start and stop)? Are any actors notified?

- Do any external events affect the system? What notifies the system about those events?
- Does the system interact with any external system?
- Does the system generate any reports?

4.3.3.2   *The use case diagram*

In the use case diagram you represent the subject of the use case model by a box labeled with the name of the subject. This box is the subject and, as we've already mentioned in Section 4.3.1, it represents the boundary of the system modeled by the use cases. You show actors outside the subject (external to the system) and use cases, which constitute the system behavior, inside the subject (internal to the system). This is illustrated in Figure 4.6.

The relationship between an actor and a use case is shown by a solid line, which is actually the UML association symbol. You'll see much more of associations in Chapter 9. The association between actor and use case indicates that the actor and the use case communicate in some way.

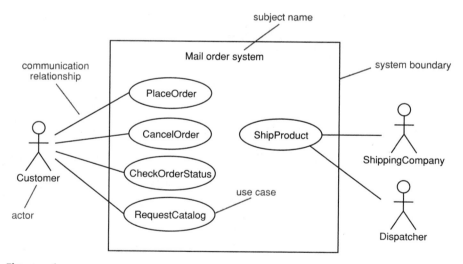

Figure 4.6

4.3.4   The project glossary

The project glossary may well be one of the most important project artifacts. Every business domain has its own unique language, and the primary purpose of requirements engineering and analysis is to understand and capture that language. The glossary provides a dictionary of key business terms

Capture business language and jargon in the project glossary.

and definitions. It should be understandable by everyone in the project, including all the stakeholders.

As well as defining key terms, the project glossary must resolve synonyms and homonyms.

- Synonyms are different words that mean the same thing. As an OO analyst you must choose one of these words (the one that seems to be used most widely) and stick with it. The other variants must be completely excluded from your models. The reason is that if you allow the use of synonyms, you may well end up with two classes that do more or less the same thing but have different names. Also, if you allow the use of all the synonyms on an ad hoc basis, you can be sure that the actual semantics of the terms will gradually diverge over time.

- Homonyms occur when the same word means different things to different people. This always gives rise to difficult communication problems as the various parties are quite literally speaking different languages when they all *believe* that they are speaking the same language. Again, the way to resolve this is to choose one meaning for the term, and perhaps introduce new terms for the other homonyms.

In the project glossary, you should record the preferred term and list any synonyms under the definition. This may involve encouraging some business stakeholders to become accustomed to different terminology. It is often a hard task to get stakeholders to change their use of language and yet, with persistence, it can be done.

UML does not set any standards for a project glossary. It is good practice to keep it as simple and concise as possible. Use a format like that of a dictionary with an alphabetically sorted list of words and definitions. A simple text-based document may suffice, but large projects may well require an online HTML- or XML-based glossary or even a simple database. Remember that the more accessible and easy the glossary is to use, the more positive an impact it is likely to have on the project.

You can see part of an example project glossary in Table 4.1. As a matter of style, we always write "None" if there are no synonyms or homonyms, rather than leaving the fields blank or omitting them. This shows that we have considered the question.

One issue with the project glossary is that terms and definitions in the glossary will also be used in the UML model. You have to ensure that the two documents are kept synchronized. Unfortunately, most UML modeling tools do not provide any support for this and so it is usually a manual activity.

Table 4.1

Project Glossary for the Clear View Training ECP (E-Commerce Platform)	
Term	**Definition**
Catalog	A listing of all of the products that Clear View Training currently offers for sale Synonyms: None Homonyms: None
Checkout	An electronic analogue of a real-world checkout in a supermarket A place where customers can pay for the products in their shopping basket Synonyms: None Homonyms: None
Clear View Training	A limited company specializing in sales of books and CDs Synonyms: CVT Homonyms: None
Credit card	A card such as VISA or Mastercard that can be used for paying for products Synonyms: Card Homonyms: None
Customer	A party who buys products or services from Clear View Training Synonyms: None Homonyms: None

4.4   UP activity: Detail a use case

Having created a use case diagram and identified the actors and key use cases, you then need to begin to specify each use case in turn. This is the UP activity known as Detail a use case; it is summarized in Figure 4.7.

It is important at this point to note that, typically, you don't do things in an exact sequence, and you can choose to specify some, or all, of the use cases as you find them. It is always difficult to present parallel activities in a book that, by its very nature, is linear!

The output of this activity is a more detailed use case. This consists of at least the use case name and a use case specification.

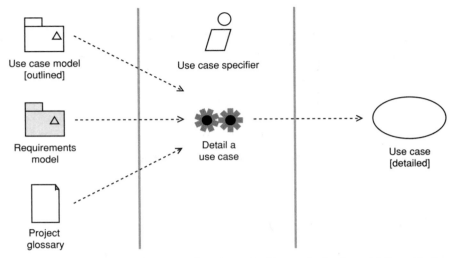

Figure 4.7   Adapted from Figure 7.14 [Jacobson 1] with permission from Addison-Wesley

4.5   Use case specification

There is no UML standard for a use case specification. However, the template shown in Figure 4.8 is in common use. There are more complex templates but, in our experience, it is best to keep use case modeling as simple as possible.

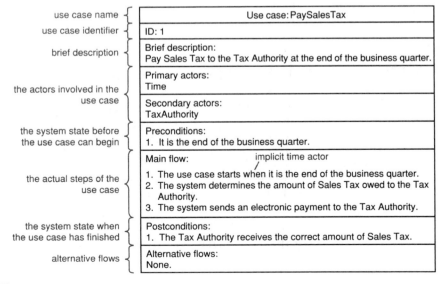

Figure 4.8

<table>
<tr><td>

Decide on a
standard for use case
specifications.

</td></tr>
</table>

It's important that your organization decides on a standard for use case specifications that is used consistently within projects. We have worked in organizations where there was no such standard, and it made the whole use case modeling process unnecessarily difficult. There were many different formats, levels of detail and even interpretations of what was, and was not, a use case—even within the same project! A simple, effective standard for use case specifications can help ensure that your project succeeds with use case analysis. We present such a standard in this chapter and the next.

Our template for a simple use case specification contains the following information:

- use case name;
- use case ID;
- brief description – a paragraph that captures the goal of the use case;
- actors involved in the use case;
- preconditions – these are things that must be true before the use case can execute—they are constraints on the state of the system;
- main flow – the steps in the use case;
- postconditions – things that must be true at the end of the use case;
- alternative flows – a list of alternatives to the main flow.

When we look at more complicated use cases later, we will add to the template to accommodate extra information.

The use case in Figure 4.8 is about paying Sales Tax—a form of tax levied on sales in many countries. In this example, the tax authority always gets its tax one way or another, and so we state this as a postcondition of the use case.

<table>
<tr><td>

Write use cases in
structured English.

</td></tr>
</table>

A good way to write a use case is to use "structured English" (or German or whatever your native language is). Over the next few sections, we introduce a simple style that you can use to express a use case effectively.

4.5.1   Use case name

There is no UML standard for naming use cases. We always name use cases in UpperCamelCase. The words of the use case name are run together, and each word starts with an uppercase letter.

Use cases describe system behavior, so the use case name should always be a verb or verb phrase such as PaySalesTax. You should always try to choose a name that is short, yet descriptive. A business reader of your use case model should be able to get a clear idea of the business function or process that the use case is modeling by the use case name alone. You will see lots of examples of use case names throughout this chapter and the next.

The use case name provides a unique identifier for the use case within your use case model.

4.5.2   Use case ID

Although use case names must be unique within your use case model, it is possible for them to change over time. You might wish therefore to add another immutable identifier that uniquely identifies a particular use case within your project. We often just use a number.

When working with alternative flows (Section 4.5.7), you may choose to use a hierarchical numbering system so that the alternative flow can be easily linked back to the main flow. For example, if a use case is numbered X, then its alternative flows are numbered X.1, X.2,..., X.n.

4.5.3   Brief description

This should be a single paragraph that summarizes the goal of the use case. Try to capture the essence of the use case—the business benefit it delivers to its actors.

4.5.4   Actors

From the point of view of a specific use case, there are two types of actors:

> Primary actors trigger the use case.

- primary actors – these actors actually trigger the use case;
- secondary actors – these actors interact with the use case after it has been triggered.

> Secondary actors do not trigger the use case.

Each use case is always triggered by a single actor. However, the same use case may be triggered by different actors at different points in time. Each actor that can trigger the use case is a primary actor. All the other actors are secondary actors.

4.5.5   Preconditions and postconditions

Preconditions and postconditions are constraints.

> Preconditions constrain the state of the system before the use case can start. Postconditions constrain the state of the system after the use case has executed.

- Preconditions constrain the state of the system before the use case can start. Think of them as gatekeepers that prevent an actor from triggering the use case until all their conditions are met.

- Postconditions constrain the state of the system after the use case has executed.

Another way of looking at this is that preconditions specify what must be true *before* the use case can be triggered, and postconditions specify what will be true *after* the use case has executed. Preconditions and postconditions help you to design systems that function correctly.

Preconditions and postconditions should always be simple statements about the state of the system that will evaluate to true or false—these are known as Boolean conditions.

If your use case doesn't have any preconditions or postconditions, then it is good style to write "None" in the appropriate section of the use case specification. This demonstrates that you have considered the matter, whereas merely leaving the section blank is ambiguous.

4.5.6 Main flow

> The main flow describes "perfect world" steps in a use case.

The steps in a use case are listed in a flow of events. You can think of a use case as being like a river delta with many branching channels. Every use case has one main flow that is the main channel through the delta. The other, smaller, channels in the delta are the alternative flows. These alternative flows can capture errors, branches, and interrupts to the main flow. The main flow is sometimes known as the *primary scenario*, and the alternative flows as *secondary scenarios*.

The main flow lists the steps in a use case that capture the "happy day", or "perfect world", situation where everything goes as expected and desired, and there are no errors, deviations, interrupts, or branches.

You can model deviations to the main flow in two ways that we will discuss shortly.

1. Simple deviations – create branches in the main flow (Section 4.5.6.1).

2. Complex deviations – write alternative flows (Section 4.5.7).

The main flow *always* begins by the primary actor doing something to trigger the use case. A good way to start a flow of events is as follows:

1. The use case starts when an <actor> <function>.

Remember that time can be an actor, so the use case may also start with a time expression in place of the actor, as in Figure 4.8.

The flow of events consists of a sequence of short steps that are declarative, numbered, and time-ordered. Each step in the use case flow should be in the form

<number> The <something> <some action>.

The use case flow of events can also be captured as prose. However, we don't recommend this, as it is generally far too imprecise.

Here is an example of a couple of steps in a PlaceOrder use case.

1. The use case starts when the customer selects "place order".
2. The customer enters his or her name and address into the form.

These are well-formed steps. In both cases we have a simple declarative statement of some thing performing some action. An example of an ill-formed use case step would be as follows:

2. Customer details are entered.

In fact, any step written in the passive voice is usually ill-formed. This particular step actually contains three important deletions.

- Who is it that enters the customer details?
- Into what are the details entered?
- What specifically are the "customer details"?

It is important that you recognize and avoid deletions when you write use case flows. Even though you may be able to tell by context, or guess what is meant, this is not really the point. The point is that the use case should be a precise statement of a piece of system functionality!

When you encounter vagueness, deletions, or generalizations during the process of analysis, it is useful to ask the following questions.

- Who specifically...?
- What specifically...?
- When specifically...?
- Where specifically...?

4.5.6.1   *Branching within a flow*

The UML specification does not specify any way to show branching within a flow.

We use an idiom that allows you to show branching in a simple way without having to write a separate alternative flow. We use the keyword If to indicate a branch.

It's worth knowing that some use case modelers may frown on branching within use cases. They argue that wherever there is a branch, a new alternative flow should be written. Strictly speaking, this argument has merit; however, we take the more pragmatic stance that a small amount of simple branching in a flow is desirable because it reduces the total number of alternative flows and leads to a more compact representation of the requirements.

Branching within a flow can simplify by reducing the number of use cases, but use sparingly!

4.5.6.2   *Keyword* If

Use the keyword If to indicate a branch in a flow. The example in Figure 4.9 shows a nicely structured flow of events with two branches. Each branch is prefixed with the keyword If, and begins with a simple Boolean expression such as If the user types in a new quantity, which is true or false. The indented text under the If statement is what will happen if the Boolean expression is true. You can clearly indicate the body of the If statement by careful use of indentation and numbering *without* needing to introduce an endif, or some other statement-closing syntax.

Use case: ManageBasket
ID: 2
Brief description: The Customer changes the quantity of an item in the basket.
Primary actors: Customer
Secondary actors: None.
Preconditions: 1. The shopping basket contents are visible.

Main flow:
1. The use case starts when the Customer selects an item in the basket.
2. If the Customer selects "delete item"
   2.1   The system removes the item from the basket.
3. If the Customer types in a new quantity
   3.1   The system updates the quantity of the item in the basket.

Postconditions: None.
Alternative flows: None.

Figure 4.9

Branching can reduce the number of use case postconditions. This is because steps within a branch may or may not occur, depending on the circumstances. They can't therefore generate postconditions, which are things that *must* be true rather than things that *may* be true.

4.5.6.3   *Repetition within a flow*

Sometimes you have to repeat an action several times within a flow of events. This doesn't occur very often in use case modeling, but when it does, it is useful to have a strategy to deal with it.

The UML specification does not specify any way to show repetition within a flow, so we introduce simple idioms using keywords For and While.

4.5.6.4 *Keyword* For

You can model repetition by using the keyword For. The format is as follows:

n. For (iteration expression)
    n.1. Do something
    n.2. Do something else
    n.3. ...
n+1.

The iteration expression is some expression that evaluates to a positive whole number of iterations. Each indented line after the For statement is repeated for the number of iterations specified in the iteration expression. An example is given in Figure 4.10.

Use case: FindProduct
ID: 3
Brief description: The system finds some products based on Customer search criteria and displays them to the Customer.
Primary actors: Customer
Secondary actors: None.
Preconditions: None.

Main flow:
1. The use case starts when the Customer selects "find product".
2. The system asks the Customer for search criteria.
3. The Customer enters the requested criteria.
4. The system searches for products that match the Customer's criteria.
5. If the system finds some matching products then
    5.1 For each product found
        5.1.1 The system displays a thumbnail sketch of the product.
        5.1.2 The system displays a summary of the product details.
        5.1.3 The system displays the product price.
6. Else
    6.1 The system tells the Customer that no matching products could be found.

Postconditions: None.
Alternative flows: None.

Figure 4.10

4.5.6.5   *Keyword* While

You use the While keyword to model a sequence of actions in the flow of events that is performed while some Boolean condition is true. The format is as follows:

n. While (Boolean condition)
    n.1. Do something
    n.2. Do something else
    n.3. ...
n+1.

Like For, the While keyword is infrequently used. An example is shown in Figure 4.11. The sequence of indented lines after the While statement is repeated until the Boolean condition specified in the While clause becomes false.

Use case: ShowCompanyDetails
ID: 4
Brief description: The system displays the company details to the Customer.
Primary actors: Customer
Secondary actors: None.
Preconditions: None.

Main flow:
1. The use case starts when the Customer selects "show company details".
2. The system displays a web page showing the company details.
3. While the Customer is browsing the company details
   3.1 The system plays some background music.
   3.2 The system displays special offers in a banner ad.

Postconditions: 1. The system has displayed the company details. 2. The system has played background music. 3. The system has displayed special offers.
Alternative flows: None.

Figure 4.11

4.5.7   Modeling alternative flows

Each use case has a main flow and may have many alternative flows. These are alternative paths through the use case that capture errors, branches, and

> Each use case has one main flow and may have many alternative flows.

> Alternative flows often do not return to the use case main flow.

interrupts to the main flow. As you have seen, the use case specification contains the main flow and a list of the names of the alternative flows.

The key point about alternative flows is that they frequently do not return to the main flow. This is because alternative flows often deal with errors and exceptions to the main flow and tend to have different postconditions. You can see alternative flows illustrated figuratively in Figure 4.12.

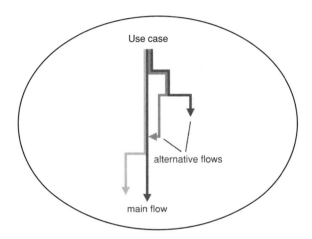

Figure 4.12

You can document alternative flows separately or append them to the end of the use case. We prefer to document them separately.

As an example of how you can model a use case with alternative flows, consider Figure 4.13.

You can see that this use case has three alternate flows, InvalidEmailAddress, InvalidPassword, and Cancel. In Figure 4.14 we have documented the InvalidEmail-Address alternative flow.

Notice that we make several changes to the use case template to accommodate alternative flows.

- Name – we use the following naming convention for alternative flows:

  Alternative flow: CreateNewCustomerAccount:InvalidEmailAddress

  This indicates that it is an alternative flow named InvalidEmailAddress for the CreateNewCustomerAccount use case.

- ID – notice how we have used a hierarchical numbering system to relate the alternative flow back to the main use case.

Use case: CreateNewCustomerAccount
ID: 5
Brief description: The system creates a new account for the Customer.
Primary actors: Customer
Secondary actors: None.
Preconditions: None.

Main flow:
 	
1. The use case begins when the Customer selects "create new customer account".
2. While the Customer details are invalid
    2.1 The system asks the Customer to enter his or her details comprising e-mail address, password, and password again for confirmation.
    2.2 The system validates the Customer details.
3. The system creates a new account for the Customer.

Postconditions: 1. A new account has been created for the Customer.
Alternative flows: InvalidEmailAddress InvalidPassword Cancel

Figure 4.13

Alternative flow: CreateNewCustomerAccount:InvalidEmailAddress
ID: 5.1
Brief description: The system informs the Customer that he or she has entered an invalid e-mail address.
Primary actors: Customer
Secondary actors: None.
Preconditions: 1. The Customer has entered an invalid e-mail address.
Alternative flow: 1. The alternative flow begins after step 2.2 of the main flow. 2. The system informs the Customer that he or she entered an invalid e-mail address.
Postconditions: None.

Figure 4.14

- Actors – list the actors used by the alternative flow.
- Preconditions and postconditions – alternative flows may have their own set of preconditions and postconditions that are different from those of the use case. If the alternative flow returns to the main flow, then its postconditions are effectively added to those of the main flow.
- Alternative flow – the steps in the alternative flow.
- An alternative flow should *not* have alternative flows. Otherwise, things rapidly get far too complex.

Alternative flows may be triggered in three different ways:

1. The alternative flow may be triggered *instead of* the main flow.
2. The alternative flow may be triggered *after a particular step* in the main flow.
3. The alternative flow may be triggered at *any time* during the main flow.

When an alternative flow executes instead of the main flow, it is triggered by the primary actor and it effectively replaces the use case entirely.

When the alternative flow is triggered after a particular step in the main flow, you should begin it as follows:

1. The alternative flow begins after step X of the main flow.

This is a form of branch, but it is different from the branching we discussed in Section 4.5.6.1 because it is a major deviation from the main flow and might not return to it.

When an alternative flow can be triggered at any time during the main flow, you should begin it as follows:

1. The alternative flow begins at any time.

You use this sort of alternative flow to model something that could happen at any point in the main flow before the final step. For example, in the use case CreateNewCustomerAccount, the Customer may choose to cancel account creation at any point. You can document Cancel as shown in Figure 4.15.

Should you wish the alternative flow to return to the main flow, you can express this as follows:

N. The alternative flow returns to step M of the main flow.

In this example the alternative flow executes its last step N, and then execution of the main flow continues at step M.

Alternative flow: CreateNewCustomerAccount:Cancel
ID: 5.2
Brief description: The Customer cancels the account creation process.
Primary actors: Customer
Secondary actors: None.
Preconditions: None.
Alternative flow: 1. The alternative flow begins at any time. 2. The Customer cancels account creation.
Postconditions: 1. A new account has *not* been created for the Customer.

Figure 4.15

4.5.7.1 Finding alternative flows

You can identify alternative flows by inspecting the main flow. At each step in the main flow, look for

- possible alternatives to the main flow;
- errors that might be raised in the main flow;
- interrupts that might occur at a particular point in the main flow;
- interrupts that might occur at *any* point in the main flow.

Each of these is a possible source of an alternative flow.

4.5.7.2 How many alternative flows?

> Only document the most important alternative flows.

As we've said, there is exactly one main flow per use case. However, there may be *many* alternative flows. The question is, "How many?" You should try to limit the number of alternative flows to the necessary minimum. There are two strategies for this.

- Pick the most important alternative flows and document those.
- Where there are groups of alternative flows that are all very similar, document one member of the group as an exemplar and (if necessary) add notes to this explaining how the others differ from it.

Going back to the river delta analogy, in addition to the main channel, there can be many branching and twisting alternative flows through the delta. You can't really afford to map them all, so you just choose the main ones. Also, many of these branches flow in pretty much the same direction with only minor differences. You can therefore map one exemplar channel in detail and just provide notes explaining how the other, smaller channels deviate from this. This is an efficient and effective way of modeling a complex use case.

The basic principle in use case modeling is to keep the amount of information captured to the *necessary minimum*. This means that many alternative flows may never be specified at all; a one-line description of them added to the use case may be enough detail to allow understanding of the functioning of the system. This is an important point. It is easy to get swamped in alternative flows, and we have seen more than one use case modeling activity fail because of this.

Remember that you are capturing use cases to *understand the desired behavior* of the system, and not for the sake of creating a complete use case model. You therefore stop use case modeling when you feel that you have achieved that understanding. Also, because the UP is an iterative life cycle, you can always go back to a use case and do more work if there is some aspect of the system's behavior that you decide you don't really understand.

4.6   Requirements tracing

> Requirements tracing links requirements in the requirements model to the use case model.

With a requirements model and a use case model, you effectively have two "databases" of functional requirements. It is important to relate the two to find out if there is anything in your requirements model that is not covered by the use case model, and vice versa. This is one aspect of requirements tracing.

Tracing functional requirements to use cases is complicated by the fact that there is a many-to-many relationship between individual functional requirements and use cases. One use case will cover many individual functional requirements, and one functional requirement may be manifest in several different use cases.

Hopefully, you will have modeling tool support for requirements tracing, and indeed requirements engineering tools such as RequisitePro and DOORS allow you to link individual requirements in their requirements database to specific use cases, and vice versa. In fact, UML provides pretty good support for requirements tracing. Using tagged values, you can associate a list of requirement ID numbers with each use case. In the requirements tool, you can link one or more use case identifiers to specific requirements.

If you have no modeling tool support, you must do the job manually. A good approach is to create a requirements traceability matrix. This is simply a grid with the ID numbers of individual requirements down one axis, and use case names (and/or ID numbers) along the other. A cross is put in all cells where a use case and requirement intersect. Requirements traceability matrices are often created in spreadsheets. An example is given in Table 4.2.

Table 4.2

		Use case			
		UC1	**UC2**	**UC3**	**UC4**
Requirement	R1	X			
	R2		X	X	
	R3			X	
	R4				X
	R5	X			

A requirements traceability matrix is a useful tool for checking consistency. If there is a requirement that doesn't map to any use case, then a use case is missing. Conversely, if there is a use case that doesn't map to any requirement, you know that your set of requirements is incomplete.

With the SUMR toolset that we discuss in Section 2.2, you can automate creation of a candidate requirements traceability matrix. The idea is simple: if a word in the project glossary occurs in a requirement and in a use case, there is a high probability that the two are related in some way. This creates a candidate requirements traceability matrix. We call it a "candidate" because such simple textual analysis will have errors and omissions and the matrix needs to be inspected manually. Still, it can be a great time saver and can help requirements engineers to perform a laborious task that might otherwise not get done at all.

4.7   When to apply use case modeling

Use cases are good at capturing system functionality. They are poor at capturing system constraints.

Use cases capture functional requirements and so are not effective for systems dominated by non-functional requirements.

Use cases are the best choice for requirements capture when

- the system is dominated by functional requirements;
- the system has many types of users to which it delivers different functionality (there are many actors);
- the system has many interfaces (there are many actors).

Use cases would be a poor choice when

● the system is dominated by non-functional requirements;

● the system has few users;

● the system has few interfaces.

Examples of systems where use cases may not be appropriate are embedded systems and systems that are algorithmically complex but with few interfaces. For these systems, you may well be much better off falling back on more conventional requirements engineering techniques. It is really just a matter of choosing the right tool for the job in hand.

4.8 What we have learned

This chapter has been all about capturing system requirements by use case modeling. You have learned the following.

● The use case modeling activity is part of the requirements workflow.

● Most of the work in the requirements workflow occurs in the Inception and Elaboration phases of the UP project life cycle.

● The key UP activities are Find actors and use cases and Detail a use case.

● Use case modeling is another form of requirements engineering that proceeds as follows:
— find the subject;
— find actors;
— find use cases.

● The subject defines what is part of the system and what is external to the system.

● Actors are roles played by things external to the system that interact directly with the system.
— You can find actors by considering who or what uses or interacts directly with the system.
— Time is often an actor.

● Use cases are functions that the system performs on behalf of, and to deliver benefit to, specific actors. You can find use cases by considering how each actor interacts with the system.
— You can find use cases by considering what functions the system offers to the actors.
— Use cases are always started by an actor.
— Use cases are always written from the point of view of the actors.

- The use case diagram shows:
  — the subject;
  — actors;
  — use cases;
  — interactions.
- The project glossary provides definitions of key business terms – it resolves synonyms and homonyms.
- The use case specification includes:
  — a use case name;
  — a unique identifier;
  — a brief description – the goal of the use case;
  — actors:
    - primary actors – trigger the use case;
    - secondary actors – interact with the use case after it has been triggered.
  — preconditions – system constraints that affect the execution of a use case;
  — main flow – the sequence of declarative, time-ordered steps in the use case;
  — postconditions – system constraints arising from the execution of a use case;
  — alternative flows – a list of alternatives to the main flow.
- You can reduce the number of use cases by allowing a limited amount of branching within the flow of events:
  — use the keyword If for branches that occur at a particular step in the flow;
  — use Alternative Flow sections in the use case to capture branches that may occur at any point in the flow.
- You can show repetition within a flow by using the keywords:
  — For (iteration expression);
  — While (Boolean condition).
- Each use case has one main flow – this is the "happy day" scenario where everything goes as planned.
- More complex use cases may have one or more alternative flows – these are paths through a use case that represent exceptions, branches, and interrupts.
- You find key alternative flows by examining the main flow and looking for:
  — alternatives;
  — error situations;
  — interrupts.

- Only decompose a use case into alternative flows when it adds value to the model.
- Requirements in the requirements model may be traced to use cases using a requirements traceability matrix.
- Use case modeling is most appropriate for systems that:
  - are dominated by functional requirements;
  - have many types of user;
  - have many interfaces to other systems.
- Use case modeling is least appropriate for systems that:
  - are dominated by non-functional requirements;
  - have few users;
  - have few interfaces.

chapter 5

Advanced use case modeling

5.1 Chapter roadmap

In this chapter, we discuss some advanced aspects of use case modeling and then finish our discussion of use cases with some hints and tips.

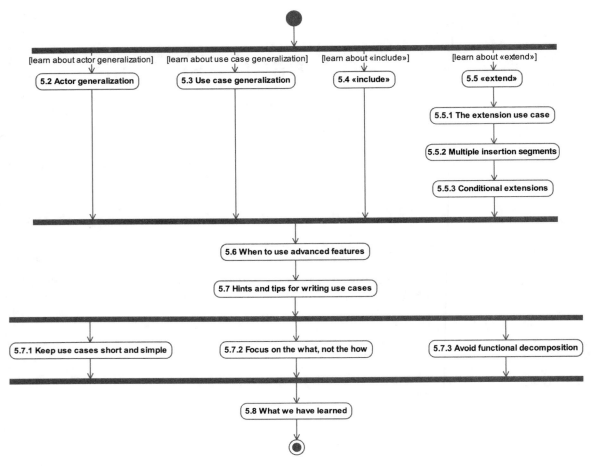

Figure 5.1

We discuss the relationships that are possible between actors and actors and between use cases and use cases. These relationships are as follows:

- actor generalization – a generalization relationship between a more general actor and a more specific actor;
- use case generalization – a generalization relationship between a more general use case and a more specific use case;
- «include» – a relationship between use cases that lets one use case include behavior from another;
- «extend» – a relationship between use cases that lets one use case extend its behavior with one or more behavior fragments from another.

It is important to keep all models as simple as possible, so use these relationships with discretion and only where they improve the overall clarity of the use case model. It is easy to go overboard with «include» and «extend» in particular, but you must avoid this.

5.2   Actor generalization

Actor generalization factors out behavior common to two or more actors into a parent actor.

In the example in Figure 5.2, you can see quite a lot of commonality between the two actors, Customer and SalesAgent, in the way that they interact with the Sales system (here, the SalesAgent can handle a sale on behalf of a Customer). Both actors trigger the use cases ListProducts, OrderProducts, and AcceptPayment. In fact, the only difference between the two actors is that the SalesAgent also triggers the CalculateCommission use case. Apart from the fact that this similarity in behavior gives lots of crossed lines on the diagram, it seems to indicate that there is some common actor behavior that could be factored out into a more *generalized* actor.

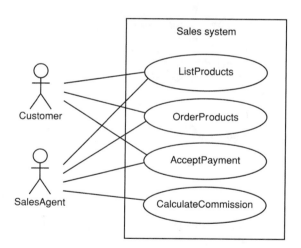

Figure 5.2

You can factor out this common behavior by using actor generalization as shown in Figure 5.3. You create an abstract actor called Purchaser that interacts with the use cases ListProducts, OrderProducts, and AcceptPayment. Customer and SalesAgent are known as concrete actors because real people (or other systems) could fulfill those roles. However, Purchaser is an abstract actor as it is an abstraction introduced simply to capture the common behavior of the two concrete actors—that they can both act in a purchasing role.

Customer and SalesAgent inherit all of the roles and relationships to use cases of their abstract parent. So, interpreting Figure 5.3, both Customer and SalesAgent have interactions with the use cases ListProducts, OrderProducts, and AcceptPayment that they inherit from their parent, Purchaser. In addition, SalesAgent has an interaction with the use case CalculateCommission that is not inherited—it is specific to the SalesAgent actor. You can see that judicious use of abstract actors can simplify use case diagrams. It also simplifies the semantics of your use case model because you are able to treat different things in the same way.

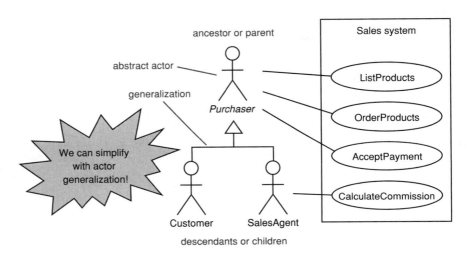

Figure 5.3

It's worth pointing out that the parent actor in actor generalization does not always have to be abstract—it may be a concrete role that a person or system could play. However, good style dictates that parent actors are usually abstract in order to keep the generalization semantics simple.

What we have seen is that if two actors communicate with the same set of use cases in the same way, we can express this as a generalization to another (possibly abstract) actor. The descendent actors inherit the roles and relationships to use cases held by the parent actor. You can substitute a descendent actor anywhere the ancestor actor is expected. This is the substitutability principle, which is an important test for correct use of generalization with *any* classifier.

In this example, it is reasonable that you can substitute a SalesAgent or a Customer anywhere a Purchaser is expected (i.e., interacting with use cases

We can use a descendant anywhere the ancestor actor is expected.

ListProducts, OrderProducts, and AcceptPayment), so actor generalization is the correct strategy.

5.3 Use case generalization

Use case generalization is used when you have one or more use cases that are really specializations of a more general case. Just like actor generalization, you should only use this when it simplifies your use case model.

In use case generalization, the child use cases represent more specific forms of the parent. The children may

> Use case generalization factors out behavior common to one or more use cases into a parent use case.

- inherit features from their parent use case;
- add new features;
- override (change) inherited features.

The child use case automatically inherits *all* features from its parent. However, not every type of use case feature may be overridden. The restrictions are summarized in Table 5.1.

Table 5.1

Use case feature	Inherit	Add	Override
Relationship	Y	Y	N
Extension point	Y	Y	N
Precondition	Y	Y	Y
Postcondition	Y	Y	Y
Step in main flow	Y	Y	Y
Alternative flow	Y	Y	Y

In UML 1.5 use cases also had attributes and operations, but in UML 2 they do not. In fact, use case attributes and operations didn't seem to add any real value, were rarely used, and were rarely supported in UML tools. According to the UML 1.5 specification, the operations of a use case were not even callable externally, so it was hard to imagine why they were ever there at all.

So how is use case generalization documented in use case specifications? The UML specification remains silent on this point, but there are several fairly standard techniques. We prefer to use a simple tag language to high-light the five possibilities in a child use case. There are two rules for applying the technique.

- Each step number in the child is postfixed by the equivalent step number in the parent if there is one. For example: 1. (2.). Some step.

- If the step in the child overrides a parent step, it is postfixed by "o" (for overridden) and then the step number in the parent.
  For example: 6. (06.) Another step.

Table 5.2 summarizes the syntax for the five options in child use cases.

Table 5.2

Feature is ...	Tag example
Inherited without change	3. (3.) The customer enters the requested criteria.
Inherited and renumbered	6.2 (6.1) The system tells the Customer that no matching products could be found.
Inherited and overridden	1. (01.) The Customer selects "find book".
Inherited, overridden, and renumbered	5.2 (05.1) The system displays a page showing details of a maximum of 5 books.
Added	6.3 The system redisplays the "find book" search page.

Figure 5.4 shows an extract from the use case diagram of a Sales system. We have the parent use case FindProduct, and then two specializations of this, FindBook and FindCD.

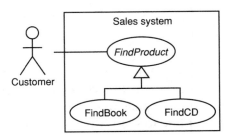

Figure 5.4

Figure 5.5 shows the specification for the parent use case FindProduct. Notice that it is expressed at a very high level of abstraction.

Use case: *FindProduct*
ID: 6
Brief description: The Customer searches for a product.
Primary actors: Customer
Secondary actors: None.
Preconditions: None.

Main flow:
1. The Customer selects "find product".
2. The system asks the Customer for search criteria.
3. The Customer enters the requested criteria.
4. The system searches for products that match the Customer's criteria.
5. If the system finds some matching products
    5.1 The system displays a list of the matching products.
6. Else
    6.1 The system tells the Customer that no matching products could be found.

Postconditions: None.
Alternative flows: None.

Figure 5.5

One of the child use cases, FindBook, is shown in Figure 5.6. This illustrates the application of our standard for indicating overridden or new features.

As you can see from Figure 5.6, the FindBook child use case is much more concrete. It specializes the more abstract parent to deal with a specific type of product, books.

If the parent use case has no flow of events or a flow of events that is incomplete, it is an abstract use case. Abstract use cases are quite common because you can use them for capturing behavior at the highest levels of abstraction. Because abstract use cases have a missing or incomplete flow of events, they can never be executed by the system. Rather than a flow of events, abstract use cases may have a plain text summary of the high-level behavior that their children will be expected to implement. You can place this in the brief description section of the use case.

As you have just seen, it's difficult to show inherited features in child use cases. You have to use some sort of tag language or typographic convention that stakeholders typically find confusing. As use cases are all about communication with the stakeholders, this is a serious drawback. Another disadvantage is that you have to manually maintain consistency between the parents and children when one of them changes. This is a laborious and error-prone task.

Use case: FindBook		
ID: 7		
Parent ID: 6		
Brief description: The Customer searches for a book.		
Primary actors: Customer		
Secondary actors: None.		
Preconditions: None.		
Main flow:		
overridden	1.	(o1.)	The Customer selects "find book".
overridden	2.	(o2.)	The system asks the Customer for book search criteria comprising author, title, ISBN, or topic.
inherited without change	3.	(3.)	The Customer enters the requested criteria.
overridden	4.	(o4.)	The system searches for books that match the Customer's criteria.
overridden	5.	(o5.)	If the system finds some matching books
added		5.1	The system displays the current best seller.
overridden and renumbered		5.2	(o5.1) The system displays details of a maximum of five books.
added		5.3	For each book on the page the system displays the title, author, price, and ISBN.
added		5.4	While there are more books, the system gives the Customer the option to display the next page of books.
inherited without change	6.	(6.)	Else
added		6.1	The system displays the current best seller.
renumbered		6.2	(6.1) The system tells the Customer that no matching products could be found.
Postconditions: None.		
Alternative flows: None.		

Figure 5.6

One approach to this problem is to restrict the parent use case so that it doesn't have any main flow, but only a brief description of its semantics. In this case, you don't have to worry about inheritance or overriding. This approach makes use case generalization easy and is a very effective way of showing that one or more use cases are really just specific variants of a more general use case. The more general use case allows you to think about the system in an abstract way, and may indicate opportunities for streamlining the software system.

5.4   «include»

Writing use cases can be very repetitive at times. Suppose you are writing a Personnel system (see Figure 5.7). Almost anything you ask the system to do

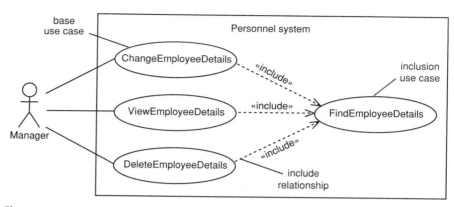

Figure 5.7

will first involve locating the details of a specific employee. If you had to write this sequence of events every time you needed employee details, your use cases would become quite repetitive. The «include» relationship between use cases allows you to include the behavior of one use case into the flow of another use case.

We refer to the *including* use case as the *base* use case, and to the *included* use case as the *inclusion* use case. The inclusion use case supplies behavior to its base use case.

You must specify the *exact* point in the base use case where you need the behavior of the inclusion use case to be included. The syntax for «include» is a bit like a function call, and indeed it has somewhat similar semantics.

The semantics of «include» are simple (see Figure 5.8). The base use case executes until the point of inclusion is reached, then execution passes over to the inclusion use case. When the inclusion use case finishes, control returns to the base use case again.

The base use case is not complete without all of its inclusion use cases. The inclusion use cases form integral parts of the base use case. However, the inclusion use cases may or may not be complete. If an inclusion use case is *not* complete, then it just contains a partial flow of events that will only make sense when it is included into a suitable base. We often refer to this as a behavior fragment. In this case, we say that the inclusion use case is not in-stantiable—that is, it can't be triggered directly by actors, it can only execute when included in a suitable base. If, however, the inclusion use cases *are* complete in themselves, they act just like normal use cases and are instantia-ble. It is then quite reasonable to trigger them by actors. You can see the inclusion use case, FindEmployeeDetails, in Figure 5.9. It is incomplete and therefore not instantiable.

> «include» factors out steps common to several use cases into a separate use case that is then included.

Use case: ChangeEmployeeDetails
ID: 1
Brief description: The Manager changes the employee details.
Primary actors: Manager
Secondary actors: None.
Preconditions: 1. The Manager is logged on to the system.
Main flow: 1. include(FindEmployeeDetails). 2. The system displays the employee details. 3. The Manager changes the employee details. ...
Postconditions: 1. The employee details have been changed.
Alternative flows: None.

Use case: ViewEmployeeDetails
ID: 2
Brief description: The Manager views the employee details.
Primary actors: Manager
Secondary actors: None.
Preconditions: 1. The Manager is logged on to the system.
Main flow: 1. include(FindEmployeeDetails). 2. The system displays the employee details. ...
Postconditions: 1. The system has displayed the employee details.
Alternative flows: None.

Use case: DeleteEmployeeDetails
ID: 3
Brief description: The Manager deletes the employee details.
Primary actors: Manager
Secondary actors: None.
Preconditions: 1. The Manager is logged on to the system.
Main flow: 1. include(FindEmployeeDetails). 2. The system displays the employee details. 3. The Manager deletes the employee details. ...
Postconditions: 1. The employee details have been deleted.
Alternative flows: None.

Figure 5.8

Use case: FindEmployeeDetails
ID: 4
Brief description: The Manager finds the employee details.
Primary actors: Manager
Secondary actors: None.
Preconditions: 1. The Manager is logged on to the system.
Main flow: 1. The Manager enters the employee's ID. 2. The system finds the employee details.
Postconditions: 1. The system has found the employee details.
Alternative flows: None.

Figure 5.9

5.5   «extend»

«extend» is a way
of inserting new
behavior into an
existing use case.

«extend» provides a way to insert new behavior into an existing use case (see Figure 5.10). The base use case provides a set of extension points that are hooks where new behavior may be added, and the extension use case provides a set of insertion segments that can be inserted into the base use case at these hooks. As you will see shortly, the «extend» relationship can be used to specify *exactly* which extension points in the base use case are being extended.

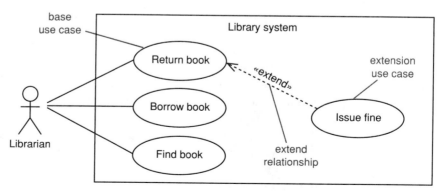

Figure 5.10

What is interesting about «extend» is that the base use case does not know anything about the extension use cases—it just provides hooks for them. In fact, the base use case is perfectly complete without its extensions. This is *very* different from «include», where the base use cases were incomplete without their inclusion use cases. Furthermore, the extension points are not actually inserted into the flow of events of the base use case; rather, they are added to an overlay on top of the flow of events.

Extension points are indicated in the flow of events of the base use case as shown in Figure 5.11. You can also show extension points on the use case diagram by listing them in a new compartment in the base use case icon.

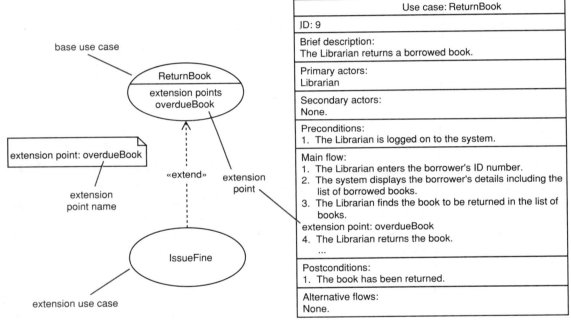

Figure 5.11

Notice that extension points in the main flow are not numbered. Instead, they appear *between* the numbered steps of the flow. In fact, UML explicitly states that extension points actually exist on an overlay on top of the main flow. They are therefore not part of the main flow at all. You can think of this overlay as being like an acetate film over the main flow where the extension points are recorded. The point of this idea of an overlay is to make the base use case flow completely independent of the extension points. In other words, the base use case flow doesn't know (or care) where it is being extended. This allows you to use «extend» to make arbitrary and ad hoc extensions to a base use case flow.

When you use «extend», the base use case acts as a modular framework into which you can plug extensions at predefined extension points. In the example in Figure 5.11, you can see that the ReturnBook base use case has an extension point called overdueBook between steps 3 and 4 in its flow of events.

You can see that «extend» provides a good way of dealing with exceptional cases or cases in which you need a flexible framework because you can't predict (or just don't know) all of the possible extensions in advance.

5.5.1   The extension use case

Extension use cases are *generally* not complete use cases and therefore can't usually be instantiated. They normally just consist of one or more behavior fragments known as insertion segments. The «extend» relationship specifies the extension point in the base use case where the insertion segment will be inserted. The following rules apply.

- The «extend» relationship must specify one or more of the extension points in the base use case or it is assumed that the «extend» relationship refers to *all* extension points.

- The extension use case must have the same number of insertion segments as there are extension points specified in the «extend» relationship.

- It is legal for two extension use cases to «extend» the same base use case at the same extension point. But if this happens, the order in which the extensions execute is indeterminate.

In the example in Figure 5.12, there is a single insertion segment in the Issue-Fine extension use case.

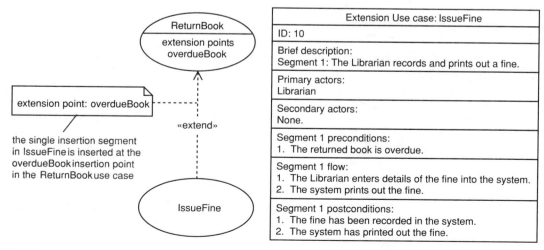

Figure 5.12

The extension use case may also have preconditions and postconditions. The preconditions must be fulfilled; otherwise, the segment does not execute. The postconditions constrain the state of the system after the segment has executed.

Extension use cases may themselves have extension use cases or inclusion use cases. However, we tend to avoid this, as it can make the use case model too complex.

5.5.2 Multiple insertion segments

You can have multiple insertion segments in an extension use case. This is useful when you can't capture the extension cleanly in a single segment because you need to go back to the main flow of the base use case to do something. In the example in Figure 5.13, you can imagine that after recording and printing a fine, we go back to the main flow to process any more overdue

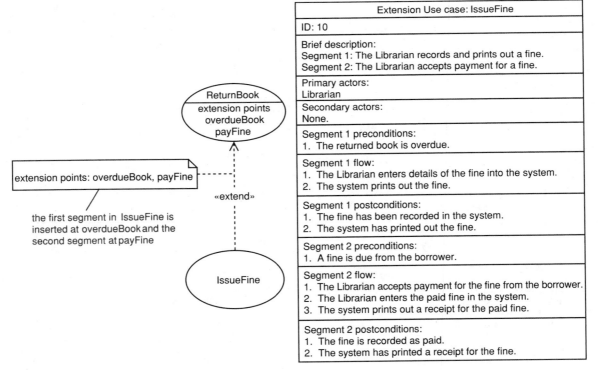

Figure 5.13

books and then, finally, at extension point payFine, we give the borrower the option to pay the total fine. This is clearly more efficient than having to accept payment for each fine individually, which would have been the case if we had combined the two segments in IssueFine.

When you create extension use cases with multiple segments, you have to clearly label each segment with a number as shown in Figure 5.13. This is because the order of the segments is important—the first segment is inserted at the first extension point and so on. You must therefore be very careful to write the segments in the right order, and to preserve this order.

5.5.3 Conditional extensions

The example in Figure 5.14 shows a slightly more benign library system in which borrowers are given a warning the first time a book is returned overdue and are fined only subsequently. We can model this by adding a new extension use case, IssueWarning, and then placing conditions on the «extend» relationships. The conditions are Boolean expressions, and the insertion is made if, and only if, the expression evaluates to true.

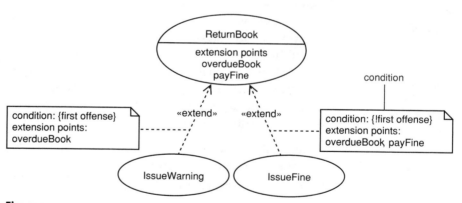

Figure 5.14

Notice that the IssueWarning extension use case only extends at the overdueBook extension point. However (as before), the IssueFine extension use case extends both at overdueBook and at payFine. This immediately tells you that IssueWarning (Figure 5.15) contains exactly one insertion segment, whereas IssueFine (as we have already seen) contains two.

Extension Use case: IssueWarning
ID: 11
Brief description: Segment 1: The Librarian issues a warning.
Primary actors: Librarian
Secondary actors: None.
Segment 1 preconditions: 1. The returned book is overdue.
Segment 1 flow: 1. The Librarian enters details of the warning into the system.
Segment 1 postconditions: 1. The warning has been recorded in the system.

Figure 5.15

5.6   When to use advanced features

> Use advanced features only when they simplify the model and make it easier to understand.

Use advanced features when they simplify your use case model. We have found time and again that the best use case models are simple. Remember that the use case model is a statement of requirements and, as such, must be accessible to the stakeholders as well as the modelers. A simple use case model that only uses advanced features sparingly, if at all, is in every respect preferable to one that overuses advanced features, even if that model is in some ways more elegant from a modeler's perspective.

Based on our experience in use case modeling in many different companies, we have found that

- generally, stakeholders can easily understand actors and use cases with just a little training/mentoring;
- stakeholders find actor generalization more difficult to grasp;
- heavy use of «include» can make use case models harder to understand—stakeholders and modelers have to look at more than one use case to get the complete picture;
- stakeholders have great difficulty with «extend»—this can be true even with careful explanation;
- a surprising number of object modelers misunderstand the semantics of «extend»;
- use case generalization should be avoided unless abstract (rather than concrete) parent use cases are used—otherwise, it adds too much complexity to the child use cases.

5.7 Hints and tips for writing use cases

In this section we give a few hints and tips on writing use cases.

5.7.1 Keep use cases short and simple

Our motto for use cases is "keep them short, keep them simple". Include only enough detail to capture the requirements. Unfortunately, some projects are scared of things that are short and simple and are enamored of large quantities of documentation. Grady Booch calls this tendency "paper envy".

A good rule of thumb is to ensure that the main flow of a use case fits on a single side of paper. Any more than this, and the use case is almost certainly too long. In fact, you will find that many use cases are less than half a page in length.

Start by simplifying the text (remember to use short declarative sentences as we describe in Section 3.6.2). Remove any design details (see next section). If it is still too long, reanalyze the problem. Perhaps there could be more than one use case there? Perhaps you can factor out alternative flows?

5.7.2 Focus on the *what*, not the *how*

Remember that you are writing use cases to work out *what* the actors need the system to do, not *how* the system should do it. The how comes later in the design workflow. Confusing the what with the how is a problem that we see over and over again. The use case writer hallucinates some solution when writing the use case. For example, consider the use case fragment below.

...
4. The system asks the Customer to confirm the order.
5. The Customer presses the OK button.
...

In this step, the use case writer has imagined some sort of user interface: a form with an OK button. Because of this, the use case is no longer a pure statement of requirements, it is a primitive design. A better way of expressing step 5 is as follows:

...
5. The Customer accepts the order.
...

Keep the details of the design (which you don't know yet!) out of the use case.

5.7.3   Avoid functional decomposition

Functional
decomposition doesn't
work for use case
models.

One common error in use case analysis is to create a set of "high level" use cases, and then break these down into a set of lower-level use cases and so on, until you end up with "primitive" use cases that are detailed enough to implement. This approach to software design is known as functional decomposition and it is invariably *wrong* when applied to use case modeling.

Let's look at an example. In Figure 5.16 the analyst has defined the operation of a library system using a single high-level use case, RunLibrary, and then decomposed this into use cases at finer and finer levels of detail, creating a functional decomposition.

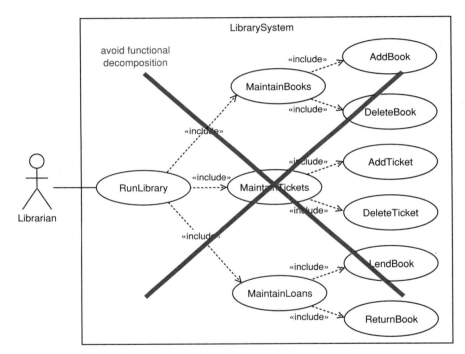

Figure 5.16

Many non-OO analysts would find Figure 5.16 quite plausible. However, as a use case model, there is a lot wrong with it.

- Rather than focusing on capturing the requirements, the model focuses on structuring those requirements in an artificial way—there are many possible decompositions.

- The model describes the system as a set of nested functions. However, OO systems are really sets of cooperating objects sending messages back and forth. There is clearly a conceptual mismatch here.

- Only the lowest level of use cases, AddBook, DeleteBook, AddTicket, Delete-Ticket, LendBook, and ReturnBook, have interesting specifications. The higher levels just call the lower ones and add nothing to the model in terms of requirements capture.

- The model is hard for stakeholders to understand—there are several rather abstract use cases (RunLibrary, MaintainBooks, MaintainTickets, and MaintainLoans) and a lot of «include» relationships to lower levels.

The use of a functional decomposition approach suggests that an analyst has been thinking about the system in the wrong way. It is often an indication that the analyst is trained in more traditional procedural programming techniques and hasn't yet grasped the OO paradigm. In this case, it's generally a good idea to employ an experienced use case modeler to provide mentoring and reviews.

Not all examples of functional decomposition are as obvious as the example in Figure 5.16. Often you find that parts of the use case model are okay, whereas other parts have been decomposed. It's a good idea to check any part of the use case model that has a deep hierarchy for possible functional decomposition.

Finally, we should point out that hierarchies often arise naturally in use case modeling. However, these natural hierarchies are generally never more than one (or at most two) levels deep, and the whole model is *never* rooted in a single use case.

5.8   What we have learned

You have learned about techniques for advanced use case modeling. Your goal always should be to produce a simple, easy-to-understand use case model that captures the necessary information as clearly and concisely as possible. Personally, we always prefer to see a use case model that does not use any of the advanced features rather than one where there is so much generalization, «include», and «extend» that it is hard to figure out what's going on. A good rule of thumb here is, "if in doubt, leave it out".

You have learned the following.

- Actor generalization allows you to factor out into a parent actor behaviors that are common to two or more actors.
    - The parent actor is more generalized than its children, and the children are more specialized than their parent.
    - You can substitute a child actor anywhere a parent actor is expected – this is the substitutability principle.
    - The parent actor is often abstract – it specifies an abstract role.

— The child actors are concrete – they specify concrete roles.

— Actor generalization can simplify use case diagrams.

● Use case generalization allows you to factor out features that are common to two or more use cases into a parent use case.

— The child use cases inherit all features of their parent use case.

— The child use cases may add new features.

— The child use cases may override parent features *except* relationships and extension points.

— We use a simple tag convention in the child use cases:

– inherited without change – 3. (3.);

– inherited and renumbered – 6.2 (6.1);

– inherited and overridden – 1. (01.);

– inherited, overridden, and renumbered – 5.2 (05.1);

– added – 6.3.

— Good style indicates that the parent use case should normally be abstract.

● «include» allows you to factor out steps repeated in several use case flows into a separate use case that you include where needed.

— include(UseCaseName) is used to include the behavior of another use case.

— The including use case is the base use case.

— The included use case is the inclusion use case.

— The base use case is not complete without all of its inclusion use cases.

— Inclusion use cases may be:

– complete – they are just normal use cases and are instantiable;

– incomplete – they contain only a behavior fragment and are not instantiable.

● «extend» adds new behavior to an existing (base) use case.

— The base use case has extension points in an overlay on its flow of events – extension points occur between the steps in the flow of events.

— Extension use cases provide insertion segments – these are behavior fragments that may be "plugged into" extension points.

— The «extend» relationship between the extension use cases and the base use case specifies the extension points into which the extension use case insertion segments are plugged.

— The base use case is complete without the insertion segments – it does not know anything about possible insertion segments, just provides hooks for them.

— The extension use case is generally not complete – usually, it just consists of one or more insertion segments; it may also be a complete use case, but this is rare.

— If the extension use case has preconditions, these must be fulfilled; otherwise, the extension use case does not execute.

- — If the extension use case has postconditions, these constrain the state of the system after the extension use case has executed.
- — An extension use case may contain many insertion segments.
- — Two or more extension use cases may extend the same base use case at the same extension point – the order of execution of each extension use case is indeterminate.
- — Conditional extensions – Boolean guard conditions on the «extend» relationship allow an insertion if true, and prevent an insertion if false.

● Use advanced features as follows:
- — actor generalization – use only where it simplifies the model;
- — use case generalization – consider *not* using, or only using with abstract parents;
- — «include» – use only where it simplifies the model; beware of overuse, as this makes a use case model turn into a functional decomposition;
- — «extend» – consider *not* using; but if you do use it, be careful to ensure that all modelers and stakeholders exposed to the model understand and agree on its semantics.

● Hints and tips for writing use cases:
- — keep use cases short and simple;
- — focus on the *what* not the *how*;
- — avoid functional decomposition.

part 3

Analysis

chapter 6

The analysis workflow

6.1 Chapter roadmap

This chapter begins our investigation of the process of OO analysis. It provides a brief overview of the UP analysis workflow and then some "rules of thumb" for analysis models, which set the scene for more detailed discussions in the other chapters in this part of the book.

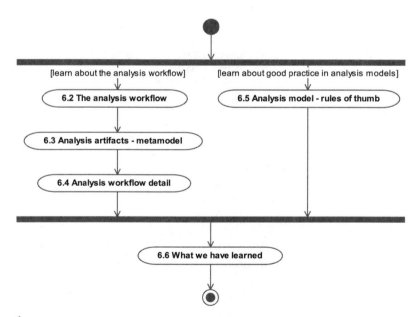

Figure 6.1

6.2   The analysis workflow

> Analysis modeling
> is strategic as we are
> trying to model the
> system's essential
> behavior.

The main work in analysis begins toward the end of the Inception phase and is the main focus of the Elaboration phase, along with requirements.

Most of the activity in Elaboration is about creating models that capture the desired behavior of the system. Notice in Figure 6.2 that analysis work overlaps to a great extent with requirements capture. In fact, these two activities often go hand-in-glove—you often need to perform some analysis on your requirements in order to clarify them and uncover any missing or distorted requirements.

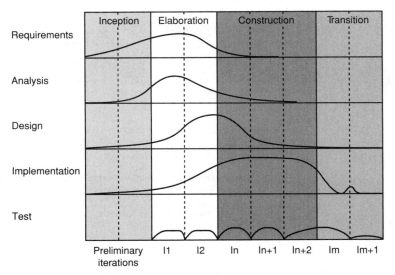

Figure 6.2   Adapted from Figure 1.5 [Jacobson 1] with permission from Addison-Wesley

The aim of the analysis workflow (from the point of view of the OO analyst) is to produce an analysis model. This model focuses on *what* the system needs to do, but leaves the details of *how* it will do it to the design workflow.

The boundary between analysis and design can be quite vague, and to some extent it is up to the individual analyst to draw the line where he or she sees fit. See Section 6.5 for some rules of thumb that can help in the production of successful analysis models.

6.3   Analysis artifacts – metamodel

In the analysis workflow, two key artifacts are produced:

● analysis classes – these model key concepts in the business domain;

● use case realizations – these illustrate how instances of the analysis classes can interact to realize system behavior specified by a use case.

We can model the analysis model itself by using UML. A metamodel of the analysis model is shown in Figure 6.3.

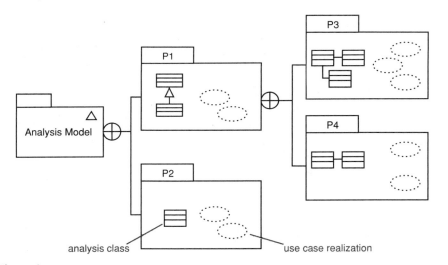

Figure 6.3

You've seen package syntax already (the things that look like folders), but the class syntax (the boxes) and the use case realization syntax (the dotted ovals) are new. We look at classes in Chapter 7, packages in Chapter 11, and use case realizations in Chapter 12.

We can model the analysis model as a package with a triangle in its top right-hand corner. This package contains one or more analysis packages. We call them "analysis packages" because they are part of the analysis model. In Figure 6.3 we have only shown four analysis packages, but the analysis model may actually contain many analysis packages and each package may in turn contain nested analysis packages.

6.4   Analysis workflow detail

Figure 6.4 shows the UP analysis workflow. We look at the relevant activities in turn in later chapters, but before you can understand these activities, you first need to understand classes and objects. We look at this topic in Chapter 7.

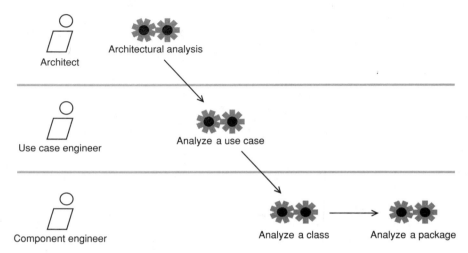

Figure 6.4   Reproduced from Figure 8.18 [Jacobson 1] with permission from Addison-Wesley

6.5   Analysis model – rules of thumb

Every system is different, so it is hard to generalize about analysis models. Still, for a system of moderate size and complexity there are probably about 50 to 100 analysis classes in the analysis model. Remember that, when constructing the analysis model, it is vitally important to restrict yourself *only* to those classes that are part of the vocabulary of the problem domain. It is always tempting to put design classes (such as communications or database access classes) in an analysis model, but you should avoid this (unless the problem domain is actually about communications or databases)! We restrict ourselves in this way to try to keep the analysis model a concise and simple statement of the system structure and behavior. All implementation decisions should be left to the design and implementation workflows.

Here are some rules of thumb for successful analysis modeling.

● The analysis model is *always* in the language of the business. The abstractions found in the analysis model should form part of the vocabulary of the business domain.

- Create models that "tell a story". Each diagram produced should elucidate some important part of the system's desired behavior. If it doesn't, then what purpose does it serve? You'll see good ways of producing such diagrams when we consider use case realizations.

- Concentrate on capturing the big picture. Don't get bogged down in the details of how the system will work—there is plenty of time for this in design.

- Distinguish clearly between the problem domain (the business requirements) and the solution domain (detailed design considerations). Always focus on abstractions that exist in the problem domain. So, for example, if you are modeling an e-commerce system, you would expect to see classes like Customer, Order, and ShoppingBasket in the analysis model. You would *not* expect to see database access classes or communications classes, as these are clearly artifacts arising from the solution domain.

- Always try to minimize coupling. Each association between classes creates coupling between them. You will see in Chapter 9 how you can apply multiplicities and navigation to associations to minimize this coupling.

- Explore inheritance *if* there seems to be a natural and compelling hierarchy of abstractions. In analysis, never apply inheritance just to reuse code. Inheritance is the strongest form of coupling between classes, as you will see in Section 17.6.

- Always ask, "Is the model useful to all the stakeholders?" There's nothing worse than producing an analysis model that is ignored by the business users or the designers and developers. Yet this happens all too often, particularly to inexperienced analysts. The key preventive strategies are to make the analysis model and modeling activity as visible as possible, to incorporate stakeholders into the process wherever possible, and to hold frequent and open reviews.

Finally—keep the model simple! This is easier said than done of course, but it has certainly been our experience that inside every complex analysis model is a simple analysis model struggling to get out. One of the ways of creating simplification is to look at the general case rather than specifics. As a case in point, a system we recently reviewed had completely separate models for how tickets, hotel reservations, and car hire were to be sold. Clearly there is a generic "selling system" model implicit in that system that could handle the different cases by using a relatively simple combination of inheritance and polymorphism.

6.6   What we have learned

You have learned the following.

- Analysis is about creating models that capture the essential requirements and characteristics of the desired system – analysis modeling is strategic.

- Most of the work in the analysis workflow occurs toward the end of the Inception phase and throughout the Elaboration phase.

- Analysis and requirements workflows overlap, especially in the Elaboration phase – it is often advantageous to analyze requirements as you find them to uncover missing or distorted requirements.

- The analysis model:
  — is always in the language of the business;
  — captures the big picture;
  — contains artifacts that model the problem domain;
  — tells a story about the desired system;
  — is useful to as many of the stakeholders as possible.

- Analysis artifacts are:
  — analysis classes – these model key concepts in the business domain;
  — use case realizations – these illustrate how instances of the analysis classes can interact to realize system behavior specified by a use case.

- UP analysis workflow comprises the following activities:
  — Architectural analysis;
  — Analyze a use case;
  — Analyze a class;
  — Analyze a package.

- Analysis model – rules of thumb:
  — expect about 50 to 100 analysis classes in the analysis model of an average system;
  — only include classes that model the vocabulary of the problem domain;
  — do *not* make implementation decisions;
  — focus on classes and associations – minimize coupling;
  — use inheritance where there is a natural hierarchy of abstractions;
  — keep it simple!

chapter **7**

Objects and classes

7.1 Chapter roadmap

This chapter is all about objects and classes. These are the basic building blocks of OO systems. If you are already familiar with the notion of objects and classes, then you may choose to skip Sections 7.2 and 7.4. You will, however, want to learn UML object notation (Section 7.3) and class notation (Section 7.5).

The chapter finishes with a discussion of the related topics of operation and attribute scope (Section 7.6) and object construction and destruction (Section 7.7).

You only use a subset of UML class syntax in analysis. However, for ease of reference, and so we don't have to come back to it later, we cover complete class syntax in this chapter.

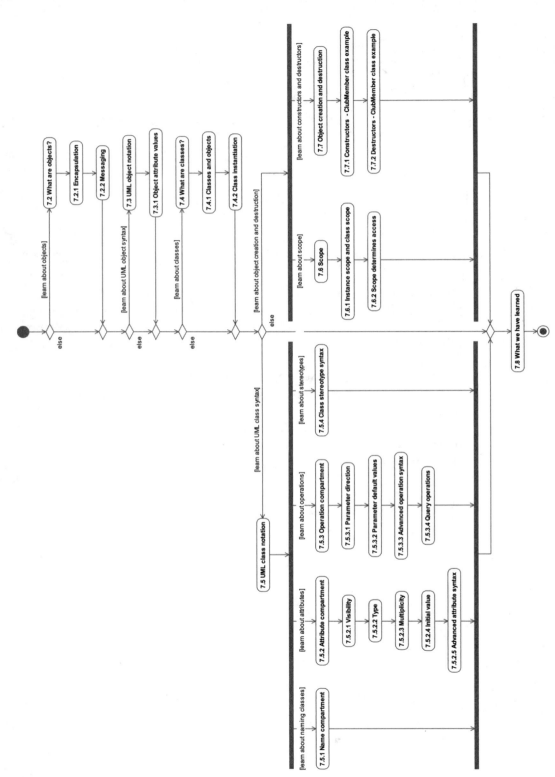

Figure 7.1

7.2   What are objects?

The UML Reference Manual [Rumbaugh 1] defines an object as "A discrete entity with a well-defined boundary that encapsulates state and behavior; an instance of a class."

Objects combine data and function in a cohesive unit.

You can think of an object as a cohesive packet of data and function. Generally, the only way to get to the data part of an object is by calling one of the functions that the object makes available. These functions are called *operations*. Hiding the data part of an object behind this layer of operations is known as encapsulation or data-hiding. Encapsulation is not enforced in UML as some OO languages do not demand it. However, to hide the data part of an object behind its set of operations is always good OO style.

Objects hide data behind a layer of functions called operations.

Every object is itself an instance of some class that defines the common set of features (attributes and operations) that are shared by all instances of that class. The idea of classes and classifiers is really very simple. Think of a printer of type "Epson Photo 1200." This describes the properties of all specific instances of this class such as the particular "Epson Photo 1200 S/N 34120098" sitting on our desk. A specific instance of a class is called an object.

Thinking about this example of an Epson printer object a bit more, you can see that it has certain properties that are common to all objects.

Every object is uniquely identifiable.

- Identity – this is the object's unique existence in time and space. It is what makes it different from all other objects. In our example, the printer's serial number can be used as the identifier to point to this particular printer on our desk and represent the unique identity of that object. A serial number is a great way to specify the identity of a physical object, and we use a similar principle, the idea of an object reference, to specify the identity of every one of the software objects we will be working with in OO analysis and design. Of course, in the real world not all objects have a serial number, but they still have unique identities because of their particular spatial and temporal coordinates. Similarly, in OO software systems every object has some sort of object reference.

Attribute values hold an object's data.

- State – this is determined by the attribute values of an object and the relationships the object has to other objects at a particular point in time. Table 7.1 gives a nonexhaustive list of the states the printer can go through. You can see from this how an object's state depends on the values of its attributes and its connection to other objects.

- Behavior – there are certain things the printer can do for us:

switchOn()
switchOff()
printDocument()

pageFeed()
clearInkJetNozzles()
changeInkCartridge()

Invoking an operation on an object will often cause a change in the values of one or more of its attributes or in its relationships to other objects, and this *may* constitute a state transition. This is a meaningful movement of the object from one state to another state. Considering Table 7.1 again, it is clear that an object's state can also affect its behavior. For example, if the printer is out of ink (object state = OutOfBlackInk), then invoking the operation printDocument() will cause it to signal an error. The actual behavior of printDocument() is therefore *state dependent*.

A method is an
implementation of
an operation.

An operation is the *specification* of a piece of behavior. An implementation of that behavior is called a *method*.

Table 7.1

Object state	Class attribute	Attribute value for object	Relationship
On	power	on	N/A
Off	power	off	N/A
OutOfBlackInk	blackInkCartridge	empty	N/A
OutOfColorInk	colorInkCartridge	empty	N/A
Connected	N/A	N/A	Connected to a computer object
NotConnected	N/A	N/A	Not connected to a computer object

7.2.1   Encapsulation

As we have already mentioned, the identity of an object is some unique handle, usually an address in memory, provided by the implementation language. We refer to these handles as object references from now on. You don't need to worry about how these are implemented in OO analysis—you can simply assume that each object has a unique identity that is managed by the implementation technology. In design you may need to consider the implementation of object references if you are targeting an OO language, such as C++, that allows the direct manipulation of special types of object references known as pointers.

In Figure 7.2 we show a conceptual picture of an object that emphasizes encapsulation. Note that Figure 7.2 is *not* a UML diagram. You'll see shortly what the UML syntax for objects is.

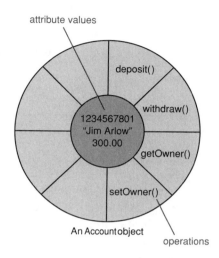

attribute values

deposit()

withdraw()

getOwner()

setOwner()

1234567801
"Jim Arlow"
300.00

An Account object

operations

Figure 7.2

> An object's state is determined by its attribute values.

The state of this object is the set of attribute values (in this case 1234567801, "Jim Arlow", 300.00) held by the object at any point in time. Typically, some of these attribute values will remain fixed, and some will change over time. For example, the account number and name will remain fixed, but we hope that the balance goes up steadily!

As the balance changes with time, we see that the object's state also changes with time. For example, if the balance is negative, then we may say that object is in the state Overdrawn. As the balance changes from negative to zero, the object makes a significant change in its nature—it makes the state transition from the state Overdrawn to the state Empty. Furthermore, as the Account object's balance becomes positive, it makes another state transition from the state Empty to the state InCredit. There may be many more possible state transitions than this. In fact, any operation invocation that leads to a substantive change in the object's nature creates a state transition. UML provides a powerful set of modeling techniques called state machines for modeling state changes; we look at those in Chapter 21.

> An object's behavior is "what it can do for us" – its operations.

The behavior of any object is basically "what it can do" for you. The object in Figure 7.2 provides the operations listed in Table 7.2.

This set of operations specifies the object's behavior. Notice that invoking some of these operations (deposit(), withdraw(), setOwner()) changes attribute

Table 7.2

Operation	Semantics
deposit()	Deposit some money in the Account object
	Increment the balance attribute value
withdraw()	Withdraw some money from the Account
	Decrement the balance attribute value
getOwner()	Return the owner of the Account object – a query operation
setOwner()	Change the owner of the Account object

values and *may* generate state transitions. The operation getOwner() does not change any attribute values and thus will *not* cause a state transition.

Encapsulation, or data-hiding, is one of the primary benefits of OO programming, and it can lead to more robust and extendible software. In this simple Account example, a user of this object need not be concerned with the structure of the data hidden inside the object, only with what the object can do—in other words, with the *services* it offers to other objects.

7.2.2   Messaging

Objects generate
system behavior by
sending messages to
one another over links.
This is collaboration.

Objects have attribute values and behavior, but how do you put objects together to create software systems? Objects collaborate to perform the functions of the system. What this means is that objects form links to other objects and send messages back and forth along those links. When an object receives a message, it looks at its set of operations to see if there is an operation whose signature matches the message signature. If there is, then it invokes that operation (see Figure 7.3). These signatures comprise the message (or operation) name, parameter types, and return value.

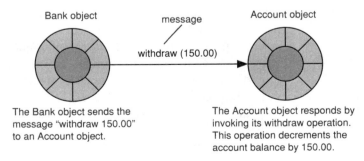

The Bank object sends the
message "withdraw 150.00"
to an Account object.

The Account object responds by
invoking its withdraw operation.
This operation decrements the
account balance by 150.00.

Figure 7.3

The runtime structure of an OO system consists of many objects being created, abiding for a time, and then perhaps being destroyed. These objects send messages to invoke one another's services. This is a radically different structure than procedural software systems that evolve over time by the progressive application of functions to data.

7.3   UML object notation

The UML object icon is a box with two compartments; an example is shown in Figure 7.4. The top compartment contains the object identifier, which is *always* underlined. This is important, as the UML notation for classes is very similar to that for objects. Being rigorous about using the underline correctly removes any confusion as to whether a modeling element is a class or an object.

UML is very flexible about how objects may be represented on object diagrams. The object identifier can consist of any of the following.

- The class name alone – for example, :Account. This signifies that you have an anonymous object, or instance of that class (i.e., you are looking at an instance of an Account but haven't identified, or don't really care, which specific instance it is). Anonymous objects are often used when only one object of a particular class is on a given diagram. If you need to show two objects of the same class, then you should give each a name to distinguish them from each other.

- The object name alone – for example, jimsAccount. This identifies a specific object but doesn't identify which class it belongs to. This notation can be useful in very early analysis when you haven't yet discovered all the classes.

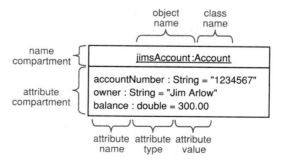

Figure 7.4

● The object name concatenated with the class name, separated from each other by a colon. You may read the colon as "is an instance of class". So, in Figure 7.4, you could read the diagram as follows: there is an object called jimsAccount that is an instance of class Account.

> Objects of the same class have the same operations and the same attributes but may have different attribute values.

Objects are usually named in mixed upper- and lowercase, starting with a lowercase letter. Special characters, such as spaces and underscores, are avoided. This is known as *lowerCamelCase* because the resulting words start with a lowercase letter and appear to have humps.

From Section 7.2, you know that a class defines the attributes and operations of a set of objects. As all objects of the *same* class have exactly the *same* set of operations, the operations are listed on the class icon, not the object icon.

Attributes may be optionally shown in the lower compartment of the object icon. Those attributes that you choose to show *must* be named and may have an optional type and value. Attributes are also named in lowerCamelCase.

7.3.1   Object attribute values

Each object attribute value has the following form:

name : type = value

You may choose to show all, some, or none of the object attribute values, depending on the purpose of the diagram.

To keep object diagrams simple and clear, you may choose to omit attribute types, since they are already defined in the class of the object. When you see how object diagrams are used in analysis in Chapter 12, it will be clear why you might choose to show only some of the information in an object icon.

7.4   What are classes?

> A class describes the features of a set of objects.

The UML Reference Manual [Rumbaugh 1] defines a class as "The descriptor for a set of objects that share the same attributes, operations, methods, relationships, and behavior." We could summarize this by saying that a class is a descriptor for a set of objects that have the same features.

Every object is an instance of exactly one class. Here are some useful ways to think about classes.

● Think of a class as being a template for objects—a class determines the structure (set of features) of all objects of that class. All objects of the *same* class must have the *same* set of operations, the *same* set of attributes, and the *same* set of relationships, but may have *different* attribute values.

● Think of a class as being like a rubber stamp, and objects as actual stamp marks on a piece of paper; or think of a class as being like a cookie cutter, and the objects as being the cookies.

> Every object is an instance of exactly one class.

Classifier and instance are one of UML's common divisions (see Chapter 1) and the most common example of this division is class and object. A class is a specification or template that all objects of that class (instances) must follow. Each object of the class has specific values for the attributes defined by the class and will respond to messages by invoking the operations defined by the class.

Depending on their state, different objects may respond to the same message in different ways. For example, if you try to withdraw $100 from a bank account object that is already overdrawn, this may give a different result than trying to withdraw $100 from a bank account object that is several hundred dollars in credit.

Classification is possibly the single most important way that human beings have of ordering information about the world. As such, it is also one of the most important OO concepts. Using the notion of classes, you can talk about a particular type of car or a type of tree without ever mentioning a specific instance. It is the same for software. Classes allow us to describe the set of features that every object of the class *must* have without having to describe every one of those objects.

Take a look at Figure 7.5 and think about classes for a minute or two. How many classes are there in this figure?

In fact, there's no answer to that question! There are an almost infinite number of ways of classifying objects in the real world. A few classes we can see are

● the class of cats;

● the class of fat food-loving cats (we have a cat who is an instance of this class!);

Figure 7.5

- the class of trees;
- the class of leaves;
- etc., etc., etc.

Given that there are so many options, choosing the most appropriate classification scheme is one of the most important aspects of OO analysis and design. You'll see how to do this in Chapter 8.

Looking at Figure 7.5 very closely, you might begin to see other types of relationships apart from class/instance. For example, you might see multiple levels of classification. We have the class of cats, and we could classify things further into the subclasses "house cat" and "wild cat"—or even the subclasses "modern cat" and "prehistoric cat". This is a relationship between classes—one class is a subclass of another. Conversely, the class "cat" is a superclass of "house cat" and "wild cat". We look at this in much more detail when we study inheritance in Chapter 10.

Also, if you consider the leaves and trees in Figure 7.5, you can see that tree objects have collections of leaf objects. There is a very strong kind of relationship between trees and leaves. Each leaf object belongs to a specific tree object and can't be swapped or shared between them, and the life cycle of the leaf is intimately tied to, and controlled by, the tree. This is a relationship between objects and is known in UML as composition.

If, however, you consider the relationship between computers and peripherals, the object relationship is very different. One peripheral, such as a pair of speakers, can be swapped between different computers—different computers can even share some peripherals. Also, even if a computer is thrown away, its peripherals may well survive it and be used by a new machine. The life cycle of the peripherals is typically independent of the life cycle of the computer. In UML this type of object relationship is known as aggregation. We discuss object relationships, and in particular composition and aggregation, in much more depth in Chapter 18.

7.4.1   Classes and objects

The relationship between a class and objects of that class is an «instantiate» relationship. This is the first example of a relationship that we have come across. *The UML Reference Manual* [Rumbaugh 1] defines a relationship as a "connection among model elements." There are many types of relationship in UML and we eventually explore them all.

The «instantiate» relationship between objects and classes is shown in Figure 7.6. The dotted arrow is actually a dependency relationship that has been given a special meaning by the stereotype «instantiate». As you saw in Chapter 1, anything inside guillemets («...») is known as a stereotype, and stereotypes are one of the three UML extensibility mechanisms. A stereotype is a way of customizing modeling elements—a way of creating variants with new semantics. In this case, the stereotype «instantiate» turns an ordinary dependency into an instantiation relationship between a class and objects of that class.

The UML Reference Manual [Rumbaugh 1] defines a dependency as "A relationship between two elements in which a change to one element (the supplier) may affect or supply information needed by the other element (the client)." From Figure 7.6 it is quite clear that the class Account must be the supplier because it determines the structure of all objects of that class, and it is clear that the objects are clients.

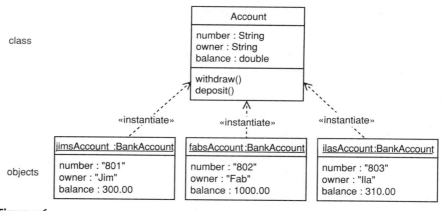

Figure 7.6

7.4.2 Class instantiation

Instantiation is the creation of new instances of model elements. In this case we are instantiating objects from classes—we are creating *new instances* of classes.

UML tries to be general, and so instantiation applies to other modeling elements as well as classes and objects. In fact, instantiation captures the general notion of creating a specific instance of something from a template.

> Class instantiation creates a new object, using the class as a template.

In most OO programming languages, there are special operations, called constructors, that really belong to the class itself rather than to the objects of that class. These special operations are said to have class scope, and we say a bit more about scope in Section 7.6. The purpose of constructor operations is to create new instances of the class. The constructor allocates memory for the new object, gives it a unique identity, and sets the initial attribute values for the object. It also sets any links to other objects.

7.5   UML class notation

The visual UML syntax for a class is very rich, and to make the syntax manageable, it is important to apply the UML notion of optional adornments. The only mandatory part of the visual syntax is the name compartment with the class name in it. All the other compartments and adornments are optional. However, we've shown the whole thing in Figure 7.7 for your reference.

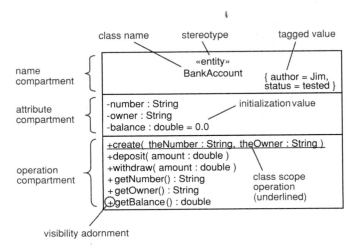

Figure 7.7

Only show the compartments and adornments that make a point.

Which compartments and adornments you actually include on a class in a class diagram depends entirely on the purpose of the diagram. If you are only interested in showing the relationships between various classes, then you may be content with just the name compartment. If the diagram is to illustrate the behavior of the classes, then you will probably add the operation compartment and the key operations on each class. On the other hand, the diagram might be more "data oriented", perhaps trying to show the mapping of classes to relational tables. In this case, you would show the name compartment and the attribute compartment, perhaps also showing attribute types. You should aim to use this UML flexibility to show just the right amount of information on class diagrams to make your point clearly and concisely.

In analysis models, you typically only need to show the following:

- class name;
- key attributes;

- key operations;
- stereotypes (if they have business significance).

You typically do *not* show the following:

- tagged values;
- operation parameters;
- visibility;
- initialization values (unless they have business significance).

In the next few subsections we look at the name, attribute, and operation compartments in detail.

7.5.1 Name compartment

While UML does not mandate any naming convention for classes, there is a convention that is almost universally followed.

- Class name is in UpperCamelCase—it begins with an uppercase letter, and then is in mixed upper- and lowercase, with each word beginning in uppercase. Special symbols such as punctuation marks, dashes, underscores, ampersands, hashes, and slashes are *always* avoided. There is a good reason for this: these symbols are used in languages such as HTML, XML, and by operating systems. Including them in class names, or the names of any other modeling element for that matter, can lead to unexpected consequences when code or HTML/XML documentation is generated from the model.

> Never abbreviate class, attribute, or operation names.

- Avoid abbreviations *at all costs*. Class names should always reflect the names of real-world entities *without* abbreviation. For example, FlightSegment is always preferable to FltSgmnt, DepositAccount is always preferable to DpstAccnt. Again, the reason for this is very simple—abbreviations make the model (and resulting code) harder to read. Any time saved typing is lost many times over when the abbreviated model or code needs to be maintained.

- If there are domain-specific acronyms (e.g., CRM – Customer Relationship Management) that are in common use and will be understood by *all* readers of the model, then you may use them. However, bear in mind that the long form of the name might still be preferable if it makes the model clearer.

Classes represent "things", so they should have a name that is a noun or a noun phrase, for example, Person, Money, BankAccount.

7.5.2   Attribute compartment

The only mandatory part of the UML attribute syntax (Figure 7.8) is the attribute name. Attributes are named in lowerCamelCase—starting with a lowercase letter and then mixed upper- and lowercase. Attribute names are usually nouns or noun phrases because attributes indicate some "thing" such as an account balance. You must avoid special symbols and abbreviations.

We look at the optional parts of attribute syntax over the next few sections.

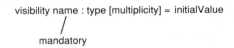

Figure 7.8

7.5.2.1   *Visibility*

> Visibility controls access to the features of a class.

The visibility adornment (Table 7.3) applies to attributes and operations within the class. It may also be applied to role names on relationships (Chapter 9). In analysis, you typically don't clutter the diagrams with visibility as this is really a statement of "how" rather than "what".

Implementation languages may differently interpret all types of UML visibility, except public. This is an important point—in fact, languages may define additional types of visibility that UML does not support by default. Typically, this is not really a problem. The most common OO languages, C++ and Java, and even common semi-OO languages such as Visual Basic, get along just fine with public, private, protected, and package visibility, at least as a first approximation.

Table 7.3

Adornment	Visibility name	Semantics
+	Public visibility	Any element that can access the class can access any of its features with public visibility
–	Private visibility	Only operations within the class can access features with private visibility
#	Protected visibility	Only operations within the class, or within children of the class, can access features with protected visibility
~	Package visibility	Any element that is in the same package as the class, or in a nested subpackage, can access any of its features with package visibility

Let's look at two OO languages in detail. Table 7.4 compares UML visibility semantics with those of Java and C#.

As you can see, visibility is dependent on the implementation language and can become quite complex. The exact type of visibility used is really a detailed implementation decision that would usually be made by the programmer rather than by the analyst/designer. For general modeling, the UML standard definitions of public, private, protected, and package are quite adequate, and we encourage you to restrict yourself to these.

Table 7.4

Visibility	UML semantics	Java semantics	C# semantics
public	Any element that can access the class can access any of its features with public visibility	Same as UML	Same as UML
private	Only operations within the class can access features with private visibility	Same as UML	Same as UML
protected	Only operations within the class, or within children of the class, can access features with protected visibility	As UML but is also accessible to all classes in the same Java package as the defining class	Same as UML
package	Any element that is in the same package as the class, or in a nested subpackage, can access any of its features with package visibility	The default visibility in Java – nested classes in nested subpackages don't automatically have access to elements in their parent package	–
private protected	–	Same as UML protected	–
internal	–	–	Accessible by any element in the same program
protected internal	–	–	Combines the semantics of protected and internal – only applicable to attributes

7.5.2.2   *Type*

The type of an attribute may be another class or a primitive type.

> An attribute's type may be another class or a primitive type.

The UML specification defines four primitive types that are used in the UML specification itself, and you can use these in your analysis models when you want to remain platform independent. These types are listed in Table 7.5.

Table 7.5

	Primitive type	Semantics
UML	Integer	A whole number
	UnlimitedNatural	A whole number >= 0 Infinity is shown as *
	Boolean	Can take the value true or false
	String	A sequence of characters String literals are quoted, e.g., "Jim"
OCL	Real	A floating point number

The Object Constraint Language (OCL) is a formal language for expressing constraints in UML models; we discuss OCL in detail in Chapter 25. OCL defines standard operations for the UML primitive types (except UnlimitedNatural) and adds a new type called Real.

If your model is targeting a specific language, such as Java or C#, then you can use the primitive types from that language. However, your model will then be tied to that language.

Sometimes you need to add a set of primitive types to your UML model so that you can use them in other classes as attribute and operation parameter types. You can add a primitive type by creating a class with the same name as the primitive type and the stereotype «primitive». The class typically has no attributes or operations since it is merely acting as a placeholder for the primitive type, adding its name to the model namespace.

7.5.2.3   *Multiplicity*

Multiplicity is widely used in design, but may also be used in analysis models as it can provide a concise way to express certain business constraints relating to the "number of things" participating in a relationship.

Multiplicity allows you to model two distinctly different things by using a multiplicity expression on an attribute (see Figure 7.9).

> Multiplicity allows you to model collections of things or null values.

- Collections – if the multiplicity expression results in an integer greater than 1, then you are specifying a collection of the type. For example, colors : Color[7] would model an attribute that is a collection of seven Color objects, which you could use to model the colors of the rainbow.

- Null values – there is a difference in most languages between an attribute that contains an empty or uninitialized object, such as the empty String, "", and an attribute that points nowhere, that is, to the null object reference. When an attribute references null, this means that the object it points to has not yet been created or has ceased to exist. It can sometimes be important in detailed design to distinguish when null is a possible value for an attribute, and you can model this by using the special multiplicity expression [0..1]. Take the emailAddress example in Figure 7.9: if the attribute emailAddress has the value "" (the empty String), you might take this to mean that you have asked for an e-mail address and it has not been given to you. On the other hand, if the attribute emailAddress points to null, you might take this to mean that you have *not yet* asked for the e-mail address and so its value is unknown. If you use distinctions like these, it's *essential* that you record in the emailAddress documentation the precise semantics of "" versus null. As you can see, this is a fairly detailed design consideration, but it can be important and useful.

Figure 7.9 gives some examples of multiplicity syntax.

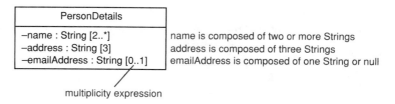

Figure 7.9

7.5.2.4   *Initial value*

> The initialValue allows you to set the value of an attribute at the point of object creation.

The initialValue allows you to specify the value an attribute will take when an object is instantiated from the class. This is known as the initial value of the attribute because it is the value that the attribute takes at the point of object creation. In design, it is good style to use initial values wherever possible—it helps to ensure that objects of the class are always created in a valid and useful state.

Initial values are only used in analysis when they can express or highlight an important business constraint. This tends to be quite rare.

7.5.2.5   *Advanced attribute syntax*

Like any other UML modeling element, you can extend the semantics of attributes by prefixing them with stereotypes. You can also extend the specification of an attribute by postfixing the attribute with tagged values, for example,

«stereotype» attribute { tag1 = value1, tag2 = value2, ... }

You can store whatever information you choose in tagged values. For example, they are sometimes used to store version information as shown here:

address { addedBy="Jim Arlow", dateAdded="20MAR2004" }

In this example, we have recorded that Jim Arlow added the address attribute to some class on 20 March 2004.

7.5.3   Operation compartment

Operations are functions that are bound to a particular class. As such, they have all of the characteristics of functions:

- name;
- parameter list;
- return type.

> An operation signature comprises its name, the type of all its parameters, and its return type.

The combination of the operation name, types of all the parameters, and the return type is the operation signature (Figure 7.10). Every operation of a class must have a unique signature as it is this signature that gives the operation its identity. When a message is sent to an object, the message signature is compared to the operation signatures defined in the object's class, and if a match is found, the appropriate operation is invoked on the object.

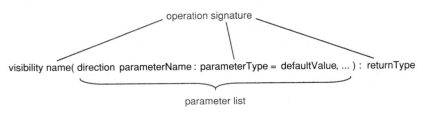

Figure 7.10

Different implementation languages have slightly different interpretations as to what constitutes an operation signature. For example, in C++ and Java the return type is ignored. This means that two operations on a class that only differ by return type will be considered to be the same operation and will generate a compiler/interpreter error. In Smalltalk, which is a weakly typed language, the parameters and return type are all of type Object, and so it is only the operation name that constitutes the signature.

Operations are named in lowerCamelCase. Operation names are usually a verb or verb phrase, and you must avoid special symbols and abbreviations.

Each operation parameter has the form shown in Figure 7.11. An operation may have zero to many parameters.

direction parameterName : parameterType = defaultValue

Figure 7.11

Parameter names are in lowerCamelCase and are usually a noun or a noun phrase since they refer to something being passed in to the operation. Each parameter has a type that is a class or primitive type.

We look at the parameter direction and default value in the next two sections.

7.5.3.1   Parameter direction

Operation parameters can be given a direction:

operation(in p1:Integer, inout p2:Integer, out p3:Integer, return p4:Integer, return p5:Integer)

If the direction is not specified, then it defaults to in. Parameter direction semantics are summarized in Table 7.6.

The semantics of in, inout, and out are quite straightforward but perhaps return needs more discussion.

We tend to expect functions to return exactly one object as shown below—

maximumValue = max(a, b)
minimumValue = min(a, b)

—where a, b, maximumValue, and minimumValue are Integers. In fact, normal operation syntax supports precisely this situation—every operation may normally have one return value. As you have seen, you can model these "normal" operations in UML as follows:

maximumValue(a:Integer, b:Integer) : Integer

Table 7.6

Parameter	Semantics
in p1:Integer	Default
	The operation uses p1 as an input parameter
	The value of p1 is used by the operation in some way
	p1 is *not* changed by the operation
inout p2:Integer	The operation accepts p2 as an input/output parameter
	The value of p2 is used by the operation in some way *and* serves to accept a value output by the operation
	p2 may be changed by the operation
out p3:Integer	The operation uses p3 as an output parameter
	The parameter serves as a repository to accept a value output by the operation
	p3 may be changed by the operation
return p4:Integer	The operation uses p4 as a return parameter
	The operation returns p4 as one of its return values
return p5:Integer	The operation uses p5 as a return parameter
	The operation returns p5 as one of its return values

However, some languages allow operations to return *more* than one value. For example, Python allows operations to have multiple return values. In Python you could write—

maximumValue, minimumValue = maxMin(a, b)

—where maxMin(a, b) returns two values, the maximum value and the minimum value. In UML, you can model this operation as follows:

maxMin(in a: Integer, in b:Integer, return maxValue:Integer, return minValue:Integer)

You can see that the return parameter direction allows you to model situations where an operation has *more than one* return value.

You can also list the return parameters after the operation name as follows:

maxMin(in a: Integer, in b:Integer) : Integer, Integer

In this case, it is bad style to use the keyword return, as the return parameters are clearly distinguished.

Parameter directions are really a design issue, and so you typically don't bother with them in analysis (unless you are using OCL).

Parameter directions can be very important in design, especially if you are generating code. Code generators will map UML parameter directions to the specific parameter passing semantics of your target language.

7.5.3.2 Parameter default values

You can give an operation parameter a default value. When the operation is called, if no value is given for that parameter, its default value will be used.

You can specify default values as shown in Figure 7.12. In this figure, the Canvas class has two operations, drawCircle(...) and drawSquare(...), that draw a square and circle respectively on the screen. We have supplied the default value of Point(0,0) for the origin parameter. If this parameter is omitted when the operations are called, the shapes will be drawn at position {0,0} on the screen.

Canvas
drawCircle(origin: Point = Point(0, 0), radius : Integer) drawSquare(origin: Point = Point(0, 0), size : Dimension)

Figure 7.12

Default values are really a design issue, and you rarely use them in analysis.

7.5.3.3 Advanced operation syntax

You can extend the semantics of operations by prefixing them with stereotypes and postfixing them with tagged values.

«stereotype» operation(...) { tag1 = value1, tag2 = value2, ... }

You can also add tagged values to operation parameters, but we have not yet come across a situation where this is useful.

7.5.3.4 Query operations

Each operation has a property called isQuery. If you set this property to true in your modeling tool, the operation is a query operation. This means that it *has no side effects* and doesn't change the state of the object it is called on. An operation that returns the value of an attribute is a query operation and should have isQuery set to true.

The default value for isQuery is false. Setting isQuery is normally a design issue. However, specifying query operations can be important if you are using OCL in your UML models (see Chapter 25). This is because OCL expressions can't change the state of the system and so can *only* use query operations. Setting isQuery allows OCL compilers to check that your OCL expressions are only calling valid operations.

A more or less universal naming standard for query operations is to construct the name of the operation by prefixing the name of whatever you are querying with get. An example is shown in Figure 7.13.

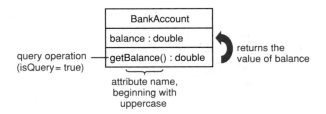

Figure 7.13

7.5.4   Class stereotype syntax

There is a lot of flexibility in how stereotypes can be displayed (Figure 7.14). However, most modelers just use the name in guillemets («stereotypeName») or the icon. The other variants don't tend to be used as much, and the modeling tool you are using often imposes limits.

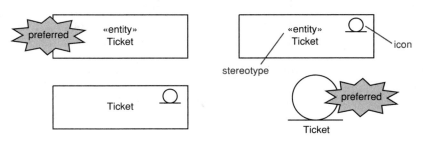

Figure 7.14

Stereotypes can also be associated with colors or textures, but this is very bad practice. Some readers, the visually impaired or the color-blind, may have difficulty interpreting such diagrams. Also, diagrams often have to be printed in black and white.

7.6   Scope

Up to now you have seen that objects have their own copies of the attributes defined in their class so that different objects can have different attribute values. Similarly, the operations that you have seen so far all act on specific objects. This is the normal case, and we say that these attributes and operations have *instance scope*.

However, sometimes you need to define attributes that have a single, shared value for *every* object of the class, and you need operations (like object creation operations) that don't operate on any particular class instance. We say that these attributes and operations have *class scope*. Class scope features provide a set of global features for an entire class of objects.

> Instance scope attributes and operations belong to, or operate on, specific objects.

> Class scope attributes and operations belong to, or operate on, the whole class of objects.

7.6.1   Instance scope and class scope

The notation for instance scope and class scope attributes and operations is shown in Figure 7.15. The semantics for instance scope and class scope attributes and operations are summarized in Table 7.7.

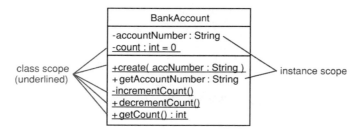

Figure 7.15

7.6.2   Scope determines access

Whether an operation can access another feature of the class is determined by the scope of the operation and the scope of the feature it is trying to access.

Instance scope operations can access other instance scope attributes and operations, and also all of the class scope attributes and operations.

Class scope operations can *only* access other class scope operations and attributes. Class scope operations can't access instance scope operations because

- there might not be any class instances created yet;
- even if class instances exist, you don't know which one to use.

Table 7.7

	Instance scope	Class scope
Attributes	By default, attributes have instance scope	Attributes may be defined as class scope
	Every object of the class gets its own copy of the instance scope attributes	Every object of the class shares the same, single copy of the class scope attributes
	Each object may therefore have different instance scope attribute values	Each object will therefore have the same class scope attribute values
Operations	By default, operations have instance scope	Operations may be defined as class scope
	Every invocation of an instance scope operation applies to a specific instance of the class	Invocation of a class scope operation does not apply to any specific instance of the class – instead, you can think of class scope operations as applying to the class itself
	You can't invoke an instance scope operation unless you have an instance of the class available – clearly, this means that you *can't* use an instance scope operation of a class to create objects of that class, as you could never create the first object	You can invoke a class scope operation even if there is no instance of the class available – this is ideal for object creation operations

7.7   Object construction and destruction

> Constructors are special operations that create new objects. They have class scope.

Constructors are special operations that create new instances of classes—these operations *must* be class scope. If they were instance scope, there would be no way to create the first instance of a class.

Constructors are a design consideration and are generally *not* shown on analysis models.

Different languages have different standards for naming constructors. A completely generic approach is just to call the constructor create(...). This makes the intention of the operation clear. However, Java, C#, and C++ all demand that the constructor name be the same as the class name.

A class may have many constructors, all with the same name but each distinguished by a different parameter list. The constructor with no parameters is known as the *default constructor*. You can use constructor parameters to initialize attribute values at the point of object construction.

Figure 7.16 shows a simple BankAccount example. Every time you create a new BankAccount object, you have to pass in a String as a parameter to the constructor. This String is used to set the accountNumber attribute (e.g., to some value

Figure 7.16

such as "XYZ001002"). The fact that the BankAccount constructor needs a parameter means that there is *no way* to create a BankAccount object *without* specifying this parameter. This ensures that every BankAccount object has the accountNumber attribute value set at the point of creation—this is very good style.

In analysis-level models, you generally don't bother specifying constructors (or, indeed, destructors). They usually have no impact on, or relationship to, the business semantics of the class. If you *do* want to show constructor operations, you can put in a create() operation with no parameters as a place-holder. Alternatively, you can specify just those parameters that are important from a business perspective.

When you come to detailed design, you need to specify the name, parameter types, and return type of *every* operation (see Section 17.4), and this will include explicit specification of constructor and destructor operations.

Object destruction is not as straightforward as object construction. Different OO languages have different semantics for object destruction. We explore object construction and destruction in more detail in the next two sections.

7.7.1   Constructors – **ClubMember** class example

The ClubMember example in Figure 7.17 shows a typical use of class scope attributes and operations. This class represents a member of a club. The numberOfMembers attribute is a private class scope attribute of type int. This attribute is therefore shared by all objects of the ClubMember class and will have the same value for each of those objects.

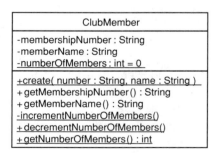

Figure 7.17

When the numberOfMembers attribute is created, it is initialized to zero. Now, if this were an instance scope attribute, each object would get its own copy of the attribute when that object was created. However, the attribute has class scope, meaning that there is only one copy and this single copy is only initialized once. Exactly *when* that happens depends on the implementation language, but, as far as we are concerned, all we have to know is that the attribute is initialized to the value zero when the program started.

Suppose that in the create(...) operation you invoke the class scope operation incrementNumberOfmembers(). As you might expect from its name, this operation increments the value of the class scope attribute numberOfMembers. Every time an instance of the class is created, numberOfMembers is incremented—a counter has been added to the class! You can query the value of numberOfMembers by using the class scope operation getNumberOfMembers(). This returns a number that is equal to the number of ClubMember objects created.

7.7.2   Destructors – **ClubMember** class example

> Destructors are special operations that "clean up" when objects are destroyed.

What happens if the program creates *and* destroys ClubMember objects? Obviously, the value of numberOfMembers would rapidly become meaningless. You can fix this by introducing an operation to the class to decrement numberOfMembers (see Figure 7.17) and then ensuring that this operation is called every time an instance of ClubMember is destroyed.

Some OO languages have special instance scope operations called destructors that are automatically called at the point of object destruction. In C++, for example, the destructor is always of the form ~ClassName(parameterList). In C++ the destructor operation is *guaranteed* to be called at the time an object is destroyed.

Java has a similar capability—every class has an operation called finalize() that is called when the object is finally destroyed. However, objects are not explicitly destroyed by the program itself, but rather are left to an automatic garbage collector. You know that finalize() will be called, but you just don't know *when*! This is obviously not going to work for our simple counter application, and you would have to explicitly decrement numberOfMembers yourself by calling the class scope operation called decrementNumberOfMembers() whenever you were finished with an object and were letting it go to garbage collection.

C# has identical destruction semantics to those of Java, except the operation is called Finalize().

7.8   What we have learned

This chapter has presented the basic groundwork on classes and objects that is used throughout the rest of the book. Classes and objects are the building blocks of OO systems, so it is important to have a thorough and detailed understanding of them.

You have learned the following.

- Objects are cohesive units that combine data and function.

- Encapsulation – the data inside an object is hidden and can only be manipulated by invoking one of the object's functions.
  - operations are specifications for object functions created in analysis;
  - methods are implementations for object functions created in implementation.

- Every object is an instance of a class – a class defines the common features shared by all objects of that class.

- Every object has the following features.
  - Identity – its unique existence – you use object references to uniquely refer to specific objects.
  - State – a meaningful set of attribute values and relationships for the object at a point in time.
    - Only those sets of attribute values and relationships that constitute a semantically important distinction from other possible sets constitute a state. For example, BankAccount object – balance < 0, state = Overdrawn; balance > 0, state = InCredit.
    - State transition – the movement of an object from one meaningful state to another.
  - Behavior – services that the object offers to other objects:
    - modeled as a set of operations;
    - invoking operations *may* generate a state transition.

- Objects collaborate to generate the behavior of the system.
  - Interaction involves objects sending messages back and forth – when a message is received, the corresponding operation is invoked; this *may* cause a state transition.

- UML object notation – every object icon has two compartments.
  - The top compartment contains the object name and/or the class name, *all* of which must be underlined.
    - Object names are in lowerCamelCase.
    - Class names are in UpperCamelCase.

- No special symbols, punctuation, or abbreviation.
- Object name is separated from class name by a single colon.

— The bottom compartment contains the attribute names and values separated by an equal sign.
- Attribute names are in lowerCamelCase.
- Attribute types may be shown but are often omitted for brevity.

- A class defines the features (attributes, operations, relationships, and behavior) of a set of objects.
— Each object is an instance of exactly one class.
— Different objects of the same class have the same set of attributes but may have different values for those attributes. Different attribute values cause objects of the same class to behave differently – for example, compare trying to withdraw $100 from a BankAccount object that is overdrawn with trying to withdraw $100 from a BankAccount object that is $200 in credit.
— There are many ways of classifying the world – finding the right classification scheme is one of the keys to successful OO analysis.
— You can show the instantiate relationship between a class and one of its objects by using a dependency stereotyped as «instantiate»:
- relationships connect things;
- a dependency relationship indicates that a change to the supplier affects the client.
— Object instantiation creates a new object by using its class as a template.
- Most OO languages provide special operations called constructors that are called when an object needs to be created – constructors set up or initialize objects; constructors are class scope (they belong to the class).
- Some OO languages provide special operations called destructors that are called when an object is destroyed – destructors clean up after objects.

- UML class notation.
— Name compartment has the class name in UpperCamelCase:
- no abbreviations, punctuation, or special characters.
— Attribute compartment – each attribute has:
- visibility – this controls access to features of a class;
- name (mandatory) – lowerCamelCase;
- multiplicity – collections, for example, [10]; null values, for example, [0..1];
- type;
- attributes may have stereotypes and tagged values.

— Operation compartment – each operation may have:
  - visibility;
  - name (mandatory) – UpperCamelCase;
  - parameter list (name and type for each parameter);
    - a parameter may optionally have a default value;
    - a parameter may optionally have a direction – in, out, inout, return.
  - return type;
  - stereotype;
  - tagged values.
— Query operations have isQuery = true – they have no side effects.
— An operation signature comprises:
  - name;
  - parameter list (types of all parameters);
  - return type.
— Every operation or method of a class must have a unique signature.

- Scope.
  — Instance scope attributes and operations belong to or operate on specific objects:
    - instance scope operations can access other instance scope operations or instance scope attributes;
    - instance scope operations can access all class scope attributes or operations.
  — Class scope attributes and operations belong to or operate on the whole class of objects:
    - class scope attributes and operations can only access other class scope operations.

chapter **8**

Finding analysis classes

8.1 Chapter roadmap

This chapter is all about the core activity of OO analysis, finding the analysis classes. If you want to understand the UP activity in which analysis classes are found, go to Section 8.2. If you need to know what an analysis class is, go to Section 8.3.

In Section 8.4 we describe how to find analysis classes. We present three specific techniques—noun/verb analysis (8.4.1), CRC analysis (8.4.2), and RUP analysis class stereotypes (8.4.3)—and also a general consideration of other possible sources for classes (8.4.4).

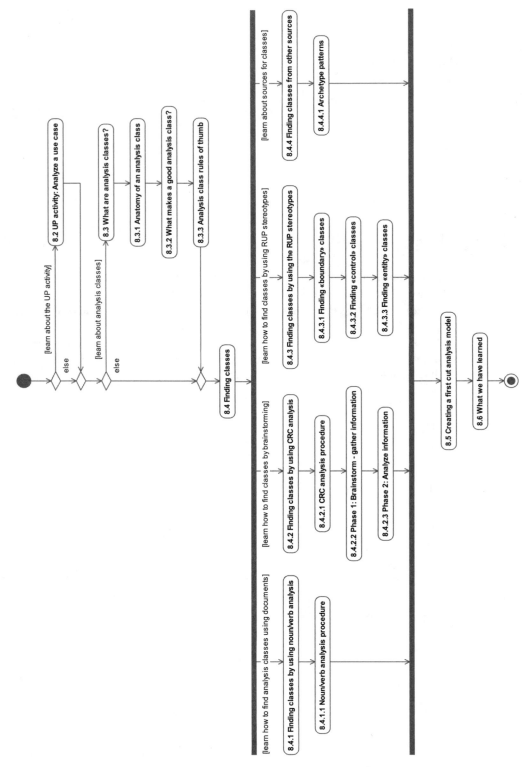

8.2 UP activity: Analyze a use case

[learn about the UP activity]

else

[learn about analysis classes]

else

8.3 What are analysis classes?

8.3.1 Anatomy of an analysis class

8.3.2 What makes a good analysis class?

8.3.3 Analysis class rules of thumb

8.4 Finding classes

[learn about sources for classes]

8.4.4 Finding classes from other sources

8.4.4.1 Archetype patterns

[learn how to find classes by using RUP stereotypes]

8.4.3 Finding classes by using the RUP stereotypes

8.4.3.1 Finding «boundary» classes

8.4.3.2 Finding «control» classes

8.4.3.3 Finding «entity» classes

[learn how to find classes by brainstorming]

8.4.2 Finding classes by using CRC analysis

8.4.2.1 CRC analysis procedure

8.4.2.2 Phase 1: Brainstorm - gather information

8.4.2.3 Phase 2: Analyze information

[learn how to find analysis classes using documents]

8.4.1 Finding classes by using noun/verb analysis

8.4.1.1 Noun/verb analysis procedure

8.5 Creating a first cut analysis model

8.6 What we have learned

Figure 8.1

8.2   UP activity: Analyze a use case

The outputs from the UP workflow Analyze a use case (see Figure 8.2) are analysis classes and use case realizations. In this chapter we focus on analysis classes. We consider use case realizations in Chapter 12; these are collaborations between objects that show how systems of interacting objects can realize the system behavior expressed in the use cases.

It's worth looking at the inputs to Analyze a use case.

> The UP activity "Analyze a use case" involves creating analysis classes and use case realizations.

- Business model – you may, or may not, have a business model available that relates to the system you are modeling. If you do, this is an excellent source of requirements.

- Requirements model – we described creation of this model in Chapter 3. These requirements (grayed to show that the artifact is modified from the original figure) provide useful input to the use case modeling process. In particular, the functional requirements will suggest use cases and actors. The non-functional requirements will suggest things you may need to keep in mind when constructing the use case model.

- Use case model – we discussed creation of the use case model in Chapters 4 and 5.

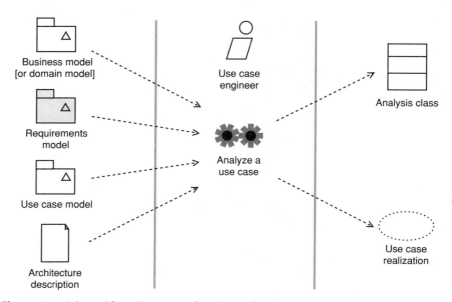

Figure 8.2   Adapted from Figure 8.25 [Jacobson 1] with permission from Addison-Wesley

- Architecture description – a snapshot of the architecturally significant aspects of the system. May include extracts from UML models embedded in an explanatory text. This is created by architects with input from analysts/ designers.

8.3 What are analysis classes?

> Analysis classes model important aspects of the problem domain such as "customer" or "product".

Analysis classes are classes that

- represent a crisp abstraction in the problem domain;
- should map on to real-world business concepts (and be carefully named accordingly).

The problem domain is the domain in which the need for a software system (and hence a software development activity) first arises. This is usually a specific area of the business such as online selling or customer relationship management. However, it is important to note that the problem domain might not be any specific business activity at all, but might arise from a piece of physical hardware that needs software to operate it. Ultimately, all commercial software development serves some business need, be that automating an existing business process or developing a new product that has a significant software component.

> An analysis class should map in a clear and unambiguous way to a real-world business concept.

The most important aspect of an analysis class is that it should map in a clear and unambiguous way to some real-world business concept such as customer, product, or account. However, this statement assumes that the business concepts themselves are clear and unambiguous, and this is rarely the case. It is therefore the job of the OO analyst to try to clarify confused or inappropriate business concepts into something that can form the basis of an analysis class. This is why OO analysis can be difficult.

So the first step in building OO software is to clarify the problem domain. If it contains clearly defined business concepts and has a simple, functional structure, the solution is virtually there for the taking. Much of this work will be done in the requirements workflow in the activities of capturing requirements and creating a use case model and project glossary. However, much more clarification occurs in the construction of analysis classes and use case realizations.

It is important that *all* classes in the analysis model are analysis classes rather than classes arising from design considerations (the solution domain). When you get down to detailed design, you may find that analysis classes are ultimately refined into one or more design classes.

> Finding the right analysis classes is the key to OO analysis and design.

Although, in the previous chapter, we necessarily began by considering specific objects, you will now understand that the real goal of OO analysis is finding the *classes* of those objects. In fact, finding the right analysis classes is the key to OO analysis and design. If the classes are not right in analysis, then the rest of the software engineering process, which is predicated on the requirements and analysis workflows, will be in jeopardy. It is therefore crucial that you spend sufficient time in the analysis workflow to ensure that the right set of analysis classes has been identified. Your time will be well spent, as it will almost certainly save time later.

In this book, we focus on development of business systems, as that is what most OO analysts and designers are involved in. However, development of embedded systems is really just a special case of normal business development and all the same principles apply. Business systems are usually dominated by functional requirements and so it is generally the requirements and analysis activities that are the most difficult. Embedded systems are often dominated by non-functional requirements that arise from the hardware in which the system is embedded. In this case analysis tends to be straightforward, but design can be difficult. Requirements are important for *all* types of system, and for some embedded systems, such as controllers for x-ray machines, they can be a matter of life and death.

8.3.1 Anatomy of an analysis class

> Analysis classes only have key attributes and very high-level responsibilities.

Analysis classes should present a very "high level" set of attributes. They *indicate* the attributes that the resultant design classes will *probably* have. We might say that analysis classes capture candidate attributes for the design classes.

Analysis class operations specify, at a high level, the key services that the class must offer. In design they will become actual, implementable operations. However, one analysis-level operation will often break down into more than one design-level operation.

We have already covered the UML syntax for classes in great detail in Chapter 7, but in analysis only a small subset of that syntax is actually used. Of course, the analyst is always free to add any adornments felt to be necessary to make the model clearer. However, the basic syntax of an analysis class *always* avoids implementation details. After all, in analysis we are trying to capture the big picture.

A minimal form for an analysis class consists of the following.

- Name – this is mandatory.
- Attributes – attribute names are mandatory although only an important subset of candidate attributes may be modeled at this point. Attribute types are considered optional.
- Operations – in analysis, operations might just be very high-level statements of the responsibilities of the class. Operation parameters and

return types are only shown where they are important for understanding the model.

- Visibility – generally not shown.
- Stereotypes – may be shown if they enhance the model.
- Tagged values – may be shown if they enhance the model.

An example is given in Figure 8.3.

The idea of an analysis class is that you try to capture the *essence* of the abstraction and leave the implementation details until you come to design.

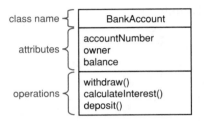

Figure 8.3

8.3.2   What makes a good analysis class?

We can summarize what makes a good analysis class in the following points:

- its name reflects its intent;
- it is a crisp abstraction that models one specific element of the problem domain;
- it maps on to a clearly identifiable feature of the problem domain;
- it has a small, well-defined set of responsibilities;
- it has high cohesion;
- it has low coupling.

> The name of an analysis class should indicate its intent.

In analysis you are trying to model one aspect of the problem domain accurately and concisely from the perspective of the system you are trying to construct. For example, if you are modeling a customer in a banking system, you would want to capture the customer's name, address, and so on, but you would be unlikely to be interested in his preference for window or aisle seats on an aircraft. You need to focus on the aspects of real-world things that are important from the perspective of the system you are building.

You can often get a first idea as to whether or not a class is a "good" class simply from its name. If you consider an e-commerce system, Customer would seem to refer to something quite precise in the real world and would be a good candidate for a class. ShoppingBasket would also seem to be a good abstraction—we know, almost intuitively, what its semantics will be. However, something like WebSiteVisitor seems to have rather vague semantics, and in fact really sounds like a role that a Customer plays in relation to the e-commerce system. You should always be looking for a "crisp abstraction"— something that has clear and obvious semantics.

A responsibility is a contract or obligation that a class has to its clients. Essentially, a responsibility is a service that a class offers to other classes. It is crucial that your analysis classes have a cohesive set of responsibilities that directly accord with the intent of the class (as expressed by its name) and with the real-world "thing" that the class is modeling. Going back to the ShoppingBasket example, you would expect this class to have responsibilities such as

> Responsibilities describe cohesive sets of operations.

- add item to basket;
- remove item from basket;
- show items in basket.

This is a cohesive set of responsibilities, all about maintaining a collection of items that the customer has chosen. It is cohesive because all the responsibilities are working toward the same goal—maintaining the customer's shopping basket. In fact, we could summarize these three responsibilities as a very high-level responsibility called "maintain basket".

Now, you could also add the following responsibilities to the ShoppingBasket:

- validate credit card;
- accept payment;
- print receipt.

But these responsibilities do not seem to fit with the intent or intuitive semantics of shopping baskets. They are not cohesive and clearly should be assigned elsewhere—perhaps to a CreditCardCompany class, a Checkout class, and a ReceiptPrinter class. It is important to distribute responsibilities appropriately over analysis classes to maximize cohesion within each class.

Finally, good classes have the minimum amount of coupling to other classes. We measure coupling between classes by the number of other classes with which a given class has relationships. An even distribution of responsibilities between classes will tend to result in low coupling. Localization of control or of many responsibilities in a single class tends to increase coupling to that class. We consider ways of maximizing cohesion and minimizing coupling in Chapter 15.

8.3.3   Analysis class rules of thumb

Here are some rules of thumb for creating well-formed analysis classes.

- About three to five responsibilities per class – typically, classes should be kept as simple as possible, and this usually limits the number of responsibilities that they can support to between three and five. Our previous example of a ShoppingBasket is a good example of a focused class with a small and manageable number of responsibilities.

- No class stands alone – the essence of good OO analysis and design is that classes collaborate with each other to deliver benefit to users. As such, each class should be associated with a small number of other classes with which it collaborates to deliver the desired benefit. Classes may delegate some of their responsibilities to other "helper" classes that are dedicated to that specific function.

- Beware of many very small classes – it can sometimes be hard to get the balance right. If the model seems to have lots and lots of very small classes with just one or two responsibilities each, then you should look at this very carefully with a view to consolidating some of the small classes into larger ones.

- Beware of few but very large classes – the converse of the above is a model that has few classes, where many of them have a large number (> 5) of responsibilities. The strategy here is to look at these classes in turn and see if each can be decomposed into two or more smaller classes with the right number of responsibilities.

- Beware of "functoids" – a functoid is really a normal procedural function disguised as a class. Grady Booch tells the amusing anecdote of a model of a very simple system that had thousands of classes. On closer inspection, each class had exactly one operation called doIt(). Functoids are always a danger when analysts accustomed to the technique of top-down functional decomposition approach OO analysis and design for the first time.

- Beware of omnipotent classes – these are classes that seem to do everything. Look for classes with "system" or "controller" in their name! The strategy for dealing with this problem is to see if the responsibilities of the omnipotent class fall into cohesive subsets. If so, perhaps each of these cohesive sets of responsibilities can be factored out into a separate class. These smaller classes would then collaborate to implement the behavior offered by the original omnipotent class.

- Avoid deep inheritance trees – the essence of designing a good inheritance hierarchy is that each level of abstraction in the hierarchy should have a well-defined purpose. It is easy to add many levels that don't really serve any useful purpose. In fact, a common mistake is to use inheritance to implement a kind of functional decomposition where each level of abstraction has only one responsibility. This is, in every respect, pointless and just leads to a complex, difficult to understand model. In analysis, inheritance is only used where there is a clear, and obvious, inheritance hierarchy arising directly from the problem domain.

In the last bullet, we need to clarify what we mean by a "deep" inheritance tree. In analysis, where the classes represent business things, "deep" would be three levels of inheritance or more. This is because business things tend to form inheritance hierarchies that are broad rather than deep.

In design, where the tree consists of classes from the solution domain, the definition of "deep" depends on the implementation language you are targeting. In Java, C++, C#, Python, and Visual Basic, we still consider three or more levels to be deep. In Smalltalk, however, inheritance trees can go much deeper than this, due to the structure of the Smalltalk system.

8.4   Finding classes

In the rest of this chapter we consider the core issue of OO analysis and design, finding the analysis classes.

As Meyer points out in *Object Oriented Software Construction* [Meyer 1], there is no simple algorithm for finding the right analysis classes. If such an algorithm did exist, then it would amount to an infallible way to design OO software and this is just as unlikely as finding an infallible way to prove mathematical theorems.

Still, there are tried and tested techniques that lead toward a good answer, and we present them here. They involve analyzing text and interviewing users and domain experts. But ultimately, despite all the techniques, finding the "right" classes depends on the perspective, skill, and experience of the individual analyst.

8.4.1   Finding classes by using noun/verb analysis

Noun/verb analysis is a very simple way of analyzing text to try to find classes, attributes, and responsibilities. In essence, nouns and noun phrases in the text indicate classes or attributes of classes, and verbs and verb phrases indicate responsibilities or operations of a class. Noun/verb analysis has been used for many years and works well as it is based on a direct analysis of the language of the problem domain. However, you have to be very aware of synonyms and homonyms as these can give rise to spurious classes.

> In noun/verb analysis you analyze text. Nouns and noun phrases indicate classes or attributes. Verbs and verb phrases indicate responsibilities or operations.

You also have to be very careful if the problem domain is poorly understood and defined. In this case, try to collect as much information about the domain from as many people as possible. Look for similar problem domains outside your organization.

Perhaps the trickiest aspect of noun/verb analysis is finding the "hidden" classes. These are classes that are intrinsic to the problem domain but that might never be mentioned explicitly. For example, in a reservation system for a holiday company, you will hear the stakeholders talk about reservations, bookings, and so on, but the single most important abstraction, Order, may never be mentioned explicitly if it does not exist in current business systems. You generally know when you have found a hidden class because the whole model seems to gel suddenly with the introduction of this single, new abstraction. This happens surprisingly often—in fact, if we're ever having trouble with an analysis model and it just doesn't seem to be making sense, we go on a search for hidden classes. If nothing else, this makes us ask some penetrating questions and improves our understanding of the problem domain.

8.4.1.1   Noun/verb analysis procedure

The first step in noun/verb analysis is to collect as much relevant information as possible. Suitable sources of information are

- the requirements model;
- the use case model;
- the project glossary;
- anything else (architecture, vision documents, etc.).

After collecting the documentation, analyze it in a very simple way by highlighting (or recording in some other way) the following:

- nouns – for example, flight;
- noun phrases – for example, flight number;
- verbs – for example, allocate;
- verb phrases – for example, verify credit card.

Nouns and noun phrases may indicate classes or class attributes. Verbs and verb phrases may indicate responsibilities of classes.

If you come across any terms that you don't understand during this process, seek immediate clarification from a domain expert and add the term to the project glossary. Take the list of nouns, noun phrases, verbs, and verb phrases and use the project glossary to resolve any synonyms and homonyms. This creates a list of candidate classes, attributes, and responsibilities.

Once you have this list of candidate classes, attributes, and responsibilities, you make a tentative allocation of the attributes and responsibilities to the classes. You can do this by entering the classes into a modeling tool and adding the responsibilities as operations to the classes. If you have found any candidate attributes, then you can tentatively assign these to classes as well. You might also have gained some idea of relationships between certain classes (the use cases are a good source of these), so you can add some candidate associations. This gives you a first-cut class model that you can refine by further analysis.

8.4.2 Finding classes by using CRC analysis

> CRC is a brainstorming technique in which you capture on sticky notes the important things in the problem domain.

A very good (and fun) way to get user involvement in finding classes is to use CRC analysis—CRC stands for class, responsibilities, and collaborators. This technique uses the world's most powerful analysis tool, the sticky note! So popular is the CRC method that there is a (possibly apocryphal) story that at one point a company actually marketed sticky notes already marked out with class name, responsibilities, and collaborators.

You begin by marking up some sticky notes as shown in Figure 8.4. The note is divided into three compartments. In the top compartment you record the name of the candidate class; in the left compartment, the responsibilities; and in the right, the collaborators. Collaborators are other classes that may collaborate with this class to realize a piece of system functionality. The collaborators compartment provides a way of recording relationships between classes. Another way to capture relationships (which we prefer) is to stick the notes on a whiteboard and draw lines between the collaborating classes.

Class name: BankAccount	
Responsibilities: Maintain balance	Collaborators: Bank

Figure 8.4

8.4.2.1 CRC analysis procedure

CRC analysis should always be used in conjunction with noun/verb analysis of use cases, requirements, glossary, and other relevant documentation, unless the system is very simple. The CRC analysis procedure is straightforward and the key is to separate information *gathering* from information *analysis*. CRC is therefore best run as a two-phase activity.

8.4.2.2   Phase 1: Brainstorm – gather the information

Stakeholder involvement is essential for CRC success.

The participants are OO analysts, stakeholders, and domain experts. You also need a facilitator. The procedure is as follows.

1. Explain that this is a true brainstorm.
   1.1. All ideas are accepted as good ideas.
   1.2. Ideas are recorded but *not* debated – never argue about something, just write it down and then move on. Everything will be analyzed later.

2. Ask the team members to name the "things" that operate in their business domain – for example, customer, product.
   2.1. Write each thing on a sticky note – it is a candidate class, or attribute of a class.
   2.2. Stick the note on a wall or whiteboard.

3. Ask the team to state responsibilities that those things might have – record these in the responsibilities compartment of the note.

4. Working with the team, try to identify classes that might work together. Rearrange the notes on the whiteboard to reflect this organization and draw lines between them. Alternatively, record collaborators in the collaborators compartment of the note.

8.4.2.3   Phase 2: Analyze information

Important business concepts generally become classes.

The participants are OO analysts and domain experts. How do you decide which sticky notes should become classes and which should become attributes? Go back and look at Section 8.3.2—analysis classes *must* represent a crisp abstraction in the problem domain. Certain sticky notes will represent key business concepts and clearly need to become classes. Other notes may become classes or attributes. If a note logically seems to be a *part* of another note, this is a good indication that it represents an attribute. Also, if a note doesn't seem to be particularly important or has very little interesting behavior, see if it can be made an attribute of another class.

If in doubt about a note just make it a class. The important point is to make a best guess and then drive this process to closure; you can always refine the model later.

8.4.3   Finding classes by using the RUP stereotypes

According to RUP, it can be helpful to look for **«boundary»**, **«control»**, and **«entity»** classes.

A useful technique comes from RUP in the form of RUP stereotypes. The idea is that you consider three distinct types of analysis class during your analysis activity. This is a way of focusing your analysis on specific aspects of the system. We consider this an optional technique that you can use to complement the core noun/verb and CRC card analysis techniques presented earlier.

Three distinct types of analysis class can be distinguished by the stereotypes shown in Table 8.1.

We look at how to find each of these types of analysis class in the next three subsections.

Table 8.1

Stereotype	Icon	Semantics
«boundary»		a class that mediates interaction between the system and its environment
«control»		a class that encapsulates use-case-specific behavior
«entity»		a class that is used to model persistent information about something

8.4.3.1   *Finding* «boundary» *classes*

These classes exist on the boundary of your system and communicate with external actors.

You find these classes by considering the subject (system boundary) and discovering what classes mediate between the subject and its environment. According to RUP there are three types of «boundary» class:

1. user interface classes – classes that interface between the system and humans;

2. system interface classes – classes that interface with other systems;

3. device interface classes – classes that interface with external devices such as sensors.

Each communication between an actor and a use case in your model must be enabled by some object in your system. These objects are instances of boundary classes. You can work out what type of boundary class is indicated by considering what the actor represents (Table 8.2).

Table 8.2

Actor	Indicates
Represents a human	User interface class
Represents a system	System interface class
Represents a device	Device interface class

When a boundary class services more than one actor, these actors should generally be of the same kind (representing a human, system, or device). It can be an indication of bad design if a boundary class services actors of different types!

Because you are still in analysis, it is important to keep these classes at the right level of abstraction. For example, when modeling a «boundary» class that represents a GUI, just model the top-level window and leave all the details of the widgets that compose the window to design. Alternatively, you can introduce a dummy class that represents the whole user interface.

Similarly, with system interface classes and device interface classes, you are concerned with capturing the fact that there *is* a class that mediates between your system and something else, but *not* with the specific details of that class. You will decide on these details later in design.

For example, if you are writing an e-commerce system that needs to interface to an Inventory system, you can represent the interface to the Inventory system by a class called InventoryInterface that is stereotyped «boundary». This is sufficient detail for an analysis model.

8.4.3.2   *Finding «control» classes*

These classes are controllers—their instances coordinate system behavior that corresponds to one or more use cases.

You find control classes by considering the behavior of the system as described by the use cases and working out how that behavior should be partitioned among the analysis classes. Simple behavior can often be distributed between boundary or entity classes, but more complex behavior, such as order processing, is generally best localized by introducing a suitable controller class such as an OrderManager. Some modelers (ourselves included!) often indicate control classes by appending Manager or Controller to the name of the class.

The key point when working with control classes is to let the classes arise naturally from the problem domain itself. Some modelers artificially introduce a control class for each use case to control or execute that use case. This is a dangerous approximation that leads to a model that looks more like a top-down functional decomposition than a true OO analysis model. In fact, this is one of the reasons that we consider using the RUP stereotypes as optional—they can lead novice modelers astray!

In the real world, controllers arising directly from the problem domain (rather than as a by-product of a specific analysis technique) tend to cut across several use cases. A good example might be a controller such as a Registrar class that is involved in many of the use cases that describe a course registration system. Similarly, a single use case may require the participation of many control classes.

If you find that a controller class has a very complicated behavior, this indicates that you may be able to break it down into two or more simpler controllers that each implement a cohesive subset of that behavior. Each of the simpler classes that you identify must still be something that naturally occurs in the problem domain. For example, when designing a course registration system, you might originally introduce a control class called CourseRegistrationController that coordinates the whole process. But such a class has a complex behavior, and so you might decide to break it up into a set of collaborating classes with each class handling one or two aspects of that behavior. The CourseRegistrationController might be decomposed into Registrar, CourseManager, and PersonnelManager classes. Notice that each of these classes represents a thing that exists in the problem domain.

A good way to explore controller classes is to imagine yourself in the role of the class. What would you have to do in that situation?

8.4.3.3   *Finding «entity» classes*

These classes model information about something and usually have very simple behavior that amounts to little more than getting and setting values. Classes that represent persistent information such as addresses (an Address class) and people (a Person class) are entity classes.

Entity classes—

- cut across many use cases;
- are manipulated by control classes;
- provide information to, and accept information from, boundary classes;
- represent key things managed by the system (e.g., Customer);
- are often persistent.

Entity classes express the logical data structure of the system. If you have a data model, then entity classes are intimately related to entities or tables in this model.

8.4.4   Finding classes from other sources

Along with noun/verb analysis, CRC analysis, and RUP stereotypes, it is worth remembering that there are many other potential sources of classes that should be considered. As you are looking for crisp abstractions that map to real-world things in the problem domain then, obviously, you can look to the real world for classes.

- Physical objects such as aircraft, people, and hotels may all indicate classes to you.

- Paperwork is another rich source of classes. Things like invoices, orders, and bankbooks may all indicate possible classes. However, you must be very careful when looking at paperwork. In many companies the paperwork has evolved over the years to support exactly the redundant business processes that the new system might be trying to replace! The last thing you want to do as an OO analyst/designer is to automate obsolete and pathological paper-based systems.

- Known interfaces to the outside world such as screens, keyboards, peripherals, and other systems can also be a source of candidate classes, especially for embedded systems.

- Conceptual entities are things that are crucial to the operation of the business but are not manifest as concrete things. An example of this might be a LoyaltyProgram such as a reward card. Clearly, the program itself is not a concrete thing (you can't kick it!), but it is still a cohesive abstraction and so may warrant modeling as a class.

8.4.4.1   *Archetype patterns*

> Archetype patterns can provide ready-made model components for your analysis models.

In our book *Enterprise Patterns and MDA* [Arlow 1] we describe a set of what we call *archetype patterns*. These are patterns of business concepts that are so pervasive in business systems that we believe that they are truly archetypal in nature. As such, they can be modeled once and then reused, rather than modeled over and over again in each new business system. The idea of the book is that you can use these patterns as-is, or modify them, to construct your analysis model from *model components*. We call this technique *component-based modeling*.

We provide the following archetype patterns:

- Customer Relationship Management;
- Inventory;
- Money;

- Order;
- Party;
- Party relationship;
- Product;
- Quantity;
- Rule.

Each of these patterns is *very* detailed and inclusive. If you can reuse one of these patterns, you can save yourself many man-days or even man-months of work. Even if the pattern isn't completely appropriate for what you are trying to model, it may give you useful ideas for your own analysis classes rather than starting from a blank page.

This is probably the most efficient way of finding classes for your models—just take them off the shelf!

8.5   Creating a first-cut analysis model

To create a first-cut analysis model, you need to consolidate the outputs of noun/verb analysis, CRC analysis, RUP stereotypes, and a consideration of other sources of classes (especially archetype patterns) into a single UML model in a modeling tool. Perform consolidation as follows.

1. Compare all sources of classes.
2. Consolidate the analysis classes, attributes, and responsibilities from the different sources and enter them into a modeling tool.
   2.1. Use the project glossary to resolve synonyms and homonyms.
   2.2. Look for differences in the results of the three techniques – differences indicate areas where there is uncertainty or where more work might be done. Resolve these differences now, or highlight for later work.
3. Collaborators (or lines between sticky notes on the whiteboard) represent relationships between classes. You will see how to model these in Chapter 9.
4. Improve the naming of classes, attributes, and responsibilities to follow any standard naming conventions that your company has, or follow the simple naming conventions described in Chapter 7.

The output from this activity is a set of analysis classes where each class *may* have some key attributes and *should* have between three to five responsibilities. This is your first-cut analysis model.

8.6   What we have learned

In this chapter we have described what analysis classes are and how to find these classes using the techniques of noun/verb analysis, CRC brainstorming, and an examination of other sources of classes.

You have learned the following.

- The UP activity Analyze a use case outputs analysis classes and use case realizations.
- Analysis classes represent a crisp, well-defined abstraction in the problem domain.
  - The problem domain is that domain in which the need for the software system has arisen.
  - Analysis classes should map in a clear, unambiguous way to a real-world business concept.
  - Business concepts often need to be clarified during analysis.
- The analysis model only contains analysis classes – any classes arising from design considerations (the solution domain) must be excluded.
- Analysis classes include:
  - a set of high-level candidate attributes;
  - a set of high-level operations.
- What makes a good analysis class?
  - Its name reflects its intent.
  - It is a crisp abstraction that models one specific element of the problem domain.
  - It maps to a clearly identifiable feature of the problem domain.
  - It has a small, well-defined set of responsibilities:
    - a responsibility is a contract or obligation that a class has to its clients;
    - a responsibility is a semantically cohesive set of operations;
    - there should only be about three to five responsibilities per class.
  - It has high cohesion – all features of the class should help to realize its intent.
  - It has low coupling – a class should only collaborate with a small number of other classes to realize its intent.
- What makes a bad analysis class?
  - It is a functoid – a class with only one operation.
  - It is an omnipotent class – a class that does everything – classes with "system" or "controller" in their name *may* need closer scrutiny.
  - It has a deep inheritance tree – in the real world inheritance trees tend to be shallow.

- — It has low cohesion.
- — It has high coupling.
- ● Noun/verb analysis.
  - — Look for nouns or noun phrases – these are candidate classes or attributes.
  - — Look for verbs or verb phrases – these are candidate responsibilities or operations.
  - — The procedure is to collect relevant information and then to analyze it.
- ● CRC analysis is a powerful and fun brainstorming technique.
  - — Important things in the problem domain are written on sticky notes.
  - — Each note has three compartments:
    - – class – contains the name of the class;
    - – responsibilities – contains a list of the responsibilities of that class;
    - – collaborators – contains a list of other classes with which this class collaborates.
  - — Procedure – brainstorm:
    - – ask the team members to name the "things" that operate in their business domain and write them on sticky notes;
    - – ask the team to state the responsibilities of the things and record them in the responsibilities compartment of the note;
    - – ask the team to identify classes that might work together and draw lines between them, or record this in the collaborators compartment of each note.
- ● RUP stereotypes can be used to focus analysis activity on three types of class:
  - — «boundary» – a class that mediates interaction between the system and its environment;
  - — «control» – a class that encapsulates use-case-specific behavior;
  - — «entity» – a class that is used to model persistent information about something.
- ● Consider other sources of classes:
  - — physical objects, paperwork, interfaces to the outside world, and conceptual entities;
  - — archetype patterns – component-based modeling.
- ● Create a first-cut analysis model:
  - — compare noun/verb analysis results with CRC results and the results of an examination of other sources of classes;
  - — resolve synonyms and homonyms;
  - — differences between the results of the different techniques indicate areas of uncertainty;
  - — consolidate results into a first-cut analysis model.

chapter **9**

Relationships

9.1 Chapter roadmap

This chapter discusses relationships between objects, and relationships between classes. To find out what a relationship is, read Section 9.2. The chapter is then organized under three separate threads. We discuss links (relationships between objects) in Section 9.3, associations (relationships between classes) in Section 9.4, and, finally, dependencies (catch-all relationships) in Section 9.5.

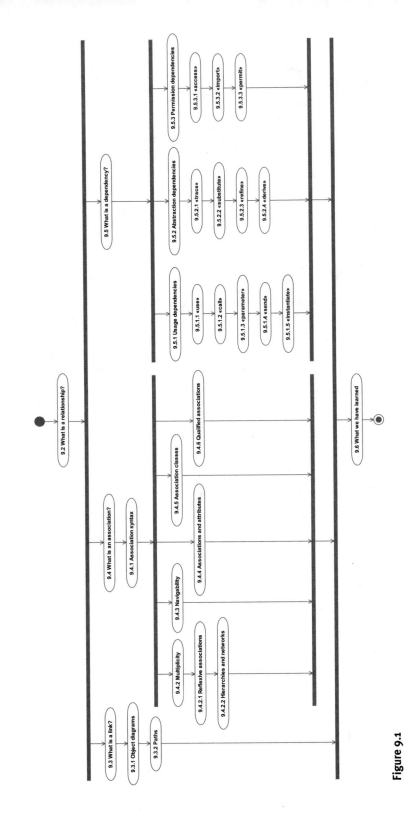

Figure 9.1

9.2 What is a relationship?

Relationships are semantic (meaningful) connections between modeling elements—they are the UML way of connecting things together. You have already seen a few types of relationships:

- between actors and use cases (association);
- between use cases and use cases (generalization, «include», «extend»);
- between actors and actors (generalization).

UML relationships connect things.

In this chapter we explore connections between objects and connections between classes. We start with links and associations, and then, in Chapter 10, look at generalization and inheritance.

To create a functioning OO system, you can't let the objects stand alone in glorious isolation. You need to connect them so that they can perform useful work of benefit to the users of the system. Connections between objects are called links, and when objects work together, we say that they collaborate.

If there is a link between two objects, there must also be some semantic connection between their classes. This is really common sense—for objects to communicate directly with each other, the classes of those objects must know about each other in some way. Connections between classes are known as associations. Links between objects are actually instances of the associations between their classes.

9.3 What is a link?

To create an object-oriented program, objects need to communicate with each other. In fact, an executing OO program is a harmonious community of cooperating objects.

Objects send messages to one another over connections called links.

A link is a semantic connection between two objects that allows messages to be sent from one object to the other. An executing OO system contains many objects that come and go, and many links (that also come and go) that join those objects. Messages are passed back and forth between objects over these links. On receipt of a message, an object will invoke its corresponding operation.

Links are implemented in different ways by different OO languages. Java implements links as object references; C++ may implement links as pointers, as references, or by direct inclusion of one object by another.

Whatever the approach, a minimal requirement for a link is that *at least one* of the objects must have an object reference to the other.

9.3.1   Object diagrams

An object diagram is a diagram that shows objects and their relationships at a point in time. It is like a snapshot of part of an executing OO system at a particular instant, showing the objects and the links between them.

Objects that are connected by links may adopt various roles relative to each other. In Figure 9.2, you can see that the ila object adopts the role of chairperson in its link with the bookClub object. You indicate this on the object diagram by placing the role name at the appropriate end of the link. You can put role names at either or both ends of a link. In this case, the bookClub object always plays the role of "club" and so there is no real point in showing this on the diagram—it would not really add anything to our understanding of the object relationships.

Figure 9.2 tells us that at a particular point in time, the object ila is playing the role of chairperson. However, it is important to realize that links are *dynamic* connections between objects. In other words, they are not necessarily fixed over time. In this example, the chairperson role may pass at some point to erica or naomi, and we could easily create an object diagram to show this new state of affairs.

Normally, a single link connects exactly two objects as shown in Figure 9.2. However, UML does allow a single link to connect more than two objects. This is known as an n-ary link and is shown as a diamond with a path to each participating object. Many modelers (ourselves included) consider this idiom to be unnecessary. It is rarely used and UML modeling tools do not always support it, so we do not say anything more about it here.

Object diagrams are snapshots of an executing OO system.

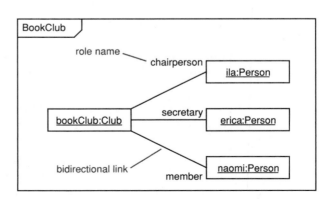

Figure 9.2

Considering Figure 9.2 in more depth, you can see that there are three links between four objects:

- a link between bookClub and ila;
- a link between bookClub and erica;
- a link between bookClub and naomi.

In Figure 9.2 the links are bidirectional, so you can just as correctly say that the link connects ila to bookClub or that the link connects bookClub to ila.

> Use navigability to specify which directions messages may pass over a link.

If a link is unidirectional, you use navigability to specify in which direction messages may pass over the link.

You can show navigability by placing an arrowhead (navigable) or cross (not navigable) on the end of a link. Think of navigability as being a bit like a one-way system in a city. Messages can only flow in the direction indicated by the arrowhead.

The UML 2 specification allows three different modeling idioms for showing navigability, which we discuss in detail in Section 9.4.3. We use the most common idiom consistently throughout this book:

- all crosses are suppressed;
- bidirectional associations have *no* arrows;
- unidirectional associations have a single arrow.

The only real disadvantage of this idiom is that there is no way to indicate that navigability is undecided, because no navigability is taken to mean "not navigable".

For example, Figure 9.3 shows that the link between :PersonDetails and :Address is unidirectional. This means that the :PersonDetails object has an object reference to the :Address object, but *not* vice versa. Messages can *only* be sent from :PersonDetails to :Address.

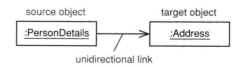

Figure 9.3

9.3.2   Paths

UML symbols, such as the object icon, use case icon, and class icon, are connected to other symbols by paths. A path is a "connected series of graphic segments" (in other words, a line!) joining two or more symbols. There are three styles for drawing paths:

- orthogonal – where the path consists of a series of horizontal and vertical segments;
- oblique – where the path is a series of one or more sloping lines;
- curved – where the path is a curve.

It is a matter of personal preference as to which style of path is used, and the styles may even be mixed on the same diagram if this makes the diagram clearer and easier to read. We usually use the orthogonal style, as do many other modelers.

In Figure 9.4, we have adopted the orthogonal path style, and the paths have been combined into a tree. You can only combine paths that have the same properties. In this case, all the paths represent links and so we can legally combine them.

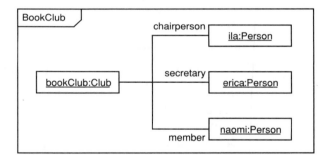

Figure 9.4

The visual neatness, readability, and general appeal of the diagrams is of crucial importance. Always remember that the majority of diagrams are drawn to be read by someone else. As such, no matter what style you adopt, neatness and clarity are vital.

9.4   What is an association?

Associations are connections between classes.

Associations are relationships between classes. Just as links connect objects, associations connect classes. The key point is that for there to be a link between two objects, there *must* be an association between the classes of those objects. This is because a link is an instance of an association, just as an object is an instance of a class.

Figure 9.5 shows the relationship between classes and objects, and between links and associations. Because you can't have a link without an association, it is clear that links *depend* on associations; you can model this with a dependency relationship (the dashed arrow) that we look at in more detail in Section 9.5. To make the semantics of the dependency between associations and links explicit, you stereotype the dependency «instantiate».

Objects are instances of classes, and links are instances of associations.

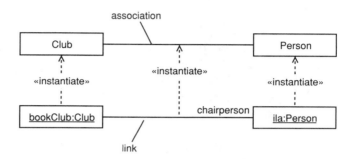

Figure 9.5

The semantics of the basic, unrefined association are very simple—an association between classes indicates that you can have links between objects of those classes. There are other more refined forms of association (aggregation and composition) that we look at in Section 18.3 in the design workflow.

9.4.1   Association syntax

Associations may have

- an association name;
- role names;
- multiplicity;
- navigability.

Association names should be verb phrases because they indicate an action that the source object is performing on the target object. The name may also be prefixed or postfixed with a small black arrowhead to indicate the direction in which the association name should be read. Association names are in lowerCamelCase.

In the example in Figure 9.6 you read the association as follows: "a Company employs many Persons." Although the arrow indicates the direction in which the association should be read, you can always read associations in the other direction as well. So in Figure 9.6 you can say, "each Person is employed by exactly one Company" at any point in time.

Association names are verb phrases that indicate the semantics of the association.

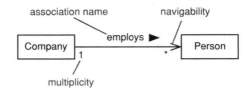

Figure 9.6

Alternatively, you can give role names to the classes on one or both ends of the association. These role names indicate the roles that objects of those classes play when they are linked by instances of this association. In Figure 9.7, you can see that a Company object will play the role employer, and Person objects will play the role employee when they are linked by instances of this association. Role names should be nouns or noun phrases as they name a role that objects can play.

Associations can have *either* an association name, *or* role names. Putting both role names *and* association names on the same association is theoretically legal, but this is very bad style—and overkill!

The key to good association names and role names is that they should read well. In Figure 9.6 a Company *employs* many Persons—this reads very well indeed. Reading the association the other way around, you can say that a Person *is employed* by exactly one Company at any point in time—it still reads very well. Similarly, the role names in Figure 9.7 clearly indicate the roles that objects of these classes will play when linked in this particular way.

Role names are noun phrases that indicate the roles played by objects linked by instances of the association.

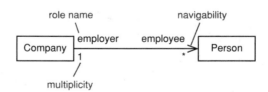

Figure 9.7

9.4.2   Multiplicity

Constraints are one of the three UML extensibility mechanisms, and multiplicity is the first type of constraint that we have seen. It is also by far the most common type of constraint. Multiplicity constrains the number of objects of a class that can be involved in a particular relationship *at any point in time*. The phrase "at any point in time" is vital to understanding multiplicities. Considering Figure 9.8, you can see that at any point in time a Person object is employed by exactly one Company object. However, *over time* a Person object might be employed by a series of Company objects.

Looking at Figure 9.8, you can see something else that is interesting. A Person object can never be unemployed—it is always employed by exactly one Company object. The constraint therefore embodies two business rules of this model:

- that Person objects can only be employed by one Company at a time;
- that Person objects must *always* be employed.

Whether or not these are reasonable constraints depends entirely on the requirements of the system you are modeling, but this is what the model actually says.

You can see that multiplicity constraints are very important—they can encode key business rules in your model. However, these rules are "buried" in the details of the model. Literate modelers call this hiding of key business rules and requirements "trivialization". For a much more detailed discussion of this phenomenon, see [Arlow 1].

Multiplicity is specified as a comma-separated list of intervals, where each interval is of the form:

minimum..maximum

minimum and maximum may be integers or any expression that yields an integer result.

> If multiplicity is not explicitly stated, then it is undecided.

If multiplicity is not explicitly stated, then it is undecided—there is no "default" multiplicity in UML. In fact, it is a common UML modeling error to assume that an undecided multiplicity defaults to a multiplicity of 1. Some examples of multiplicity syntax are given in Table 9.1.

> Multiplicity specifies the number of objects that can participate in a relationship at any point in time.

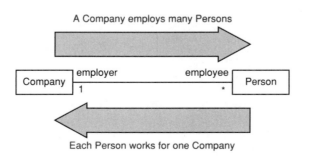

Figure 9.8

Table 9.1

Adornment	Semantics
0..1	Zero or 1
1	Exactly 1
0..*	Zero or more
*	Zero or more
1..*	1 or more
1..6	1 to 6
1..3, 7..10, 15, 19..*	1 to 3 *or* 7 to 10 *or* 15 exactly *or* 19 to many

Always read the
model exactly as
written.

The example in Figure 9.9 illustrates that multiplicity is actually a powerful constraint that often has a big effect on the business semantics of the model.

If you read the example carefully, you see that

- a Company can have exactly seven employees;
- a Person can be employed by exactly one Company (i.e., in this model a Person can't have more than one job at a time);
- a BankAccount can have exactly one owner;
- a BankAccount can have one or many operators;
- a Person may have zero to many BankAccounts;
- a Person may operate zero to many BankAccounts.

When reading a UML model, it is vital to figure out exactly what the model actually says, rather than making any assumptions or hallucinating semantics. We call this "reading the model as written".

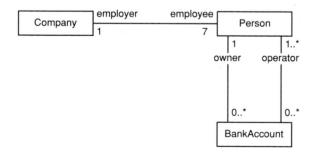

Figure 9.9

For example, Figure 9.9 states that a Company may have exactly seven employees, no more and no less. Most people would consider these semantics to be rather odd, or even incorrect (unless it is a very strange company), but this is what the model actually says. You must never lose sight of this.

There is a certain amount of debate as to whether multiplicity should be shown on analysis models. We think that it should, because multiplicity describes business rules, requirements, and constraints and can expose unwarranted assumptions made about the business. Clearly, such assumptions need to be exposed and challenged as early as possible.

9.4.2.1   *Reflexive associations*

> When a class has an association to itself, this is a reflexive association.

It is quite common for a class to have an association to itself. This is called a reflexive association and it means that objects of that class have links to other objects of the same class. A good example of a reflexive association is shown in Figure 9.10. Each Directory object can have links to zero or more Directory objects that play the role subdirectory, and to zero or one Directory object that plays the role parent. In addition, each Directory object is associated with zero or more File objects. This models a generic directory structure quite well, although it's worth mentioning that specific file systems (such as Windows) may have different multiplicity constraints to this model.

The top half of Figure 9.10 shows the class diagram, and the bottom half shows an example object diagram that accords with that class diagram.

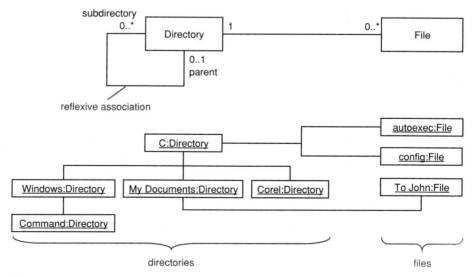

Figure 9.10

9.4.2.2   *Hierarchies and networks*

When modeling, you'll find that objects often organize themselves into hierarchies or networks. A hierarchy has one root object, and every other node in the hierarchy has exactly one object directly above it. Directory trees naturally form hierarchies. So do part breakdowns in engineering, and elements in XML and HTML documents. The hierarchy is a very ordered, structured, and somewhat rigid way of organizing objects. An example is shown in Figure 9.11.

In a hierarchy an object may have zero or one object above it.

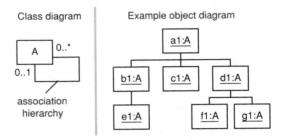

Figure 9.11

In the network, however, there is often no root object, although that is not precluded. In networks, each object may have many objects directly connected to it. There is no real concept of "above" or "below" in a network. It is a much more flexible structure in which it is possible that no node has primacy over another. The World Wide Web forms a complex network of nodes, as illustrated in a simple way in Figure 9.12.

In a network an object may have zero or many objects above it.

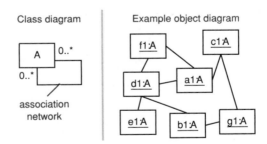

Figure 9.12

As an example to illustrate hierarchies and networks, let's consider products. There are two fundamental abstractions:

- ProductType – a type of product, such as "Inkjet Printer";
- ProductItem – a specific ink jet printer, serial number 0001123430.

ProductType and ProductItem are discussed in great detail in [Arlow 1]. Product-Types often tend to form networks, so a ProductType such as a computer package may consist of a CPU, screen, keyboard, mouse, graphics card, and other ProductTypes. Each of these ProductTypes describes a *type* of product, not an individual item, and these types of products may participate in other composite ProductTypes, such as different computer packages.

However, if we consider the ProductItems, which are specific instances of a ProductType, any ProductItem, such as a specific CPU, can only be sold and delivered *once* as part of one package of goods. ProductItems, therefore, form hierarchies.

9.4.3   Navigability

> Navigability indicates that objects of the source class "know about" objects of the target class.

Navigability shows us that it is possible to traverse from an object of the source class to one or more objects of the target class, depending on the multiplicity. You can think of navigability as meaning "messages can only be sent in the direction of the arrow". In Figure 9.13, Order objects can send messages to Product objects, but not vice versa.

One of the goals of good OO analysis and design is to minimize coupling between classes, and using navigability is a good way to do this. By making the association between Order and Product unidirectional, you can navigate easily from Order objects to Product objects, but there is no navigability back from Product objects to Order objects. So Product objects *do not know* that they may be participating in a particular Order and therefore have no coupling to Order.

Navigability is shown by appending either a cross or an arrowhead to an end of the relationship as shown in Figure 9.13.

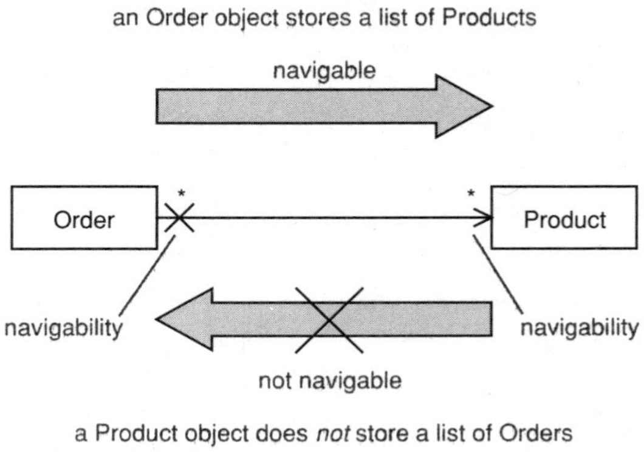

Figure 9.13

The UML 2.0 specification [UML2S] suggests three modeling idioms for using navigability on your diagrams.

1. Make navigability completely explicit. All arrows and crosses must be shown.

2. Make navigability completely invisible. No arrows or crosses are shown.

3. Suppress all crosses. Bidirectional associations have no arrows. Unidirectional associations have a single arrow.

These three idioms are summarized in Figure 9.14.

Idiom 1 makes navigability fully visible, but it can tend to clutter the diagrams.

Idiom 2 should usually be avoided, because it hides far too much valuable information.

Idiom 3 is a reasonable compromise. In fact, idiom 3 is the option that is used, almost exclusively, in practice. Because it represents current best practice, it is the option we use consistently throughout this book. The main advantages of idiom 3 are that it doesn't clutter the diagrams with too many

UML 2 navigability idioms			
UML 2 syntax	Idiom 1: Strict UML 2 navigability	Idiom 2: No navigability	Idiom3: Standard practice
A ←→ B	A to B is navigable B to A is navigable		
A ✕→ B	A to B is navigable B to A is not navigable		
A → B	A to B is navigable B to A is undefined		A to B is navigable B to A is not navigable
A — B	A to B is undefined B to A is undefined	A to B is undefined B to A is undefined	A to B is navigable B to A is navigable
A ✕—✕ B	A to B is not navigable B to A is not navigable		

Figure 9.14

arrows or crosses and that it is backwards compatible with earlier versions of UML. However, it does have disadvantages.

- It is not possible to tell from the diagram if navigability is present or if it has not yet been defined.

- It changes the meaning of the single arrowhead from navigable/undefined to navigable/not navigable. This is unfortunate but is just the way it is.

- You can't show associations that are not navigable in either direction (a cross at each end). These are useless in day-to-day modeling so it is not really an issue.

You can see a summary of idiom 3 in Figure 9.15.

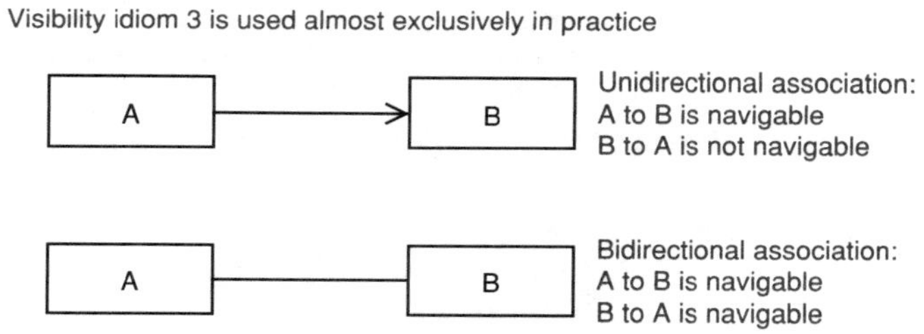

Visibility idiom 3 is used almost exclusively in practice

Figure 9.15

> Even if an association is not navigable, it may still be possible to traverse the association but the cost will be high.

Even if an association is not navigable in a particular direction, it might *still* be possible to traverse the relationship in that direction. However, the computational cost of the traversal is likely to be very high. In the example in Figure 9.13, even though you can't navigate *directly* back from Product to Order, you could still find the Order object associated with a particular Product object by searching through all of the Order objects in turn. You have then traversed a non-navigable relationship, but at high computational cost. One-way navigability is like a one-way street—you might not be able to go down it directly, but you might still be able to get to the end of it by some other (longer) route.

If there is a role name on the target end of the relationship, objects of the source class may reference objects of the target class by using this role name.

In terms of implementation in OO languages, navigability implies that the source object holds an object reference to the target object. The source object may use this object reference to send messages to the target object. You could represent that on an object diagram as a unidirectional link with associated message.

9.4.4   Associations and attributes

There is a close link between class associations and class attributes.

An association between a source class and a target class means that objects of the source class can hold an object reference to objects of the target class. Another way to look at this is that an association is equivalent to the source class having a pseudo-attribute of the target class. An object of the source class can refer to an object of the target class by using this pseudo-attribute; see Figure 9.16.

If a navigable relationship has a role name, then it is as though the source class has a pseudo-attribute with the same name as the role name and the same type as the target class

Figure 9.16

There is no commonly used OO programming language that has a specific language construct to support associations. Therefore, when code is automatically generated from a UML model, one-to-one associations turn into attributes of the source class.

In Figure 9.17, the generated code has a House class that contains an attribute called address, which is of type Address. Notice how the role name provides the attribute name, and the class on the end of the association provides the attribute class. The Java code below was generated from the model in Figure 9.17:

```
public class House
{
    private Address address;
}
```

Figure 9.17

You can see that there is a class House that has one attribute called address that is of type Address. Notice that the address attribute has private visibility—this is typically the default for most code generation.

Target multiplicities greater than 1 are implemented as either

- an attribute of type array (a construct that is supported in most languages); or

- an attribute of some type that is a collection.

Collections are just classes whose instances have the specialized behavior of being able to store and retrieve references to other objects. A common Java example of a collection is a Vector, but there are many more. We discuss collections in more detail in Section 18.10.

This notion of pseudo-attributes is fine for one-to-one and one-to-many relationships, but it begins to break down when you consider many-to-many relationships. You will see how these are implemented in Chapter 18.

You use associations only when the target class is an important part of the model. Otherwise, you model the relationship by using attributes. Important classes are business classes that describe part of the business domain. Unimportant classes are library components such as String classes and Date and Time classes.

To some extent, the choice of explicit associations versus attributes is a matter of style. The best approach is always one in which the model and the diagrams express the problem clearly and precisely. Often it is clearer to show an association to another class than to model the same relationship as an attribute that would be much harder to see. When the target multiplicity is greater than 1, this is a pretty good indication that the target is important to the model, and so you generally use associations to model the relationship.

If the target multiplicity is exactly 1, the target object may actually be just a part of the source, and so not worth showing as an association—it may be better modeled as an attribute. This is especially true if the multiplicity is exactly 1 at *both* ends of the relationship (as in Figure 9.17) where neither source nor target can exist alone.

9.4.5 Association classes

A common problem in OO modeling is this: when you have a many-to-many relationship between two classes, there are sometimes some attributes that can't easily be accommodated in either of the classes. We can illustrate this by considering the simple example in Figure 9.18.

Figure 9.18

At first glance, this seems like a fairly innocuous model:

- each Person object can work for many Company objects;
- each Company object can employ many Person objects.

However, what happens if you add the business rule that each Person has a salary with each Company they are employed by? Where should the salary be recorded—in the Person class or in the Company class?

You can't really make the Person salary an attribute of the Person class, as each Person instance may work for many Companies and may have a different salary with each Company. Similarly, you can't really make the Person salary an attribute of Company, as each Company instance employs many Persons, all with potentially different salaries.

The answer is that the salary is actually a *property of the association itself*. For each employment association that a Person object has with a Company object, there is a specific salary.

UML allows you to model this situation with an association class as shown in Figure 9.19. It is important to understand this syntax—many people think that the association class is just the box hanging off the association. However, nothing could be further from the truth. The association class is actually the association line (including all role names and multiplicities), the dashed descending line, and the class box on the end of the dashed line. In short, it is the whole lot—everything shown in the indicated area.

> An association class is an association that is also a class.

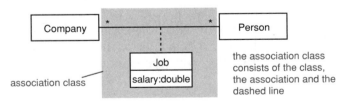

association class · · · the association class consists of the class, the association and the dashed line

Figure 9.19

In fact, an association class is an association that is *also* a class. Not only does it connect two classes like an association, it defines a set of features that belong to the association itself. Association classes can have attributes, operations, and other associations.

> An association class means that there can only be one link between any two objects at any point in time.

Instances of the association class are really *links* that have attributes and operations. The unique identity of these links is determined *exclusively* by the identities of the objects on either end. This factor constrains the semantics of the association class—you can only use it when there is a *single unique link* between two objects at any point in time. This is simply because each link, which is an instance of the association class, must have its own unique identity. In Figure 9.19, using the association class means that you constrain the model such that for a given Person object and a given Company object, there can only be *one* Job object. In other words, each Person can only have one Job with a given Company.

If, however, you have the situation where a given Person object can have more than one Job with a given Company object, then you can't use an association class—the semantics just don't match!

> A reified association allows more than one link between any two objects at a particular point in time.

But you still need somewhere to put the salary for each Company/Job/Person combination, and so you reify (make real) the relationship by expressing it as a normal class. In Figure 9.20, Job is now just an ordinary class, and you can see that a Person may have many Jobs where each Job is for exactly one Company.

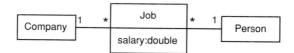

Figure 9.20

To be frank, many object modelers just don't understand the semantic difference between association classes and reified relationships, and the two are therefore often used interchangeably. However, the difference is really very simple: you can use association classes *only* when each link has a unique identity. Just remember that link identity is determined by the identities of the objects on the ends of the link.

9.4.6   Qualified associations

You can use a qualified association to reduce an n-to-many association to an n-to-one association by specifying a unique object (or group of objects) from the target set. They are very useful modeling elements as they illustrate how you can look up, or navigate to, specific objects in a collection.

Consider the model in Figure 9.21. A Club object is linked to a set of Member objects, and a Member object is likewise linked to exactly one Club object.

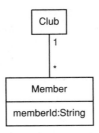

Figure 9.21

A qualified association selects a single member from the target set.

The following question arises: given a Club object that is linked to a set of Member objects, how could you navigate to one specific Member object? Clearly, you need some unique key that you can use to look up a particular Member object from the set. This is known as a qualifier. Many qualifiers are possible (name, credit card number, social security number), but in the example above, every Member object has a memberId attribute value that is unique to that object. This, then, is the look-up key in this model.

You can show this look-up on the model by appending a qualifier to the Club end of the association. It is important to recognize that this qualifier belongs to the *association end* and *not* to the Club class. This qualifier specifies a unique key, and in doing so resolves the one-to-many relationship to a one-to-one relationship as shown in Figure 9.22.

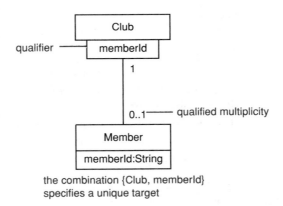

Figure 9.22

Qualified associations are a great way of showing how you select a specific object from a set by using a unique key. Qualifiers *usually* refer to an attribute on the target class, but may be some other expression provided it is understandable and selects a single object from the set.

9.5   What is a dependency?

A dependency indicates a relationship between two or more model elements whereby a change to one element (the supplier) may affect or supply information needed by the other element (the client). In other words, the client depends in some way on the supplier. We use dependencies to model relationships between classifiers where one classifier depends on the other in some way, but the relationship is not really an association or generalization.

> In a dependency relationship, the client depends in some way on the supplier.

For example, you may pass an object of one class as a parameter to an operation of an object of a different class. There is clearly some sort of relationship between the classes of those objects, but it is not really an association. You can use the dependency relationship (specialized by certain predefined stereotypes) as a catch-all to model this kind of relationship. You have already seen one type of dependency, the «instantiate» relationship, but there are many more. We look at the common dependency stereotypes in the next sections.

UML 2 specifies three basic types of dependency, shown in Table 9.2. We include a discussion of these for completeness, but in day-to-day modeling you rarely use anything other than a plain dashed dependency arrow and you typically don't bother specifying the type of dependency.

Table 9.2

Type	Semantics
Usage	The client uses some of the services made available by the supplier to implement its own behavior – this is the most commonly used type of dependency
Abstraction	This indicates a relationship between client and supplier, where the supplier is more abstract than the client.
	What do we mean by "more abstract"? This could mean that the supplier is at a different point in development than the client (e.g., in the analysis model rather than the design model)
Permission	The supplier grants some sort of permission for the client to access its contents – this is a way for the supplier to control and limit access to its contents

Dependencies don't just occur between classes. They can commonly occur between

- packages and packages;
- objects and classes.

They can also occur between an operation and a class, although it is quite rare to show this explicitly on a diagram because it is usually too great a level of detail. Some examples of different types of dependency are shown in Figure 9.23, and we discuss these in the remaining sections of this chapter.

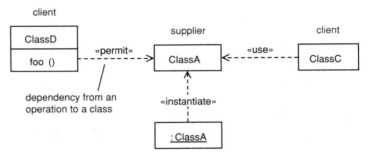

Figure 9.23

Most of the time, you just use an unadorned dotted arrow to indicate a dependency and don't worry about what type of dependency it is. In fact, the type of the dependency is often clear without a stereotype just from context. However, if you want or need to be more specific about the type of dependency, then UML defines a whole range of standard stereotypes that you can use.

9.5.1   Usage dependencies

There are five usage dependencies: «use», «call», «parameter», «send», and «instantiate». We look at each of these in the next few subsections.

9.5.1.1   «use»

The most common dependency stereotype is «use», which simply states that the client makes use of the supplier in some way. If you see just a dashed dependency arrow with no stereotype, then you can be pretty sure that «use» is intended.

Figure 9.24 shows two classes, A and B, that have a «use» dependency between them. This dependency is generated by any of the following cases.

1. An operation of class A needs a parameter of class B.

2. An operation of class A returns a value of class B.

3. An operation of class A uses an object of class B somewhere in its implementation, but *not* as an attribute.

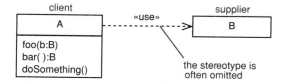

Figure 9.24

Cases 1 and 2 are straightforward, but case 3 is more interesting. You would have this case if one of the operations of class A created a transient object of class B. Here is a Java code fragment for this case:

```
class A
{
  ...
  void doSomething()
    {
      B myB = new B();
      // Use myB in some way
      ...
    }
}
```

Although you can use a single «use» dependency as a catch-all for the three cases listed above, there are other more specific dependency stereotypes that you could apply.

You can model cases 1 and 2 more accurately by a «parameter» dependency, and case 3 by a «call» dependency. However, this is a level of detail that is rarely (if ever) required in a UML model, and most modelers find it much clearer and easier to just put a single «use» dependency between the appropriate classes as shown above.

9.5.1.2   «call»

The «call» dependency is between operations—the client operation invokes the supplier operation. This type of dependency tends not to be very widely used in UML modeling. It applies at a deeper level of detail than most modelers are prepared to go. Also, very few modeling tools currently support dependencies between operations.

9.5.1.3   «parameter»

The supplier is a parameter of the client operation.

9.5.1.4   «send»

The client is an operation that sends the supplier (which must be a signal) to some unspecified target. We discuss signals in Section 15.6 but, for now, just think of them as special types of classes used to transfer data between the client and the target.

9.5.1.5   «instantiate»

The client is an instance of the supplier.

9.5.2   Abstraction dependencies

Abstraction dependencies model dependencies between things that are at different levels of abstraction. An example might be a class in an analysis model, and the same class in the design model. There are four abstraction dependencies: «trace», «substitute», «refine», and «derive».

9.5.2.1   «trace»

You often use a «trace» dependency to illustrate a relationship in which the supplier and the client represent the same concept but are in different models. For example, the supplier and the client might be at different stages of development. The supplier could be an analysis view of a class, and the client a more detailed design view. You could also use «trace» to show a relationship between a functional requirement such as "The ATM shall allow the withdrawal of cash up to the credit limit of the card" and the use case that supports this requirement.

9.5.2.2   «substitute»

The «substitute» relationship indicates that the client may be substituted for the supplier at runtime. The substitutability is based on the client and the supplier conforming to common contracts and interfaces, that is, they must both make available the same set of services. Note that this substitutability is *not* achieved through specialization/generalization relationships between the client and supplier (we discuss specialization/generalization in Section 10.2). In fact, «substitute» is specifically designed to be used in those environments that do *not* support specialization/generalization.

9.5.2.3   «refine»

Whereas the «trace» dependency is between elements in different models, «refine» may be used between elements in the same model. For example, you may have two versions of a class in a model, one of which is optimized for performance. As performance optimization is a type of refinement, you can model this as a «refine» dependency between the two classes, along with a note stating the nature of the refinement.

9.5.2.4   «derive»

You use the «derive» stereotype when you want to show explicitly that a thing can be derived in some way from some other thing. For example, if you have a BankAccount class and the class contains a list of Transactions where each Transaction contains a Quantity of money, you can always calculate the current balance on demand by summing Quantity over all the Transactions. There are three ways of showing that the balance of the account (a Quantity) can be derived. These are shown in Table 9.3.

Table 9.3

Model	Description
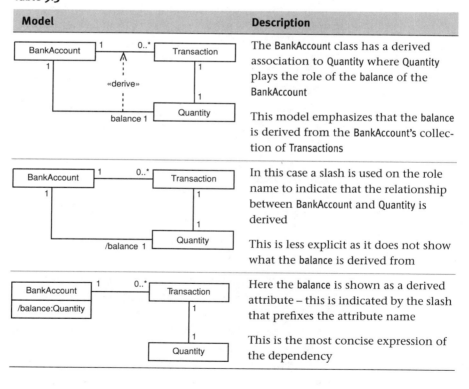	The BankAccount class has a derived association to Quantity where Quantity plays the role of the balance of the BankAccount This model emphasizes that the balance is derived from the BankAccount's collection of Transactions
	In this case a slash is used on the role name to indicate that the relationship between BankAccount and Quantity is derived This is less explicit as it does not show what the balance is derived from
	Here the balance is shown as a derived attribute – this is indicated by the slash that prefixes the attribute name This is the most concise expression of the dependency

All of these ways of showing that balances can be derived are equivalent, although the first model in Table 9.3 is the most explicit. We tend to prefer explicit models.

9.5.3   Permission dependencies

Permission dependencies are about expressing the ability of one thing to access another thing. There are three permission dependencies: «access», «import», and «permit».

9.5.3.1   «access»

The «access» dependency is between packages. Packages are used in UML to group things. The essential point here is that «access» allows one package to access all of the public contents of another package. However, packages each define a namespace and with «access» the namespaces remain separate. This means that items in the client package must use pathnames when they want to refer to items in the supplier package. See Chapter 11 for a more detailed discussion.

9.5.3.2   «import»

The «import» dependency is conceptually similar to «access» except that the namespace of the supplier is merged into the namespace of the client. This allows elements in the client to access elements in the supplier without having to qualify element names with the package name. However, it can sometimes give rise to namespace clashes when an element in the client has the same name as an element in the supplier. Clearly, in this case you must use pathnames to resolve the conflict. Chapter 11 provides a more detailed discussion.

9.5.3.3   «permit»

The «permit» dependency allows a *controlled* violation of encapsulation, but on the whole it should be avoided. The client element has access to the supplier element, whatever the *declared* visibility of the supplier. There is often a «permit» dependency between two very closely related classes where it is advantageous (probably for performance reasons) for the client class to access the private members of the supplier. Not all computer languages support «permit» dependencies—C++ allows a class to declare friends that have permission to access its private members, but this feature has, perhaps wisely, been excluded from Java and C#.

9.6   What we have learned

In this chapter you have begun to look at relationships, which are the glue of UML models. You have learned the following.

- Relationships are semantic connections between things.
- Connections between objects are called links.
  - A link occurs when one object holds an object reference to another object.
  - Objects realize system behavior by collaborating:
    - collaboration occurs when objects send each other messages across links;
    - when a message is received by an object, it executes the appropriate operation.
  - Different OO languages implement links in different ways.
- Object diagrams show objects and their links at a particular point in time.
  - They are snapshots of an executing OO system at a particular time.
  - Objects may adopt roles with respect to each other – the role played by an object in a link defines the semantics of its part in the collaboration.
  - N-ary links may connect more than two objects – they are drawn as a diamond with a path to each object but are not widely used.
- Paths are lines connecting UML modeling elements:
  - orthogonal style – straight lines with right-angled bends;
  - oblique style – slanted lines;
  - curved style – curved lines;
  - be consistent and stick to one style or the other, unless mixing styles increases the readability of the diagram (it usually doesn't).
- Associations are semantic connections between classes.
  - If there is a link between two objects, there *must* be an association between the classes of those objects.
  - Links are instances of associations just as objects are instances of classes.
  - Associations may optionally have the following.
    - Association name:
      - may be prefixed or postfixed with a small black arrowhead to indicate the direction in which the name should be read;
      - should be a verb or verb phrase;
      - in lowerCamelCase;
      - use either an association name or role names but *not* both.

- Role names on one or both association ends:
  - should be a noun or noun phrase describing the semantics of the role;
  - in lowerCamelCase.
- Multiplicity:
  - indicates the number of objects that can be involved in the relationship at any point in time;
  - objects may come and go, but multiplicity constrains the number of objects in the relationship at any point in time;
  - multiplicity is specified by a comma-separated list of intervals, for example, 0..1, 3..5;
  - there is no default multiplicity – if multiplicity is not explicitly shown, then it is undecided.
- Navigability:
  - shown by an arrowhead on one end of the relationship – if a relationship has no arrowheads, then it is bidirectional;
  - navigability indicates that you can traverse the relationship in the direction of the arrow;
  - you may also be able to traverse back the other way, but it will be computationally expensive to do so.

— An association between two classes is equivalent to one class having a pseudo-attribute that can hold a reference to an object of the other class:
  - you can often use associations and attributes interchangeably;
  - use association when you have an important class on the end of the association that you wish to emphasize;
  - use attributes when the class on the end of the relationship is unimportant (e.g., a library class such as String or Date).
— An association class is an association that is also a class:
  - it may have attributes, operations, and relationships;
  - you can use an association class when there is exactly one unique link between any pair of objects at any point in time;
  - if a pair of objects may have many links to each other at a given point in time, then you reify the relationship by replacing it with a normal class.
— Qualified associations use a qualifier to select a unique object from the target set:
  - the qualifier must be a unique key into the target set;
  - qualified associations reduce the multiplicity of n-to-many relationships, to n-to-one;
  - they are a useful way of drawing attention to unique identifiers.

- Dependencies are relationships in which a change to the supplier affects or supplies information to the client.
  — The client depends on the supplier in some way.
  — Dependencies are drawn as a dashed arrow from client to supplier.
  — Usage dependencies:
    - «use» – the client makes use of the supplier in some way – this is the catch-all;
    - «call» – the client operation invokes the supplier operation;
    - «parameter» – the supplier is a parameter or return value from one of the client's operations;
    - «send» – the client sends the supplier (which must be a signal) to the specified target;
    - «instantiate» – the client is an instance of the supplier.
  — Abstraction dependencies:
    - «trace» – the client is a historical development of the supplier;
    - «substitute» – the client can be substituted for the supplier at runtime;
    - «refine» – the client is a version of the supplier;
    - «derive» – the client can be derived in some way from the supplier:
      - you may show derived relationships explicitly by using a «derive» dependency;
      - you may show derived relationships by prefixing the role or relationship name with a slash;
      - you may show derived attributes by prefixing the attribute name with a slash.
  — Permission dependencies:
    - «access» – a dependency between packages where the client package can access all of the public contents of the supplier package – the namespaces of the packages remain separate;
    - «import» – a dependency between packages where the client package can access all of the public contents of the supplier package – the namespaces of the packages are merged;
    - «permit» – a controlled violation of encapsulation where the client may access the private members of the supplier – this is not widely supported and should be avoided if possible.

chapter 10

Inheritance
and polymorphism

10.1 Chapter roadmap

In this chapter we focus on the key concepts of inheritance (Section 10.3) and polymorphism (Section 10.4). But before getting into these topics, it is important to understand the concept of generalization, which we discuss in Section 10.2.

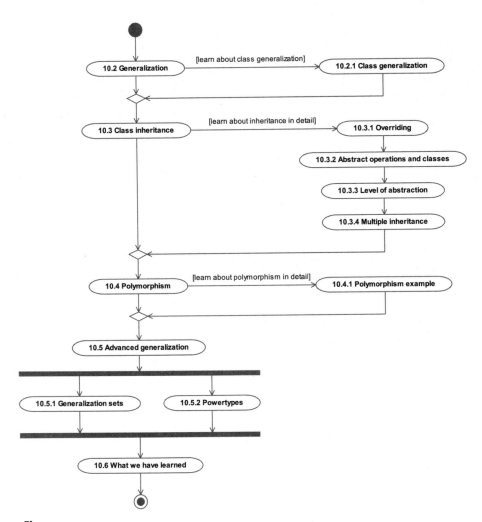

Figure 10.1

10.2   Generalization

Generalization
is a relationship
between a more
general thing and a
more specific thing.

Before we can discuss inheritance and polymorphism, we need to have a solid understanding of the idea of generalization. Generalization is a relationship between a more general element and a more specific element, where the more specific element is *entirely consistent* with the more general element but contains more information.

The two elements obey the substitutability principle—we can use the more specific element *anywhere* the more general element is expected without breaking the system. Clearly this is a much stronger type of relationship than association, and indeed, generalization implies the very highest level of dependency (and therefore coupling) between two elements.

10.2.1   Class generalization

Conceptually, generalization is a simple idea. You are already familiar with the notion of general things such as a tree, and then more specific things such as an oak tree, which is a particular type of tree.

Generalization applies to all classifiers. You have already seen generalization applied to use cases and actors, and now you will see how it is applied to classes.

In Figure 10.2, we have a class called Shape—this is clearly a very general notion! From that, we derive children, subclasses, descendants (all these terms are in common use) that are more specific variants of the general idea of Shape. By the substitutability principle, we can use an instance of any of these subclasses *anywhere* an instance of the Shape superclass is expected.

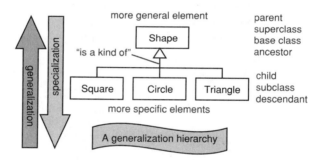

Figure 10.2

> We create a generalization hierarchy by generalizing from more specialized things and specializing from more general things.

As you will see when we look at the detailed attributes and operations of these classes, we could arrive at the above hierarchy in one of two ways: through either a process of specialization or a process of generalization. In specialization, we would first identify the general concept of Shape in analysis and then specialize this to specific types of shape. In generalization, we would identify the more specialized Square, Circle, and Triangle in analysis and then notice that they all have common features that we could factor out into a more general superclass.

OO analysts tend to use both specialization and generalization hand-in-hand, although in our experience it is wise to train oneself to see the more general case as early in the analysis process as possible.

10.3   Class inheritance

When you arrange classes into a generalization hierarchy as shown in Figure 10.2, you implicitly have inheritance between the classes whereby the subclasses inherit all the features of their superclasses. To be more specific, subclasses inherit

- attributes;
- operations;
- relationships;
- constraints.

Subclasses can also add new features and override superclass operations. We look at all these aspects of inheritance in detail in the next few sections.

> Subclasses inherit features from their superclass.

10.3.1   Overriding

In the example in Figure 10.3, the Shape subclasses Square and Circle inherit all of the attributes, operations, and constraints from the Shape superclass. This means that although you don't see these features in the subclasses, they are implicitly there. We say that Square and Circle are types of Shape.

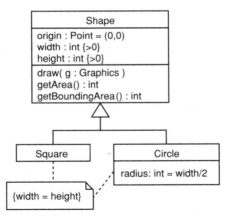

Figure 10.3

Notice that the operations draw() and getArea() defined in Shape can in no way be appropriate for the subclasses. You would expect a Square object, when sent the message draw(), to draw a square, and a Circle object, when sent the message draw(), to draw a circle. The default draw() operation that both subclasses have inherited from their parent clearly won't do. In fact, this operation may not draw anything at all as, after all, what should a Shape look like? The same arguments apply to getArea(). How do you calculate the area of a Shape?

These problems clearly point to the need for subclasses to be able to change superclass behavior. Square and Circle need to implement their own draw() and getArea() operations that override the default operations supplied by the parent and provide a more appropriate behavior.

Figure 10.4 shows this in action: the subclasses Square and Circle have provided their own draw() and getArea() operations that have the appropriate behaviors.

- Square::draw(g : Graphics) – draws a square.
- Square::getArea() : int – calculates and returns the area of the square.
- Circle::draw(g : Graphics) – draws a circle.
- Circle::getArea() : int – calculates and returns the area of the circle.

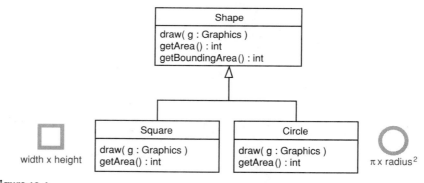

Figure 10.4

> Subclasses override inherited operations by providing a new operation with the same signature.

To override a superclass operation, a subclass must provide an operation with *exactly* the same signature as the superclass operation it wishes to override. UML defines operation signature as the operation name, its return type, and the types of all of the parameters listed in order. The parameter names don't count, as they are just a convenient way of referring to a specific parameter within an operation body and so are not really part of the signature.

This is all well and good, but it is important to know that different languages may define "operation signature" differently. For example, in C++ and Java, the operation return type is *not* part of the operation signature. So, if you override a superclass operation by a subclass operation that is identical apart from the return type, you will get a compiler or interpreter error in these languages.

10.3.2   Abstract operations and classes

Sometimes we would like to defer implementation of an operation to the subclasses. In our Shape example, the operation Shape::draw(g : Graphics) is a case in point. We can't really provide any sensible implementation of this operation in the Shape class itself, as we just don't know how "shapes" should be drawn—the concept of "drawing a shape" is too abstract to have any concrete implementation.

You can specify that an operation lacks an implementation by making it an abstract operation. In UML you do this simply by writing the operation name in italics.

When you think about it, a class with one or more abstract operations is incomplete as there are some operations that don't have an implementation. This means that you can't instantiate such classes, and they are therefore known as abstract classes. You write the class name in italics to show that it is abstract.

In the example in Figure 10.5, we have the abstract class *Shape*, which has two abstract operations: *Shape::draw(g : Graphics)* and *Shape::getArea() : int*. The implementations for these operations are provided by both the Square and the Circle subclasses. Although *Shape* is incomplete and can't be instantiated, both of its subclasses provide the missing implementations, are complete, and can be instantiated. Any class that can be instantiated is known as a concrete class.

> Abstract operations have no implementation.

> Abstract classes have one or more abstract operations, and they can't be instantiated.

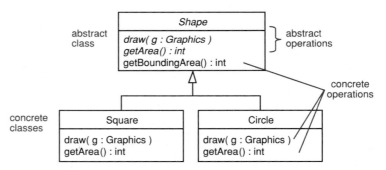

Figure 10.5

The operation getBoundingArea() is a *concrete* operation of *Shape* because the bounding area of every kind of *Shape* is calculated in the exactly the same way—it is always the width of the shape multiplied by its height.

There are a couple of big advantages of using abstract classes and operations.

● You can define a set of abstract operations in the abstract superclass that must be implemented by all *Shape* subclasses. You can think of this as defining a "contract" that all concrete *Shape* subclasses *must* implement.

- You can write code to manipulate *Shapes* and then substitute Circle, Square, and other *Shape* subclasses as appropriate. According to the substitutability principle, code written to manipulate *Shapes* should also work for all *Shape* subclasses.

We look at these advantages in greater depth when we discuss polymorphism in Section 10.4.

10.3.3 Level of abstraction

Before we get into polymorphism, it's a good idea to understand something about levels of abstraction. What's wrong with the model in Figure 10.6?

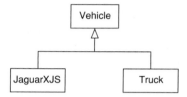

Figure 10.6

> Things at the same level in a generalization hierarchy should be at the same level of abstraction.

The answer is "levels of abstraction". A generalization hierarchy defines a set of levels of abstraction from the most general at the top to the most specific at the bottom. You should always try to maintain a uniform level of abstraction at each level of the generalization hierarchy. In the example above, we have *not* achieved this. JaguarXJS is a *type* of car. Clearly this is a lower level of abstraction than Truck. You can fix the model quite easily by introducing a Car superclass between JaguarXJS and Vehicle.

10.3.4 Multiple inheritance

> Multiple inheritance – a class can have more than one direct superclass.

UML allows a class to have more than one direct superclass. This is called *multiple inheritance*. The subclass inherits from *all* of its direct superclasses.

Multiple inheritance is usually considered to be a design issue, and so we defer discussion to Section 17.6.2.

10.4 Polymorphism

Polymorphism means "many forms". A polymorphic operation is one that has many implementations. You have already seen two polymorphic operations in the *Shape* example. The abstract operations *draw()* and *getArea()* in the

Shape class have two different implementations—an implementation in the Square class and a different implementation in the Circle class. The operations have "many forms" and are therefore polymorphic.

Figure 10.7 illustrates polymorphism perfectly. We define an abstract *Shape* class with abstract operations *draw()* and *getArea()*.

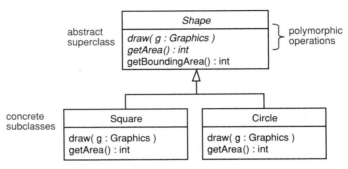

Figure 10.7

Polymorphism means "many forms". Polymorphic operations have many implementations.

A concrete subclass must implement all the abstract operations that it inherits.

Square and Circle inherit from *Shape* and provide implementations for the polymorphic operations *Shape::draw()* and *Shape::getArea()*. All concrete subclasses of *Shape must* provide concrete draw() and getArea() operations because they are abstract in the superclass. This means that for draw() and getArea() you can treat all subclasses of Shape in a similar way. A set of abstract operations is therefore a way to define a set of operations that *all* concrete subclasses *must* implement. This is known as a contract.

Clearly the implementation of draw() and getArea() will be different for Squares and Circles. The draw() operation will draw a square for objects of the Square class and will draw a circle for objects of the Circle class. You can see that the getArea() operation will also have different implementations. It will return width*height for a square and $\pi*r^2$ for a circle. This is the essence of polymorphism—objects of different classes have operations with the *same* signature but *different* implementations.

Encapsulation, inheritance, and polymorphism are the "three pillars" of OO. Polymorphism allows you to design simpler systems that can more easily accommodate change because it allows you to treat different objects in the same way.

In fact, what makes polymorphism an essential aspect of OO is that it allows you to send objects of *different* classes the *same* message and have the objects respond appropriately. So if you send objects of the Square class the message draw(), they will draw a square, and if you send objects of the Circle class the same message, they will draw a circle. The objects seem to exhibit a kind of intelligence.

10.4.1   Polymorphism example

Here is an example of polymorphism in action. Suppose you have a Canvas class that maintains a collection of *Shapes*. Although this is a somewhat simplified picture, many graphics systems actually work in very much this way. The model for this simple graphics system is shown in Figure 10.8.

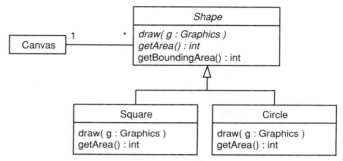

Figure 10.8

Now, you know that you can't create an instance of *Shape* (because it is abstract), but according to the substitutability principle, you can create instances of its concrete subclasses and substitute these anywhere a *Shape* is called for.

So, although Figure 10.8 shows that objects of type Canvas contain a collection of many *Shape* objects, the only objects that you can actually put in the collection are instances of concrete subclasses of *Shape* because *Shape* itself is abstract and can't be instantiated. In this case there are two concrete subclasses, Circle and Square, so the collection may contain Circle objects and/or Square objects.

In Figure 10.9 we have created an object model from the class diagram in Figure 10.8. This object model shows that a :Canvas object holds a collection of four *Shape* objects s1, s2, s3, and s4 where s1, s3, and s4 are objects of class Circle, and s2 is an object of class Square. What happens when the :Canvas object iterates over this collection and sends each object in the collection the message draw()? Well, not surprisingly, each object does the right thing—Square objects draw squares, and Circle objects draw circles. It is the object's class that determines *what* the object draws; in other words, the object's class determines the semantics of the set of operations that the object offers.

The key point here is that each object responds to a message by invoking the corresponding operation specified by its class. All objects of the same class will respond to the same message by invoking the same operation. This doesn't necessarily mean that all objects of the same class respond to the

> With polymorphism, objects of different classes respond to the same message in different ways.

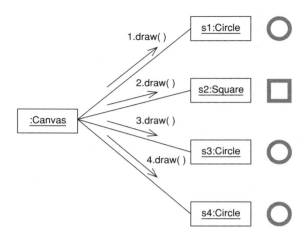

Figure 10.9

same message in exactly the same way. The results of an operation invocation often depend on the state of the object—the values of all its attributes
and the state of all its relationships. For example, you might have three
objects of class Square with different attribute values for width and height.
When you send the message draw() to each of these objects in turn, they will
each draw a square (i.e., the meaning, or semantics, of the operation remains
the same) but each square will have a different size depending on the attribute
values of width and height.

Here is another example. The business rules about making withdrawals
and calculating interest are different depending on the type of bank account.
For example, checking accounts tend to have an overdraft limit and therefore
may have a negative balance, while deposit accounts will not let the balance
fall below zero. Similarly, interest is often calculated and accrued to the
account differently. One simple way to model this is shown in Figure 10.10.
An abstract class *Account* is defined, and then concrete subclasses CheckingAccount
and DepositAccount are provided. The abstract class defines abstract operations
for *withdraw()* and *calculateInterest()*, and these are implemented in different
ways by each of the concrete subclasses.

Notice that we have also overridden the concrete deposit() operation by
providing a new implementation in the ShareAccount class. Remember that to
override a base class operation, all you need to do is provide the subclass
with an operation that has exactly the same signature. We have done this for
ShareAccounts because there happen to be business rules that make the process
of depositing to a ShareAccount different from other types of *Account*. For
example, there might be business rules that determine the minimum value
of deposit that can be made. There are now two implementations of deposit():

> Concrete
> operations may also
> be polymorphic – but
> this is bad style.

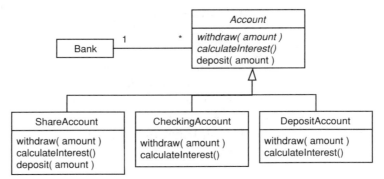

Figure 10.10

one implementation in *Account* and another in ShareAccount. This means that deposit() is now a polymorphic operation. So even concrete operations like deposit() can be polymorphic!

You have to be very careful when you override concrete operations. This is because, rather than just providing an implementation for an abstract superclass operation, you are now changing an existing implementation. You only know that it is safe to do this by examining the specification of the superclass operation and ensuring that you abide by its contract. Abstract operations can always be safely overridden because that is what they are designed for. However, overriding concrete operations can have unexpected side effects and might be dangerous. Often, the subclass operation just does something extra and then calls the superclass operation. In other words, it *adds* its own behavior to the superclass operation. This particular idiom is a good way of reusing and extending the behavior of a concrete superclass operation as it is generally safe.

Some languages allow you to prevent subclasses from overriding a concrete superclass operation. In Java, appending the keyword final to the operation signature explicitly prevents that operation from being overridden. In fact, in Java it is good style to define *all* operations as final except those you explicitly want to be polymorphic.

10.5   Advanced generalization

In this section, we look at two advanced aspects of generalization: generalization sets and powertypes. The notion of generalization sets can be quite useful. However, you will use powertypes rarely, if at all. We include them mainly for completeness.

10.5.1 Generalization sets

You can organize the subclasses of any superclass into one or more generalization sets.

> Generalization sets partition subclasses according to a specific rule.

A generalization set groups subclasses according to a particular rule, or basis of specialization. Here's an example. Figure 10.11 illustrates that the superclass *Shape* has many subclasses. On examination of these subclasses, you can see that there are two distinctly different groups of *Shapes*: two-dimensional shapes and three-dimensional shapes.

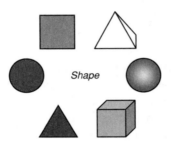

Figure 10.11

You can indicate this partitioning of subclasses on a class diagram by associating each group of shapes with a different generalization set as illustrated in Figure 10.12.

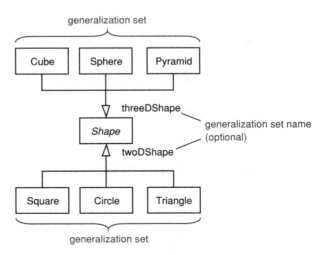

Figure 10.12

Generalization sets can have constraints applied to them. These constraints determine whether the sets are

- {complete} – the subclasses in the generalization set cover *all* of the possibilities. For example, a generalization set gender of class Person containing the two subclasses Male and Female could be considered to be {complete} *provided* that you only recognize two genders;

- {incomplete} – there may be subclasses other than those in the generalization set. The generalization set twoDShape is clearly {incomplete} as there are potentially very many twoDShapes;

- {disjoint} – an object can be an instance of *one and only one* of the members of the generalization set. This is by far the most common case;

- {overlapping} – an object can be an instance of *more than one* of the members of the generalization set. This is quite uncommon as it requires multiple inheritance or multiple classification.

Generalization set constraints can be combined as shown in Table 10.1.

Table 10.1

Constraint	The set is complete	Members of the set may have instances in common
{incomplete, disjoint} – the default	N	N
{complete, disjoint}	Y	N
{incomplete, overlapping}	N	Y
{complete, overlapping}	Y	Y

Figure 10.13 illustrates generalization set constraints applied to the *Shape* example.

As you've seen, generalization sets are an analysis concept that allow you to partition a set of subclasses. When it comes to implementation, none of the commonly used OO languages directly support generalization sets, and the concept is redundant from an implementation perspective.

In implementation, generalization sets are either ignored or resolved into a new layer in the inheritance hierarchy, provided there is a benefit in doing so. Looking at the analysis model in Figure 10.13, you can imagine that there might be some attributes or operations common to all twoDShapes and to all threeDShapes. This gives you a basis to resolve the generalization sets into new classes in the inheritance hierarchy, as illustrated in Figure 10.14.

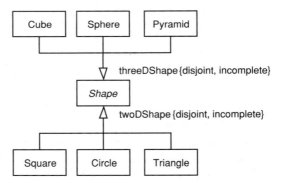

Figure 10.13

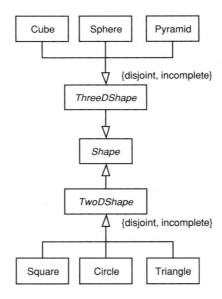

Figure 10.14

10.5.2   Powertypes

Powertypes are an analysis concept that you will hardly ever come across in normal day-to-day modeling. This section is included largely for completeness and as a reference should you happen to encounter the idiom.

A powertype is a class whose instances are classes. These instances are *also* subclasses of another class.

Any class whose instances are classes is called a *metaclass* (the class of a class). A powertype is therefore a special type of metaclass whose instances are also subclasses of another class.

> A powertype is a class whose instances are classes that are also subclasses of another class.

The idea of powertypes is quite complex and is best illustrated with a simple example as shown in Figure 10.15.

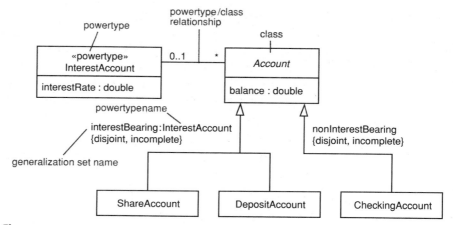

Figure 10.15

The first thing to note about Figure 10.15 is that InterestAccount is not a normal class. It is a powertype, as indicated by the stereotype. The second thing to note about this figure is that the association between InterestAccount and *Account* doesn't have normal association semantics. In this case it indicates that the *Account* class (and by inheritance its subclasses) can optionally (0..1) have an InterestAccount as a powertype.

To use the powertype, you partition the subclasses into one or more generalization sets and apply the powertype to one or more of these sets. All classes in a powertyped generalization set are then instances of that powertype.

You apply a powertype to a generalization set by listing the powertype name after the generalization set name and a colon, much as you would list the type of an attribute after an attribute name. You can think of the powertype as providing an extra type for the members of the generalization set in addition to the type they get from their superclass.

In Figure 10.15, we have partitioned the subclasses of *Account* into two generalization sets, interestBearing and nonInterestBearing—those that bear interest and those that don't. The interestBearing generalization set is typed by the powertype InterestAccount. This means that ShareAccount and DepositAccount are simultaneously subclasses of *Account and* instances of InterestAccount. They inherit the balance attribute from *Account* and get the attribute interestRate by virtue of being instances of InterestAccount.

The nonInterestBearing generalization set contains a single class, CheckingAccount, that is a simple subclass of *Account*. As such, ShareAccount inherits the balance attribute from *Account* but gets nothing from InterestAccount.

None of the mainstream OO languages support powertypes, and so you may be wondering how you can implement this idiom in practice. Figure 10.16 shows a simple solution to the problem where we implement powertyping by delegation. In this example, we have introduced new classes *AccountType* and NonInterestAccount to create a well-formed inheritance hierarchy of *AccountTypes*. We have used constraints to indicate the type for each different *Account*. This is a pretty standard way of dealing with powertypes.

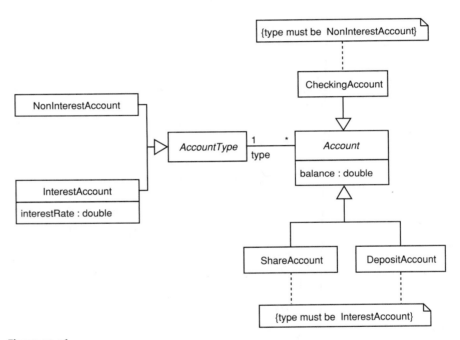

Figure 10.16

In theory, powertypes provide a concise and convenient modeling idiom for use in analysis models. However, in practice we find that they are not widely understood or used. Thus, when they are used they can cause a lot of confusion. Powertypes add nothing new to your modeling repertoire and may not even be supported by your modeling tool. Our advice is that you avoid them.

10.6   What we have learned

In this chapter we looked at class inheritance and polymorphism. You have learned the following.

- Generalization is a relationship between a more general thing and a more specific thing:
  - the more specific thing is consistent in every way with the more general thing;
  - the substitutability principle states that you can substitute the more specific thing anywhere the more general thing is expected;
  - generalization applies to all classifiers and some other modeling elements;
  - generalization hierarchies may be created by generalizing from specific things or by specializing from general things;
  - all things at the same level in a generalization hierarchy should be at the same level of abstraction.

- Class inheritance occurs in a generalization relationship between classes.
  - The subclass inherits the following features from its parents – attributes, operations, relationships, and constraints.
  - Subclasses may:
    - add new features;
    - override inherited operations:
      - the subclass provides a new operation with the same signature as the parent operation it wishes to override;
      - the operation signature consists of an operation name, types of all parameters in order, and return type.
  - Abstract operations are designed to have no implementation:
    - they serve as placeholders;
    - all concrete subclasses must implement all inherited abstract operations.
  - An abstract class has one or more abstract operations:
    - abstract classes can't be instantiated;
    - abstract classes define a contract as a set of abstract operations that concrete subclasses must implement.
  - Polymorphism means "many forms". It allows you to design systems to use with an abstract class, then substitute concrete subclasses at runtime – such systems are very flexible and easy to extend; just add more subclasses.

— Polymorphic operations have more than one implementation:
  - different classes may implement the same polymorphic operation differently;
  - polymorphism allows instances of different classes to respond to the same message in different ways.

- Generalization set – a set of subclasses organized according to a particular rule.
  — Constraints:
    - {complete} – the generalization set contains all possible members;
    - {incomplete} – the generalization set does not contain all possible members;
    - {disjoint} – an object may be an instance of no more than one of the members of the generalization set;
    - {overlapping} – an object may be an instance of more than one of the members of the generalization set;
    - {incomplete, disjoint} – the default.

- Powertype – a class whose instances are classes that are also subclasses of another class.
  — A powertype is a metaclass whose instances are subclasses of another class:
    - «powertype» – indicates that the class is a powertype.
  — An association between a class and a powertype indicates that the class can be an instance of the powertype.
  — To use powertypes:
    - partition the subclasses into one or more generalization sets;
    - apply powertypes to type the generalization sets.

chapter 11

Analysis packages

11.1 Chapter roadmap

In this chapter we look at the UML grouping mechanism, packages, and the way in which they are used in analysis.

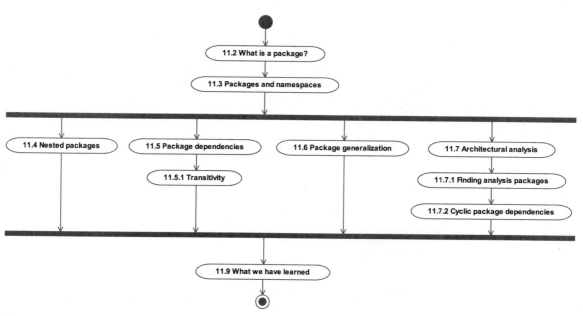

Figure 11.1

11.2   What is a package?

If you go back to the basic UML principles (Section 1.8), then you know that the set of UML building blocks consists of things, relationships, and diagrams. A package is the UML grouping thing—it is a container and owner for model elements. Each package has its own namespace within which all names must be unique.

In fact, a package is a general-purpose mechanism for organizing model elements (including other packages) and diagrams into groups. It can be used to

> The package is the UML mechanism for grouping things.

- provide an encapsulated namespace within which all names must be unique;
- group semantically related elements;
- define a "semantic boundary" in the model;
- provide units for parallel working and configuration management.

Packages let you create a navigable and well-structured model by allowing you to group things that have close semantic ties. You can create semantic boundaries in the model where different packages describe different aspects of the system functionality.

It's important to note that in UML 2 a package is a *logical* grouping mechanism that provides a namespace for its members. If you want to physically group model elements then you should use a component as we discuss in Section 22.2.

> Every model element is owned by one package. The packages form a hierarchy.

Every model element is owned by exactly one package, and the ownership hierarchy forms a tree rooted in a top-level package. A special UML stereotype, «topLevel», can be used to mark this package. If you don't explicitly place a modeling element in a package, then it goes into the top-level package by default. The package hierarchy also forms a namespace hierarchy where the top-level package is the root of the namespace.

Analysis packages should contain

- use cases;
- analysis classes;
- use case realizations.

UML package syntax is quite straightforward. The package icon is a folder, and the package name may be shown on the tab if package contents are shown, or on the body of the folder. The syntax is summarized in Figure 11.2, which shows three different ways of representing the same package at different levels of detail.

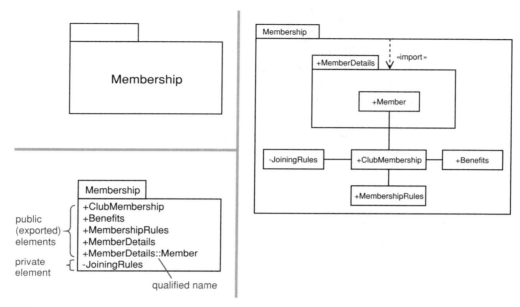

Figure 11.2

Elements inside a package can be given a visibility that indicates whether they are visible to clients of the package. The possible visibilities are summarized in Table 11.1.

Table 11.1

Symbol	Visibility	Semantics
+	public	Elements with public visibility are visible to elements outside the package – they are *exported* by the package
–	private	Elements with private visibility are completely hidden inside the package

> Visibility determines whether a package element is visible outside the package.

You can use the visibility of package elements to control the amount of coupling between packages. This can be done because the exported elements of a package act as the interface to, or the window into, the rest of the package. You must try to make this interface as small and simple as possible.

To ensure that a package has a small, simple interface, you need to minimize the number of public package elements and maximize the number of private package elements. This may be difficult to achieve in analysis unless navigability is applied to the associations. Otherwise, there will be many bi-directional associations between classes, and so the classes involved in the association must either both be in the same package, or both be public. In design, relationships between classes become unidirectional, and so it is only the supplier class that needs to be public.

UML provides two standard stereotypes, listed in Table 11.2, to tailor the semantics of packages for specific purposes.

Table 11.2

Stereotype	Semantics
«framework»	A package that contains model elements that specify a reusable architecture
«modelLibrary»	A package that contains elements that are intended to be reused by other packages

11.3   Packages and namespaces

A package defines what is known as an encapsulated namespace. All this really means is that the package creates a boundary within which all the element names must be unique. It also means that when an element in one namespace needs to refer to an element in a different namespace, it has to specify both the name of the element it wants *and* a way to navigate through the namespaces to that element. This navigation path is known as the *qualified name* or *pathname* of the element.

You create a qualified name by prefixing the element name with the names of the packages in which it resides, separated by a double colon. You list the outermost package first, and then each package in order of nesting until you get to the element. Qualified names are very similar to pathnames in directory structures.

For example, the qualified name of the class Librarian in Figure 11.3 is

Library::Users::Librarian

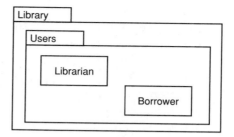

Figure 11.3

11.4   Nested packages

Packages may be nested inside other packages to any depth. However, just two or three levels of nesting are generally enough. Much more than this, and the model may become difficult to understand and navigate.

UML gives two ways to show nesting. The first is very graphic, as it shows modeling elements physically contained in the package. An example is shown in Figure 11.3.

An alternative nesting syntax is shown in Figure 11.4. This is useful when there is a lot of nesting, or complex nesting, that might be confusing to show with embedding.

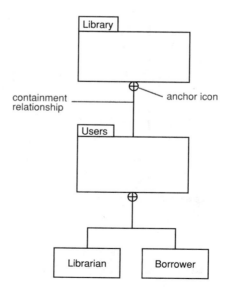

Figure 11.4

Nested packages have access to the namespace of their owning package. So, in Figure 11.4, elements in the Users package can access all elements in the Library package by using *un*qualified names. However, the converse is not true. The owning package must use qualified names to access the contents of its owned packages. So in the example, elements in Library must use the fully qualified names Users::Librarian and Users::Borrower to access the two elements in the Users package.

You'll see how you can use dependencies to merge package namespaces in the next section.

11.5   Package dependencies

> A dependency relationship indicates that one package depends in some way on another.

Packages may be related to each other by a dependency.

Consider the example in Figure 11.5. Any package that has a dependency relationship with the Membership package will be able to see the public elements of that package (ClubMembership, Benefits, etc.) but will *not* be able to see the private element JoiningRules.

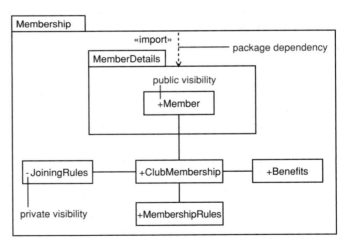

Figure 11.5

There are five different types of package dependencies, each with different semantics. These are summarized in Table 11.3.

The «use» dependency means that there are dependencies between *elements* in the packages rather than between the packages themselves.

Table 11.3

Package dependency	Semantics
Supplier ◄----«use»---- Client	An element in the client package uses a public element in the supplier package in some way – the client depends on the supplier If a package dependency is shown without a stereotype, then «use» should be assumed
Supplier ◄----«import»---- Client	Public elements of the supplier namespace are added as public elements to the client namespace Elements in the client can access all public elements in the supplier using unqualified names
Supplier ◄----«access»---- Client	Public elements of the supplier namespace are added as private elements to the client namespace Elements in the client can access all public elements in the supplier using unqualified names
Analysis Model △ ◄----«trace»---- Design Model △	«trace» usually represents a historical development of one element into another more developed version – it is usually a relationship between models rather than elements (an extra-model relationship)
Supplier ◄----«merge»---- Client	Public elements of the supplier package are merged with elements of the client package This dependency is only used in metamodeling – you should not encounter it in ordinary OO analysis and design

Both «import» and «access» merge client and supplier namespaces. This allows client elements to use unqualified names to access supplier elements. The difference between the two is that «import» performs a public merge, that is, merged supplier elements become public in the client, while «access» performs a private merge, that is, merged elements become private in the client.

«trace» is the odd man out. Whereas the other package dependencies are between things in the same model, «trace» usually represents some historical development of one package into another. It therefore often shows relationships between *different* models. A complete UML model can be represented by a package with a small triangle in its right-hand corner, and in Table 11.3 we show the extra-model «trace» dependency between the analysis model and the design model. Clearly, such a diagram is a metamodel where we model the relationships between models! As such, it is not used very often.

«merge» is a complex relationship that indicates a set of transformations between the elements in the supplier package and the client package. Elements in supplier package are merged with client elements to create new, expanded, client elements. This dependency is only used in metamodeling (e.g., it is widely used in the UML metamodel) and should *not* be used in ordinary OO analysis and design. We do not discuss it any further here, but if you need to find out more, you can look in [Rumbaugh 1].

11.5.1   Transitivity

Transitivity is a term that applies to relationships. It means that if there is a relationship between thing A and thing B and a relationship between thing B and thing C, then there is an implicit relationship between thing A and thing C.

«**import**» is transitive. «**access**» is not.

It is important to note that the «import» dependency is transitive, but the «access» dependency is not. This is because, as you saw above, when there is an «import» dependency between a client and a supplier package, public elements in the supplier package become public elements in the client. These imported public elements are accessible outside the client package. On the other hand, when there is an «access» dependency between a client and a supplier package, public elements in the supplier package become private elements in the client. These private elements are *not* accessible outside the client package.

Consider the example in Figure 11.6. Package A accesses package B, and package B accesses package C.

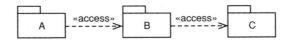

Figure 11.6

Lack of transitivity in «access» means that

- public elements in package C become private elements in package B;
- public elements in package B become private elements in package A;
- elements in package A therefore *can't* access elements in package C.

This lack of transitivity in «access» allows you to actively manage and control coupling and cohesion in the model. Nothing is accessed unless it is *explicitly* accessed.

11.6   Package generalization

Package generalization is similar in many ways to class generalization. In package generalization, the more specialized child packages inherit the public elements from their parent package. Child packages may add new elements and may override elements in the parent package by providing an alternative element with the same name.

In the example in Figure 11.7, the Hotels and CarHire packages inherit all the public members of their parent Product package. Both the Hotels and CarHire packages override the Item class inherited from their parent by providing an alternative class with the same name. Child packages may also add new elements; the Hotels package adds classes Hotel and RoomType and the CarHire package adds class Car.

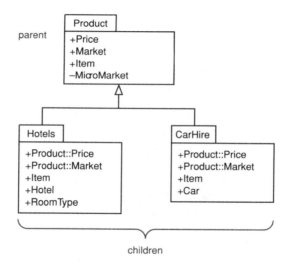

Figure 11.7

Child packages inherit elements from their parent. They may override parent elements. They may add new elements.

Just like class inheritance, the substitutability principle must apply— anywhere we might use the Product package, we should be able to use either the Hotels or CarHire package.

11.7   Architectural analysis

In architectural analysis, all the analysis classes are organized into a set of cohesive analysis packages, and these are further organized into partitions and layers as illustrated in Figure 11.8. Each analysis package within a layer is a partition.

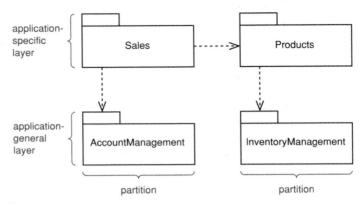

Figure 11.8

One of the goals in architectural analysis is to try to minimize the amount of coupling in the system. You can do this in three ways:

- minimize the dependencies between analysis packages;
- minimize the number of public elements in each analysis package;
- maximize the number of private elements in each analysis package.

Reduction in coupling is one of the most important considerations in architectural analysis because systems that exhibit a high degree of coupling are typically complex and difficult to build and maintain. You should always try to keep coupling to the necessary minimum.

As the model deepens into a design model, so the number of layers will tend to increase. In analysis, however, you can just arrange packages into application-specific and application-general layers. The application-specific layer contains functionality that is entirely specific to the particular application. The application-general layer contains functionality that is more generally useful. In Figure 11.8, AccountManagement and InventoryManagement might be reusable across several different applications, and so these packages naturally live in the application-general layer.

11.7.1   Finding analysis packages

You find analysis packages by identifying groupings of model elements that have strong semantic connections. Analysis packages are often discovered over a period of time as the model develops and matures. It is imperative that the analysis packages reflect real, semantic groupings of elements, rather than just some idealized (but fictitious) view of the logical architecture.

Where do you begin looking for such groupings? The static model is the most useful source of packages. Look for

- cohesive clusters of classes in the class diagrams;
- inheritance hierarchies.

You may also consider the use case model as a source of packages because it is important that you try to make packages as cohesive as possible from a business process perspective. However, it is common for use cases to cut *across* analysis packages—one use case may be realized by classes from several different packages. Still, one or more use cases that support a particular business process or actor, or a set of related use cases, *may* indicate a potential package.

After a set of candidate packages has been identified, you should then attempt to minimize the public members of the packages and the dependencies between the packages by

- moving classes between packages;
- adding packages;
- removing packages.

The keys to good package structure are high cohesion *within* a package and low coupling *between* packages. A package should contain a group of closely related classes. Classes are most closely related by inheritance (Chapter 10), next by composition (Chapter 18), then by aggregation (Chapter 18), and finally by dependencies (Chapter 9). Classes that are in inheritance or composition hierarchies are prime candidates for co-location in the same package. This will lead to high cohesion within the package and will probably lead to lower coupling with other packages.

As always, you should keep things simple when creating the analysis package model. It is more important to get the right set of packages than to make extensive use of features such as package generalization and dependency stereotypes. These can be added later if, and only if, they make the model more comprehensible. Part of keeping things simple is avoiding nested packages. The more deeply something is buried in a nested package structure, the more obscured it becomes. We have seen models with very deeply nested packages where each package contained only one or two classes. These models were more like a standard top-down functional decomposition than an object model.

As a rule of thumb, expect to have between four and ten analysis classes per package. However, as with all rules of thumb, there will be exceptions, and if breaking this rule makes the model clearer, then do so! Sometimes you need to introduce packages with just one or two classes because you need to break cyclic dependencies in the package model. In such circumstances, this is a perfectly reasonable thing to do.

Figure 11.9 shows an example of an analysis package model from a simple e-commerce system. We provide this system as a worked example on our website www.umlandtheunifiedprocess.com.

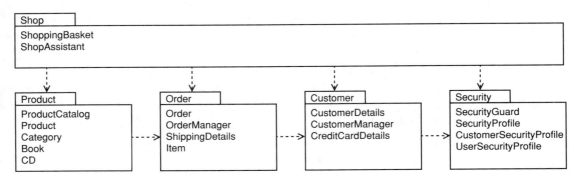

Figure 11.9

11.7.2   Cyclic package dependencies

You should try to avoid cyclic dependencies in the analysis package model. When you think about it, if package A depends in some way on package B, and vice versa, there is a very strong argument for just merging the two packages, and this is a perfectly valid way of removing cyclic dependencies. But a better approach, which very often works, is to try to factor the common elements out into a third package C. The dependency relationships are then recalculated to remove the cycle. This is shown in Figure 11.10.

Many modeling tools allow you to check the dependencies between packages automatically. The tool creates a list of access violations if an element in one package accesses an element in another package but there is no visibility or dependency between the two packages.

In an analysis model, it can be impossible to create a package diagram that is free of access violations. This is because in analysis you often use bidirectional relationships between classes. Suppose we have a very simple model with one class in package A and another class in package B. If the class in package A has a bidirectional relationship with the class in package B, then package A depends on package B, but package B also depends on package A—we have a cyclic dependency between the two packages. The only ways to remove this violation are to refine the relationship between A and B by making

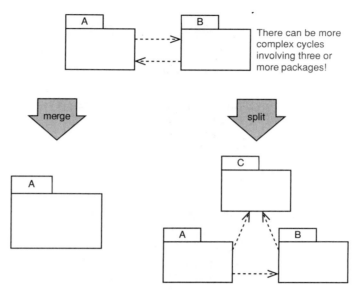

Figure 11.10

it unidirectional or to put the two classes in the same package. Package dependencies thus provide an excellent argument for using navigability in analysis models! On the other hand, classes that truly have mutual dependencies (rather than dependencies that are just a feature of the incompleteness of the model) should normally live in the same package.

11.8   What we have learned

In this chapter we have looked at analysis packages. In particular, you have seen how you can maximize the cohesion within an analysis package and minimize the coupling between analysis packages. This helps create more robust and maintainable systems. You have learned the following.

- The package is the UML mechanism for grouping things.
- Packages serve many purposes:
  — they group semantically related elements;
  — they create a "semantic boundary" in the model;
  — they provide units of configuration management;
  — in design, they provide units for parallel working;

— they provide an encapsulated namespace in which all names must be unique – to access an element within the namespace you must specify both the element name and the namespace name.

- Every model element is owned by one package:
  — the packages form a hierarchy;
  — the root package may be stereotyped «topLevel»;
  — by default, model elements are placed in the «topLevel» package.
- Analysis packages may contain:
  — use cases;
  — analysis classes;
  — use case realizations.
- Package elements may have visibility:
  — visibility is used to control the coupling between packages;
  — there are two levels of visibility:
    – public (+) – elements are visible to other packages;
    – private (-) – elements are completely hidden.
- Package stereotypes:
  — «framework» – a package that contains model elements that specify a reusable architecture;
  — «modelLibrary» – a package that contains elements that are intended to be reused by other packages.
- A package defines an encapsulated namespace:
  — use qualified names to refer to elements in other packages, for example,

    Library::Users::Librarian

- Nested packages:
  — the inner package can see all of the public members of its outer packages;
  — the outer package can't see any of the members of its inner packages unless it has an explicit dependency on them (usually «access» or «import») – this allows you to hide implementation details in nested packages.
- A dependency relationship between packages indicates that the client package depends in some way on the supplier package.
  — «use» – an element in the client package uses a public element in the supplier package.
  — «import» – public elements of the supplier namespace are added as *public* elements to the client namespace. Elements in the client can access all public elements in the supplier by using unqualified names.
  — «access» – public elements of the supplier namespace are added as *private* elements to the client namespace. Elements in the client can access all public elements in the supplier by using unqualified names.

— «trace» – the client is a historical development of the supplier. This usually applies to models rather than elements.

— «merge» – public elements of the supplier package are merged with elements of the client package. Only used in metamodeling.

- Transitivity: If A has a relationship to B and B has a relationship to C, then A has a relationship to C.
  — «import» is transitive.
  — «access» is not transitive.

- Package generalization:
  — very similar to class generalization;
  — the child packages:
    - inherit elements from their parent package;
    - can add new elements;
    - can override parent elements.

- Architectural analysis:
  — partitions cohesive sets of analysis classes into analysis packages;
  — layers analysis packages according to their semantics;
  — attempts to minimize coupling by:
    - minimizing package dependencies;
    - minimizing the number of public elements in all packages;
    - maximizing the number of private elements in all packages.

- Finding analysis packages.
  — Examine analysis classes – look for:
    - cohesive clusters of closely related classes;
    - inheritance hierarchies;
    - classes are most closely related by (in order) inheritance, composition, aggregation, dependency.
  — Examine use cases:
    - clusters of use cases that support a particular business process or actor *may* have analysis classes that should be packaged together;
    - related use cases *may* have analysis classes that should be packaged together;
    - be careful – analysis packages often cut across use cases!
  — Refine the package model to maximize cohesion within packages and minimize dependencies between packages by:
    - moving classes between packages;
    - adding packages;
    - removing packages;
    - remove cyclic dependencies by merging packages or by splitting them to factor out coupled classes.

chapter 12

Use case realization

12.1 Chapter roadmap

This chapter discusses the process of use case realization in which you model interactions between objects.

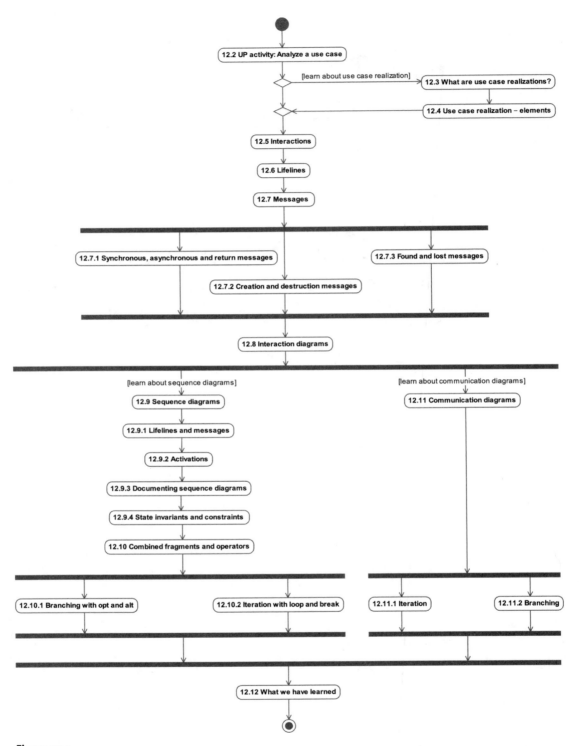

Figure 12.1

12.2   UP activity: Analyze a use case

In previous chapters, you have seen how the analysis class artifact of the Analyze a use case activity is produced. The second artifact produced by this activity is the use case realization, as shown in Figure 12.2. We discuss the inputs to this activity in Section 8.2.

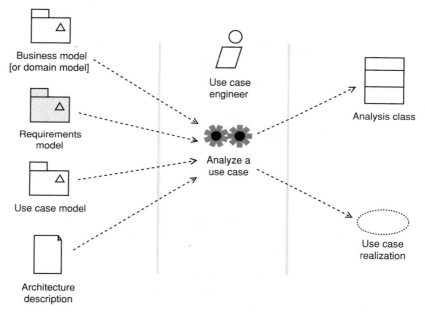

Business model [or domain model]

Requirements model

Use case model

Architecture description

Use case engineer

Analyze a use case

Analysis class

Use case realization

Figure 12.2   Adapted from Figure 8.25 [Jacobson 1] with permission from Addison-Wesley

Analysis classes model the static structure of a system, and use case realizations show how instances of the analysis classes interact to realize the functionality of the system. This is part of the dynamic view of the system.

Your goals for use case realization in analysis are as follows.

- Find out which analysis classes interact to realize the behavior specified by a use case—you may uncover new analysis classes as you perform use case realization.

- Find out what messages instances of these classes need to send to each other to realize the specified behavior. As you will see in this chapter, this tells you

  — the key operations your analysis classes need to have;
  — the key attributes of the analysis classes;
  — important relationships between analysis classes.

● Update your use case model, requirements model, and analysis classes with the information you get from use case realization. Keep all models consistent and in step with each other.

In use case realization in analysis, it is essential that you focus on capturing *key* attributes, operations, and relationships between analysis classes. At this point you are not concerned with details such as operation parameters—you will discover this information in design.

Also, you don't need to create a use case realization for every use case. Pick the key use cases, and work on these. Keep realizing use cases until you feel that you have sufficient information to understand how the analysis classes work together. When you have this information, stop. UP is an iterative process, so if you decide you need to do more work on use case realization later, you will have an opportunity to do so.

At the end of use case realization in analysis, you will have an analysis model that gives a high-level picture of the dynamic behavior of the system.

12.3   What are use case realizations?

Use case realizations show how classes collaborate to realize system functionality.

The key to analysis, after finding the analysis classes, is finding the use case realizations. These consist of sets of classes that realize the behavior specified in a use case. For example, if you have a use case BorrowBook and have identified the analysis classes Book, Ticket, Borrower, and the actor Librarian, you need to create a use case realization that demonstrates how these classes and objects of these classes interact to realize the behavior specified in BorrowBook. In this way, you turn a use case, which is a specification of functional requirements, into class diagrams and interaction diagrams, which are a high-level specification of a system.

Use case realizations are an implicit part of the model backplane – you typically don't show them on diagrams.

Although UML provides a symbol for use case realizations, as shown in Figure 12.3, they are rarely modeled explicitly. This is simply because each use case has *exactly one* use case realization, so there is no extra information to be captured in creating a use case realization diagram. Instead, you just add the appropriate elements (see Table 12.1) to the modeling tool and let the use case realizations be an implicit part of the backplane of the model.

Figure 12.3

Table 12.1

Element	Purpose
Analysis class diagrams	Show the analysis classes that interact to realize the use case
Interaction diagrams	Show interactions between specific instances that realize the use case – they are "snapshots" of the running system
Special requirements	The process of use case realization may well uncover new requirements specific to the use case – these must be captured
Use case refinement	New information may be discovered during realization that means the original use case has to be updated

12.4   Use case realization – elements

Use case realizations consist of the elements shown in Table 12.1.

Use case realization is fundamentally a process of refinement. You take a specification of one aspect of the system's behavior as captured in a use case and any associated requirements, and model how this may be realized by interactions between instances of the analysis classes that you have identified. You go from a general specification of required behavior to a fairly detailed description of the interactions between classes and objects that will actually make this behavior real.

Analysis class diagrams are a vital part of a use case realization. They should "tell a story" about the system—about how a set of classes are related such that instances of those classes can collaborate to realize the behavior specified in one (or more) use cases.

As well as analysis class diagrams, you can create diagrams that demonstrate explicitly how instances of those analysis classes collaborate and interact to realize some or all of the use case behavior. These diagrams are known as interaction diagrams, and there are four types: sequence diagrams, communication diagrams, interaction overview diagrams, and timing diagrams. We look at sequence and communication diagrams in this chapter, interaction overview diagrams in Section 15.12, and timing diagrams in Section 20.7.

OO modeling is an iterative process, so you should not be too surprised if you uncover new requirements or if you need to modify existing use cases once you begin to model in more depth. This is all part of use case

> Analysis class diagrams "tell a story" about one or more use cases.

> Interaction diagrams show how classifier instances interact to realize system behavior.

realization—you must keep existing documents up to date as you uncover more information about the system. As such, you must update the use case model, requirements model, and analysis classes to keep them all consistent.

12.5   Interactions

> Interaction – a unit of behavior of a context classifier.

Interactions are simply units of behavior of a classifier. This classifier, known as the *context classifier*, provides the context for the interaction.

An interaction may use any of the features of its context classifier or any features that the context classifier has access to (e.g., temporary or global variables).

In use case realization, the context classifier is a use case, and you create one or more interactions to demonstrate how the behavior specified by the use case can be realized by instances of classifiers (in this case, analysis classes) passing messages back and forth.

As you work on interaction diagrams, you begin to uncover more and more of the operations and attributes of the analysis classes. The analysis class diagrams should be updated with this information as part of the use case realization process.

The key elements in interaction diagrams are lifelines and messages. We look at these in detail in the next two sections.

12.6   Lifelines

> Lifeline – a participant in an interaction.

A *lifeline* represents a single participant in an interaction, that is, it represents how an instance of a specific classifier participates in the interaction. Lifeline syntax is summarized in Figure 12.4.

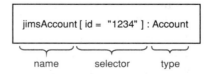

Figure 12.4

Each lifeline has an optional name, a type, and an optional selector.

- Name – used to refer to the lifeline within the interaction.
- Type – the name of the classifier of which the lifeline represents an instance.

● Selector – a Boolean condition that may be used to select a single instance that satisfies the condition. If there is no selector, a lifeline refers to an arbitrary instance of the classifier. Selectors are only valid if the type has a multiplicity greater than one so that there are many instances from which to choose. In Figure 12.4, the selector selects an instance of Account that has an id of "1234".

Lifelines are drawn with the same icon as their type and have a vertical dashed "tail" when they are used in sequence diagrams. Some examples of lifelines are shown in Figure 12.5.

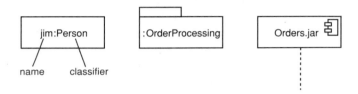

Figure 12.5

> Lifelines represent how an instance of a classifier participates in an interaction.

You can think of a lifeline as representing *how* an instance of the classifier may participate in the interaction. However, it does not represent any *particular* instance of the classifier. This is a subtle, but important, distinction. The interaction describes how instances of the classifier interact in a general way, rather than specifying just one particular interaction between a set of particular instances. You can therefore think of the lifeline as representing a *role* that an instance of the classifier may play in the interaction.

You can show true instances directly on an interaction diagram if you want to. Just use normal instance notation—the classifier symbol with the instance name, selector (if any), colon, and classifier name, all underlined.

This distinction between lifelines and instances gives rise to two different forms of interaction diagrams. A *generic form* interaction diagram shows the interaction between lifelines that represent arbitrary instances. An *instance form* interaction diagram shows the interaction between particular instances. The generic form diagrams tend to be the most common and useful.

To complete the interaction you need to specify messages that are sent between the lifelines. We look at messages in the next section.

12.7   Messages

> Message – a specific communication between lifelines.

A message represents a specific kind of communication between two lifelines in an interaction. This communication may involve

- calling an operation—a call message;
- creating or destroying an instance—a creation or destruction message;
- sending a signal.

When a lifeline receives a call message, this is a request for the invocation of an operation that has the same signature as the message. So, for every call message received by a lifeline, there must be a corresponding operation in the classifier of that lifeline. UML allows messages on interaction diagrams to get out of step with operations so that you can work on the model dynamically and flexibly. However, by late analysis they *must* be brought into step.

When a lifeline is executing a message it has *focus of control* or *activation*. As the interaction progresses over time, the activation moves between lifelines—this movement is called the *flow of control*.

Messages are drawn as arrows between lifelines. If the lifeline has a dashed tail (as in sequence diagrams), the messages are generally drawn between the tails. Otherwise the messages are drawn between the lifeline boxes; you'll see many examples of this shortly. There are seven types of message as illustrated in Table 12.2.

12.7.1   Synchronous, asynchronous, and return messages

In a synchronous message call, the sender waits for the receiver to finish executing the requested operation. In an asynchronous message call, the sender does *not* wait but continues to the next step.

In analysis models, the distinction between synchronous and asynchronous messages is usually too great a level of detail. In analysis, you are not concerned with the detailed semantics of message sending, merely with the fact that a message is sent. As such, you can show all messages as synchronous or asynchronous—it really doesn't matter. Our preference is to show all messages as synchronous because this is the most constrained case. Synchronous messages indicate a strict sequencing of operation calls, whereas asynchronous messages indicate the possibility of concurrency.

In design, it can be important to distinguish between those messages that are synchronous and those that are asynchronous so that you can design concurrent flows of control.

Table 12.2

Syntax	Name	Semantics
aMessage(aParameter) ▶	Synchronous message	The sender waits for the receiver to return from executing the message
aMessage(aParameter) →	Asynchronous message	The sender sends the message and continues executing – it does *not* wait for a return from the receiver
←- - - - - - - - - - - - - - - -	Message return	The receiver of an earlier message returns focus of control to the sender of that message
«create» aMessage() → :A	Object creation	The sender creates an instance of the classifier specified by the receiver
«destroy» → ✕	Object destruction	The sender destroys the receiver If its lifeline has a tail, this is terminated with an X
●——————→	Found message	The sender of the message is outside the scope of the interaction Use this when you want to show a message receipt, but don't want to show where it came from
——————→●	Lost message	The message never reaches its destination May be used to indicate error conditions in which messages are lost

You can show return messages on analysis-level use case realizations or not as you choose. They are generally not that important. We tend to show them if they don't clutter the diagram.

12.7.2   Creation and destruction messages

In OO analysis you generally don't need to worry about the exact semantics of object creation or destruction, but it is important that you understand what is going on, so we cover the topic here.

The object creation message is always drawn as a solid line with an open arrowhead. You can show object creation by simply sending a message stereotyped «create», or you can send a specific, named, object creation message that you may also stereotype «create». In C++, C#, or Java, object creation operations are special operations known as constructors—these have the same name as the class of the object, no return value, and zero or more parameters. So, for example, if you wanted to create a new Account object, you might send a message called Account() to create an Account object and initialize its account-Number attribute to some value. Not all OO languages have constructors however; in Smalltalk, for example, you would probably send the message «create» init: accountNumber.

Object destruction is shown as a solid line with an open arrowhead stereotyped «destroy». Destruction means that the classifier instance referred to by the target lifeline is no longer available for use. If the lifeline has a tail, you must terminate the tail with a large cross at the point of destruction. There is no return value from object destruction.

Different languages have different destruction semantics. For example, in C++, destruction is usually explicitly handled by the programmer, and when an object is destroyed, a special method called a destructor is guaranteed to be invoked (if it exists). This method is often used to perform cleanup activities such as releasing resources like files or database connections. After the destructor is called, the object's memory allocation is freed.

In languages such as Java and C#, object destruction is handled by the virtual machine by a strategy called garbage collection. For example, when an object in a Java program is no longer referenced by any other object, it is marked as ready for destruction. Destruction *will* occur at some future time according to the garbage collection algorithm, but you don't know when that will be! Java and C# objects can have a "finalize" method that will be executed at the point of true destruction by the garbage collector. However, this method is dangerous to use as you don't know when the garbage collector will call it.

12.7.3   Found and lost messages

You can generally ignore found and lost messages in analysis. We include them here mostly for completeness.

Found messages can be useful if you need to show a message receipt by a class, but you don't know (at that point in time) where that message originated. We find that this doesn't happen too often in practice.

Lost messages allow you to show that a message is lost—it never reaches its destination. This could be useful in design to show how messages might be lost during an error condition. However, we have never felt a compelling need to use this idiom.

12.8   Interaction diagrams

UML interaction diagrams can be used to model any type of interaction between classifier instances. In use case realization they are specifically used to model interactions between objects that realize a use case, or part of a use

The four types of interaction diagram provide different perspectives on object interactions.

case. There are four different types of interaction diagram, each of which emphasizes a different aspect of the interaction.

- Sequence diagrams – these emphasize the time-ordered sequence of message sends between lifelines. Users tend to be able to understand sequence diagrams better than communication diagrams as they are much easier to read. Communication diagrams have a tendency to get cluttered very quickly. We discuss sequence diagrams in Section 12.9.

- Communication diagrams – these emphasize the structural relationships between objects and are very useful in analysis, especially for creating a quick sketch of an object collaboration. In UML 2, these diagrams offer only a subset of the functionality of sequence diagrams. We discuss communication diagrams in Section 12.11.

- Interaction overview diagrams – these show how complex behavior is realized by a set of simpler interactions. These are a special case of activity diagram in which the nodes refer to other interactions. They are useful for modeling the control flow within a system. We discuss interaction overview diagrams in Section 15.12.

- Timing diagrams – these emphasis the real-time aspects of an interaction. Their primary purpose is to help you reason about time. We discuss timing diagrams in Section 20.7.

Sequence and communication diagrams are the most important diagrams from the perspective of use case realization, and we look at them in detail in the rest of this chapter.

12.9   Sequence diagrams

Sequence diagrams show interactions between lifelines as a time-ordered sequence of events.

Sequence diagrams show interactions between lifelines as a time-ordered sequence of events. They are the richest, and most flexible, form of interaction diagram.

When modeling, you sometimes start out by sketching a use case realization, using a communication diagram (see Section 12.11) because it is easy to place lifelines on the diagram and connect them. However, when you need to focus on the actual *sequencing* of events, it is always much easier to use a sequence diagram.

12.9.1   Lifelines and messages

To investigate lifelines and messages, we take an example from a simple course registration system. Consider realizing the use case AddCourse shown in

Figure 12.6. We have kept this use case at a very high level to provide a simple example.

Use case: AddCourse
ID: 8
Brief description: Add details of a new course to the system.
Primary actors: Registrar
Secondary actors: None.
Preconditions: 1. The Registrar has logged on to the system.
Main flow: 1. The Registrar selects "add course". 2. The Registrar enters the name of the new course. 3. The system creates the new course.
Postconditions: 1. A new course has been added to the system.
Alternative flows: CourseAlreadyExists

Figure 12.6

Initial analysis of the use case created the high-level analysis class diagram in Figure 12.7. Given the use case specification and the class diagram, you have enough information to create a sequence diagram.

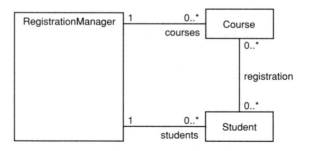

Figure 12.7

Figure 12.8 shows a sequence diagram that realizes the behavior specified by the AddCourse use case. According to the UML 2 specification, interaction diagram names may be prefixed by sd to indicate that the diagram is an interaction diagram. Strangely enough, sd is used as a prefix for *all* types of interaction diagrams, not just sequence diagrams!

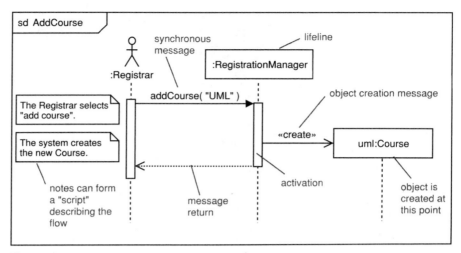

Figure 12.8

At this point it's worth reminding you that when you start to create sequence diagrams as part of the use case realization, you may find that you need to modify the analysis class diagram or even the use case. This is OK—it is all part of the analysis process. The use case, analysis class diagram, and sequence diagram artifacts all evolve together over time.

Consider the sequence diagram in Figure 12.8. Sequence diagrams have time running from top to bottom, and lifelines running from left to right. Lifelines are placed horizontally to minimize the number of crossing lines on the diagram and are placed vertically according to when they are created. Stretching beneath each lifeline is a dashed line that indicates the duration of the lifeline over time.

Notice that Figure 12.8 shows how the use case behavior is realized, but it is not an exact representation of every step in the use case. This is an important point. Steps 1 and 2 of the use case involve some sort of user interface that we won't really look at until design, so we have omitted these from the sequence diagram. In design, we can add a user interface layer to the sequence diagram that helps to clarify things (see Section 20.4). In analysis, we are only concerned with capturing the essential behavior of the analysis classes.

Let's look at another example use case from the course registration system, DeleteCourse (Figure 12.9).

In this use case, we are destroying an object. To indicate object destruction, you terminate the lifeline with a large cross, as shown in Figure 12.10. If you don't know when the object is destroyed, or don't care, you just terminate the lifeline normally.

> Interaction diagrams are not verbatim transcriptions of a use case; they are illustrations of how the use case behavior is realized by analysis classes.

Use case: DeleteCourse
ID: 8
Brief description: Remove a course from the system.
Primary actors: Registrar
Secondary actors: None.
Preconditions: 1. The Registrar has logged on to the system.
Main flow: 1. The Registrar selects "delete course". 2. The Registrar enters the name of the course. 3. The system deletes the course.
Postconditions: 1. A course has been removed from the system.
Alternative flows: CourseDoesNotExist

Figure 12.9

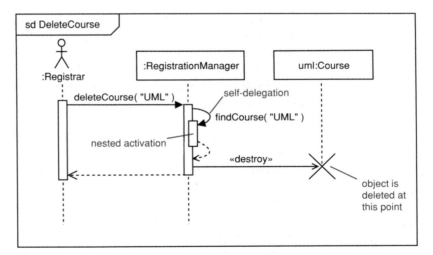

Figure 12.10

Figure 12.10 also shows self-delegation, that is, a lifeline sends a message to itself. This creates a nested activation (see next section). Self-delegation is common in OO systems. Objects offer a set of public services (the public operations) that can be called by client objects, but they also generally have a set of private "helper" operations that are specifically designed to be called by the object itself. In this example, the :RegistrationManager lifeline sends itself the message findCourse("UML") to find a UML course object if one exists. Private operations of an object can *only* be called by that object itself by means of self-delegation.

12.9.2 Activations

Activations indicate when a lifeline has focus of control.

You place long thin rectangles on the dashed line below the lifeline to indicate when a particular lifeline has the focus of control. These rectangles are called *activations* or *focus of control*.

We note in passing that *The Unified Modeling Language Reference Manual, Second Edition* [Rumbaugh 1] refers to activation as "a UML 1 term replaced by execution specification". However, as we go to press, the term "execution specification" occurs nowhere in the *Unified Modeling Language: Superstructure, version 2.0* [UML2S], whereas both "activation" and "focus of control" do. We can only conclude that "activation" and "focus of control" are the standard terms. We mention this because you may come across the term "execution specification" as a synonym for activation because of its inclusion in [Rumbaugh 1].

In Figure 12.8 the :Registrar actor starts with the focus of control. It sends the message addCourse("UML") to :RegistrationManager, which invokes its addCourse(...) operation with the parameter "UML". During the execution of this operation, :RegistrationManager has focus of control. However, notice that this focus of control is *nested* within the focus of control of the :Registrar actor. This is quite normal—one object starts with focus of control and invokes an operation on another object nesting the focus of control. This object may then invoke an operation on another object nesting focus of control yet further, and so on.

Within the execution of the addCourse(...) operation, the :Registration-Manager creates a new object, the uml:Course object.

Activations seem to have gone out of favor in recent years, and you will find that many modelers just don't bother to show them. This is partly because some UML tools don't support activations very well and partly because they generally aren't that important, especially in analysis models. In an executing OO system, activations take care of themselves through the normal semantics of operation invocation. In fact, complex sequence diagrams can be slightly easier to read *without* activations. Our style is to use activations unless they make the diagram harder to read.

12.9.3 Documenting sequence diagrams

One very nice feature of sequence diagrams is that you can add a "script" to a diagram by placing notes down the left-hand side (see Figure 12.8). This makes the diagram much more accessible to nontechnical stakeholders, such as users and business domain experts. The script may consist of actual steps from a use case or just a textual summary of what is happening in the diagram. Either way, a script can be a useful addition to a sequence diagram, especially if the diagram is complex.

12.9.4   State invariants and constraints

When an instance receives a message, this can cause it to change state.

A state is defined as "a condition or situation during the life of an object during which it satisfies some condition, performs some activity, or waits for some event" [Rumbaugh 1]. Every classifier can have a state machine that describes the life cycle of its instances in terms of the states they can be in and the events that cause them to transition between those states.

Not all messages cause a state change. For example, a message that simply returns the value of some attribute and has no side effects never generates a state change. You can show the state of the instances on the lifelines by using *state invariants*.

Adding state invariants to a sequence diagram can be a very useful analysis technique because it allows you to capture the key states in the life cycle of a lifeline. These states indicate important states of the system and can be the basis of the state machines that we discuss in Chapter 21.

Let's look at a specific example: Figure 12.11 shows a use case from a simple order processing system that is subject to the following constraints:

- the order must be paid for in full by a *single* payment;
- the items specified in the order can only be delivered *after* payment;
- the items are delivered to the customer within 28 days of payment.

Real-world order processing is usually much more complex and flexible than this! Nevertheless, the example serves to illustrate state invariants. Figure 12.12 shows a sequence diagram for ProcessAnOrder.

You can see that when an Order instance is created, it immediately transitions to the state unpaid (drawn as a rounded rectangle). This tells you that all Orders are created in the unpaid state. On receipt of the acceptPayment() message, which must be for payment in full, the Order instance transitions to the state paid. At some later time, the DeliveryManager instance is sent the message deliver(). It forwards this message to the Order instance, causing it to transition to the state delivered.

If the Order class also has a state machine, the states in that machine must correspond to any state invariants it may have on its sequence diagrams.

Use case:ProcessAnOrder
ID: 5
Brief description: The Customer raises an order that is then paid for and delivered.
Primary actors: Customer
Secondary actors: None.
Preconditions: None.
Main flow: 1. The use case begins when the Customer actor creates a new order. 2. The Customer pays for the order in full. 3. The goods are delivered to the Customer within 28 days of the date of the final payment.
Postconditions: 1. The order has been paid for. 2. The goods have been delivered within 28 days of the final payment.
Alternative flows: ExcessPayment OrderCancelled GoodsNotDelivered GoodsDeliveredLate PartialPayment

Figure 12.11

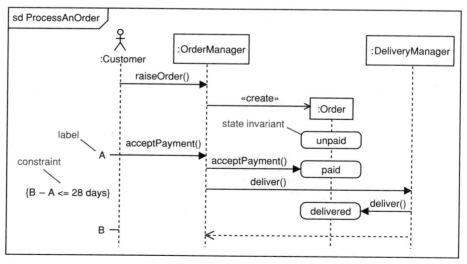

Figure 12.12

Figure 12.12 illustrates the use of constraints that are written in braces and placed on (or near) the lifelines. A constraint placed on a lifeline indicates something that must be true about instances from that point onwards. Constraints are often stated in informal language, although UML does have a formal constraint language (OCL) that we discuss in Chapter 25.

The figure shows a duration constraint. The :Customer lifeline has two labels, A and B, and a constraint, {B – A <= 28 days}. This says that the distance in time between the points A and B must be less than or equal to 28 days. Point A marks the point at which payment is made, and point B marks the point at which the products are delivered to the customer. In plain English, the constraint means that "the order shall be delivered no more than 28 days after payment has been received".

Any type of constraint may be placed on a lifeline. Constraints that constrain attribute values of instances are quite common.

Finally, notice that in Figure 12.12 we have used neither activations nor message returns. This is because the emphasis in this diagram is on timing and state invariants and these features would add nothing.

12.10   Combined fragments and operators

Combined fragments divide a sequence diagram into different areas with different behavior.

Sequence diagrams may be divided into areas called *combined fragments.* Figure 12.13 illustrates combined fragment syntax, which is quite rich.

Each combined fragment has one *operator,* one or more *operands,* and zero or more *guard conditions.*

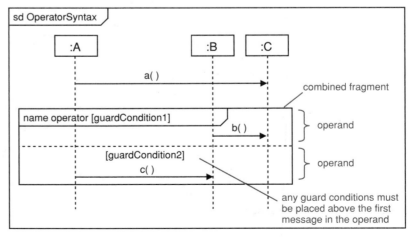

Figure 12.13

The operator determines *how* its operands are executed.

Guard conditions determine *whether* their operands execute. Guard conditions are Boolean expressions, and the operand executes if, and only if, the expression evaluates to true. A single guard condition may apply to all operands, or each operand may have its own unique guard condition.

The full list of operators is given in Table 12.3.

The most important operators are opt, alt, loop, break, ref, par, and critical. We discuss opt, alt, loop, and break in detail in the next few subsections and cover ref in the next chapter. The operators par and critical are about concurrency, which is a design issue. We discuss these in Section 20.5 when we discuss concurrency. The other operators are rarely used, and you have enough information in the table to enable you to apply them should you need to.

> The operator determines *how* its operands execute.

> Guard conditions determine *whether* their operands execute.

Table 12.3

Operator	Long name	Semantics	Section
opt	option	There is a single operand that executes if the condition is true (like if … then)	12.10.1
alt	alternatives	The operand whose condition is true is executed. The keyword else may be used in place of a Boolean expression (like select … case)	12.10.1
loop	loop	This has a special syntax: loop min, max [condition] loop min times, then while condition is true, loop (max – min) times	12.10.2
break	break	If the guard condition is true, the operand is executed, *not* the rest of the enclosing interaction	12.10.2
ref	reference	The combined fragment refers to another interaction	13.2
par	parallel	All operands execute in parallel	20.5.2
critical	critical	The operand executes atomically without interruption	20.5.2
seq	weak sequencing	All operands execute in parallel subject to the following constraint: events arriving on the *same* lifeline from *different* operands occur in the same sequence as the operands occur This gives rise to a weak form of sequencing – hence the name	12.10
strict	strict sequencing	The operands execute in strict sequence	12.10
neg	negative	The operand shows invalid interactions Use this when you want to show interactions that *must not* happen	12.10

Continued on next page

Table 12.3 *Continued*

Operator	Long name	Semantics	Section
ignore	ignore	Lists messages that are intentionally omitted from the interaction – the names of the ignored messages are placed in braces in a comma-delimited list after the operator name, e.g., {m1, m2, m3} For example, an interaction might represent a test case in which you choose to ignore some of the messages	12.10
consider	consider	Lists messages that are intentionally included in the interaction – the names of the messages are placed in braces in a comma-delimited list after the operator name For example, an interaction might represent a test case in which you choose to include a subset of the set of possible messages	12.10
assert	assertion	The operand is the only valid behavior at that point in the interaction – any other behavior would be an error Use this as a way of indicating that some behavior *must* occur at a certain point in the interaction	12.10

12.10.1 Branching with **opt** and **alt**

Figure 12.14 illustrates the syntax of opt and alt.

> **opt** creates a single branch.

The opt operator indicates that its single operand executes if, and only if, the guard condition is true. Otherwise, execution continues after the combined fragment.

opt is equivalent to the programming construct:

```
if (condition1) then
    action1
```

> **alt** creates multiple branches.

The alt operator represents a choice between alternatives. Each of its operands has its own guard condition and will only execute if the guard condition is true. An optional operand with a guard condition of [else] executes if *none* of the other guard conditions are true.

It's worth noting that *only one* of the alt operands can execute. This means that all the operand guard conditions must be mutually exclusive. If at any time more than one of the guard conditions is true, this is an error condition and the resulting behavior of alt is not defined by the UML specification.

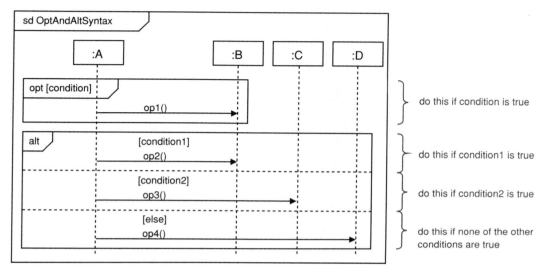

Figure 12.14

alt is equivalent to the programming construct:

```
if (condition1) then
   operand 1
else if (condition2) then
   operand 2
...
else if (conditionN) then
   operand N
else
   operand M
```

You can see that opt is semantically equivalent to an alt operator with exactly one operand.

As an example of using opt and alt, consider the use case in Figure 12.15. We first saw this ManageBasket use case in Section 4.5.6. It is part of a simple e-commerce system, and it describes updating the quantity of an item in the Customer's ShoppingBasket or removing an item entirely.

Figure 12.16 is the analysis class diagram for this use case. You can see that the ShoppingBasket holds one or more Items. Each of these Items is a quantity of a particular Product. In analysis class diagrams, you only show the classes, attributes, and operations that illustrate the point you are trying to make. In

Use case: ManageBasket
ID: 2
Brief description: The Customer changes the quantity of an item in the basket.
Primary actors: Customer
Secondary actors: None.
Preconditions: 1. The shopping basket contents are visible.

Main flow:
1. The use case starts when the Customer selects an item in the
    basket.
2. If the Customer selects "delete item"
    2.1 The system removes the item from the basket.
3. If the Customer types in a new quantity
    3.1 The system updates the quantity of the item in the basket.

Postconditions: None.
Alternative flows: None.

Figure 12.15

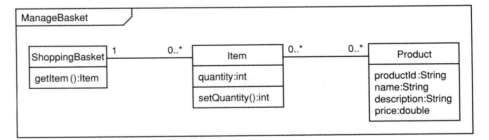

Figure 12.16

this diagram, we are trying to show the collaboration between the Shopping-Basket, Items, and Products.

Finally, Figure 12.17 shows the sequence diagram that realizes this use case. Notice that in this sequence diagram, we have described the policy that when an Item's quantity falls to zero, it is destroyed. This is perfectly reasonable as an Item only exists to represent a quantity of a particular Product in the ShoppingBasket. However, you could argue that this level of detail is unnecessary in analysis and that a sequence diagram that did not show the explicit deletion of Items would be equally acceptable.

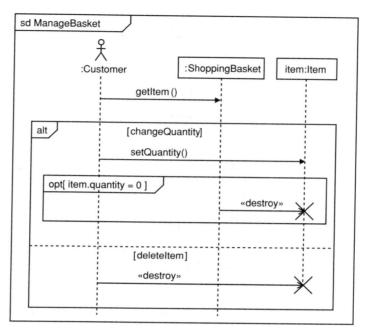

Figure 12.17

Iteration with **loop** and **break**

> **loop** allows you to model iteration.

Very often you need to show loops in sequence diagrams. You can do this by using the loop and break operators as illustrated in Figure 12.18.

The loop operator works as follows:

loop min times then
  while (condition is true)
    loop (max - min) times

You should note the following points about loop syntax:

- a loop *without* max, min, or a condition is an infinite loop;
- if only min is given, then max = min;
- the condition is usually a Boolean expression but it may also be arbitrary text, provided that its intent is clear.

> When the **break** guard condition evaluates to true, the **break** operand executes, and the loop terminates.

loop might seem to be quite complex at first, but it can be used to support a great variety of looping idioms. Some of the more common idioms are listed in Table 12.4.

You can use break to indicate under what conditions the loop is broken out of and what happens then. The break operator has a single guard condition,

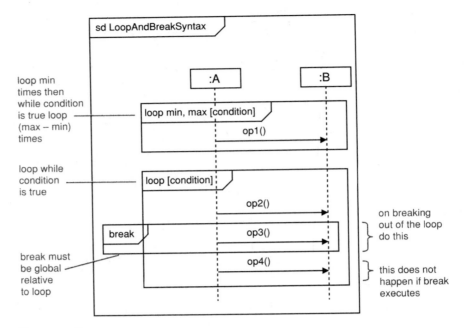

Figure 12.18

Table 12.4

Type of loop	Semantics	Loop expression
while(true) { body }	Keep looping forever	loop or loop *
for i = n to m { body }	Repeat (m − n) times	loop n, m
while(booleanExpression) { body }	Repeat while booleanExpression is true	loop [booleanExpression]

repeat
{ body }
while(booleanExpression)
	Execute once then repeat while booleanExpression is true	loop 1, * [booleanExpression]

forEach object in collection { body }	Execute the body of the loop once for each object in a collection of objects	loop [for each object in collectionOfObjects]
forEach object of class { body }	Execute the body of the loop once for each object of a particular class	loop [for each object in ClassName]

and if this is true, the body of break executes and the loop terminates. The essential point is that the rest of the loop after break does *not* execute.

The break combined fragment is logically outside the loop—it is *not* part of it. You must therefore always draw the break fragment outside the loop but overlapping it, as shown in Figure 12.18.

One of the commonest looping idioms is to traverse a collection of objects. For example, you could use a loop over a collection as a possible implementation for the findCourse(...) operation of the RegistrationManager class (Figure 12.19).

The operation returns the Course object with the right name or null, as shown in Figure 12.20. You can use the name of an association end with multiplicity greater than 1 as a collection of objects. In this case we use courses to represent a collection of Course objects.

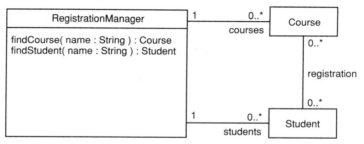

Figure 12.19

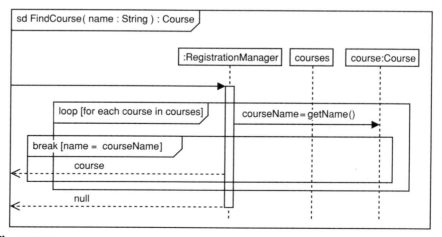

Figure 12.20

12.11   Communication diagrams

> Communication diagrams emphasize the structural aspects of an interaction.

Communication diagrams emphasize the structural aspects of an interaction—how lifelines connect. In UML 2, they are semantically quite weak compared to sequence diagrams.

You have already seen some communication diagrams. According to the UML 2.0 specification [UML2S], the object diagrams you saw in Chapter 7 can be considered to be special cases of class diagrams *or* to be special cases of instance form communication diagrams where each lifeline represents a class instance (object).

Communication diagrams have a syntax similar to that of sequence diagrams except that the lifelines don't have tails. Instead, they are connected by links that provide communication channels for the messages to pass over. Sequencing is indicated by numbering each message hierarchically.

Figure 12.21 shows a simple communication diagram for the AddCourses use case that shows the :Registrar adding two new Courses. Note how the messages are numbered to indicate their sequence and their nesting within other messages.

Here is the walkthrough for Figure 12.21.

1. addCourse("UML") – The message addCourse(...) is sent to the :RegistrationManager lifeline with the parameter "UML". The :RegistrationManager instance invokes an operation called addCourse(...) with the parameter "UML" and focus of control passes to this operation.

   1.1. «create» – As the sequence number is 1.1, this tells us that we are still within the focus of control of the operation addCourse(...). The :RegistrationManager sends an anonymous message that is stereo-

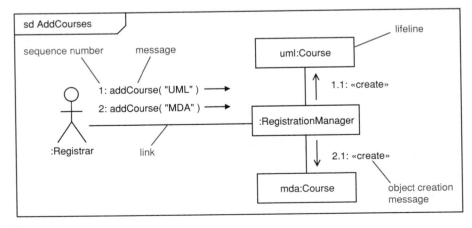

Figure 12.21

typed «create». These «create» messages create new objects, and this particular message creates a new object, uml:Course. You will give this anonymous message a name, and possibly parameters, later in analysis or design but for now it is sufficient to show that you are creating a new uml:Course object. After object creation, no more messages are sent within the focus of control of addCourse(...), and this flow returns.

2. addCourse("MDA") – The message addCourse(...) is sent to the :RegistrationManager with the parameter "MDA". Focus of control passes to the operation addCourse(...).

   2.1. «create» – As the sequence number is 2.1, this tells us that we are still within the focus of control of addCourse(...). The :RegistrationManager sends an anonymous message, stereotyped «create», that creates a new object, mda:Course. After object creation, the focus of control of addCourse(...) returns and the interaction finishes.

At first, communication diagrams can be somewhat tricky to read as quite a lot is going on. The key points to realize are that a message send results in an operation being called on an instance and that the sequence numbering of messages indicates the nesting of operation calls within operation calls (i.e., nested focus of control).

12.11.1 Iteration

> An iteration expression specifies the number of times to repeat a message send.

You can show iteration on communication diagrams by using an iteration expression. This comprises an iteration specifier (*) and an (optional) iteration clause as shown in Figure 12.22.

UML 2 does not prescribe any particular syntax for iteration clauses, so you can use anything that makes sense. Generally, code or pseudocode is a

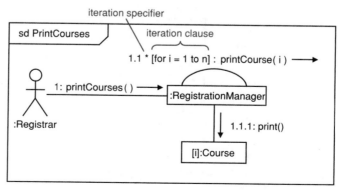

Figure 12.22

good option. You might think that communication diagrams would by default use the iteration syntax for sequence diagrams that we described in Section 12.10.2. However, the UML specification doesn't mention this! If you do decide to use the same iteration syntax, an iteration expression could be written as

* [loop min, max [condition]]

This has the advantage of consistency but has some syntactic redundancy as both loop and * are effectively iteration specifiers. Nevertheless, we think that this is a very good approach.

In the example in Figure 12.22 we have used pseudocode to indicate that the iteration clause loops, incrementing i from 1 to n. We then use i as a selector for a specific Course instance to which we send the message print(). This has the effect of printing out all the Course instances. However, this approach assumes that the Course instances are stored in some kind of indexed collection. If you don't want to make that assumption, you can use the alternative approach shown in Figure 12.23.

In Figure 12.23 we have done two things.

1. We have shown the role name and multiplicity on the :RegistrationManager to :Course link. This indicates that :RegistrationManager is connected to a collection of :Course objects via the courses role name (see the class diagram in Figure 12.7).

2. We have added the iteration specifier to the message print(). This indicates that the print() message is sent to *each object* in the collection.

The standard iteration specifier (*) means that the messages will be executed sequentially. If you wish to indicate that the messages are all executed in parallel, you must use the parallel iteration specifier */ /.

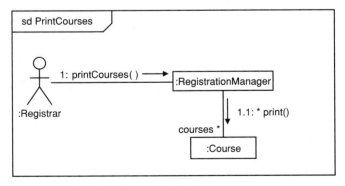

Figure 12.23

12.11.2   Branching

> Branching – the message is only sent if the condition is true.

You can model branching simply by adding guard conditions to the messages. The message is only sent when the guard condition evaluates to true.

Figure 12.24 shows an example of branching in our course registration system. This communication diagram realizes the use case RegisterStudentForCourse. In this registration system, registration is a three-step process:

- find the right student record—we can't register students for courses unless they are in the system;
- find the right course;
- register the student for the course.

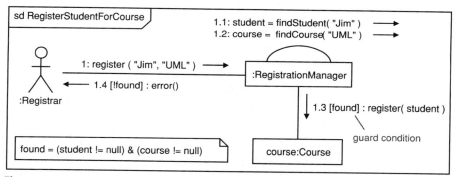

Figure 12.24

In Figure 12.24, we have made extensive use of conditions to show how you can use them in communication diagrams. Conditions have no formal syntax but are often expressions that involve temporary variables in the scope of the current focus of control, or attributes of the classes involved in the interaction. In Figure 12.24, we record the results of the findStudent(...) and findCourse(...) operations in two temporary variables: student and course. We then use the values of these variables to calculate the value of the temporary Boolean variable found. We use found to make a branch at step 1.3. We also use found to decide whether to raise an error condition to the :Registrar at step 1.4.

Here is the walkthrough for Figure 12.24.

1. registerStudent("Jim", "UML") – The :Registrar actor sends the message registerStudent("Jim", "UML") to the :RegistrationManager.

    1.1. findStudent("Jim") – The :RegistrationManager sends itself the message findStudent("Jim"). The return value from this operation is stored in the variable student. It will be null if the search failed.

1.2. findCourse("UML") – The :RegistrationManager sends itself the message findCourse("UML"). The return value from this operation is stored in the variable course. It will be null if the search failed.

1.3. [found] register(student) – The :RegistrationManager sends the message register(student) to the course object. This message is protected by a condition and will only be sent if both student and course are not null. In other words, we only attempt to register the student with the course if both the student and the course objects have been found successfully.

1.4. [!found] : error() – If found is false, call the error() operation on the :Registrar.

It is quite difficult to show branching clearly on communication diagrams—the conditions seem to spread out all over the diagram and it can get complex quite quickly. As a general style guideline, only show very simple branching on these diagrams. It is much easier to show complex branches on sequence diagrams.

12.12   What we have learned

Use case realization is an essential part of the analysis process. It allows you to test your theories against reality by explicitly demonstrating how objects of your classes can interact to deliver the specified system behavior. Interaction diagrams show how classes and objects realize requirements as specified in use cases.

You have learned the following.

- The UP activity Analyze a use case is where you create use case realizations – this activity creates part of the dynamic view of the system.
- Use case realizations show how instances of analysis classes interact to realize the functional requirements specified by a use case.
  — Each use case realization realizes exactly one use case.
  — Use case realizations consist of:
    – analysis class diagrams – these should "tell a story" about one (or more) use cases;
    – interaction diagrams – these demonstrate how objects interact to realize the use case behavior;
    – special requirements – you always uncover new requirements during use case realization and you need to record these;
    – use case refinement – you may need to change a use case as you begin to realize it.

- Interactions are units of behavior of a context classifier.
  - Interactions can use any of the features of the context classifier.
  - In use case realization the context classifier is a use case.
  - Generic form interaction diagrams show interactions between roles that classifier instances may play in the interaction.
  - Instance form interaction diagrams show interactions between specific classifier instances:
    - use normal instance notation for lifelines.
- A lifeline represents a participant in an interaction – how an instance of a classifier participates in the interaction.
  - Each lifeline has an optional name, a type, and an optional selector.
  - Each lifeline is drawn with the same icon as its type.
  - Underline the name, type, and selector to show actual instances.
- A message represents a specific kind of communication between two lifelines in an interaction.
  - Synchronous message (solid arrow head).
  - Asynchronous message (open arrow head).
  - Message return (open arrow head, dashed line).
  - Create message (open arrow head, solid line, stereotyped «create»).
  - Destroy message (open arrow head, solid line, stereotyped «destroy»).
  - Found message (open arrow head, originates from a filled circle).
  - Lost message (open arrow head, terminates in a filled circle).
- Interaction diagrams.
  - Sequence diagrams – emphasize time-ordered sequence of message sends.
  - Communication diagrams – emphasize structural relationships between objects.
  - Interaction overview diagrams – emphasize relationships between interactions.
  - Timing diagrams – emphasize real-time aspects of interactions.
- Sequence diagrams.
  - Time runs top to bottom.
  - Lifelines run left to right:
    - lifelines have dashed vertical tails that indicate the duration of the lifeline;
    - lifelines may have activations to indicate when the lifeline has focus of control;
    - organize lifelines to minimize the number of crossing lines.
  - Place explanatory scripts down the left-hand side of the sequence diagram.

— State invariants – place state symbols on the lifeline at the appropriate points.
— Constraints – place constraints in {} on or near lifelines.

- Combined fragments – areas within a sequence diagram with different behavior.
  — The operator defines *how* its operands execute.
  — The guard condition defines *whether* its operand executes.
  — The operand contains the behavior.

- Operators.
  — opt – there is a single operand that executes if the condition is true (like if ... then).
  — alt – the operand whose condition is true is executed.
  — loop – loop min, max [condition]:
    – loop or loop * – loop forever;
    – loop n, m – loop (m - n) times;
    – loop [booleanExpression] – loop while booleanExpression is true;
    – loop 1, * [booleanExpression] – loop once then loop while booleanExpression is true;
    – loop [for each object in collectionOfObjects] – execute the body of the loop once for each object in the collection;
    – loop [for each object in className] – execute the body of the loop once for each object of the class.
  — break – if the guard condition is true, the operand is executed, not the rest of the enclosing interaction.
  — ref – the combined fragment refers to another interaction.
  — par – all operands execute in parallel.
  — critical – the operand executes atomically without interruption.
  — seq – operands execute in parallel subject to the following constraint: events arriving on the same lifeline from different operands occur in the same sequence as the operands occur.
  — strict – the operands execute in strict sequence.
  — neg – the operand shows invalid interactions.
  — ignore – lists messages that are intentionally omitted from the interaction.
  — consider – lists messages that are intentionally included in the interaction.
  — assert – the operand is the only valid behavior at that point in the interaction.

- Communication diagrams – emphasize the structural aspects of an interaction:
  — lifelines are connected by links;
  — messages have a sequence number – they are numbered hierarchically according to the nesting of the focus of control.

- Iteration – use an iteration specifier (*) and an optional iteration clause on the message.
  — The iteration clause specifies the number of times to loop.
  — You can use natural language, pseudocode, source code, or sequence diagram loop notation for the iteration clause.
  — You can show iteration over a collection of objects by showing the role name and multiplicity (>1) on the target end of the link and prefixing the message with the iteration specifier (*). The message is sent to each object in turn.
  — Use the parallel iteration specifier */ / to indicate that messages are executed in parallel.
- Branching – prefix messages with guard conditions. The message executes if the guard condition is true.
  — It can be hard to show branching clearly on a communication diagram – for complex branching, use sequence diagrams instead.

chapter 13

Advanced use case realization

13.1 Chapter roadmap

This chapter introduces some advanced features of interaction diagrams that help you deal with complexity. This complexity can arise in both analysis and design, depending on the nature of the system on which you are working. While you should always try to keep interaction diagrams as simple as possible, sometimes there is irreducible complexity. This is when you should see if any of the techniques presented in this chapter can help.

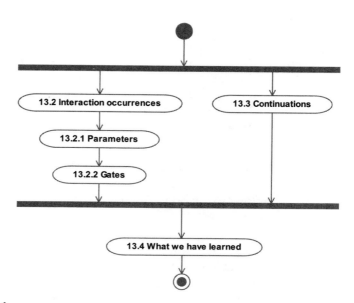

Figure 13.1

13.2   Interaction occurrences

Interaction occurrences are references to another interaction.

Very often you have a sequence of message sends that occurs again and again in many different sequence diagrams. Clearly, it is both error-prone and tiresome to have to redraw the same interaction fragment over and over again, so instead you use *interaction occurrences*.

Interaction occurrences are references to an interaction. When an interaction occurrence is placed into an interaction, the flow of the interaction it references is included at that point.

As a specific example, let us look at a fragment from the simple course registration system that we discussed Chapter 12. The analysis class diagram for the part of the system we are interested in is shown in Figure 12.7.

Consider a specific example. Before the Registrar actor in Figure 12.6 can use the system in any way, he or she first has to log on. You can realize this requirement by adding a SecurityManager class to Figure 12.7 as illustrated in Figure 13.2.

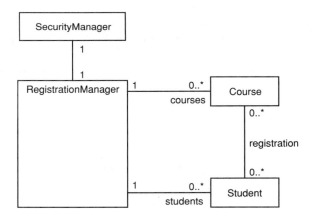

Figure 13.2

Let's look at the use case LogOnRegistrar. This is illustrated in Figure 13.3. This use case is one that will be included by any use case that first needs the Registrar to log on to the system.

The interaction fragment for logging on the Registrar can potentially occur at the beginning of a large number of sequence diagrams. It makes sense to factor this common behavior out into its own sequence diagram and then reference it when needed. Figure 13.4 shows the sequence diagram LogOnRegistrar that contains the reusable interaction fragment.

In Figure 13.5, you can see another sequence diagram, ChangeStudentAddress, that includes the LogOnRegistrar interaction.

Use case: LogOnRegistrar
ID: 4
Brief description: The Registrar logs on to the system.
Primary actors: Registrar
Secondary actors: None.
Preconditions: 1. The Registrar is not logged on to the system.
Main flow: 1. The use case starts when the Registrar selects "log on". 2. The system asks the Registrar for a user name and password. 3. The Registrar enters a user name and password. 4. The system accepts the user name and password as valid.
Postconditions: 1. The Registrar is logged on to the system.
Alternative flows: InvalidUserNameAndPassword RegistrarAlreadyLoggedOn

Figure 13.3

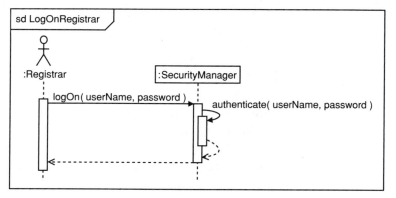

Figure 13.4

The complete sequence of events in ChangeStudentAddress is summarized in Table 13.1.

There are several points to bear in mind when you use interaction occurrences.

- The interaction referenced by the interaction occurrence is inserted into the including interaction at the point where the interaction occurrence first appears.

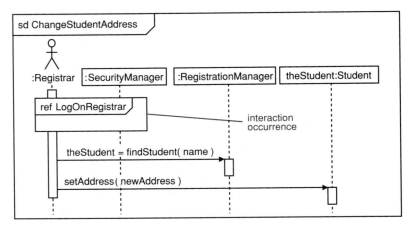

Figure 13.5

Table 13.1

Diagram	Source lifeline	Message	Target lifeline
LogOnRegistrar	:Registrar	logOn(...)	:SecurityManager
LogOnRegistrar	:SecurityManager	authenticate(...)	:SecurityManager
ChangeStudentAddress	:Registrar	findStudent(...)	:RegistrationManager
ChangeStudentAddress	:Registrar	setAddress	theStudent:Student

- When the included interaction ends, be very aware of where it leaves the focus of control! The very next message send in the including interaction must be consistent with this.
- All lifelines used in the interaction occurrence must also exist in the including interaction.
- To indicate the scope of the interaction occurrence, draw it across the lifelines it uses.

13.2.1   Parameters

> Parameters provide specific values for the interaction to use.

Interactions may be parameterized. This allows you to supply different values to the interaction in each of its occurrences. You can specify parameters by using the normal syntax for operations that we discussed in Section 7.5.3.

Figure 13.6 shows FindStudent(...) and FindCourse(...), two parameterized interactions.

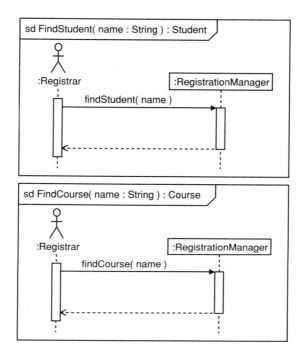

Figure 13.6

Figure 13.7 shows an example of how these parameterized interactions can be used. Notice how you can pass specific values in to the interactions as parameters. This gives you great power and flexibility!

In Figure 13.7 you can see that the two interaction occurrences have return values that are assigned to the temporary variables theStudent and theCourse. These temporary variables exist in the scope of the sequence diagram.

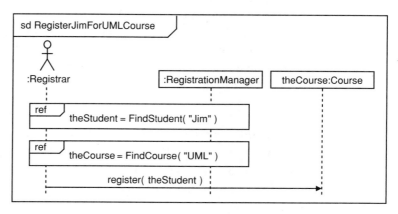

Figure 13.7

13.2.2   Gates

Gates are the inputs and outputs of interactions.

> Gates are the inputs and outputs of interactions.

You use gates when you want an interaction to be triggered by a lifeline that is *not* part of the interaction. You can easily adapt the examples in Figure 13.6, FindStudent and FindCourse, to use gates. This is illustrated in Figure 13.8.

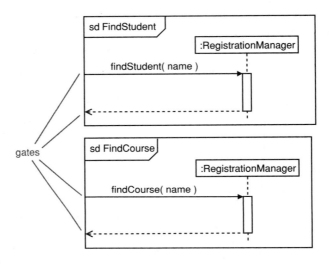

Figure 13.8

As you can see from the figure, a gate is a point on the sequence diagram frame. This point connects a message *outside* the frame to a message *inside* the frame. Both these messages *must* have a matching signature.

You can modify Figure 13.7 to use these new sequence diagrams with gates as shown in Figure 13.9.

Now that FindStudent and FindCourse have explicit inputs and outputs, they have even more flexibility. Consider Figure 13.10, which shows another possible use of the FindCourse interaction.

Given that both gates and parameters allow flexibility in the reuse of interactions, when should you use gates and when should you use parameters?

- You use parameters when you know the source and destination lifelines of all messages within the interaction.

- You use gates when some of the messages arise from outside the interaction frame and you don't know in advance where they might come from.

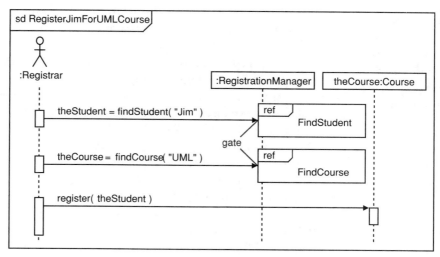

Figure 13.9

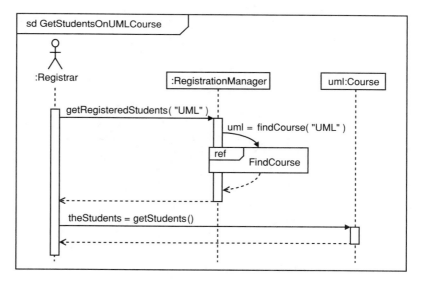

Figure 13.10

13.3   Continuations

Continuations allow an interaction fragment to indicate that its flow terminates in such a way that it can be picked up and continued by another interaction fragment. The continuation is drawn as a label inside a rounded rectangle.

When a continuation is the *last* item in an interaction fragment, it indicates the point at which the fragment finishes but may be continued by other fragments.

When a continuation is the *first* item in an interaction fragment, it indicates that this fragment is continuing from a previous fragment.

Continuations provide a way to connect different interactions. Essentially, one interaction finishes, leaving its lifelines in a specific state, and other interactions may pick up at that point and continue.

Continuations have the same visual syntax as the state invariants that we discussed in Section 12.9.4. However, a continuation is just a way of connecting different interactions at labelled points and doesn't necessarily map to a specific state in the state machine of the context classifier.

Figure 13.11 shows a simple sequence diagram in which the :RegistationUI (UI stands for user interface) prompts the :Registrar actor first for a course name, and then for one of the three options: add, remove, or find. Depending on which option is selected, the interaction terminates at one of the three continuations addCourse, removeCourse, or findCourse.

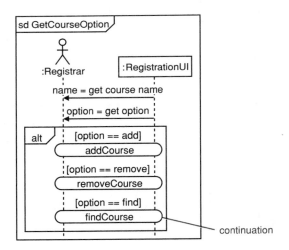

Figure 13.11

In Figure 13.12 you can see an interaction called HandleCourseOption that includes GetCourseOption and then picks up at each of its continuations. You can see that continuations have allowed you to

- decouple the interactions GetCourseOption and HandleCourseOption;
- potentially reuse GetCourseOption and HandleCourseOption with other interactions that have the same continuations.

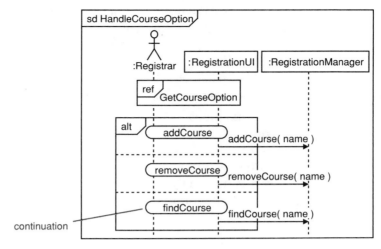

Figure 13.12

When using continuations be aware that

- continuations start and end interactions—they must therefore be either the first or last thing in an interaction;
- in the context of a given classifier, continuations with the same name *must* cover the same set of lifelines;
- continuations only make sense when there is at least weak sequencing in an interaction—clearly, if there was no sequencing, you could not know where the continuation occurred;
- continuations must cover *all* lifelines in their enclosing fragment (i.e., they are *global* within that fragment).

Continuations are often used with the alt operator, as shown in Figure 13.12, to create branch points within an interaction.

13.4   What we have learned

In this section we have looked at advanced features of interaction diagrams. You have learned the following.

- Interaction occurrences – references to another interaction.
  - The flow of the referenced interaction is included in the flow of the referencing interaction.
  - Parameters – interaction occurrences may have parameters – use normal parameter notation.

— Gates – inputs and outputs of interactions:
  - – a point on the sequence diagram frame that connects a message outside the frame to a message with the same signature inside the frame.
— Use parameters when you know the source and destination of all messages – use gates when you don't.

- Continuations – terminate an interaction fragment so that it can be continued by another fragment:
  — first item in the fragment – the fragment is continuing from another fragment;
  — last item in the fragment – the fragment terminates but may be continued by another fragment.

chapter 14
Activity diagrams

14.1 Chapter roadmap

Activity diagrams are "OO flowcharts". They allow you to model a process as an activity that consists of a collection of nodes connected by edges. UML 2 introduces new semantics for activity diagrams that gives them much more power and flexibility than they have ever had before. In this chapter we cover basic activity diagrams—this should be all you need for most of your activity modeling. For completeness, we present more advanced topics in the next chapter.

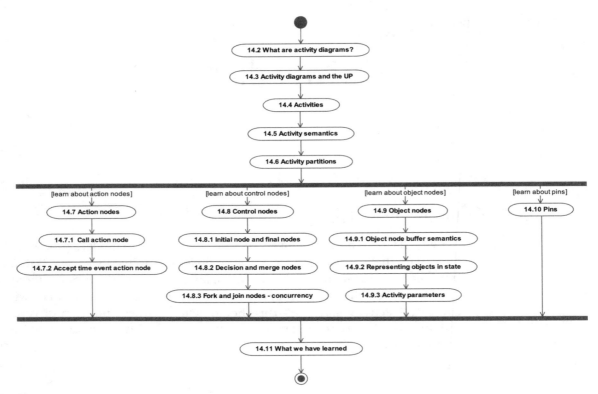

Figure 14.1

14.2   What are activity diagrams?

Activity diagrams
are OO flowcharts.

Activity diagrams are often called "OO flowcharts". They allow you to model a process as an activity that consists of a collection of nodes connected by edges.

In UML 1, activity diagrams were really just special cases of state machines (see Chapter 21), where every state had an entry action that specified some process or function that occurred when the state was entered. In UML 2, activity diagrams have completely new semantics based on Petri Nets. This has two advantages.

1. The Petri Net formalism provides greater flexibility in modeling different types of flow.

2. There is now a clear distinction in UML between activity diagrams and state machines.

An activity can be attached to *any* modeling element for the purpose of modeling its behavior. The element provides the context for the activity, and the activity may refer to features of its context. Activities are typically attached to

- use cases;
- classes;
- interfaces;
- components;
- collaborations;
- operations.

You can also use activity diagrams to model business processes and workflows. We indicate how you can do this, but it can be a complex topic and is beyond the scope of this book.

Although a common use of activity diagrams is to flowchart operations, it's worth considering that the source code for an operation, in code or pseudocode, might be its best and most concise representation! So judge each case on its merits.

The essence of a good activity diagram is that it is focused on communicating one specific aspect of a system's dynamic behavior. As such, it must be at the correct level of abstraction to communicate that message to its target audience, and it should contain the minimum amount of information necessary to make the point. It is easy to adorn activity diagrams with object states and objects flows, etc., but you must always ask yourself whether those adornments clarify or obscure the diagram. As usual, it's best to keep it simple if possible.

14.3   Activity diagrams and the UP

Activity diagrams can be used in many UP workflows.

Because of their flexibility, there is no single place where activity diagrams fit into the UP. They provide a general-purpose mechanism for modeling behaviors and you may use them wherever they add value. We cover them here in the analysis workflow as this is where we tend to use them the most.

The unique capability of activity diagrams is that they let you model a process *without* having to specify the static structure of classes and objects that realize that process. Clearly, this is very useful when you are in the early stages of analysis and are trying to uncover what a particular process is.

In our experience, activity diagrams are most commonly used in the following ways.

- In the analysis workflow:
  — to model the flow in a use case in a graphical way that is easy for stakeholders to understand;
  — to model the flow between use cases. This uses a special form of activity diagram called an interaction overview diagram (see Section 15.12).
- In design:
  — to model the details of an operation;
  — to model the details of an algorithm.
- In business modeling:
  — to model a business process.

Activity diagrams are usually easily understood by stakeholders. This is because most stakeholders will have had some exposure to flowcharts in some form or another. Activity diagrams can therefore be a great communication mechanism *provided* you keep them simple.

As you will see in this chapter and the next, UML 2 introduces a lot of powerful new syntax and semantics for activity diagrams, and it's important not to get carried away with this. When constructing *any* UML diagram, always keep in mind your target audience and use UML features accordingly. There's no point in using all the latest features if no one understands the diagram.

14.4   Activities

Activities are networks of nodes connected by edges.

Activities are networks of *nodes* connected by *edges*. There are three categories of node:

1. action nodes – represent discrete units of work that are atomic *within the activity;*
2. control nodes – control the flow through the activity;
3. object nodes – represent objects used in the activity.

Edges represent flow through the activity. There are two categories of edge:

1. control flows – represent the flow of control though the activity;
2. object flows – represent the flow of objects through the activity.

We look at each of these types of node and edge in detail in subsequent sections.

Let's look at an example. Figure 14.2 shows a simple activity diagram for the business process Send letter. Note that activities can have preconditions and postconditions much like use cases. Preconditions are things that must be true before the activity can start, and postconditions are things that will be true after the activity has finished. Actions within the activity can also have their own local preconditions and postconditions, as illustrated.

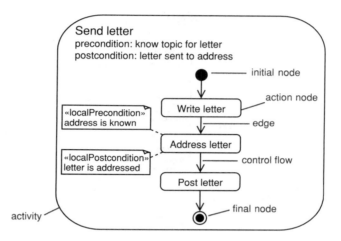

Figure 14.2

Activities often start with a single control node, the initial node, that indicates the place where execution will begin when the activity is invoked. One or more final nodes indicate places where the activity terminates.

In the example in Figure 14.2, the activity begins at the initial node and then control transitions to the action node Write letter via an edge. This node indicates a piece of work or behavior that is atomic as far as its containing activity is concerned. Flow progresses to Address letter, Post letter, and then to the final node where the activity terminates.

A common use of activity diagrams is to model a use case as a series of actions. Figure 14.3 shows the use case PaySalesTax from Chapter 4. This use case can be expressed as an activity diagram, as shown in Figure 14.4.

Notice that the activity diagram gives you a more compact and graphical form of the use case. The activity diagram expresses the use case as two actions, Calculate sales tax and Send electronic payment. Each of these actions could itself be expressed as an activity diagram, and this would probably occur in the design workflow when you need to uncover how the actions are implemented. The actor and its interaction with the system are structural features, and these are absent from the diagram.

Use case: PaySalesTax
ID: 1
Brief description: Pay Sales Tax to the Tax Authority at the end of the business quarter.
Primary actors: Time
Secondary actors: TaxAuthority
Preconditions: 1. It is the end of the business quarter.

Main flow:
  1. The use case starts when it is the end of the business quarter.
  2. The system determines the amount of Sales Tax owed to the Tax
      Authority.
  3. The system sends an electronic payment to the Tax Authority.

Postconditions: 1. The Tax Authority receives the correct amount of Sales Tax.
Alternative flows: None.

Figure 14.3

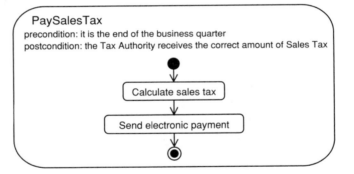

Figure 14.4

Use cases express system behavior as an interaction between an actor and the system, whereas activity diagrams express it as a series of actions. These are complementary views of the same behavior.

14.5   Activity semantics

Activity diagrams are based on Petri Nets.

Activity diagrams have quite intuitive semantics, as you may have noticed from the previous sections. In this section we look at activity semantics in depth.

UML 2 activity diagrams are based on Petri Nets. Petri Nets are out of scope for this book, but you can find out more about them at www.daimi.au.dk/ PetriNets/ if you are interested.

Activity diagrams model behavior by using the *token game*. This game describes the flow of tokens around a network of nodes and edges according to specific rules. Tokens in UML activity diagrams can represent

- the flow of control;
- an object;
- some data.

The state of the system at any point in time is determined by the disposition of its tokens.

In the example in Figure 14.2, the token is the flow of control as there are no objects or data being passed between nodes in this particular case.

Tokens are moved from a source node to a target node across an edge. Movement of a token is subject to conditions, and it can only occur when *all* of the conditions are satisfied. The conditions vary depending on the type of node. For the nodes in Figure 14.5 (action nodes) these conditions are

- the postconditions of the source node;
- guard conditions on the edge;
- the preconditions of the target node.

As well as action nodes there are control nodes and object nodes. Control nodes have special semantics that control how tokens are passed from their input edges to their output edges. For example, the initial node begins an activity, the final node ends an activity, and a join node will offer a token on its single output edge if, and only if, there are tokens on all of its input edges. Object nodes represent objects flowing around the system. We discuss control nodes and object nodes in more detail in Sections 14.8 and 14.9 respectively.

Consider how the token game works for the activity illustrated in Figure 14.5. When the activity is executed, a flow of control token starts on the initial node. There are no conditions on this node, its output edge, or the target node, and so the token automatically traverses the output edge to the target node, Write letter. This causes the action specified by the Write letter action node to execute. When Write letter has finished, the flow of control token traverses to the action node Address letter if, and only if, its precondition, address is known, is satisfied. When the postcondition, letter is addressed, is satisfied, control flows from Address letter to Post letter. Finally, as there are no conditions impeding flow out of Post letter, the flow of control moves to the final state and the activity finishes.

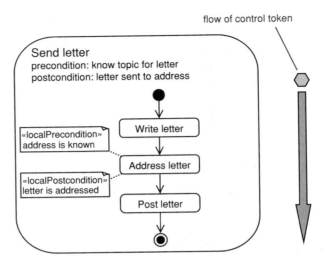

Figure 14.5

In this simple example the flow of control passes through each action node in turn, causing it to execute. This is core activity semantics.

As we've mentioned, the state of the executing system may be represented at any point in time by the disposition of its tokens. For example, when the token is in the Write letter action node, you could say that the system is in the state Writing letter. However, not every action execution or token flow constitutes a notable change in state of the system from the point of view of its state machines (see Chapter 21). Nevertheless, the disposition of tokens provides a link between activity diagrams and state machines. You must ensure that the activity diagrams and state machines for a particular model element are consistent with each other.

Although the semantics of UML 2 activities are *described* with the token game, they are hardly ever implemented in that way. In fact, an activity is just a specification for which there may be many possible implementations. For example, in Figure 14.5, we are describing a simple business process, rather than a software system, and implementations of this process would generally *not* involve token passing!

14.6   Activity partitions

Each activity partition represents a high-level grouping of related actions.

To make your activity diagrams easier to read, you can divide activities into partitions by using vertical, horizontal, or curved lines. Each activity partition represents a high-level grouping of related actions. Activity partitions are sometimes called swimlanes. Partitioning is a powerful technique—when used well, it can make activity diagrams much easier to understand.

In UML 2, the modeler defines the semantics of activity partitions—they have no inherent semantics. You can therefore use them to partition activity diagrams in any way you like! Activity partitions are commonly used to represent

- use cases;
- classes;
- components;
- organizational units (in business modeling);
- roles (in workflow modeling).

However, these are not the only possibilities. For example, in design models for distributed systems, you can even use activity partitions to model the distribution of processes across physical machines.

Each set of partitions should have a single dimension that describes the base semantics of the set. Within this dimension, partitions may be hierarchically nested. Figure 14.6 shows an activity that has a hierarchically nested set of activity partitions.

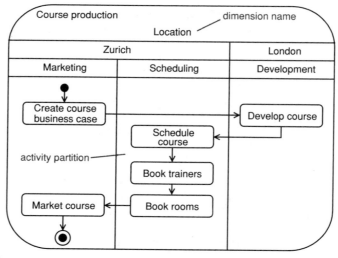

Figure 14.6

The dimension is Location, and within this dimension there is a hierarchy of partitions, as shown in Figure 14.7. This diagram actually models the course production business process in our partner company Zuhlke Engineering AG. Many of their courses are developed in London by us.

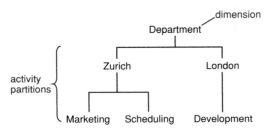

Figure 14.7

There is often a connection between activity partitions and concurrent flows of control. We discuss modeling concurrency in activity diagrams in detail in Section 14.8.3. For example, it is common for separate departments or business units to perform concurrent lines of work and then to synchronize at some point. Activity diagrams with activity partitions are an excellent way of modeling this.

Sometimes it's not really feasible to arrange the nodes into vertical or horizontal partitions without making the diagram hard to read. In this case, you could use curved lines to create irregular partitions, or you could indicate partitions by using text. UML has a textual notation for activity partitions, illustrated in Figure 14.8. However, you would typically only use this notation as a last resort because the graphical notation is usually so much clearer.

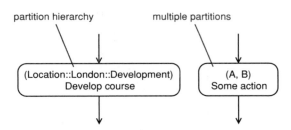

Figure 14.8

You can specify an action's position within the partition hierarchy by using a double-colon-delimited pathname in brackets above the action name. If an action resides in more than one partition, you list each partition pathname separated by commas.

Very occasionally you may need to show behavior on an activity diagram that is, strictly speaking, outside the scope of the system. This might be to show how the system interacts with some other external system. Activity diagrams can accommodate this—simply add the stereotype «external» directly

«external»
partitions are not part of your system.

above the partition name. Note that the external partition is *not* a part of the system and therefore can't be nested within any model partition hierarchies.

You can certainly add a lot of useful information to an activity diagram by careful choice of dimensions and activity partitions. However, these features can also complicate diagrams, particularly when there are multiple dimensions and complex partition hierarchies! In practice, try to use no more than three levels in a hierarchy (including the dimension) and no more than two dimensions per diagram.

Always use your judgment and apply activity partitions only when they add real value to the model.

14.7   Action nodes

Action nodes execute when

- there is a token simultaneously on each of their input edges AND
- the input tokens satisfy all of the action node local preconditions.

This is illustrated in Figure 14.9.

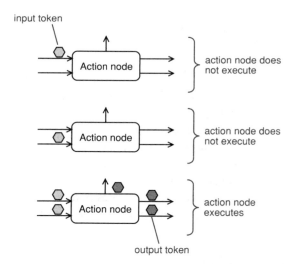

Figure 14.9

Action nodes perform a logical **AND** on their input tokens—the node isn't ready to execute until tokens are present on *all* of its input edges. Even when the required tokens are present, the node will only execute when its local precondition is satisfied.

Action nodes offer control tokens on *all* their output edges – an implicit fork.

When the action node has finished execution, the local postcondition is checked; if it is satisfied, the node simultaneously offers tokens on *all* of its output edges. This is an implicit fork as one action node may give rise to many flows. Unlike conventional flowcharts, activity diagrams are inherently concurrent.

Because action nodes do something, they are usually named with a verb or verb phrase. The UML specification doesn't give any guidelines on naming action nodes. The convention we use is to name the node by starting with an uppercase letter and continuing in lowercase, using spaces where appropriate. The only exception to this rule occurs when an action node contains a reference to another model element. In this case, we always use the model element name as it is *without* changing case or adding spaces. Figure 14.10 shows two examples. The top example refers to something called "order", whereas the bottom example refers explicitly to a class called Order that can be found somewhere else in the model.

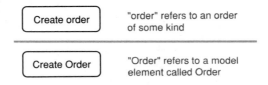

Figure 14.10

Details of the action are captured in the action node specification. It is often just a simple textual description such as "Write a letter", but in design, it might be structured text, pseudocode, or actual code. If the activity diagram is modeling a use case, then it could be one or more steps from the use case flow. However, be aware that this can create a maintenance problem because you have to keep the use case and associated activity diagram in step if one or the other changes.

There are four types of action nodes. These are summarized in Table 14.1 and discussed in detail in the sections listed in the table.

14.7.1   Call action node

A call action node can invoke an activity, a behavior, or an operation.

The most common type of action node is the *call action node*. This type of node can invoke

- an activity;
- a behavior;
- an operation.

Table 14.1

Syntax	Name	Semantics	Section
Some action	Call action node	Invokes an activity, behavior, or operation	14.7.1
SignalName	Send signal	Send signal action – sends a signal asynchronously (the sender *does not* wait for confirmation of signal receipt) It may accept input parameters to create the signal	15.6
AcceptEvent	Accept event action node	Accepts an event – waits for events detected by its owning object and offers the event on its output edge Is enabled when it gets a token on its input edge If there is *no* input edge, it starts when its containing activity starts and is always enabled	15.6
time expression	Accept time event action node	Accepts a time event – responds to time Generates time events according to its time expression	14.7.2

Some examples of call action node syntax are illustrated in Figure 14.11. As you can see from the figure, call action node syntax is very flexible!

- You can indicate that the action invokes another activity by using the special rake symbol in the lower right-hand corner of the node icon. The name of the node is the name of the activity that it calls.

- You can call a behavior—this is a direct invocation of a behavior of the context of the activity *without* specifying any particular operation.

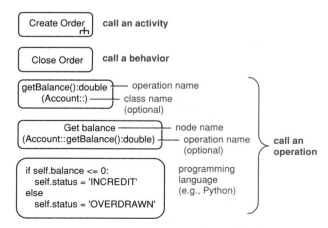

Figure 14.11

- You can call an operation by using the standard operation syntax described in Section 7.5.3.

- You can call an operation by specifying the details of the operation in a particular programming language. This can be particularly useful if you are using a UML tool that lets you generate code from activity diagrams (e.g., iUML from Kennedy Carter, www.kc.com).

- You can refer to features of the context of the activity by using the keyword self.

When you use call action nodes in analysis-level activity diagrams, you will usually be calling a behavior. Call action nodes that invoke specific operations tend to be used for more detailed activity modeling in design.

14.7.2   Accept time event action node

An accept time event action node responds to time.

An accept time event action node responds to time. This type of node has a time expression, and it generates a time event when this expression becomes true. This node behaves differently depending on whether or not it has an input edge.

For example, Figure 14.12 shows an accept time event action node that has no input edge. When its owning activity is triggered, this node will become active and will generate a time event whenever its time expression becomes true. In the example shown, a time event is generated at the end of every business year, and this causes the activity Send company tax return to execute.

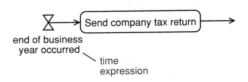

Figure 14.12

In the example in Figure 14.13, however, the accept time event action has an input edge and will only become active when a token is received on

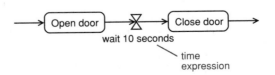

Figure 14.13

that edge. This example is a fragment from an elevator system. The first action opens the elevator door and triggers the accept time event action. This action waits for ten seconds, and then offers a token to the action Close door.

Note that the time expression may refer to

- an event in time (e.g., end of business year);
- a point in time (e.g., on 11/03/1960);
- a duration (e.g., wait 10 seconds).

14.8   Control nodes

Control nodes manage the flow of control within an activity. Table 14.2 summarizes all of the UML 2 control nodes. We discuss each of these nodes in detail in the next few sections.

Table 14.2

Syntax	Name	Semantics		Section
●—→	Initial node	Indicates where the flow starts when an activity is invoked		14.8.1
—→◉	Activity final node	Terminates an activity	Final nodes	14.8.1
—→⊗	Flow final node	Terminates a specific flow within an activity – the other flows are unaffected		14.8.1
«decisionInput» decision condition	Decision node	The output edge whose guard condition is true is traversed May optionally have a «decisionInput»		14.8.2
⟫◇→	Merge node	Copies input tokens to its single output edge		14.8.2
—▐⟨	Fork node	Splits the flow into multiple concurrent flows		14.8.3
{join spec} ⟩▐→	Join node	Synchronizes multiple concurrent flows May optionally have a join specification to modify its semantics		14.8.3

14.8.1   Initial node and final nodes

As we already mentioned in Section 14.4, the initial node is the point at which flow starts when an activity is invoked. An activity may have more than one initial node. In this case, flows start at all of the initial nodes simultaneously and execute concurrently.

> The initial node indicates where an activity starts.

An activity can also be started by an accept event action (Section 15.6) or by an activity parameter node (Section 14.9.3), so initial nodes are *not* mandatory provided there is some other way of starting the activity.

> The activity final node stops *all* flows within an activity.

The activity final node stops *all* flows within an activity. An activity may have many activity final nodes, and the first one to be activated terminates all other flows and the activity itself.

> The flow final node stops *one* flow within an activity.

The flow final node simply stops *one* of the flows within the activity—the other flows continue. See Figure 15.10 for an example.

14.8.2   Decision and merge nodes

A decision node has one input edge and two or more alternate output edges. A token arriving at the input edge will be offered to *all* of the output edges but will traverse at most *one* of them. The decision node acts like a crossroads in the flow where the token must take one direction only.

> A decision node outputs a token on an output edge whose guard condition evaluates to true.

Each of the output edges is protected by a *guard condition* such that the edge will accept a token if, and only if, the guard condition evaluates to true. It's important to ensure that the guard conditions are mutually exclusive so that only *one* of them can be true at any point in time. If not, the behavior of the decision node is formally undefined according to the UML 2 specification!

The keyword else can be used to specify the edge traversed if none of the guard conditions is true.

Figure 14.14 shows a simple example of a decision node. After the action Get mail, the flow of control hits a decision node. If the condition [is junk] is true, then the mail is binned, else the mail is opened.

A note stereotyped «decisionInput» provides a decision condition for a decision node. The result of this condition is used by the guard conditions on the outgoing edges. An example activity fragment is shown in Figure 14.15. In this fragment, the decision condition compares the requested amount of the withdrawal with the account balance. If the balance is greater than or equal to the requested amount, then the condition evaluates to true and the flow traverses to Withdraw amount. Otherwise, a failure is logged.

Figure 14.14 shows a merge node. Merge nodes have two or more input edges and a single output edge. They merge all their incoming flows into a single outgoing flow. The semantics of merge is very simple—all tokens

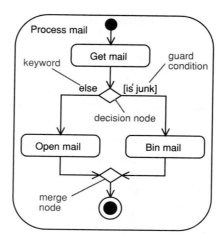

Figure 14.14

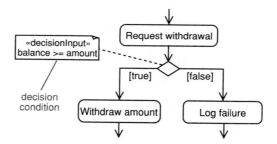

Figure 14.15

offered on the incoming edges are offered on the outgoing edge and there is no modification of the flow or the tokens.

A merge node and an immediately following decision node can be combined into a single symbol as shown in Figure 14.16. However, we don't particularly recommend this shorthand notation as it is usually clearer to show separate merge and decision nodes.

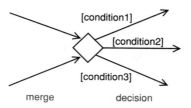

Figure 14.16

14.8.3   Fork and join nodes – concurrency

> A fork node splits a flow into multiple concurrent flows.

You can create concurrent flows within an activity by using a fork node to split a single flow into multiple concurrent flows. While concurrency is usually a design decision, you often need to show concurrent activities when you are modeling business processes. You will, therefore, often use fork and join nodes in the analysis workflow as well as in design.

A fork node has one incoming edge and two or more outgoing edges. Tokens arriving at the incoming edge are duplicated and offered on *all* of the outgoing edges simultaneously. This splits the single incoming flow into multiple parallel outgoing flows. Each outgoing edge may have a guard condition and, like decision nodes, a token can only traverse the outgoing edge if the guard condition is true.

> A join node synchronizes and joins multiple input flows into a single output flow.

Join nodes have multiple incoming edges and a single outgoing edge. They synchronize flows by offering a token on their single output edge when there is a token on *all* of their input edges. They perform a logical AND on their input edges.

Figure 14.17 shows a simple example of a Product process that uses fork and join nodes. In this example,

● the product is designed first;

● the product is marketed and manufactured concurrently;

● the product is sold *only* after both the marketing and manufacturing processes are complete.

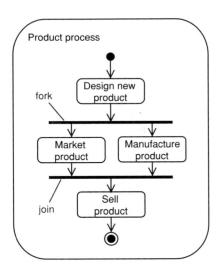

Figure 14.17

In Figure 14.17 the Product process activity starts with the action Design new product. After this action, a fork node splits the single flow into two concurrent flows. In one of these flows the product is marketed (Market product), and in the other it is manufactured (Manufacture product). The join node synchronizes the two concurrent flows because it waits for a token from each of the concurrent actions. When it has a token from each action, it offers a token on its output edge and flow traverses to the action Sell product.

When you model join nodes, it is important to ensure that all of the input edges to the join will receive a token. For example, in Figure 14.17, if there were mutually exclusive guard conditions on the output flows of the fork, the join could never be offered sufficient tokens to activate and this would cause the activity to hang.

14.9   Object nodes

> Object nodes indicate that instances of a classifier are available.

Object nodes are special nodes that indicate that instances of a particular classifier are available at a specific point in the activity. They are labelled with the name of the classifier and represent instances of that classifier or its subclasses. The activity fragment in Figure 14.18 shows an object node that represents instances of the classifier Order or Order subclasses.

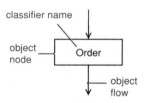

Figure 14.18

> Object flows represent the movement of objects around an activity.

The input and output edges of object nodes are *object flows*. These are special types of flows that represent the movement of objects around the activity. The objects themselves are created and consumed by action nodes.

Figure 14.19 shows the simple Product process activity introduced in Figure 14.17, updated to include partitions and to show the creation of a ProductSpecification object by the Design new product action. The ProductSpecification object is consumed by the Manufacture product action that uses it to define the manufacturing process.

> The output edges of an object node compete for each output token.

When an object node receives an object token on one of its input edges, it offers this token on all of its output edges simultaneously and these edges

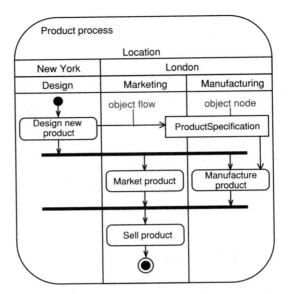

Figure 14.19

compete for the token. The key point is that there is still only one token—the token is *not* replicated on the edges! The first edge to accept the token gets it.

14.9.1   Object node buffer semantics

Object nodes act as buffers.

Object nodes have very interesting semantics. They act as buffers—places in the activity where object tokens can reside while waiting to be accepted by other nodes.

By default, each object node can hold an infinite number of object tokens. However, sometimes you need to indicate that the buffer is a finite size. You can do this by giving the object node an *upper bound* that indicates the maximum number of tokens it is capable of holding at any time. When object tokens are offered to the object node, it accepts them until it is full. An example of an object node with an upper bound specified is shown in Figure 14.20.

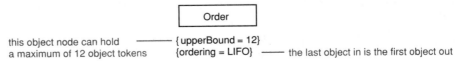

Figure 14.20

You can specify two aspects of the buffer semantics for object nodes.

- Object nodes have an *ordering* (Figure 14.20) that specifies how the buffer behaves. The default ordering is FIFO (first-in, first-out). This means that the first object into the node is the first one offered to its output edges. The other ordering is LIFO (last-in, first-out).

- Object nodes may have a *selection behavior*. This is a behavior attached to the node that selects objects from the input edges according to some modeler-defined criterion. Selection is specified by a note stereotyped «selection» as shown in Figure 14.21. In this example, the object node selects only those Order objects that were created in the month of December. It offers these to its output edges by using the default ordering (FIFO).

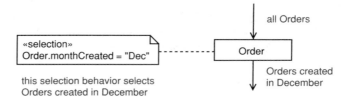

Figure 14.21

You can use an object node to collect objects from multiple incoming object flows or to distribute objects to multiple outgoing object flows. In these cases, you are using the node specifically for its buffering semantics, and you can give it the stereotype «centralBuffer» to highlight this fact.

As well as buffering individual objects, object nodes can buffer *sets* of objects. A set is a collection of objects in which there is no duplicate, that is, each object has a unique identity. To show this, you simply prefix the classifier name with Set of. You can see an example of this in Figure 14.23.

We discuss «selection» and «centralBuffer» in a little more depth in Sections 15.8.2 and 15.11, respectively.

14.9.2 Representing objects in state

> Object nodes can represent objects in a particular state.

Object nodes can represent objects in a particular state. For example, Figure 14.22 shows a fragment from an order-processing activity that accepts Order objects that are in the state Open and dispatches them. The object states referenced by object nodes can be modeled with state machines, as we describe in Chapter 21.

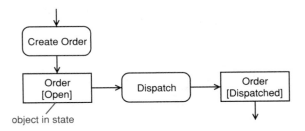

Figure 14.22

14.9.3   Activity parameters

> Activity parameters are object nodes input to or output from an activity.

You can use object nodes to provide inputs to and outputs from activities, as illustrated in Figure 14.23. The input and output object nodes should be drawn overlapping the activity frame. Input object nodes have one or more output edges *into* the activity, and output object nodes have one or more input edges *out of* the activity.

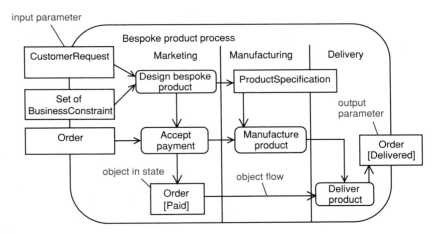

Figure 14.23

In Figure 14.23, the activity Bespoke product process has three input parameters, CustomerRequest, Set of BusinessConstraint, and Order, and one output parameter, Order. The Set of BusinessConstraint node contains a set of BusinessConstraint objects.

There are several business requirements for this process.

- Products are designed based on a CustomerRequest. This creates a ProductSpecification.

- Product design takes into account any BusinessConstraints.

- Payment is required only after the product has been designed.
- The product can't be manufactured until payment has been received and there is a ProductSpecification.
- Delivery can't occur until the product has been manufactured.

Here is a walkthrough for the activity.

1. The activity begins when there is a CustomerRequest AND a Set of Business-Constraint on the input object flows of the Design bespoke product action. This action consumes its input objects and outputs a ProductSpecification object.

2. When the Accept Payment action receives a control token from Design bespoke product AND is offered an Order object on its input object flow it executes. It changes the state of the Order object to Paid and outputs it on its single output object flow.

3. Flow of control then passes to the Manufacture product action. This consumes the ProductSpecification object output by Design bespoke product and offers a control token to Deliver product.

4. Deliver product executes when a control token is available from Manufacture product AND an Order object in the state Paid is available on its input object flow. It outputs the Order object in the state Delivered. This Order object is the output parameter of the activity.

You can see that we have been able to satisfy the business requirements quite easily as follows.

- We don't Design bespoke product until we have a CustomerRequest AND a Set of BusinessConstraint.
- We can't Accept payment until we have an Order object AND the Design bespoke product action has finished.
- We can't Manufacture product until we have a ProductSpecification AND the Accept payment action has finished (in other words, we won't manufacture it until it has been paid for!).
- We can't Deliver product until it has been manufactured (Manufacture product has finished) AND it has been paid for (Order is in state Paid).

This illustrates some of the power of activity diagrams. They can model complex processes in a concise and accurate way.

14.10 Pins

An activity that has a lot of object flows can get very messy. You can use pins to clean things up a bit!

A pin is an object node that represents one input to or output from an action.

A pin is simply an object node that represents one input to or output from an action. Input pins have exactly one input edge, and output pins have exactly one output edge. Apart from this, they have the same semantics and syntax as object nodes. However, because they are so small, you have to write all the information, such as the classifier name, outside the pin but as close to it as you can.

Figure 14.24 shows a Log on activity that has two object flows. The activity begins with the Get UserName action. This outputs a valid UserName object. The next action is Get Password, which outputs a valid Password object. The activity Authenticate User executes when it receives a valid UserName and a valid Password in its input object flows. The user is authenticated, and the activity finishes.

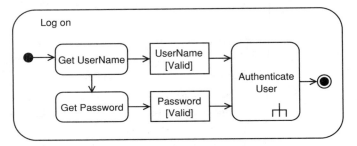

Figure 14.24

Figure 14.25 shows exactly the same activity, but drawn using pins. You can see that the pin notation is more compact and keeps the diagram a bit neater.

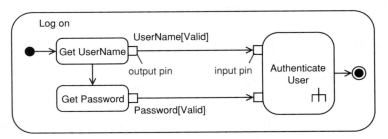

Figure 14.25

Comparing Figure 14.24 and Figure 14.25, you can see that the UserName object node is exactly equivalent to the combination of the output pin on Get UserName and the input pin on Authenticate User. Because of this, an object node is sometimes referred to as a *stand-alone style pin*.

14.11   What we have learned

In this chapter, you have seen that you can use activity diagrams to model many different kinds of processes. You have learned the following.

- Activity diagrams are OO flowcharts:
  — you use them to model all types of processes;
  — you can attach activity diagrams to *any* modeling element to capture its behavior;
  — a good activity diagram communicates one specific aspect of a system's behavior;
  — in UML 2, activity diagrams have Petri Net semantics.
- Activities are networks of nodes connected by edges.
  — Categories of nodes:
    – action nodes – atomic units of work within the activity;
    – control nodes – control the flow through the activity;
    – object nodes – represent objects used in the activity.
  — Categories of edges:
    – control flows – represent the flow of control though the activity;
    – object flows – represent the flow of objects through the activity.
  — Tokens flow around the network and can represent:
    – the flow of control;
    – an object;
    – some data.
  — Tokens move from a source node to a target node across an edge depending on:
    – source node postconditions;
    – edge guard conditions;
    – target preconditions.
  — Activities can have preconditions and postconditions.
- Action nodes.
  — Execute when there is a token simultaneously on each of their input edges AND their preconditions are satisfied.
  — After execution, action nodes offer tokens *simultaneously* on all output edges whose postconditions are satisfied:
    – an implicit fork.
  — Call action node:
    – call an activity – use the rake symbol;
    – call a behavior;
    – call an operation.
  — Send signal action node – see Section 15.6.
  — Accept event action node – see Section 15.6.

— Accept time event action node – executes when its time expression is true:
  - an event in time (e.g., end of business year);
  - a point in time (e.g., on 11/03/1960);
  - a duration (e.g., wait 10 seconds).

- Control nodes:
  — initial node – indicates where the flow starts when an activity is invoked;
  — activity final node – terminates an activity;
  — flow final node – terminates a specific flow within an activity;
  — decision node – the output edge whose guard condition is true is traversed:
    - may have a «decisionInput»;
  — merge node – copies input tokens to its single output edge;
  — fork node – splits the flow into multiple concurrent flows;
  — join node – synchronizes multiple concurrent flows:
    - may have a {join spec}.

- Activity partitions – a high-level grouping of related actions.
  — Partitions form a hierarchy rooted in a dimension.

- Object nodes represent instances of a classifier.
  — Input and output edges are object flows – represent the movement of objects.
  — Object node output edges compete for each output token.
  — Object nodes act as buffers:
    - { upperBound = n };
    - { ordering = FIFO } XOR { ordering = LIFO };
    - { ordering = FIFO } is the default;
    - may have a «selection».
  — Object nodes can represent objects in a particular state:
    - must be consistent with state machine.
  — Activity parameters are object nodes input to or output from an activity:
    - drawn overlapping the activity frame;
    - input parameters have one or more output edges *into* the activity;
    - output parameters have one or more input edges *out of* the activity.

- Pins.
  — An object node that represents one input to or output from an action or activity.

chapter 15

Advanced activity diagrams

15.1 Chapter roadmap

In this section we look at some of the more advanced features of activity diagrams. These are features that you are unlikely to use every day but that can be very useful in certain modeling situations. The sections in this chapter can be read in any order. Alternatively, you could just skim this chapter to get an idea of what's in it, then refer to the appropriate section when you need to use a specific feature.

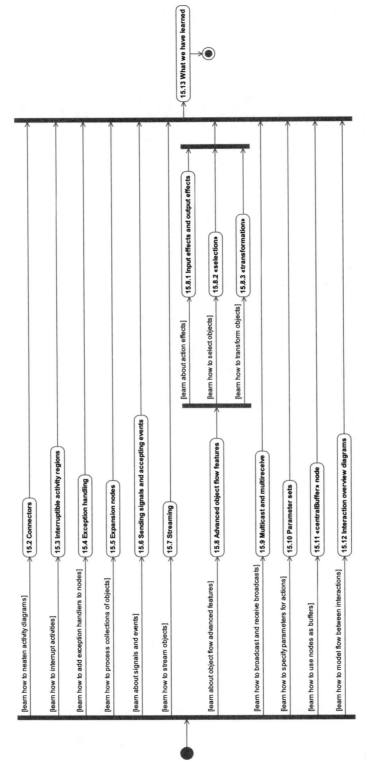

Figure 15.1

310

15.2   Connectors

Connectors can break long edges that are hard to follow and untangle edges that cross.

As a general principle, you should avoid using connectors. However, should you encounter irreducible complexity, you can use connectors to break long edges that are hard to follow or to untangle edges that cross. This can simplify an activity diagram and make it easier to read.

Connector syntax is shown in Figure 15.2. For a given activity, each outgoing connector *must* have exactly one incoming connector with the same label. Labels are merely identifiers for the connector and have no other semantics. They are often just letters of the alphabet.

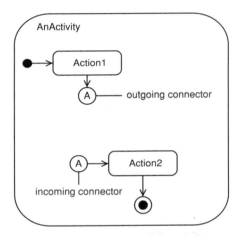

Figure 15.2

15.3   Interruptible activity regions

Interruptible regions – regions of an activity that are interrupted when a token traverses an interrupting edge.

Interruptible activity regions are regions of an activity that are interrupted when a token traverses an interrupting edge. When the region is interrupted, all flows within the region are immediately aborted. Interruptible activity regions give you a useful way of modeling interrupts and asynchronous events. They are most often used in design but can also be used to advantage in analysis to show handling of asynchronous business events.

Figure 15.3 shows a simple Log on activity that has an interruptible region. The region is shown as a dashed rounded rectangle that encloses the actions Get UserName, Get Password, and Cancel. If the Cancel accept event action gets a Cancel event while control is in the region, it outputs a token on an interrupting edge and interrupts the region. The Get UserName, Get Password, and Cancel actions all terminate.

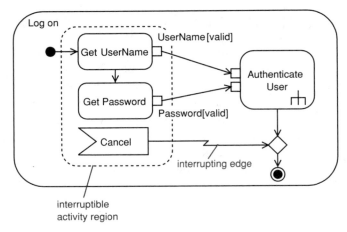

Figure 15.3

Interrupting edges are drawn as a zigzag arrow as shown in Figure 15.3, or as a normal arrow with a zigzag icon drawn above it as shown in Figure 15.4.

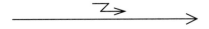

Figure 15.4

15.4   Exception handling

Modern computer languages often handle errors through a mechanism called *exception handling.* If an error is detected in a protected piece of code, an exception object is created and flow of control jumps to an exception handler that processes the exception object in some way. The exception object contains information about the error that may be used by the exception handler. The exception handler may terminate the application or try to make a recovery. The information in the exception object is often saved to an error log.

You can model this exception handling in activity diagrams by using exception pins, protected nodes, and exception handlers.

In Figure 15.5 we have updated our Log on activity to make the Authenticate User activity output a LogOnException object if the user can't be authenticated. This object is consumed by the action Log error that writes the error information to an error log. You can show that a pin represents the output of an exception object by annotating it with a small equilateral triangle as shown in the figure. The Log error node acts as an exception handler that processes

A protected node has an exception handler.

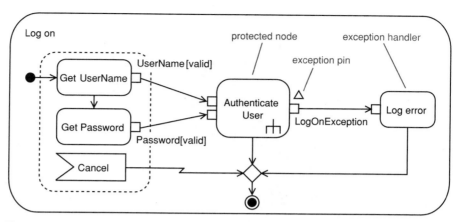

Figure 15.5

exceptions generated by Authenticate User. When a node has an associated exception handler, it is known as a protected node.

As exception handling is often a design issue rather than an analysis issue, you tend to use protected nodes more in design than in analysis. However, it can sometimes be useful to model a protected node in analysis if it has important business semantics.

15.5   Expansion nodes

Expansion nodes allow you to show how a collection of objects is processed by a part of the activity diagram called an *expansion region*. This can be a useful technique in both analysis and design as it can otherwise be quite difficult and verbose to show how a collection is processed.

An expansion node is an object node that represents a collection of objects flowing into or out of an expansion region. The expansion region is executed once per input element. Figure 15.6 shows an example of an expansion region, shown as a dashed rounded rectangle, with input and output expansion nodes. An expansion node looks like a pin, but with three boxes. This representation is to indicate that it accepts a collection rather than a single object.

There are two constraints on expansion nodes.

> Expansion node – a collection of objects flowing into or out of an expansion region that is executed once for each object.

- The type of the output collection *must* match the type of the input collection.

- The type of object held in the input and output collections *must* be the same.

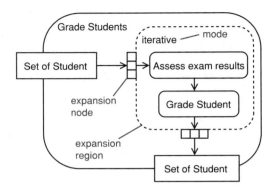

Figure 15.6

These constraints mean that expansion regions can't be used to transform input objects of one type into output objects of another type.

The number of output collections can be different from the number of input collections, so expansion regions can be used to combine or split collections.

Every expansion region has a mode that determines the order in which it processes the elements of its input collection. The mode can be

- iterative – process each element of the input collection sequentially;
- parallel – process each element of the input collection in parallel;
- stream – process each element of the input collection as it arrives at the node.

You must always explicitly specify the mode as the UML specification doesn't define any default mode.

In Figure 15.6 the expansion region accepts a set of Student objects. It processes each of these objects in turn (mode = iterative) and outputs a set of processed Student objects. The two actions inside the region first assess a Student's exam results and then assign a grade. In this case, the output Set of Student is only offered at the output expansion node when *all* Students have been processed. If, however, the mode was stream, then each Student object would be offered at the output expansion node as soon as it was processed.

15.6   Sending signals and accepting events

A signal represents information that is passed asynchronously between objects. A signal is modeled as a class stereotyped «signal». The information to be passed is held in the attributes of the signal. You can use signals in analysis to show sending and receiving of asynchronous business events (such as

> Signals represent information that is passed asynchronously between objects.

OrderReceived), and you can use them in design to illustrate asynchronous communication between different systems, subsystems, or pieces of hardware.

Figure 15.7 shows two signals that are used in the activity shown in Figure 15.8.

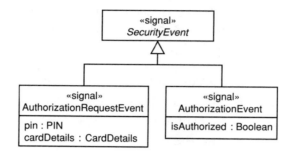

Figure 15.7

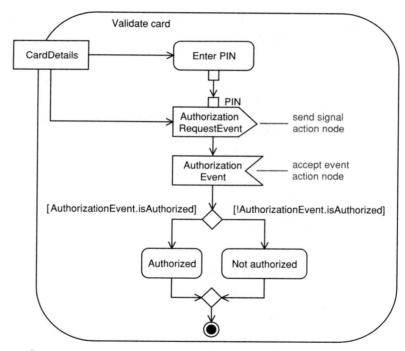

Figure 15.8

These two signals are both types of *SecurityEvent*. The AuthorizationRequest-Event signal holds a PIN and card details. These are probably encrypted. The AuthorizationEvent holds a Boolean flag to indicate whether the card and PIN have been authorized.

You can send a signal by using a send signal action node. This sends the signal asynchronously—the sending activity *does not* wait for confirmation of signal receipt. The semantics of the send signal action are as follows.

- The send signal action is started when there is a token simultaneously on *all* of its input edges. If the signal has input pins, it must receive an input object of the right type for each of its attributes.

- When the action executes, a signal object is constructed and sent. The target object is not usually specified, but if you need to specify it, you can pass it into the send signal action on an input pin.

- The sending action does not wait for confirmation of signal receipt—it is asynchronous.

- The action ends and control tokens are offered on its output edges.

An accept event action node has zero or one input edges. It waits for asynchronous events detected by its owning context and offers them on its single output edge. It has the following semantics.

- The accept event action is started by an incoming control edge, or, if it has no incoming edge, it is started when its owning activity starts.

- The action waits for receipt of an event of the specified type. This event is known as the *trigger*.

- When the action receives an event trigger of the right type, it outputs a token that describes the event. If the event was a signal event, the token is a signal.

- The action continues to accept events while the activity executes.

Figure 15.8 shows a Validate card activity that sends AuthorizationRequestEvents and receives AuthorizationEvents.

Here is a walkthrough for the Validate card activity.

1. The Validate card activity begins when it gets CardDetails as an input parameter. It then prompts the user to Enter PIN.

2. The AuthorizationRequestEvent action executes once it gets a PIN object and a CardDetails object on its input edges. It constructs an AuthorizationRequestEvent signal, using these input parameters, and sends it. Signal send actions are represented as convex pentagons as shown in the figure.

3. Signal sends are asynchronous and flow of control progresses immediately to the AuthorizationEvent accept event action, which is represented as a concave pentagon. This action waits for receipt of an AuthorizationEvent signal.

4. On receipt of the signal, flow moves to the decision node. If AuthorizationEvent.isAuthorized is true, the Authorized action executes, else the Not authorized action executes.

Here is another example of accept event actions. Figure 15.9 models a Show news activity that has two accept event actions that start automatically when the activity starts. When the NewsEvent accept event action receives a NewsEvent, this event is passed to the action Display news. Control then flows to a flow final node and this particular flow terminates. The activity continues to execute, however, and both accept event actions continue waiting for events. When the activity gets a TerminateEvent, control then moves to an activity final node and the whole activity, including both accept event actions, terminates immediately.

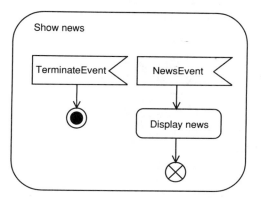

Figure 15.9

Should you need to show how signals move around activity diagrams, you can represent them as object nodes. Although signals have the same semantics as other object nodes, they have a special syntax. This is shown in Figure 15.10. The symbol is a combination of those for the send signal action and the accept event action, so it is easy to remember.

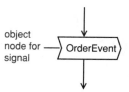

Figure 15.10

15.7 Streaming

Actions normally only take tokens off their input edges when they start executing, and offer them to their output edges when they have finished. However,

> Streaming – an action executes continuously while accepting and offering tokens.

sometimes you need an action to execute *continuously* while periodically accepting and offering tokens. This behavior is called streaming, and in UML 2, you can illustrate it in any of the four ways shown in Figure 15.11.

In fact, we think this is too many ways to represent streaming, and we recommend that you decide on just one way and stick with it, unless you have a compelling reason to do otherwise. Option 1 is the most concise option—pins filled with black—and it is the one that we recommend.

The example in Figure 15.11 illustrates a typical use of streaming. The Read mouse port action *continuously* reads the mouse port and offers information about mouse activity as MouseEvents streamed on its single output edge. These MouseEvents are consumed by the Handle MouseEvent action.

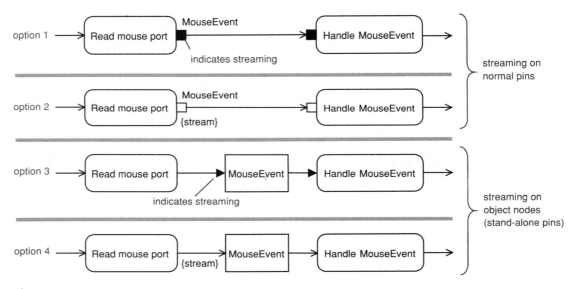

Figure 15.11

Any situation in which you need to *continuously* receive and process information is a good candidate for streaming.

15.8   Advanced object flow features

In this section we look at some advanced features of object flows. You probably won't need to use these features very often, but it's nice to know about them in case you do!

We have summarized these features in Figure 15.12.

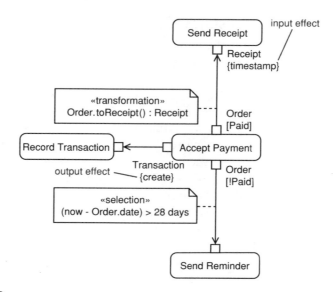

Figure 15.12

15.8.1   Input effects and output effects

> Input and output effects show the effects an action has on its input and output objects.

Input effects and output effects show the effect an action has on the objects that it inputs or outputs. You show these effects by putting a short description of the effect in braces as near to the input or output pin as you can.

There is an example of an input effect near the Send Receipt action in Figure 15.12. This effect specifies that the Send Receipt action timestamps each Receipt it receives. The Accept Payment action has an output effect, {create}. This indicates that Accept Payment creates each Transaction object that it outputs.

15.8.2   «selection»

> A selection is a condition on an object flow that causes it to accept only those objects that satisfy the condition.

A selection is a condition attached to an object flow that causes it to accept only those objects that satisfy the condition. The selection condition is shown in a note stereotyped «selection».

In Figure 15.12, you can see a selection attached to the object flow between Accept Payment and Send Reminder. The selection condition is (now - Order.date) > 28 days. The output pin on Accept Payment offers Order objects that are in the state !Paid and the selection accepts only those Order objects that have been outstanding for more than 28 days. The net effect of this flow is to select all unpaid Orders that have been outstanding for longer than 28 days and pass them to the Send Reminder action.

15.8.3   «transformation»

A transformation transforms objects in an object flow to objects of a different type. The transformation expression is shown in a note stereotyped «transformation».

In Figure 15.12, you can see a transformation attached to the object flow between Accept Payment and Send Receipt. This transformation specifies that the Order objects output by Accept Payment will be transformed into the Receipt objects expected by Send Receipt. In this example, the transformation is accomplished by invoking the toReceipt() operation on each Order object as it traverses the edge. This operation takes the information in the Order and creates a Receipt object.

You use transformations when you need to connect an output pin for instances of one classifier to an input pin that expects instances of a different classifier.

> A transforma tion transforms objects in an object flow to a different type.

15.9   Multicast and multireceive

Usually an object is sent to exactly one receiver. However, sometimes you need to show that an object is sent to multiple receivers. This is called a *multicast*. Similarly, you might need to show that objects are received from multiple senders—this is called a *multireceive*. Multicast and multireceive often occur in symmetrical pairs as shown in Figure 15.13.

> Multicast sends an object to many receivers.

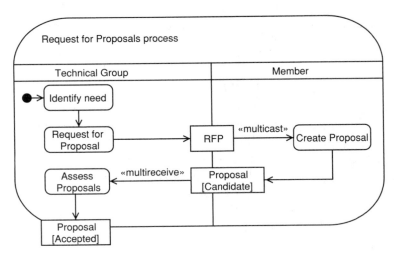

Figure 15.13

Multireceive receives objects from many senders.

To indicate that an object flow originates from a multicast or arises from a multireceive, you stereotype the flow as illustrated in Figure 15.13. This figure shows a simple business process similar to the one the OMG uses for requesting proposals for their standards. The Technical Group first identifies the need for a solution and then formulates this into a RFP (Request For Proposal). This is multicast to many Members who create candidate Proposals. These are multireceived by the Technical Group, which assesses them and finally outputs an Accepted Proposal.

15.10   Parameter sets

Parameter sets allow an action to have alternative sets of input and output pins.

Parameter sets allow an action to have *alternative sets* of input and output pins. These sets of pins are called *parameter sets*. Input parameter sets contain input pins and output parameter sets contain output pins. You *can't* have a mixed set of input and output pins.

To illustrate why you might want to use parameter sets, consider Figure 15.14. In this figure there are three types of authentication action.

1. Get UserName and Password – outputs a UserName and a Password object.
2. Get UserName and Passphrase – outputs a UserName and a Passphrase object.
3. Get Card and PIN – outputs a Card and a PIN object.

As you can see, each of these actions outputs a different set of objects. One solution to this problem would be to have a separate authenticate action

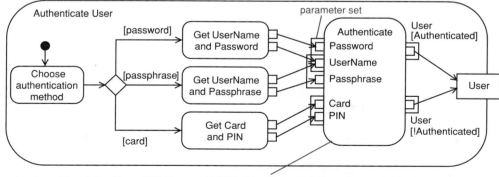

input condition: (UserName AND Password) XOR (UserName AND Passphrase) XOR (Card AND PIN)
output: (User [Authenticated]) XOR (User [!Authenticated])

Figure 15.14

for each set of objects such as AuthenticateUserNameAndPassword, AuthenticateUser-NameAndPassphrase, and AuthenticateCardAndPIN. This is a reasonable solution, but it does have a couple of drawbacks.

- It makes the activity diagram quite verbose.
- Authentication is now distributed over three actions rather than being localized in one place.

Using parameter sets you can create a *single* Authenticate action that can handle the three different sets of input parameters.

In Figure 15.14, you can see that Authenticate has three input parameter sets and two output parameter sets. The input parameter sets are

- UserName AND Password;
- UserName AND Passphrase;
- Card AND PIN.

One and only one of these input parameter sets may be used per execution of the action. There is therefore an XOR relationship between them.

Notice that the sets {UserName, Password} and {UserName, Passphrase} have the UserName pin in common. As the figure shows, you can indicate this by overlapping the two parameter sets so that common pins are in the overlap region. However, this idiom can easily get quite messy, so you might choose instead to have two UserName pins, one in each of the input parameter sets. We prefer the latter solution, and the diagram is as it is merely to illustrate the syntax for overlapping pins should you wish to use them.

The Authenticate action has the following output parameter sets, each of which contains a single pin:

- User[Authenticated];
- User[!Authenticated].

Again, only one of these output parameter sets will be used per execution of the activity.

15.11   «centralBuffer» node

As we mentioned in Section 14.9.1, all object nodes have buffering capability.

Central buffer nodes are object nodes that are used *specifically* as buffers between input and output object flows. They allow you to combine multiple input object flows and to distribute the objects among multiple output object flows. When an object node is being used as a central buffer, it should be given the stereotype «centralBuffer».

Central buffer nodes are object nodes that are used *specifically* as buffers.

Figure 15.15 shows a simple example in which a central buffer is used to accumulate different types of Order object streaming in from multiple sales channels. The Order objects are held in the buffer while waiting for the Process Order action to accept them. The Order central buffer can hold objects of type Order or its subclasses WebOrder, PhoneOrder, and PostOrder.

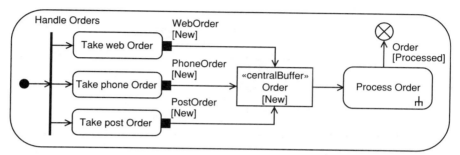

Figure 15.15

15.12 Interaction overview diagrams

Interaction overview diagrams are activity diagrams that show interactions and interaction occurrences.

Interaction overview diagrams, a special form of an activity diagram, show interactions and interaction occurrences. They are used to model the high-level flow of control between interactions. We discuss interactions and inter-action diagrams in detail in Chapter 12.

One particularly powerful use for interaction overview diagrams is to illustrate the flow of control between use cases. If you represent each use case as an interaction, you can use activity diagram syntax to show how flow of control moves between them.

Figure 15.16 shows an interaction overview diagram, ManageCourses, that shows the flow between the lower-level interactions LogOn, GetCourseOption, FindCourse, RemoveCourse, and AddCourse. Each of these interactions represents a use case, so the interaction overview diagram captures the flow of control between these use cases.

Note that the lifelines that participate in the interaction may be listed after the keyword lifelines in the header of the diagram. This can be useful documentation as lifelines are often hidden inside interaction occurrences.

Interaction overview diagrams have the same syntax as activity diagrams except that you show inline interactions and interaction occurrences rather than activity and object nodes. You can show branching, concurrency, and looping as described in Table 15.1. This table also provides an overview of the differences between sequence diagram and interaction overview diagram syntax.

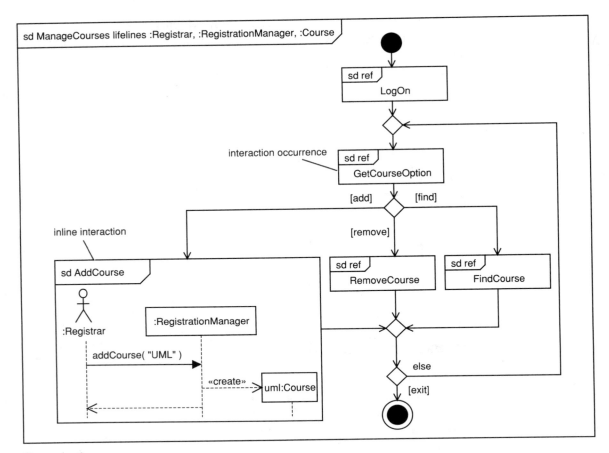

Figure 15.16

Table 15.1

Action	Sequence diagrams	Interaction overview diagram
Branching	alt and opt combined fragments (Section 12.10.1)	Decision node and merge node (Section 14.8.2)
Concurrency	par combined fragment (Section 20.5)	Fork and join nodes (Section 14.8.3)
Iteration	loop combined fragment (Section 12.11.1)	Cycles in the diagram

Sequence diagrams can do everything an interaction overview diagram can do, so you might wonder why we bother with them. The reason is that interaction overview diagrams express branching, concurrency, and iteration in a visual way that is clear and easy to read. At the same time, they de-emphasize other features, such as the lifelines, putting the focus of the diagram squarely on the flow of control. You should therefore use them when you want to emphasize flow of control across many interactions.

In use case realization, interactions express the behavior specified in a use case, so interaction overview diagrams can be used to illustrate business processes that cut across use cases.

15.13 What we have learned

In this chapter, you have seen some advanced features of activity diagrams. You have learned the following.

- Interruptible activity regions:
  - interrupted when a token traverses an interrupting edge;
  - all flows in the region are aborted when it is interrupted;
  - interrupting edges are drawn as a zigzag arrow or as a normal arrow with a zigzag icon above it.
- Exception pins:
  - output an exception object from an action;
  - are indicated with an equilateral triangle.
- Protected nodes:
  - have an interrupting edge leading to an exception handler;
  - abort when an exception of the right type is raised, and flow passes to the exception handler node;
  - are instantaneous.
- Expansion nodes:
  - represent a collection of objects flowing into or out of an expansion region;
  - the region is executed once per input element.
  - Constraints:
    - the type of the output collection *must* match the type of the input collection;
    - the type of object held in the input and output collections *must* be the same.
  - Modes:
    - iterative – process each element of the input collection sequentially;
    - parallel – process each element of the input collection in parallel;
    - stream – process each element of the input collection as it arrives at the node;
    - there is no default mode.

- Sending signals and accepting events.
  - Signals:
    - information that is passed asynchronously between objects;
    - class stereotyped «signal»;
    - the information is held in the attributes.
  - Send signal action node:
    - starts when there is a token on all input pins;
    - executes – a signal object is constructed and sent;
    - then ends and offers control tokens on its output edges.
  - Accept event action node:
    - started by an incoming control edge *or* if no incoming edge, when its owning activity starts;
    - waits for an event of the specified type:
      - outputs a token that describes the event;
      - continues to accept events while the owning activity executes;
    - for a signal event, the output token is a signal.
- Advanced object flow:
  - input and output effects show the effects an action has on its input and output objects:
    - write the effect in braces close to the pin;
  - selection – a condition on an object flow that causes it to accept only those objects that satisfy the condition:
    - put the selection condition in a note stereotyped «selection», attached to the object flow;
  - transformation – transforms objects in an object flow to a different type:
    - put the transformation expression in a note stereotyped «transformation», attached to the object flow.
- Multicast sends an object to many receivers:
  - stereotype the object flow «multicast».
- Multireceive receives objects from many senders:
  - stereotype the object flow «multireceive».
- Parameter sets allow an action to have alternative sets of input and output pins:
  - input parameter sets contain input pins;
  - output parameter sets contain output pins;
  - only one input parameter set and one output parameter set may be used per execution of the action.
- Central buffer node – object nodes that are used specifically as buffers:
  - stereotype the object node «centralBuffer».

- Interaction overview diagrams show flow between interactions and interaction occurrences:
  — branching – decision and merge nodes;
  — concurrency – fork and join nodes;
  — iteration – cycles in the diagram.

part **4**

Design

chapter 16

The design workflow

16.1 Chapter roadmap

This chapter is about the UP design workflow. One of the main issues we consider is how the analysis model evolves into the design model, and whether or not you need to maintain the analysis and design models separately—we discuss this important topic in Section 16.3.2. The rest of the chapter is about the design workflow detail and artifacts.

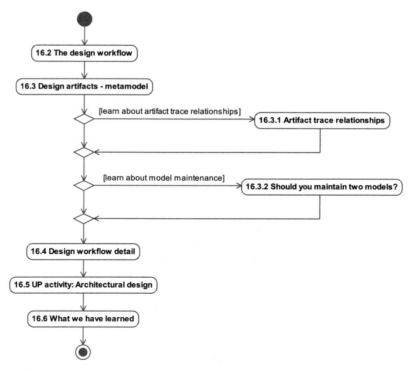

Figure 16.1

16.2   The design workflow

The design workflow is the primary modeling activity during the last part of the Elaboration phase and the first half of the Construction phase. As you can see from Figure 16.2, the main focus of the early iterations is requirements and analysis, and as the analysis activity becomes more and more complete, the modeling focus shifts to design. To a great extent, analysis and design can occur in parallel. However, as you will see, it is important to distinguish clearly between the artifacts of these two workflows—the analysis model and the design model.

> Most design work is done as you move from the Elaboration to the Construction phase.

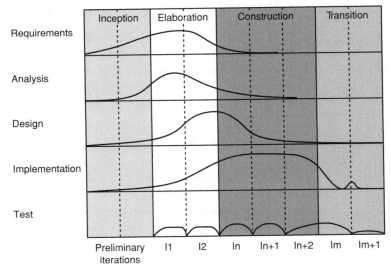

Figure 16.2   Adapted from Figure 1.5 [Jacobson 1] with permission from Addison-Wesley

Rather than have a team of analysts and a separate team of designers, UP recommends that one team be responsible for taking an artifact (such as a use case) from requirements through analysis and design, and ultimately to implementation. Instead of organizing the team around specific activities, UP organizes the team around deliverables and milestones. UP provides a "goal" focus rather than a "task" focus.

In analysis, the focus was on creating a logical model of the system that captured the functionality that the system must provide to satisfy the user requirements. The purpose in design is to specify fully how this functionality will be implemented. One way of looking at this is to consider the problem domain on the one hand and the solution domain on the other. Requirements come from the problem domain, and you can think of analysis as being the exploration of this domain from the point of view of the system stakeholders. Design involves merging in technical solutions from the solution domain (class libraries, persistence mechanisms, etc.) to provide a model of the system (the design model) that can actually be implemented.

In design, OO designers decide on strategic design issues such as object persistence and distribution, and create a design model accordingly. The project manager and architect should also create policies to deal with any tactical design issues.

16.3   Design artifacts – metamodel

A subsystem is a part of the physical system.

Figure 16.3 shows a metamodel for the design model. The design model contains many design subsystems (we only show two such subsystems here). These subsystems are components (see Chapter 19) that can contain many different types of modeling elements.

Although you might have identified several key interfaces in analysis, when you come to design you put much more emphasis on interfaces. This is because it is ultimately the interfaces between design subsystems that hold your system together. Interfaces, therefore, have a strong architectural role in design, and you will spend quite a lot of time looking for, and modeling, key interfaces. In the example in Figure 16.3, you can see that subsystem c1 requires interface I, and this interface is provided by subsystem c2. The provided and required interfaces connect these two subsystems like a plug and socket. We discuss interfaces in more detail in 19.

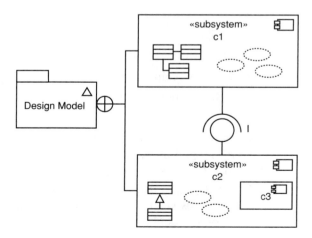

Figure 16.3

There is a simple «trace» relationship between the analysis and design models: the design model is based on the analysis model and can be considered to be just a refinement and elaboration thereof (this is shown in Figure 16.4).

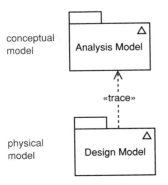

Figure 16.4

You can think of the design model as being an elaboration of the analysis model with added detail and specific technical solutions. The design model contains the same sorts of things as the analysis model, but all the artifacts are more fully formed and must now include implementation details. For example, an analysis class may be little more than a sketch with few attributes and only key operations. A design class, however, must be fully specified—all attributes and operations (including return types and parameter lists) must be complete.

Design models are made up of

- design subsystems;
- design classes;
- interfaces;
- use case realizations–design;
- a deployment diagram.

One of the key artifacts that you produce in design are interfaces. You will see in 19 that these allow you to decouple your system into subsystems that can be developed in parallel.

In design, you also produce a first-cut deployment diagram that shows how your software system is distributed over physical computational nodes. Clearly, this is an important and strategic diagram. However, as most of the work on the deployment diagram occurs in implementation, we defer discussion of them until 24.

16.3.1   Artifact trace relationships

Figure 16.5 shows the relationships between the key analysis and design artifacts.

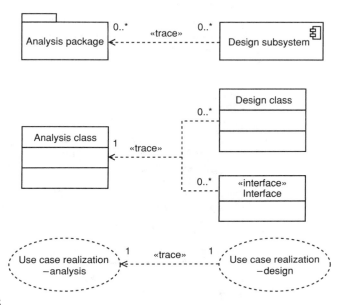

Figure 16.5

The relationship between analysis packages and design subsystems can be complex. Sometimes, one analysis package will «trace» to one design subsystem, but this isn't always the case. You might have good architectural and technical reasons for breaking down a single analysis package into more than one subsystem. In component-based development, a design subsystem represents a single coarse-grained component, and in this case, depending on the desired granularity of the components, you may find that one analysis package actually resolves to several subsystems.

An analysis class may be resolved into one or more interfaces or design classes. This is because analysis classes are a high-level conceptual view of the classes in the system. When we get down to physical modeling (design), these conceptual classes may well need to be implemented as one or more physical design classes and/or interfaces.

The Use case realization–analysis has a simple one-to-one «trace» relationship with Use case realization–design. In design, the use case realization simply has more detail.

16.3.2   Should you maintain two models?

In an ideal world, you would have a single model of your system, and your modeling tool would be able to give either an analysis view of that model or a design view. However, this is a more difficult requirement than it at first appears, and no UML modeling tool currently on the market does an entirely satisfactory job of providing analysis and design views of the same underlying model. It seems that we are left with the four strategies described in Table 16.1.

Table 16.1

Strategy	Consequences
1 Take the analysis model and refine it into a design model	You have a single design model, but you have lost the analysis view
2 Take the analysis model, refine it into a design model and use a modeling tool to recover an "analysis view"	You have a single design model, but the analysis view recovered by the modeling tool might not be satisfactory
3 Freeze the analysis model at some point in the Elaboration phase – refine a copy of the analysis model into a design model	You have two models, but they are out of step
4 Maintain two separate models – an analysis model and a design model	You have two models – they are in step, but there is a maintenance burden

There is no best strategy—it depends on your project. However, the fundamental question you need to ask is, "Do we need to preserve an analysis view of the system?" Analysis views give you the "big picture" of your system. An analysis view may only have between 1% and 10% of the classes that are in the detailed design view, and they are therefore much more understandable. They are invaluable for

Keep an analysis model for large, complex, or strategic systems.

- introducing new people to the project;
- understanding the system months or years after delivery;
- understanding how the system satisfies user requirements;
- providing requirements traceability;

- planning maintenance and enhancements;
- understanding the logical architecture of the system;
- outsourcing the construction of the system.

If you need to do any of the above, you definitely need to preserve an analysis view. Typically, you should preserve an analysis view for any system that is large, complex, strategic, or potentially long-lived. This means that you need to choose between strategies 3 and 4. Always think very carefully about allowing the analysis and design models to get out of step. Is this really acceptable to your project?

If your system is small (say, less than 200 design classes) then the design model itself is small enough to be understandable, so a separate analysis model may not be needed. Also, if the system is not strategic or has a short projected life span, separate analysis and design models may be overkill. Your choice is then between strategies 1 and 2, and the deciding factor will be the capabilities of your UML modeling tool. Some modeling tools maintain a single underlying model and allow filtering and information-hiding to try to recover an "analysis" view from the design model. This is a reasonable halfway house for many medium-sized systems, but it is probably still not good enough for very large systems.

Finally, a word of caution—it is wise to remember that many systems long outlive their projected life span!

16.4 Design workflow detail

The UP workflow for design is shown in Figure 16.6. The main participants in design are the architect, the use case engineer, and the component engineer. In most OO projects, one or more dedicated individuals perform the architect role, but it is often the same individual who will act as use case engineer and component engineer at different points in time.

One of the UP goals is that individuals take ownership and responsibility for part of the system right through from analysis to implementation. Thus, the individual or team responsible for creating a particular piece of OO analysis will often refine this into a design and, perhaps with some extra programming expertise mixed into the team, into code. The advantage of this approach is that it prevents "passing the buck" between analysts, designers, and programmers—this can be common in OO projects.

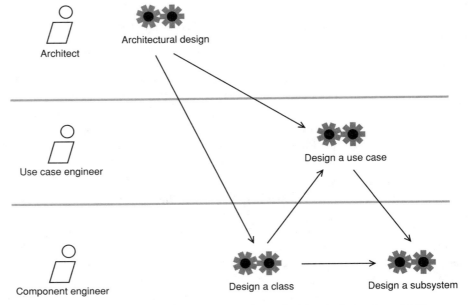

Figure 16.6   Reproduced from Figure 9.16 [Jacobson 1] with permission from Addison-Wesley

16.5   UP activity: Architectural design

In UP, the activity that kicks off the whole design process is Architectural design. This activity is performed by one or more architects. You can see the details for this activity in Figure 16.7.

As you can see, there are a lot of artifacts output from Architectural design, and we look at each of these in detail—what they are, how you find them—in the subsequent chapters in this part of the book (the grayed artifacts are modified from the original figure). The key thing to understand is that architectural design is about outlining the architecturally significant artifacts to give a big picture of the system architecture. These outlined artifacts provide inputs to more detailed design activities in which they are fleshed out.

Architectural design is not usually a separate step. Remember that UP is an iterative process, so this design occurs *throughout* the late Elaboration and early Construction phases as the details of the system architecture are developed.

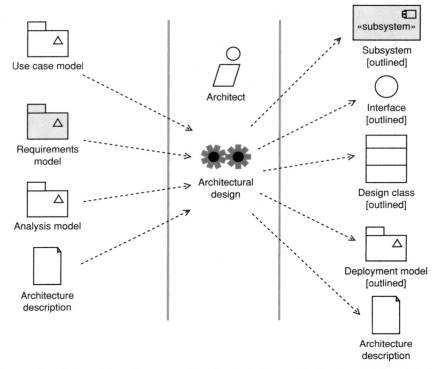

Figure 16.7   Adapted from Figure 9.17 [Jacobson 1] with permission from Addison-Wesley

16.6   What we have learned

The design workflow is about determining how the functionality specified in the analysis model will be implemented. You have learned the following.

- The design workflow is the primary modeling activity in the last part of the Elaboration phase and the first part of the Construction phase.
  - Analysis and design can occur in parallel to some extent.
  - One team should take an artifact through analysis into design.
  - OO designers should focus on strategic design issues such as distributed component architectures – policies and standards should be introduced to deal with tactical design issues.

- The design model contains:
  - design subsystems;
  - design classes;

      — interfaces;
      — use case realizations–design;
      — a deployment diagram (first-cut).

- There are trace relationships between:
  - the design model and analysis model;
  - one or more design subsystems and an analysis package.

- Maintain separate analysis and design models if the system is:
  - large;
  - complex;
  - strategic;
  - subject to frequent change;
  - expected to be long-lived;
  - outsourced.

- The UP activity Architectural design is an iterative process that occurs through-out the late Elaboration and early Construction phases:
  - it creates outlined artifacts that are then fleshed out.

chapter 17
Design classes

17.1 Chapter roadmap

This chapter is about design classes. These are the building blocks of the design model, and it is vital for you, as an OO designer, to understand how to model these classes effectively.

After providing the UP context, we describe the anatomy of a design class and then, in Section 17.5, move on to a consideration of what makes a well-formed design class. We discuss the requirements of completeness and sufficiency, primitiveness, high cohesion, low coupling, and the applicability of aggregation versus inheritance.

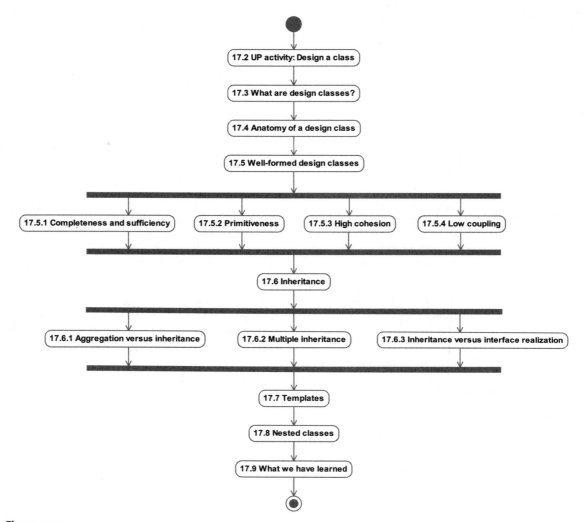

Figure 17.1

17.2   UP activity: Design a class

In the UP design workflow detail (Figure 16.6) after Architectural design, the next activities are Design a class and Design a use case (see Section 20.2). These two activities occur concurrently and iteratively.

In this section we look at the UP activity Design a class. This activity is shown in Figure 17.2. We have extended the activity to show interface [complete] as an explicit output of Design a class. The artifact is grayed to show it is a modification; in the original description of the activity it was an implicit output.

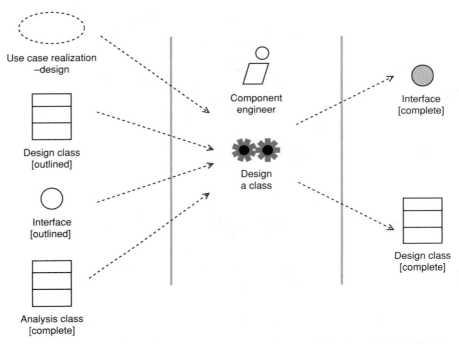

Figure 17.2   Adapted from Figure 9.39 [Jacobson 1] with permission from Addison-Wesley

You have seen how to create the analysis class [complete] input artifact in the analysis part of this book, and so we say no more about it here.

It's worth considering the design class [outlined] artifact in some depth. It looks from the activity as though there are two separate and distinct artifacts, the design class [outlined] and the design class [complete]. However, this is *not* the case. These two artifacts merely represent the same artifact (a design class) in different stages in its evolution.

If you take a snapshot of the artifacts of a UP project in late Elaboration or early Construction, you will not find artifacts labeled design class [outlined] or design class [complete]. Rather, there will just be design classes, and each of these will be at a different stage in its development.

A "complete" design class from the UP perspective is one that is suffi-ciently detailed to serve as a good basis for creating source code. This is a key point, and one that novice modelers often miss. Design classes only need to be modeled in sufficient detail that code can be developed from them, so they are rarely modeled exhaustively. The necessary level of detail depends on your project. If you are going to generate code directly from the model, your design classes will have to be modeled in great detail. On the other hand, if they are merely going to serve as a blueprint for programmers, they can be modeled in less detail. In this chapter we show you how to model design classes in sufficient detail for any project.

The considerations for design class [outlined] and design class [complete] also apply for interface [outlined] and interface [complete].

The use case realization–design input artifact is just a use case realization at a late point in its life cycle. Although it is shown flowing into Design a class, it actually includes design classes as part of its structure and is developed in parallel with them. We defer discussion of use case realizations–design until Chapter 20 because we find it more effective (and easier on the reader) to discuss their component parts first.

17.3   What are design classes?

Design classes are classes whose specifications have been completed to such a degree that they can be implemented.

In analysis, the source of classes is the problem domain. This is the set of requirements that describes the problem you are trying to solve. You have seen that use cases, requirements specifications, glossaries, and any other pertinent information can be used as a source of analysis classes.

Design classes come from two places.

Design classes come from the problem domain and the solution domain.

- The problem domain via a refinement of analysis classes – this refinement involves adding implementation details. As you do this, you often find that you need to break a very high level analysis class into two or more detailed design classes. There is a «trace» relationship between an analysis class and the one or more design classes that describe its implementation.

- The solution domain – the solution domain is the realm of utility class libraries and reusable components such as Time, Date, String, collections, etc. Middleware, such as communications middleware, databases (both relational and object), and component frameworks, such as .NET, CORBA, or Enterprise JavaBeans, live here as well. The solution domain also contains GUI frameworks. This domain provides the technical tools that allow you to implement a system.

This is illustrated in Figure 17.3.

Analysis is about modeling *what* the system should do. Design is about modeling *how* that behavior may be implemented.

Why may an analysis class refine into one or more design classes or interfaces? Well, an analysis class is specified at a very high level of abstraction. You don't bother with the complete set of attributes, and the set of operations is really only a sketch that captures the key services offered by the class.

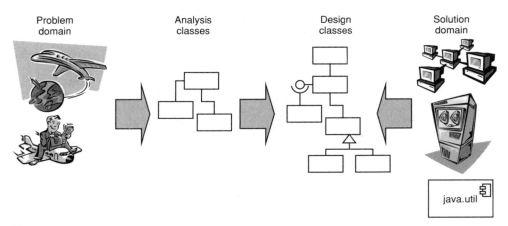

Figure 17.3

When you move this class into design, you must fully specify all of the operations and attributes, so it is quite common to find that the class has become too large. If this happens, you should break it down into two or more smaller classes. Remember that you should always be trying to design classes that are small, self-contained, cohesive units that do one or two things really well. You must avoid, at all costs, the large "Swiss Army Knife" type of class that tries to do everything.

Your chosen method of implementation determines the degree of completeness you need in the design class specifications. If the design class model will be given to programmers who will use it primarily as a guide for writing code, then the design classes only need to be complete enough to enable them to perform that task efficiently. This depends on how skilled the programmers are and how well they understand the problem and solution domains—you need to find this out for your particular project.

If, however, you intend to generate code from the design classes with a suitably equipped modeling tool, the design class specifications must be complete in all respects since a generator, unlike a programmer, can't fill in the gaps. Throughout the rest of this chapter, we assume you need a very high degree of completeness.

17.4   Anatomy of a design class

With analysis classes, you are trying to capture the required behavior of the system without worrying about how this behavior is going to be implemented.

With design classes, you have to specify exactly how each class will fulfill its responsibilities. To do this, you must do the following:

- complete the set of attributes and fully specify them including name, type, visibility, and (optionally) a default value;

- complete the set of operations and fully specify them including name, parameter list, and return type.

This process of refinement is illustrated with a very simple example in Figure 17.4.

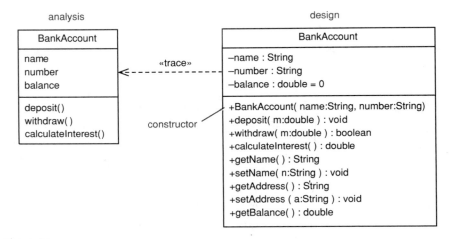

Figure 17.4

As you saw in Chapter 8, an operation in an analysis class is a high-level logical specification of a piece of functionality offered by a class. In the corresponding design classes, each analysis class operation is refined into one or more detailed and fully specified operations that can be implemented as source code. Therefore, one high-level analysis operation may actually resolve into one or more implementable design operations. These detailed design-level operations are sometimes know as methods.

To illustrate this, consider the following example. In an airline check-in system, you may specify in analysis a high-level operation called checkIn(). However, as you'll know if you have ever waited in line to check in to a flight, check-in is actually a fairly complex business process that involves collecting and verifying a certain amount of information from the passenger, taking baggage, and allocating a seat on a plane. It is reasonable, therefore, to suppose that the high-level checkIn() analysis operation will break down into a cascade of lower-level operations when you do the detailed design of the process. It might be that you still maintain a high-level checkIn() operation, but in design this operation will call a cascade of "helper" operations to discharge its responsibility. It may even be that the check-in process is sufficiently complex to require some new helper classes that were not identified in analysis.

17.5 Well-formed design classes

The design model will be passed to programmers to produce actual source code, or code may be generated directly from the model itself if the modeling tool supports this. Design classes, therefore, need to be sufficiently specified, and part of this specification process is deciding if the classes are "well formed" or not.

> Always assess a design class from the point of view of the users of that class.

When creating a design class, it is important always to look at the class from the point of view of its potential clients. How will they see the class—is it too complex? Are any bits missing? Is it highly coupled to other classes or not? Does it do what they might expect from its name? These are important considerations and may be summarized in the following four minimal characteristics that a design class must have to be considered well formed:

- complete and sufficient;
- primitive;
- high cohesion;
- low coupling.

17.5.1 Completeness and sufficiency

> The public operations of a class define a contract between the class and clients of the class.

The public operations of a class define a contract between the class and clients of that class. Just like a business contract, it is important that this contract is clear, well defined, and acceptable to all parties.

Completeness is about giving the clients of a class what they might expect. Clients will make assumptions from the class name about the set of operations that it should make available. To take a real-world example—if you buy a new car, you can reasonably expect it to have wheels! It is the same with classes—when you name a class and describe its semantics, clients of the class will infer from this information what operations should be available. For example, a BankAccount class that provides a withdraw(...) operation will also be expected to have a deposit(...) operation. Again, if you design a class such as a ProductCatalog, any client could reasonably expect this class to allow them to add, remove, and find Products in the catalog. These semantics are clearly implied just by the class name. Completeness is about making sure that the classes satisfy all reasonable client expectations.

Sufficiency, on the other hand, is making sure that all operations of the class are entirely focused on realizing the intent behind the class. A class should never surprise a client. It should contain exactly the expected set of operations and no more. For example, a typical beginner's mistake is to take a simple, sufficient class like BankAccount and then add operations to process credit cards, or manage insurance policies, etc. Sufficiency is about keeping the design class as simple and focused as possible.

The golden rule for completeness and sufficiency is that a class should do what the users of the class expect—no more and no less.

> A complete and sufficient class gives users of the class the contract they expect – no more and no less.

17.5.2   Primitiveness

Operations should be designed to offer a single primitive, atomic service. A class should *not* offer multiple ways of doing the same thing as this is confusing to clients of the class and can lead to maintenance burdens and consistency problems.

> Primitiveness – services should be simple, atomic, and unique.

For example, if a BankAccount class has a primitive operation for making a single deposit, it should *not* have a more complex operation that makes two or more deposits. This is because you can achieve the same effect by repeated application of the primitive operation. Your aim is that classes should always make available the simplest and smallest possible set of operations.

Although primitiveness is a good rule, there are occasions when it may need to be relaxed. A common reason to relax the primitiveness constraint is to improve performance. For example, if there were a sufficient performance increase on making bank deposits in a batch, rather than individually, then you might relax the primitiveness constraint in order to let a BankAccount class have a more complex deposit(...) operation that handled several transactions at once. However, your starting point in design should *always* be the most primitive possible set of operations. You should only add complexity by relaxing primitiveness if there is a genuine and proven case for doing so.

This is an important point. Many so-called design "optimizations" are based more on faith than on solid facts. As such, they may have little or no impact on the actual runtime performance of the application. For example, if an application will spend only 1% of its time in a given operation, optimization of that operation can only ever speed up the application by less than 1%. A useful rule of thumb is that most applications spend about 90% of their time in 10% of their operations. These are the operations you must identify and optimize to get real performance increases. This performance tuning can only be done by using a code profiling tool such as jMechanic for

Java (http://jmechanic.sourceforge.net) to gather performance metrics on executing code. This is clearly an implementation task that might impact the design model.

17.5.3   High cohesion

Each class should model a single abstract concept and should have a set of operations that support the intent of the class—this is cohesion. If a class needs to have many different responsibilities, you can create "helper" classes to implement some of these. The main class can then delegate responsibilities to its helpers.

Cohesion is one of the most desirable features of a class. Cohesive classes are generally easy to understand, reuse, and maintain. A cohesive class has a small set of responsibilities that are all intimately related. Every operation, attribute, and association of the class is specifically designed to implement this small, focused set of responsibilities.

We came across the perplexing model in Figure 17.5 in a selling system. There is a HotelBean class, a CarBean class, and a HotelCarBean class (the "beans" are Enterprise JavaBeans (EJBs)). The HotelBean was responsible for selling room stays in hotels, the CarBean for selling car hire, and the HotelCarBean for selling a package of car hire with a hotel stay. Clearly, this model is wrong from several perspectives.

> Each class should capture a single, well-defined abstraction, using the minimal set of features.

- The classes are badly named—HotelStay and CarHire would be much better names.
- The suffix "Bean" is unnecessary as it just refers to a specific implementation detail.
- The HotelCarBean class has very poor cohesion—it has two primary responsibilities (selling hotel stays and selling car hire) that are already carried out by two other classes.
- It is neither an analysis model (it contains design information in the "Bean" suffixes) nor a design model (it is insufficiently complete).

From a cohesion perspective, HotelBean and CarBean are quite plausible (provided they were renamed), but HotelCarBean is just absurd.

HotelBean	HotelCarBean	What's wrong with this model?

CarBean

Figure 17.5

17.5.4   Low coupling

A particular class should be associated with *just enough* other classes to allow it to realize its responsibilities and you should only associate classes if there is a genuine semantic link between them—this is low coupling.

> A class should be associated with the minimum number of other classes to allow it to fulfill its responsibilities.

One of the common mistakes of the novice OO designer is to connect everything in the model to everything else on a more or less ad hoc basis. In fact, coupling is your worst enemy in object modeling, and you must be really proactive about trying to limit the relationships between classes in order to minimize coupling as much as you can.

A highly coupled object model is the equivalent of "spaghetti code" in the non-OO world and will lead to a system that is incomprehensible and unmaintainable. You will find that highly coupled OO systems often result from projects in which there is no formal modeling activity, where the system is simply allowed to evolve in an ad hoc manner over time.

If you are a novice designer, you must be careful *not* to make connections between classes just because one class has some code that another class could use. This is the worst sort of reuse, as you sacrifice the architectural integrity of the system for a small saving in development time. In fact, you need to think very carefully about all associations between classes. Many of the associations in the design model will come directly from the analysis model, but there is a whole set of associations that are introduced by implementation constraints or by the desire to reuse code. These are the associations that you need to examine most carefully.

Of course, some coupling is good and is desirable. High coupling within a subsystem is generally OK as this indicates high cohesion within the component. You only compromise the architecture when coupling is *between* subsystems, and you must actively seek to reduce this sort of coupling.

17.6   Inheritance

When you get to design, you have to consider inheritance much more than in analysis. In analysis, you would *only* use inheritance if there were a clear and unambiguous "is a" relationship between analysis classes. In design, however, you may also choose to use inheritance in a tactical way to reuse code. This is a different strategy, as you are really using inheritance to ease the implementation of a child class rather than to express a business relationship between a parent and child.

We look at some strategies for using inheritance effectively in design in the next few sections.

17.6.1   Aggregation versus inheritance

Inheritance is a very powerful technique—it is a key mechanism for generating polymorphism in strongly typed languages such as Java, C#, and C++. However, novice OO designers and programmers often abuse it. You should realize that inheritance has certain undesirable characteristics.

> Inheritance is the strongest form of coupling between classes. It is an inflexible relationship.

- It is the strongest form of coupling possible between two or more classes.

- Encapsulation is weak within a class hierarchy. Changes in the base class ripple down to change the subclasses. This leads to what is known as the "fragile base class" problem, where changes to base classes have a large impact on other classes in the system.

- It is a very inflexible type of relationship. In all commonly used OO languages, inheritance relationships are fixed at runtime. You can modify both aggregation and composition hierarchies at runtime by creating and destroying relationships, but inheritance hierarchies remain fixed. This makes it is the most inflexible type of relationship between classes.

The example in Figure 17.6 is a typical beginner's solution to the problem of modeling roles in an organization. At first glance, it looks quite plausible, but it has problems. Consider this case: the object john is of type Programmer, and you wish to promote it to be of type Manager. How can you do this? You have seen that you can't change john's class at runtime, and so the only way you can achieve the promotion is to create a new Manager object (called john:Manager), copy all of the relevant data from the john:Programmer object, and then delete the john:Programmer object to maintain consistency in the application. This is clearly complex, and not at all how the real world works.

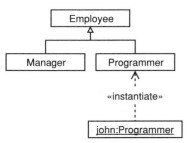

Figure 17.6

In fact, there is a fundamental semantic error in the model in Figure 17.6. Is an employee *just* his or her job, or is it rather that an employee *has* a job? This question leads us to the solution to the problem shown in Figure 17.7.

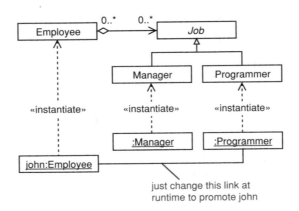

Figure 17.7

Using aggregation you get the correct semantics—an Employee *has* a *Job*. With this more flexible model, Employees can also have more than one *Job* if required.

We have achieved a much more flexible and semantically correct model by replacing inheritance with aggregation as the mechanism for assigning jobs to employees. There is an important general principle here—subclasses should always represent "is kind of", rather than "is role played by". When we think about the business semantics of companies, employees, and jobs, it is clear that a job is a *role played* by an employee and does not really indicate a *kind of* employee. As such, inheritance is definitely the wrong choice for modeling this sort of business relationship. On the other hand, there are many *kinds of* jobs in a company. This indicates that an inheritance hierarchy of jobs (rooted in the abstract base class *Job*) is probably a good model.

> Subclasses should always represent a "special kind of" rather than a "role played by".

17.6.2   Multiple inheritance

> Multiple inheritance allows a class to have more than one parent.

Sometimes you may want to inherit from more than one parent. This is multiple inheritance and it is not supported by all OO languages. For example, Java and C# only allow single inheritance. In practice, this lack of support for multiple inheritance is not a problem, as it can always be replaced by single inheritance and delegation. Even though multiple inheritance sometimes offers the most elegant solution to a design problem, it can *only* be used if the target implementation language supports it.

The important points about multiple inheritance are the following.

> Parents must be semantically disjoint.

● All the parent classes involved must be semantically disjoint. If there is any overlap in semantics between the base classes, there is the possibility of unforeseen interactions between them. This could lead to strange behavior in the subclass. We say that the base classes must all be orthogonal (at right angles to each other).

- The "is kind of" and substitutability principles must apply between the subclass and all of its superclasses.

- Typically, the superclasses should have no parent in common. Otherwise, you have a cycle in the inheritance hierarchy and there may be multiple paths whereby the same features could be inherited from the more abstract classes. Languages that support multiple inheritance (such as C++) have specific, language-dependent ways of resolving cycles in the inheritance hierarchy.

> Mixin classes are designed to be "mixed in" using multiple inheritance. This is a safe and powerful idiom.

One common idiom for using multiple inheritance effectively is the "mixin" class. These are classes that are not really stand-alone classes, but rather are designed specifically to be "mixed in" with other classes using inheritance. In Figure 17.8, the Dialer class is a simple mixin. All it does is dial a phone number, and thus is not too useful on its own. However, it does provide a cohesive package of useful behavior that can be widely reused by other classes via multiple inheritance. This mixin is an example of a general utility class that could become part of a reuse library.

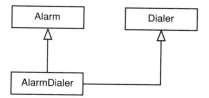

Figure 17.8

17.6.3 Inheritance versus interface realization

With inheritance you get two things:

- interface – the public operations of the base classes;
- implementation – the attributes, relationships, protected and private operations of the base classes.

With interface realization (see Chapter 19) you get exactly one thing:

- an interface – a set of public operations, attributes, and relationships that have *no* implementation.

Inheritance and interface realization have something in common as both mechanisms allow you to define a contract that subclasses must implement. However, the two techniques have very different semantics and usage.

You only need to use inheritance when you are concerned about inheriting some implementation details (operations, attributes, relationships) from a superclass. This is a kind of reuse, and in fact in the early days of OO it was often considered to be the primary mechanism for reuse. However, the world has moved on since then, and designers have recognized the sometimes unacceptable constraints that inheritance imposes and have moved away from this usage to some extent.

Interface realization is useful whenever you want to define a contract but are *not* concerned about inheriting implementation details. While interface realization gives you no actual reuse of code, it does give a very clean mechanism for defining contracts and ensuring that implementing classes conform to those contracts. Because nothing is really inherited in interface realization, it is more flexible and robust in some ways than inheritance.

17.7   Templates

Up to now, when we have defined a design class, we have had to explicitly specify the types of the attributes, the return types of all operations, and the types of all operation parameters. This is fine and works well in most of the cases but it can sometimes limit the ability to reuse code.

In the example in Figure 17.9 we have defined three classes that are all bounded arrays. One is a bounded array of int, the next is a bounded array of double, and the last is a bounded array of String. When you examine these classes, you see that they are identical except for the type that is stored in the array. Yet, despite this similarity, we have had to define three separate classes.

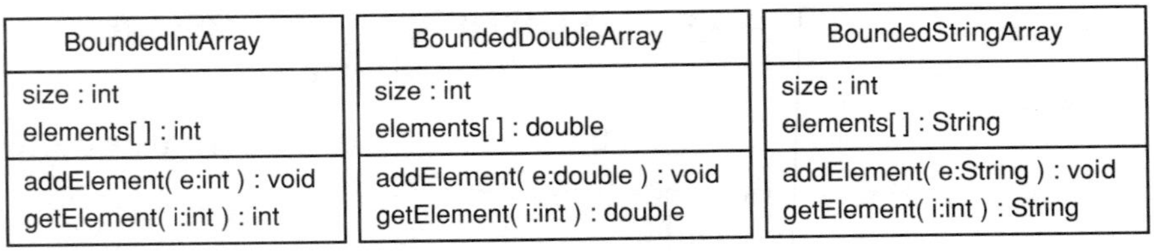

BoundedIntArray	BoundedDoubleArray	BoundedStringArray
size : int elements[ ] : int	size : int elements[ ] : double	size : int elements[ ] : String
addElement(e:int) : void getElement(i:int) : int	addElement(e:double) : void getElement(i:int) : double	addElement(e:String) : void getElement(i:int) : String

Figure 17.9

Templates allow you to parameterize a type. What this means is that instead of specifying the actual types of attributes, operation return values, and operation parameters, you can define a class in terms of placeholders or parameters. These may be replaced by actual values to create new classes.

In Figure 17.10, we have defined the class BoundedArray in terms of the parameters type (which is by default a classifier) and size, which is an int. Notice that the template specifies a default value of 10 for size. The default value will be used if size is *not* specified when the template is instantiated.

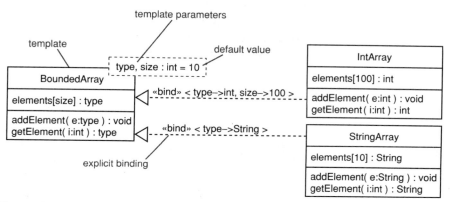

Figure 17.10

By binding specific values to these formal parameters you can create new classes—this is known as template instantiation. Notice that when you instantiate a template, you get a class, and this class may then be instantiated to get objects.

As Figure 17.10 shows, a template may be instantiated by using a realization relationship stereotyped with «bind»—this is known as explicit binding. To instantiate a template, you have to specify the actual values that will be bound to the template parameters, and you list these in angle brackets after the «bind» stereotype. When you instantiate the template, these values are substituted for the template parameters, and this gives a new class. Notice the syntax for parameter binding: the expression type->int means that the template parameter type is replaced by int on instantiation. You can think of the symbol -> as reading, "replaced by" or "bound to".

Templates are clearly a powerful mechanism for reuse—you can define a class very generally as a template, and then create many customized versions of this class by binding the template parameters to appropriate actual values.

In Figure 17.10, we actually use binding in two ways. First, we bind a classifier to the parameter type. When a template parameter has no type, then it defaults to a classifier. Second, we bind an actual integer value to the parameter size. This allows us to specify the bound for the bounded array as a template parameter.

The template parameter names are local to a particular template. This means that if two templates have a parameter called type, it is a different type in each case.

There is a variation on template syntax known as implicit binding. Here you don't use an explicit «bind» realization to show template instantiation, but rather you bind implicitly by using a special syntax on the instantiated classes. To instantiate a template implicitly, you simply list the actual values in angle brackets after the template class name as shown in Figure 17.11. The disadvantage of this approach is that you can't give the instantiated class its own name.

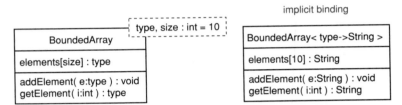

Figure 17.11

Our feeling is that it is better style to use explicit binding so that the template instantiation classes can each have their own descriptive name.

While templates are a very powerful feature, at the moment C++ and Java are the only commonly used OO languages that currently support them (see Table 17.1). Clearly, templates can only be used in design when the implementation language supports them.

Table 17.1

Language	Template support
Java	Yes
C++	Yes
Smalltalk	No
Python	No
Visual Basic	No
C#	No

17.8 Nested classes

A nested class is a class defined inside another class.

Some languages, such as Java, allow you to place a class definition inside another class definition. This creates what is known as a nested class. In Java, this is also known as an inner class.

A nested class is declared within the namespace of its outer class and is *only* accessible by that class or by objects of that class. Only the outer class or its objects can create and use instances of the nested class.

Nested classes tend to be a design issue as they are usually about *how* some functionality can be implemented rather than *what* the functionality is.

For example, nested classes are used widely in Java event handling. The example in Figure 17.12 shows a simple window class called HelloFrame. It inherits basic window behavior from its parent Frame class. HelloFrame has a nested class called MouseMonitor that inherits the ability to handle mouse events from its parent MouseAdapter class.

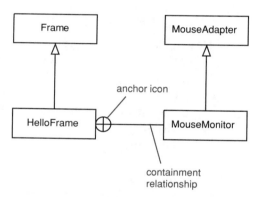

Figure 17.12

Each HelloFrame instance uses a MouseMonitor instance to process its mouse events. To achieve this, the HelloFrame instance must

- create an instance of MouseMonitor;
- set this MouseMonitor to be its mouse event listener.

This approach makes quite a lot of sense. The mouse handling code gets its own MouseMonitor class, separating it from the rest of the HelloFrame code, and MouseMonitor is completely encapsulated within HelloFrame.

17.9   What we have learned

Design classes are the building blocks of the design model. You have learned the following.

- Design classes are developed during the UP activity Design a class.
- Design classes are classes whose specifications have been completed to such a degree that they can be implemented.
- Design classes come from two sources:
  — the problem domain:
    - a refinement of analysis classes;
    - one analysis class may become zero, one, or more design classes;
  — the solution domain:
    - utility class libraries;
    - middleware;
    - GUI libraries;
    - reusable components;
    - implementation-specific details.
- Design classes have complete specifications:
  — complete set of attributes including:
    - name;
    - type;
    - default value when appropriate;
    - visibility;
  — operations:
    - name;
    - names and types of all parameters;
    - optional parameter values if appropriate;
    - return type;
    - visibility.
- Well-formed design classes exhibit certain characteristics:
  — the public operations of the class define a contract with the clients of the class;
  — completeness – the class does no less than its clients may reasonably expect;
  — sufficiency – the class does no more than its clients may reasonably expect;
  — primitiveness – services should be simple, atomic, and unique;
  — high cohesion:
    - each class should embody a single, well-defined abstract concept;
    - all the operations should support the intent of the class;

— low coupling:
  - a class should be coupled to just enough other classes to fulfill its responsibilities;
  - only couple two classes when there is a true semantic relationship between them;
  - avoid coupling classes just to reuse some code.
— Always assess a design class from the point of view of the clients of that class.

- Inheritance.
  — Only use inheritance when there is a clear "is a" relationship between two classes or to reuse code.
  — Disadvantages:
    - it is the strongest possible coupling between two classes;
    - encapsulation is weak within an inheritance hierarchy, leading to the "fragile base class" problem – changes in the base class ripple down the hierarchy;
    - very inflexible in most languages – the relationship is decided at compile time and fixed at runtime.
  — Subclasses should always represent "is kind of" rather than "is role played by" – always use aggregation to represent "is role played by".

- Multiple inheritance allows a class to have more than one parent.
  — Of all the common OO languages only C++ has multiple inheritance.
  — Design guidelines:
    - the multiple parent classes must all be semantically disjoint;
    - there must be an "is kind of" relationship between a class and all of its parents;
    - the substitutability principle must apply to the class and its parents;
    - the parents should themselves have no parent in common;
    - use mixins – a mixin is a simple class designed to be mixed in with others in multiple inheritance; this is a safe and powerful idiom.

- Inheritance versus interface realization.
  — Inheritance:
    - you get interface – the public operations;
    - you get implementation – the attributes, associations, protected and private members.
  — Interface realization – you only get interface.
  — Use inheritance when you want to inherit some implementation.
  — Use interface realization when you want to define a contract.

- Templates.
  — Of all the commonly used OO languages, only C++ and Java currently support templates.

- — Templates allow you to "parameterize" a type – you create a template by defining a type in terms of formal parameters, and you instantiate the template by binding specific values for the parameters.
    - – Explicit binding uses a dependency stereotyped «bind»:
        - – you show the actual values on the relationship;
        - – you can name each template instantiation.
    - – Implicit binding:
        - – you specify the actual values on the class inside angle brackets (< >);
        - – you can't name the template instantiations – names are constructed from the template name and the argument list.
- Nested classes:
    - — you define a class inside another class;
    - — the nested class exists in the namespace of the outer class – only the outer class can create and use instances of the nested class;
    - — nested classes are known as inner classes in Java, and are used extensively for event handling in GUI classes.

chapter 18

Refining analysis relationships

18.1 Chapter roadmap

This chapter presents techniques for refining analysis relationships into design relationships. You use these techniques in every activity in the Design workflow (Figure 16.6).

The first part of the chapter discusses converting analysis relationships into one of the whole-part relationships—aggregation (Section 18.4) or composition (Section 18.5).

The second part discusses how to deal with multiplicities in analysis associations. We provide specific techniques for refining analysis associations where the multiplicity is one-to-one (Section 18.7), many-to-one (Section 18.8), one-to-many (Section 18.9), and many-to-many (Section 18.11.1). We also cover bidirectional associations (Section 18.11.2) and association classes (Section 18.11.3).

In the final part, we see how UML 2 allows us to explore the relationship of a composite classifier to its parts.

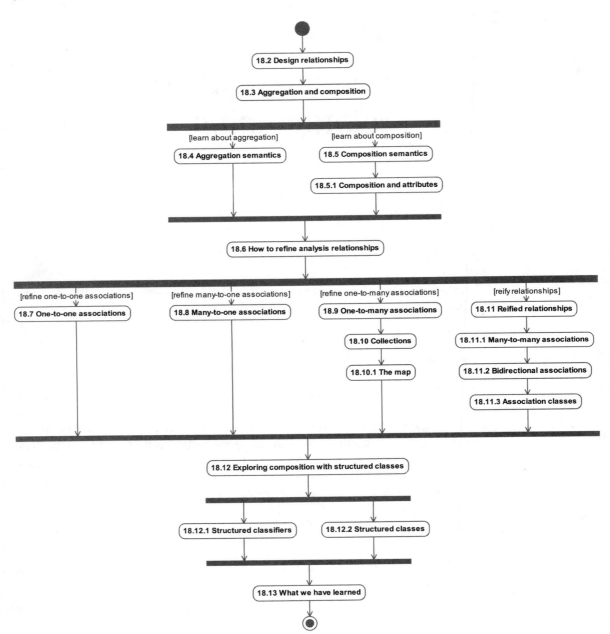

Figure 18.1

18.2 Design relationships

Analysis associations must be refined to design relationships that are directly implementable in the target OO language.

When you move to design, you have to refine the relationships between analysis classes into relationships between design classes. Many of the relationships captured in analysis are not directly implementable as they stand, and they must be made so. For example, there is no commonly used OO programming language that directly supports bidirectional associations, association classes, or many-to-many associations. To create a design model, you have to specify *how* these associations are going to be realized.

Refining analysis associations to design associations involves several procedures:

- refining associations to aggregation or composition relationships where appropriate;
- implementing one-to-many associations;
- implementing many-to-one associations;
- implementing many-to-many associations;
- implementing bidirectional associations;
- implementing association classes.

All design associations *must* have

- navigability;
- multiplicity on both ends.

All design associations *should* have an association name, or a role name on at least the target end.

18.3 Aggregation and composition

In design, you can refine an association relationship into an aggregation relationship or a stronger form of aggregation known as the composition aggregation relationship if the semantics of the association warrant it. We normally refer to composition aggregation simply as composition.

You can get a good idea about the semantic differences between the two types of aggregation by thinking about some real-world examples.

- Aggregation – this is a loose type of relationship between objects—an example might be a computer and its peripherals.
- Composition – this is a very strong type of relationship between objects— it is like a tree and its leaves.

If you consider these examples, illustrated in Figure 18.2, you can see that a computer is only weakly related to its peripherals. These peripherals may come and go, may be shared between computers, and are not in any meaningful sense "owned" by any particular computer—this is aggregation. On the other hand, a tree is intimately related to its leaves. Leaves are owned by exactly one tree, they can't be shared between trees, and when the tree dies the leaves go with it—this is composition.

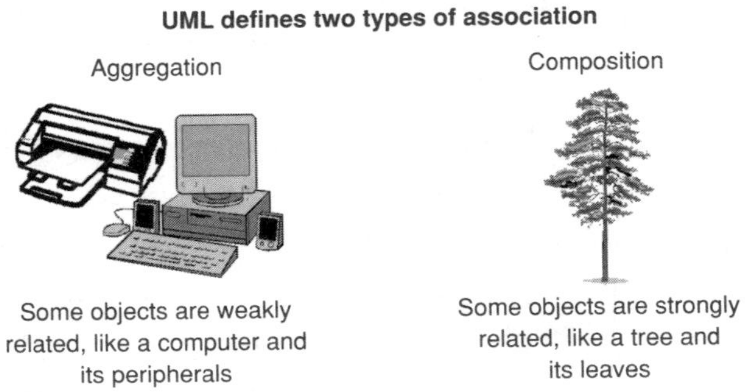

UML defines two types of association

Aggregation   Composition

Some objects are weakly   Some objects are strongly
related, like a computer and   related, like a tree and
its peripherals   its leaves

Figure 18.2

It will be very useful to keep these simple analogies in mind as you study the detailed semantics of aggregation and composition in the rest of this chapter.

18.4   Aggregation semantics

Aggregation is a type of whole-part relationship in which the aggregate is made up of many parts. In a whole-part relationship, one object (the whole) uses the services of another object (the part). As such, the whole tends to be the dominant and controlling side of the relationship, whereas the part just tends to service requests from the whole and is therefore more passive. Indeed, if you only have navigability from the whole to the part, the part doesn't even know that it is part of a whole.

Consider the particular aggregation example in Figure 18.3.

You can see that

● a Computer may be attached to 0 or more Printers;

● at any *one point in time*, a Printer is connected to 0 or 1 Computer;

● *over time*, many Computers may use a given Printer;

Aggregation is a
whole-part
relationship.

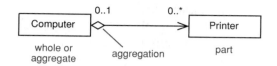

Figure 18.3

- the Printer may exist even if there are no attached Computers;
- the Printer is, in a very real sense, independent of the Computer.

We can summarize aggregation semantics as follows:

- the aggregate can sometimes exist independently of the parts, sometimes not;
- the parts can exist independently of the aggregate;
- the aggregate is in some sense incomplete if some of the parts are missing;
- it is possible to have shared ownership of the parts by several aggregates.

Aggregation is transitive. Consider the example in Figure 18.4. Transitivity means that if C is part of B and B is part of A, then C is also part of A.

Aggregation is
transitive.

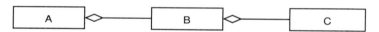

aggregation is transitive: if C is part of B and B is part of A, then C is part of A

Figure 18.4

Aggregation is asymmetric. This means that an object can never, either directly or indirectly, be part of itself. This limits how you can use aggregation in your models. In the aggregation example in Figure 18.5, you can see

Aggregation is
asymmetric. An object
can never be part of
itself.

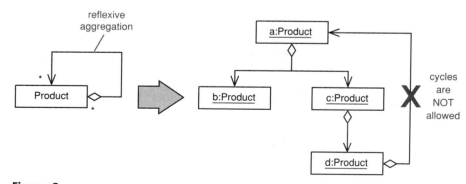

Figure 18.5

that Product objects may be composed of other Product objects. This is fine provided they are all *different* objects and the asymmetry constraint is preserved.

Considering Figure 18.5 further, sometimes you might need to model the case where object <u>d</u> has a link to object <u>a</u> as shown. This would occur when object <u>d</u> needed to *call back* and use some of the services of the aggregate object <u>a</u>. But how would you model this on the class diagram? The reflexive aggregation relationship on the Product class won't do because the asymmetry constraint on aggregation precludes object <u>a</u> from being, either directly or indirectly, a part of itself. You therefore need to use a reflexive, unrefined *association* between class Product and itself to handle the link between objects <u>d</u> and <u>a,</u> as shown in Figure 18.6.

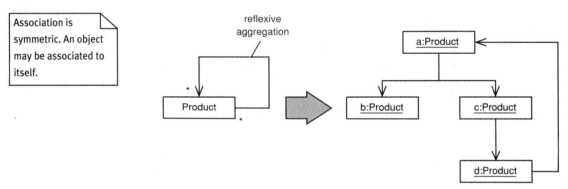

Figure 18.6

The example in Figure 18.7 shows another typical example of aggregation. You can model a home computer (the whole) as a set of parts. These

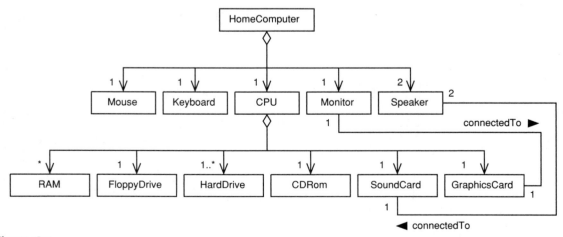

Figure 18.7

parts are quite loosely related to the whole as they are interchangeable with other computers and may be shared with other computers, so you can use aggregation semantics in your model. The model says that a home computer can be thought of as an aggregate of the following parts: a Mouse, a Keyboard, a CPU, a Monitor, and two Speakers. The CPU can itself be modeled as an aggregate of various hardware components such as RAM, HardDrives, etc.

18.5   Composition semantics

Composition is a stronger form of aggregation and has similar (but more constrained) semantics. Like aggregation, it is a whole-part relationship and is both transitive and asymmetric.

The key difference between aggregation and composition is that in composition the parts have *no* independent life outside of the whole. Furthermore, in composition each part belongs to at most one and only one whole, whereas in aggregation a part may be shared between wholes.

In the example in Figure 18.8, Button objects have no independent existence apart from their owning Mouse object. If you destroy the Mouse object, you destroy its Button objects as they are an integral part of it. Each Button object can belong to exactly one Mouse object. This is just like leaves and trees—the life of the leaf is determined by the life of the tree, and a leaf can only belong to exactly one tree.

> Composition is a strong form of aggregation.

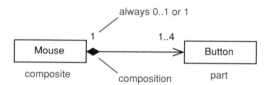

Figure 18.8

We can summarize composition semantics as follows:

> The composite has sole ownership and responsibility for its parts.

- the parts can only belong to one composite at a time—there is no possibility of shared ownership of a part;
- the composite has sole responsibility for the disposition of all its parts—this means responsibility for their creation and destruction;
- the composite may release parts, provided responsibility for them is assumed by another object;
- if the composite is destroyed, it must either destroy all its parts, or give responsibility for them over to some other object.

Because the composite has sole responsibility for the life cycle and disposition of its parts, when you create a composite, the composite object will often create its parts. Similarly, when you destroy a composite, the composite must destroy all of its parts *or* arrange for them to be adopted by another composite.

Another difference between aggregation and composition is that although you may have reflexive aggregation hierarchies *and* networks, you can only have reflexive composition hierarchies. This is because in composition, a part object can only be part of *one* composite at any point in time.

18.5.1   Composition and attributes

> A part in a composite is equivalent to an attribute.

When you think about composition semantics, you should see that they are very similar to the semantics of attributes. Both have life cycles that are controlled by their owners, and both have no independent existence outside of their owners. In fact, attributes are exactly equivalent to a composition relationship between the composite class and the class of the attribute. Why, then, do we need two ways to express the same thing? There are two reasons.

- Attributes may be primitive data types. Some hybrid OO languages like C++ and Java have primitive types such as int and double that are not classes. Now, you could model these as classes stereotyped «primitive», but this would just clutter the model. These primitive types should *always* be modeled as attributes.

- There are certain utility classes like Time, Date, and String that are used pervasively. If you were to model every usage of one of these classes by a composition relationship to the class itself, pretty soon your models would be entirely obscured. It is much better to model classes like these as attributes.

The bottom line is that if you have a primitive type or a utility class, or even a class that is just not very interesting or useful to show explicitly on the model, you should consider using an attribute rather than a composition relationship. There is no hard and fast rule here, but the key guiding points to keep in mind are always the clarity, usefulness, and readability of the model.

18.6   How to refine analysis relationships

In analysis, you use simple associations without really considering the semantics of the relationship (or how the relationship is finally to be implemented) in any great detail. In design, however, you should always try to be as specific as possible, and so you refine associations into one of the aggregation relationships wherever you can. In fact, the only case where you *must* use an association in design is where there would otherwise be a cycle in the aggregation graph (see Section 18.4). This is quite rare, and so most analysis associations end up as either aggregation or composition.

Having decided to use aggregation or composition, you should proceed as follows:

- add multiplicities and role names to the association if they are absent;
- decide which side of the association is the whole, and which is the part;
- look at the multiplicity of the whole side—if it is 0..1 or exactly 1, you *may* be able to use composition; otherwise, you *must* use aggregation;
- add navigability *from* the whole *to* the part—design associations *must* be unidirectional.

This gets you to the stage where you have refined the association into either an aggregation or a composition.

If the multiplicities on either the whole or the part end are greater than 1, you have to decide how you will implement this. This is the next step in the refinement.

18.7 One-to-one associations

Whenever you see a one-to-one association, this almost always becomes composition. In fact, a one-to-one association implies such a strong relationship between two classes that it is often worth seeing if they could be merged into a single class without breaking any of the design rules for design classes (see Section 17.5). Assuming that they can't be merged, you refine a one-to-one relationship to composition as shown in Figure 18.9.

One-to-one associations generally mean composition.

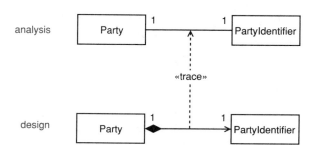

Figure 18.9

You might also consider making PartyIdentifier an attribute of Party if Party-Identifier is not a particularly important class. This certainly simplifies the diagram (Figure 18.10), but it has the disadvantage that you can't show any attributes or operations of PartyIdentifier.

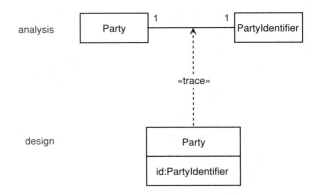

Figure 18.10

18.8   Many-to-one associations

In a many-to-one association, there is a multiplicity of many on the whole side and a multiplicity of exactly 1 on the part side.

Because there are many on the whole side, you know immediately that you *can't* use composition as the part is shared between many wholes. But you *may* be able to use aggregation. You should check at this point for cycles in the aggregation graph (see Section 18.4). Provided there are none, you can refine the analysis association to aggregation as shown in Figure 18.11. You

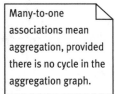

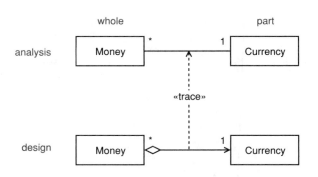

Figure 18.11

can see from this example that a single Currency object is shared between many Money objects. This correctly captures the relationship between Money and Currency—Money is an amount of a single Currency. You can find a much more complete money model in [Arlow 1].

18.9   One-to-many associations

In one-to-many associations, there is a *collection* of objects on the part side of the relationship. To implement such a relationship, you have to use either native support for collections provided by the implementation language, or a collection class.

Most OO languages provide minimal built-in support for collections of objects. In fact, most languages only offer arrays. An array is an indexed collection of object references that is normally bounded to some maximum size. The advantage of built-in arrays is that they tend to be very fast. However, this speed is offset by their inflexibility compared to other types of collection.

Collection classes are typically much more powerful and flexible than native collections. They offer a whole range of different semantics, of which array semantics is just one possibility. We look at designing with collection classes in the rest of this chapter.

18.10   Collections

Collection classes are classes whose instances hold collections of objects.

A collection class is a class whose instances specialize in managing collections of other objects. Most languages have standard libraries of collection classes (and other utilities) available.

One of the keys to excellent OO design and implementation is having a mastery of collection classes. All collection classes have operations for

- adding objects to the collection;
- removing objects from the collection;
- retrieving a reference to an object in the collection;
- traversing the collection, that is, stepping through the collection from the first object to the last.

There are many different types of collections, and each is specialized to handle collections of objects in a particular way. Choosing the right collection for the job in hand is an important aspect of OO design and implementation. We look at this in the next section.

As an example of using collections, Figure 18.12 shows a one-to-many association in analysis being implemented by a collection class called Vector. This class comes from the Java standard library java.util. The relationship from the whole (Order) to the Vector is usually a composition as the Vector typically is just a part of the implementation of the whole and has no life outside of this. However, the relationship between the Vector and the parts (OrderLine) may be an aggregation or a composition. If the whole is responsible for the life cycle of the parts, as in this example, you can use composition. Otherwise, you must use aggregation.

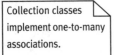

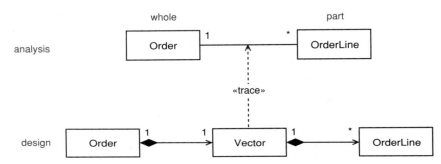

Figure 18.12

In terms of modeling with collections, there are four fundamental strategies.

- Model the collection class explicitly – this is the case shown in Figure 18.12. It has the advantage of being very explicit, but also the big disadvantage of adding a lot of clutter to the design model. If you replace every one-to-many association in the model with a collection class, the model rapidly becomes bloated. Choice of a collection class is usually a tactical implementation decision and can be left to the programmers. We recommend that you should *only* replace one-to-many associations with specific collection classes when the choice of collection is strategic.

- Tell the modeling tool how each specific one-to-many association is to be implemented. Many modeling tools that generate code allow a specific collection class to be assigned to each one-to-many association. This is usually accomplished by adding tagged values to the association to specify the code generation properties for that relationship. This approach is shown in Figure 18.13, where we have added the property {Vector} to the appropriate end of the relationship. Notice that we only use the name part of the tagged value—the value part is redundant in this case.

Figure 18.13

<aside>Don't "overmodel" when using collections.</aside>

- Specify the semantics of the collection by adding a property to the relationship, but don't specify any implementation class (see Figure 18.14). It is important not to "overmodel" when using collections. As we've said, the actual type of collection used is often a tactical, rather than a strategic, issue and it can be left to the programmer to make a reasonable assumption at implementation time. This is often a good option as it is quite concise and allows you to give a hint to the programmers about what collection class should be used. This approach usually precludes automatic code generation, however.

- Don't bother refining one-to-many relationships to collection classes— leave it up to the programmers.

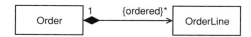

Figure 18.14

UML provides standard properties that you can apply to multiplicities to indicate the required semantics of the collection. These are summarized in Table 18.1.

Ordering determines whether the elements in the collection are maintained in a strict order with respect to one another. Uniqueness determines whether each object in the collection has a unique identity. The default semantics for a one-to-many relationship are {unordered, unique}.

Table 18.1

Standard property	Semantics
{ordered}	Elements in the collection are maintained in a strict order
{unordered}	There is no ordering of the elements in the collection
{unique}	Elements in the collection are all unique – an object appears in the collection at most once
{nonunique}	Duplicate elements are allowed in the collection

For example, assuming you need an ordered collection of OrderLines, you can express Figure 18.13 as shown in Figure 18.14.

The permutations of the order property and the uniqueness property give rise to the set of collections listed in Table 18.2. These collections are part of the Object Constraint Language (OCL) (Chapter 25), although all languages will have a similar set of collections.

Table 18.2

Property	OCL collection
{unordered, nonunique}	Bag
{unordered, unique}	Set
{ordered, unique}	OrderedSet
{ordered, nonunique}	Sequence

18.10.1   The map

Another very useful type of collection class is the map, also sometimes known as the dictionary. These classes act a bit like a database table with just two columns—the key and the value. Given a key, maps are designed so that you can *rapidly* find the associated value. If you need to store collections of objects that need to be accessed according to the value of a unique key or if you need to build fast access indexes into other collections, a map is a good choice.

> Maps are optimized to quickly return a value, given a key.

Maps usually work by maintaining a set of nodes where each node points to two objects—the key object and the value object. They are optimized to find a value object quickly when given a specific key object.

Figure 18.15 shows a simplified representation of a Java HashMap. Finding a value (given a particular key) is very fast as the collection is indexed with a hash table.

UML has no standard property to indicate a map, and maps are not part of OCL. If you want to indicate that a map is required on your design model, either indicate the specific type of collection (e.g., {HashMap}) or use the following tagged value:

{map keyName}

If you choose to use this nonstandard idiom, add a note to your model to explain it!

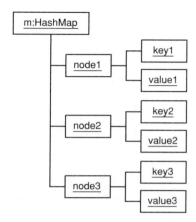

Figure 18.15

18.11   Reified relationships

Some types of relationship are pure analysis artifacts and are not themselves directly supported by any of the commonly used OO languages. The process of taking these analysis relationships and implementing them is known as *reification* (to make concrete, or real). You need to reify the following analysis relationships:

● many-to-many associations;

● bidirectional associations;

● association classes.

18.11.1   Many-to-many associations

Many-to-many associations are not directly supported in any of the commonly used OO languages (although some object databases do support them directly) so they must be reified into normal classes, aggregations, compositions, and dependencies. In analysis, you could be quite vague about issues such as ownership and navigation, but there is no room for such vagueness in design. That being the case, you first have to decide which side of the many-to-many association is the whole and then use aggregation or composition as appropriate.

In the example in Figure 18.16 we have reified the allocation relationship into an Allocation class. This resolves the many-to-many association into two aggregations as shown. Based on the requirements of the system, we have decided that Resource is the whole. This is because the system is mainly about

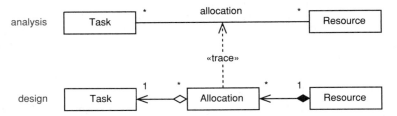

Figure 18.16

managing the lines of work associated with Resources, that is, it is resource-centric. However, if the system were task-centric, we would make Task the whole, reversing the relationships shown in the figure.

We've also chosen to give Resource responsibility for the life cycle of its Allocation objects, and so have used a composition relationship.

If the system tries to present *both* points of view, then we might say it is allocation-centric, and so we would introduce a new object (AllocationManager perhaps), which maintains a list of Allocation objects where each object points to both a Resource and a Task object.

18.11.2   Bidirectional associations

Often you need to model the circumstance in which an object a of class A uses the services of an object b of class B, and object b needs to call back and use the services of object a. An example of this might be a GUI Window control owning one or more Button objects where each of these Button objects needs to call back and use the services of their owning Window.

In analysis, this is straightforward—you model it as a single bidirectional association. In design, however, none of the commonly used OO languages support true bidirectional associations, and so you must reify this bidirectional association into two unidirectional associations or dependencies, as illustrated in Figure 18.17.

When you are modeling callbacks, you need to be aware of the asymmetry constraint on aggregation and composition—an object must *never* directly or

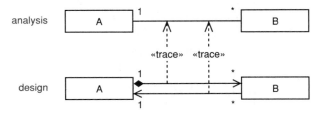

Figure 18.17

indirectly be a part of itself. This means that if class A has an aggregation or composition relationship to class B, you have to model the callback relationship from B back to A as an unrefined association. If instead you used an aggregation relationship from B back to A, then object <u>b</u> would be part (by composition or aggregation) of object <u>a</u>, and object <u>a</u> would be part (by aggregation) of object <u>b</u>. This cycle of ownership clearly breaks the aggregation asymmetry constraint.

Bidirectional associations also exist where the whole passes a reference to itself as a parameter to one of the part's operations, or where the part instantiates the whole in one of its operations. In these cases, you should use a dependency relationship from the part to the whole rather than an association.

18.11.3   Association classes

Association classes are pure analysis artifacts that are not directly supported by any commonly used OO programming language. Thus, they have no direct analog in design, and you need to remove them from your design model.

You reify the association class into a normal class and use a combination of association, aggregation, composition, or even dependency to capture the association class semantics. This may involve adding constraints to the model. You decide which side of the association is the whole and use composition, aggregation, and navigability accordingly. An example is shown in Figure 18.18.

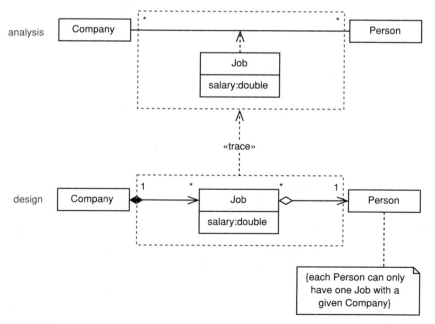

Figure 18.18

Notice that when you reify an association class, you lose the association class semantics. These semantics state that the objects on each end of the association class must form a unique pair (see Section 9.4.5). However, as shown in Figure 18.18, you can easily restore these semantics by adding a note containing the appropriate constraint.

18.12   Exploring composition with structured classes

Up to now, we have been taking analysis relationships and turning them into one or more design relationships—this is the core activity of refining analysis relationships. However, UML 2 also allows us to explore the relationship of a composite classifier to its parts. This can be an important part of the UP activities Design a class, Design a use case, and Design a subsystem as it allows you to focus on the internal workings of one of these classifiers. The key concept is the structured classifier, which we explore in the next section.

18.12.1   Structured classifiers

A structured classifier is a classifier (such as a class) that has an internal structure. This structure is modeled as parts that are joined with connectors. The interaction of a structured classifier with its environment is modeled by its interfaces and ports, but we defer discussion of these to Chapter 19.

A structured
classifier is a classifier
that has an internal
structure.

A part is a role that one or more instances of a classifier can play in the context of the structured classifier. Each part may have

- a role name – a descriptive name for the role that instances play in the context of the structured classifier;
- a type – only instances of this type (or a subtype of this type) can play the role;
- a multiplicity – the number of instances that can play the role at any particular time.

Connectors are
relationships between
roles (parts).
Connectors and parts
only exist within the
context of a particular
structured classifier.

A connector is a relationship between parts in the context of a structured classifier. It indicates that parts can communicate with one another and that there is a relationship between the instances playing the parts over which this communication can occur. These relationships might map to associations between the classes of the parts, or they might simply be ad hoc relationships in which the parts are brought together by the structured classifier in a temporary collaboration to perform some task.

Structured classifier syntax is illustrated in Figure 18.19 for the structured class SomeClass.

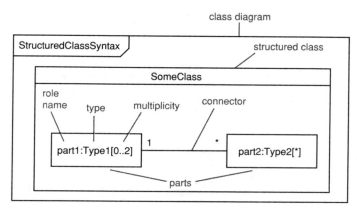

Figure 18.19

The key points of structured classifier syntax are

- the parts collaborate in the context of the structured classifier;
- the parts represent roles that instances of a classifier can play in the context of the structured classifier—the parts do *not* represent classes;
- the connector is a relationship between two parts that indicates that the instances playing the roles specified by the parts can communicate in some way.

You can see from the previous list that when you model a structured classifier, you are only considering the internal implementation and external interface of a single classifier and are ignoring all classifiers that are not parts of the structured classifier. As such, this can be a very focused modeling technique.

18.12.2 Structured classes

A structured class has the extra constraint that it owns all of its parts, connectors, and ports (see Section 19.6). It has an implicit containment relationship with them.

Lets's look an example of using structured classes in practice. Figure 18.20 shows the class diagram for a simple library management system. It is subject to the following business constraints:

- there are two types of Borrower, StudentBorrowers and StaffBorrowers;
- StudentBorrowers can have a maximum of four books on loan simultaneously;
- StaffBorrowers can have a maximum of eight books on loan simultaneously;
- only one Librarian can be logged on to the system at any particular time—it is a single-user system.

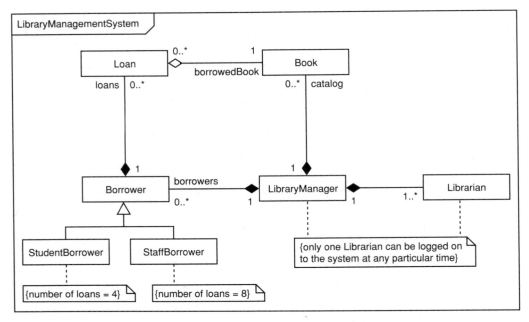

Figure 18.20

We have hidden all of the attributes and operations in this figure because we are focusing on the structural aspects of the system.

You can see that LibraryManager has an internal structure—it is a composite of Borrowers, Books, and Librarians. Because of the transitive nature of composition, Loans are also part of this composite structure. It is possible to express the LibraryManager as a structured class as shown in Figure 18.21. Notice that StudentBorrower and StaffBorrower are also shown as structured classes. In fact, you can nest structured classes to any level.

Figure 18.21 gives us a slightly different perspective on the system and allows us to look at the LibraryManager class in a bit more detail, investigating the roles that class instances play in its implementation.

- From the perspective of the LibraryManager, there are two types of Borrower that are handled slightly differently in terms of the maximum number of Loans. We introduce new roles, student and staff, to express this.

- student and staff can each have a different maximum number of Loans outstanding at any point in time. We show this by creating two different Loan roles, studentLoan and staffLoan, and adding the appropriate multiplicity to each of them.

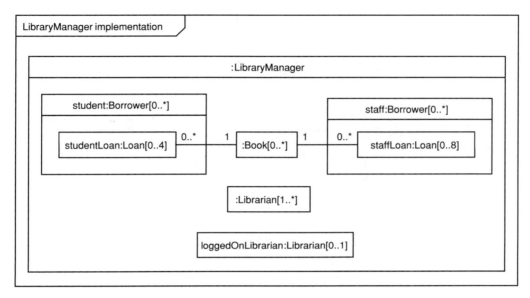

Figure 18.21

- The LibraryManager allows only one Librarian to be logged on at any point in time, so we have introduced the role loggedOnLibrarian with a multiplicity of 0..1.

> Some association roles may map to part roles.

As you can see, we have been able to make explicit the internal roles that instances play within the context of the LibraryManager. Notice that these roles can be *different* from the roles that classes play in their associations with LibraryManager. For example, in Figure 18.20 the Borrower class has the role borrowers in its association with LibraryManager, but in Figure 18.21 we have refined this role into more specific roles played by the Borrower subclasses, student and staff. Generally, some association roles map to part roles and some do not.

Similarly, connectors may map to associations between classes or merely to transient relationships created in the context of the structured class. In this simple example, each connector can be traced to an association.

As well as showing the internal structure of structured classifiers on class diagrams, you can show this structure on a special type of diagram called a *composite structure diagram*. The diagram name is the name of the structured classifier, and the diagram contents are just the contents of the structured classifier. Figure 18.22 shows the LibraryManager class in its own composite structure diagram.

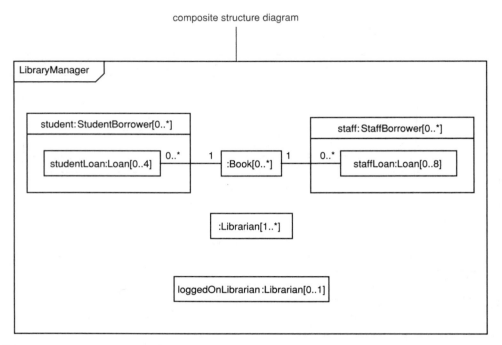

Figure 18.22

18.13   What we have learned

In this chapter you have seen how relationships in analysis are converted to implementable design relationships. You have learned the following.

- Refining analysis relationships to design relationships involves:
  — refining associations into aggregation or composition aggregation where appropriate;
  — implementing association classes;
  — implementing one-to-many associations;
  — implementing many-to-one associations;
  — implementing many-to-many associations;
  — implementing bidirectional associations;
  — adding navigability;
  — adding multiplicity to both ends of the association;
  — adding a role name at both ends of the association, or at least on the target end of the association;
  — using structured classifiers.

- Aggregation and composition.
  - These are whole-part types of relationship where objects of one class act as the whole or aggregate, and objects of the other class act as the parts:
    - the whole uses the services of the parts; the parts service the requests of the whole;
    - the whole is the dominant, controlling side of the relationship; the part tends to be more passive.
  - These relationships are transitive – if C is part of B and B is part of A, then C is part of A.
  - These relationships are asymmetric:
    - a whole can never directly or indirectly be a part of itself;
    - there must never be a cycle in the aggregation graph.
  - There are two types of aggregation relationship:
    - aggregation;
    - composition aggregation – usually referred to simply as composition.

- Aggregation.
  - Aggregation semantics:
    - the aggregate can sometimes exist independently of the parts, sometimes not;
    - the parts can exist independently of the aggregate;
    - the aggregate is in some way incomplete if some of the parts are missing;
    - it is possible to have shared ownership of the parts by several aggregates;
    - aggregation hierarchies and aggregation networks are possible;
    - the whole always knows about the parts, but if the relationship is one-way from the whole to the part, the parts don't know about the whole.
  - Aggregation is like a computer and its peripherals:
    - a computer is only weakly related to its peripherals;
    - peripherals may come and go;
    - peripherals may be shared between computers;
    - peripherals are not in any meaningful sense "owned" by any particular computer.

- Composition.
  - This is a strong form of aggregation:
    - the parts belong to exactly one composite at a time;
    - the composite has sole responsibility for the disposition of all its parts – this means responsibility for their creation and destruction;

- the composite may also release parts, provided responsibility for them is assumed by another object;
- if the composite is destroyed, it must destroy all its parts or give responsibility for them over to some other object;
- each part belongs to exactly one composite so you can only have composition hierarchies – composition networks are impossible.

— Composition is like a tree and its leaves:
- leaves are owned by exactly one tree;
- leaves can't be shared between trees;
- when the tree dies, its leaves go with it.

— A part in a composite is equivalent to an attribute:
- use explicit composition when the parts are important and interesting;
- use attributes when the parts are neither important nor interesting.

● Refining analysis associations.
— Analysis associations should be refined into one of the aggregation relationships wherever possible. If this would create a cycle in the aggregation graph, then it is impossible, and you must use an association or a dependency.
— Procedure for refining associations to aggregation relationships:
- add multiplicities and role names;
- decide which side of the relationship is the whole and which is the part;
- look at the multiplicity of the whole side:
  - if it is 1, you may be able to use composition – check that the association has composition semantics, then apply composition;
  - if it is not 1, you *must* use aggregation;
- add navigability from the whole to the part.

● Different types of association.
— One-to-one association – this almost always becomes composition. However, you may also choose to use an attribute instead or to merge the two classes.
— Many-to-one association:
- use aggregation – as there are many on the whole side, you can't use composition;
- check for cycles in the aggregation graph.
— One-to-many association:
- there is a collection of objects on the part side;
- use an inbuilt array (most OO languages directly support arrays) – they are generally quite inflexible but are usually fast;
- use a collection class – they are more flexible than inbuilt arrays and are faster than arrays when searching the collection is required (otherwise they are slower).

— Collections:
  - These are classes specialized so that their instances can manage a collection of other objects.
  - All collection classes have operations for:
    - adding objects to the collection;
    - removing objects from the collection;
    - retrieving a reference to an object in the collection;
    - traversing the collection – stepping through the collection from the first object to the last.
  - Modeling with collections – there are four options:
    - model the collection class explicitly;
    - tell the modeling tool which collection to use by adding a property to the relationship – e.g., {Vector};
    - tell the programmer what collection semantics are required by adding a property to the relationship:
      • {ordered} – the collection is maintained in a strict order;
      • {unordered} – the collection is not maintained in a strict order;
      • {unique} – all elements in the collection are unique;
      • {nonunique} – duplicate elements are allowed in the collection;
    - instead of refining one-to-many relationships to collection classes, leave it up to the programmers.
    - Don't "overmodel" – the choice of a specific collection class is often a tactical issue that can be left to the programmer at implementation time.
  - Types of collection:
    - OCL collections:
      • Bag – {unordered, nonunique};
      • Set – {unordered, unique};
      • OrderedSet – {ordered, unique};
      • Sequence – {ordered, nonunique}.
    - The map:
      • also known as the dictionary;
      • given a key, the corresponding value may be found very quickly;
      • acts like a database table with two columns, the key and the value;
      • keys must be unique.
— Reified relationships.
  - Some relationships are pure analysis artifacts and must be made implementable by the process of reification.
  - Many-to-many associations:
    - reify the relationship into a class;
    - decide which side is the whole and use aggregation, composition, or association as appropriate.

- Bidirectional associations:
  - replace with a unidirectional aggregation or composition from whole to part, and a unidirectional association or dependency from part to whole.
- Association classes:
  - decide which side is the whole and which is the part;
  - replace with a class (usually with the same name as the association class);
  - add a constraint in a note to indicate that objects on each end of the reified relationship must form a unique pair.

- Exploring composition with structured classes.
  - Structured classifier – a classifier (such as a class) that has an internal structure.
    - Modeled as parts that are joined with connectors:
      - part – a *role* that one or more instances of a classifier can play in the context of the structured classifier;
        - name – the name of the part;
        - type – the type of objects that can play the role;
        - multiplicity – the number of objects that can play the role at any time;
      - connector – a relationship between parts in the context of a structured classifier.
    - Internal structure can be shown on class diagrams or on a composite structure diagram.
  - Structured class:
    - a class that has an internal structure;
    - has the extra constraint that it owns (has an implicit containment relationship with) all of its parts, connectors, and ports.

chapter **19**

Interfaces and components

This chapter has two main threads—interfaces and components. We discuss these two topics together because, as you will see, they are intimately related. You will also see, in Section 19.10, how using interfaces combined with a special type of component called a subsystem allows the creation of flexible system architectures.

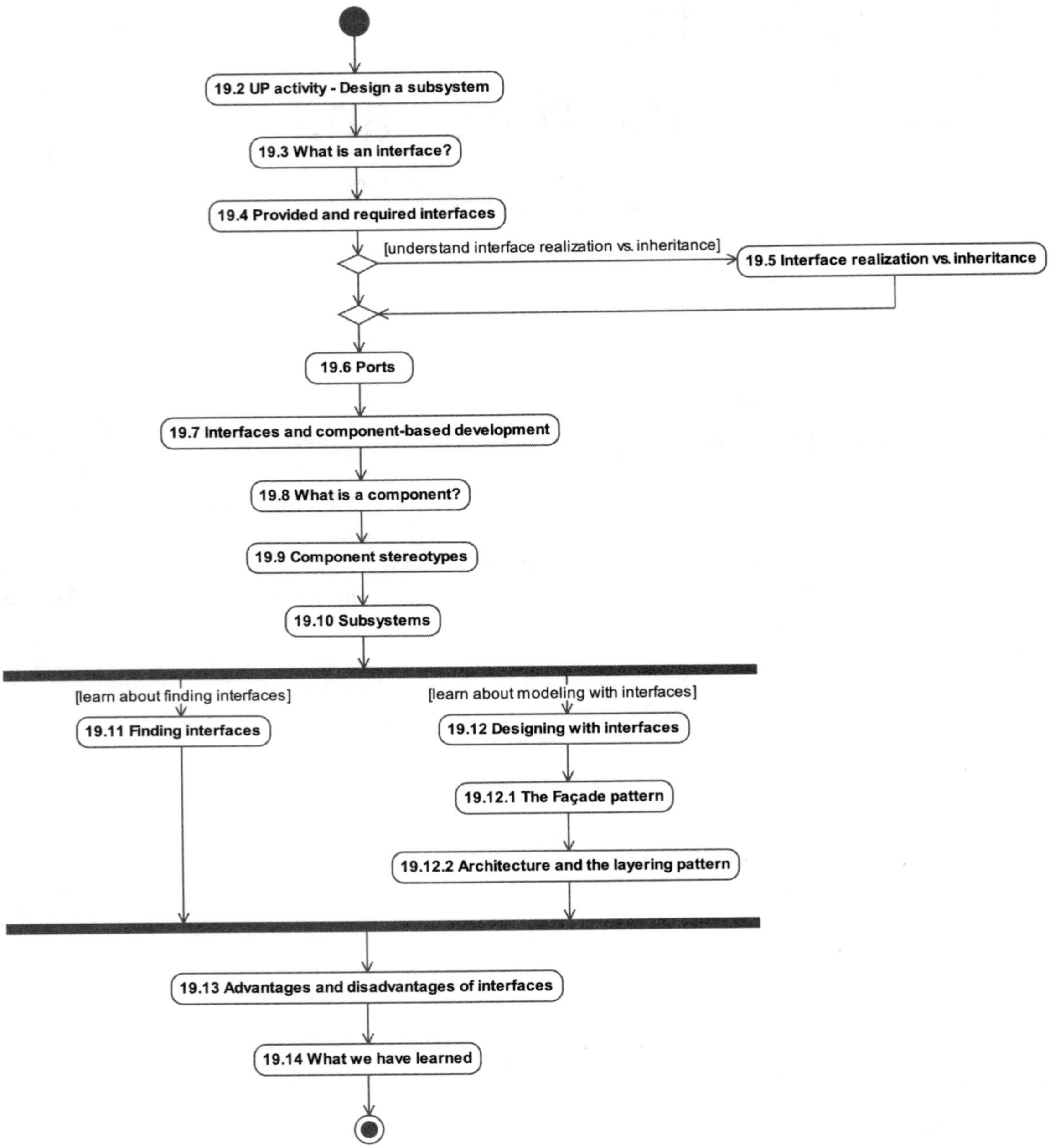
19.2 UP activity - Design a subsystem
19.3 What is an interface?
19.4 Provided and required interfaces
[understand interface realization vs. inheritance]
19.5 Interface realization vs. inheritance
19.6 Ports
19.7 Interfaces and component-based development
19.8 What is a component?
19.9 Component stereotypes
19.10 Subsystems
[learn about finding interfaces]
19.11 Finding interfaces
[learn about modeling with interfaces]
19.12 Designing with interfaces
19.12.1 The Façade pattern
19.12.2 Architecture and the layering pattern
19.13 Advantages and disadvantages of interfaces
19.14 What we have learned

Figure 19.1

19.2 UP activity: Design a subsystem

This chapter is primarily about the UP activity Design a subsystem. A subsystem is just a special type of component, so in this chapter we discuss components and component-based development along with subsystems. The topics in this chapter also have an impact on the other UP design activities, as you will see.

The UP activity Design a subsystem is shown in Figure 19.2. We have modified the original figure to bring it into line with UML 2 where subsystems are types of components, rather than stereotyped packages. Changed artifacts are shown in gray in the figure.

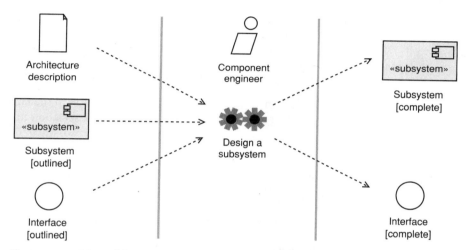

Figure 19.2 Adapted from Figure 9.44 [Jacobson 1] with permission from Addison-Wesley

The activity Design a subsystem is about breaking up the system into parts that are as independent as possible. These parts are called subsystems. Interactions between subsystems are mediated by interfaces. The goals of subsystem design are to minimize coupling in the system by designing appropriate interfaces and to ensure that each subsystem correctly realizes the behavior specified by its interfaces.

19.3 What is an interface?

An interface
specifies a named set
of public features.

An interface specifies a named set of public features.

The key idea behind interfaces is to separate the *specification* of functionality (the interface) from its *implementation* by a classifier such as a class or

Interfaces separate the specification of functionality from its implementation.

subsystem. An interface can't be instantiated—it simply declares a contract that may be realized by zero or more classifiers. Anything that realizes an interface accepts and agrees to abide by the contract that the interface defines.

Interfaces can specify the features listed in Table 19.1. This table also shows the responsibilities of realizing classifiers with respect to the interface.

Table 19.1

Interface specifies	Realizing classifier
Operation	Must have an operation with the same signature and semantics
Attribute	Must have public operations to set and get the value of the attribute – the realizing classifier is *not* required to actually have the attribute specified by the interface, but it must behave as though it has
Association	Must have an association to the target classifier – if an interface specifies an association to another interface, the implementing classifiers of these interfaces must have an association between them
Constraint	Must support the constraint
Stereotype	Has the stereotype
Tagged value	Has the tagged value
Protocol (e.g., as defined by a protocol state machine – see Section 21.2.1)	Must realize the protocol

Interfaces also need specifications of the semantics of their features (usually in text or pseudocode) to guide implementers.

The attributes and operations in an interface should be fully specified and should include the following:

● the complete operation signature (name, types of all parameters, and return type);

● the semantics of the operation—this can be recorded as text or pseudocode;

● the name and type of the attributes;

● any operation or attribute stereotypes, constraints, and tagged values.

It is important to remember that an interface only defines a *specification* for its features and that it *never* implies any particular implementation.

> Interfaces define a contract.

Interfaces can have a profound effect on the way you design. Up to now, we have been designing by connecting specific classes—we might call this "designing to an implementation". However, it is more flexible to "design to a contract" where you connect to an interface and this interface may then be realized by any number of classes and other classifiers. The Java standard libraries bear testament to the flexibility and power of this approach. We often say that an interface defines a *service* offered by a class, subsystem, or component. Modern software architectures are often service based.

> If the implementation language doesn't directly support interfaces, just use abstract classes.

Java is the first commonly used language to introduce a specific language construct for interfaces. However, it is quite possible to program using interfaces in languages that have no construct for interfaces. For example, in C++ you would simply define a pure abstract class—this is an abstract class whose operations are all abstract.

19.4   Provided and required interfaces

> Interfaces that are realized by a classifier are its provided interfaces.

The set of interfaces realized by a classifier is known as its *provided* interfaces.

> Interfaces that a classifier needs are its required interfaces.

When a classifier requires one or more interfaces for its operation, these are known as its *required* interfaces.

The UML syntax for provided interfaces is shown in Figure 19.3. There are two variants, the "class" style notation (on which you may show the attributes and operations) and the concise "lollipop" style notation (on which you may *not* show the attributes and operations).

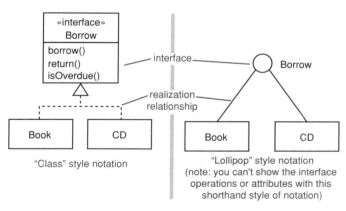

Figure 19.3

The example in Figure 19.3 is taken from a simple library management system where the Library class maintains a collection of Books and a collection of CDs. Each Book and CD realizes the Borrow interface that specifies the protocol for a borrowable item. Although Books and CDs are semantically quite different, the Borrow interface allows the Library to treat them in a uniform way, at least as far as their borrowing protocol is concerned.

Interfaces are typically named just like classes—in UpperCamelCase. However, in Visual Basic and C# there is a common standard to prefix each interface name with uppercase I, for example, IBorrow. Another naming idiom is to add "able" to the end of the name, for example, Borrowable or IBorrowable.

The realization relationship is the relationship between a specification (in this case, an interface) and the things that realize the specification (in this case, the classes Book and CD). We'll see later that it is not just classes that can realize an interface—other classifiers such as packages and components can as well.

Notice that in the class style notation, the realization relationship is drawn as a dotted line with an unfilled arrowhead, while in the lollipop style notation it becomes a single solid line with no arrowhead. The idea here is that the lollipop notation is kept as concise as possible. You use the class notation when you want to show the interface features, and the lollipop notation when you don't. However, they both mean exactly the same thing.

Figure 19.4 shows the Library class that requires the Borrow interface. You can show a required interface as a dependency to an interface (in either class or lollipop notation) or as a socket into which the required interface fits. Either way, what this notation tells us is that the Library understands and

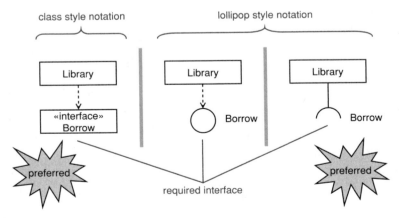

Figure 19.4

requires the specific protocol defined by the Borrow interface. Anything that realizes this interface may potentially be plugged into the Library and the Library will understand that it can be borrowed and returned.

Figure 19.5 shows the Library system assembled. The assembly connector indicates that Book and CD both provide the set of services (defined by Borrow) that the Library requires.

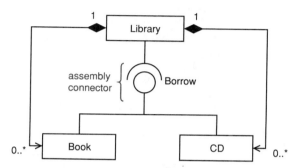

Figure 19.5

Another good example of interfaces with multiple implementations can be found in the collection classes in the Java standard libraries (Figure 19.6). Although eight interfaces are defined, Java provides many different implementations, all of which have different characteristics. By designing to an interface, the Java designer can leave the actual realization of the interface to implementation time, and let the Java programmer choose the implementation with the most appropriate characteristics.

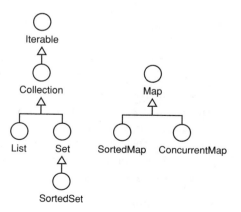

Figure 19.6

19.5   Interface realization vs. inheritance

Interface realization – "realizes a contract specified by".

Inheritance – "is a".

At this point, it's worth considering the difference between interface realization and inheritance. The semantics of interface realization are "realizes contract specified by" whereas the semantics of inheritance are "is a". The substitutability principle applies both for inheritance and for interface realization, so both types of relationship can generate polymorphism.

To illustrate the differences between interface realization and inheritance we have created an alternative solution for the library problem based on inheritance (see Figure 19.7). This seems to be a perfectly plausible and in some ways simpler solution for the library system, but there are issues.

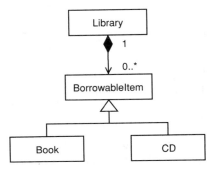

Figure 19.7

Most importantly, this inheritance-based model doesn't seem quite right because we are making a very definite statement that Books and CDs are of type BorrowableItem. But is this ability of Books and CDs to be borrowed really sufficient to specify their type? Perhaps their ability to be borrowed could be considered to be just one particular aspect of their behavior that they happen to have in common in the context of the library system. It is semantically more correct to view BorrowableItem as a particular *role* that both Books and CDs play with respect to the Library, rather than as a common supertype.

To illustrate a practical problem with the model in Figure 19.7, consider adding Journals to the Library. Journals are periodicals, such as *Nature*, and are not borrowable. This gives rise to the inheritance-based model in Figure 19.8.

Notice that the Library now has to maintain two lists of objects—those that are borrowable and those that are not. This solution would work, but it is not very elegant as it mixes two very different concerns of the Library:

- storing objects;
- borrowing objects.

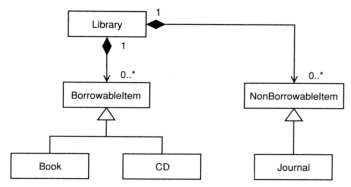

Figure 19.8

We can improve this model somewhat by adding an extra level in the inheritance hierarchy, as illustrated in Figure 19.9. This gets rid of one of the composition relationships by introducing a LibraryItem class. This solution is about as good as it gets using single inheritance. We have factored out the "borrowable" protocol of an item into a separate level in the inheritance hierarchy. This is a common solution to this sort of problem.

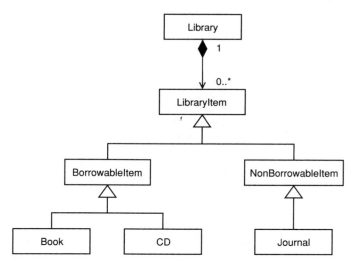

Figure 19.9

As illustrated in Figure 19.10, a model that uses both interfaces and inheritance provides a more elegant solution.

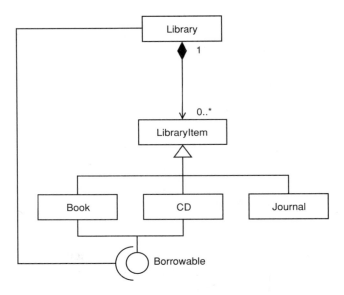

Figure 19.10

The advantages of this interface-based solution are as follows:

- every item in the Library is a LibraryItem—this makes intuitive sense;
- we have factored out the notion of "borrowability" into a separate interface, Borrowable, that we can apply to LibraryItems as needed;
- we have fewer classes—five classes and one interface, as opposed to seven classes for the other solution;
- we have fewer composition relationships—one as opposed to two in the other solution;
- we have a simpler inheritance hierarchy with only two levels;
- we have fewer inheritance relationships—three as opposed to five in the other solution.

All in all, the interface-based solution is simpler and has better semantics. We put things like catalogNumber, which all LibraryItems have, in the LibraryItem base class so that they can be inherited, and we define the "borrowable" protocol separately in the Borrowable interface.

To illustrate the flexibility of interfaces, let's take this example one step further. Suppose you need to export details of Books and Journals (but not CDs) to XML files. The business drivers for this are to allow information exchange with other libraries and to enable the display of the catalog of printed material on the Web. We design the solution as follows:

- introduce an XMLExporter class to perform the XML export;
- introduce an interface, XMLExportable, that defines the protocol that every exportable item must have to work with the XMLExporter.

We have the following non-functional requirements:

- the implementation language shall be Java;
- the JDOM library shall be used for XML processing (JDOM is a simple but powerful Java library for working with XML documents—see www.jdom.org).

The XMLExportable protocol is just a single operation, getElement(), that returns a representation of the exportable item as an Element, a class defined in the JDOM library. The XMLExporter class uses JDOM to write Elements out to an XML file.

The complete solution is shown in Figure 19.11.

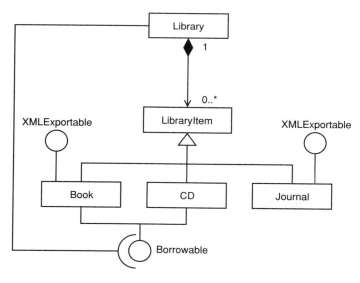

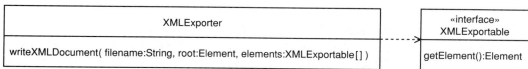

Figure 19.11

Use interfaces to
specify the common
protocols of classes that
should *not* normally be
related by inheritance.

With this solution we have managed to separate the concerns of storability (the composition relationship), borrowability (Borrowable), and exportability (XMLExportable). We have used interfaces to specify the common protocols of classes that should *not* normally be related by inheritance.

19.6   Ports

A port groups
a semantically
cohesive set of
provided and required
interfaces.

A port groups a semantically cohesive set of provided and required interfaces. It indicates a specific point of interaction between a classifier and its environment.

The example in Figure 19.12 illustrates port notation. It shows a Book class that has a port called presentation. This port consists of a required interface, DisplayMedium, and a provided interface, Display. The name of the port is optional. The figure shows two variants of the port notation. The left-hand side of the figure shows the normal case, and the right-hand side shows a more concise alternative. However, this alternative is *only* applicable if the port has a *single type* of provided interface (it may still have zero or more required interfaces). You show the type name after the port name as shown in the figure.

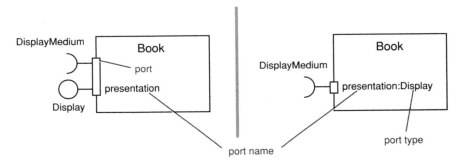

Figure 19.12

Ports are a very useful way of structuring a classifier's provided and required interfaces. They can also be used to simplify a diagram. For example, Figure 19.13 shows a Viewer class that connects to the presentation port of the Book class. For ports to be connected, their provided and required interfaces must match. Using ports is clearly much more concise than showing all of the provided and required interfaces but can be more demanding to read.

Ports may have a visibility. When a port is drawn overlapping the boundary of the classifier, it is public, and this means that the provided and required interfaces are public. If the port rectangle is shown inside the classi-

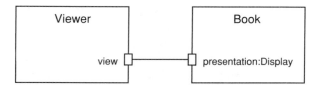

Figure 19.13

fier boundary (as illustrated in Figure 19.14), then the port has either protected visibility (the default) or private visibility. The actual visibility is not shown graphically but is recorded in the specification of the port.

Figure 19.14

Ports may have a multiplicity, and this can be shown in square brackets after the port name and type name (e.g., presentation:Display[1]). This multiplicity indicates the number of instances of the port that instances of the classifier will have.

19.7   Interfaces and component-based development

> Component-based development is about constructing software from plug-in parts.

Interfaces are the key to component-based development (CBD). This is about constructing software from plug-in parts. If you want to create flexible component-based software for which you can plug in new implementations at will, you must design with interfaces. Because an interface only specifies a contract, it allows for *any number* of specific implementations, provided each abides by that contract.

In the next few sections we look at components and then explore how components and interfaces may be combined in CBD.

19.8   What is a component?

The UML 2.0 specification [UML2S] states, "A component represents a modular part of a system that encapsulates its contents and whose manifestation is replaceable within its environment". A component acts as a black box

A component is a modular and replaceable part of a system that encapsulates its contents.

whose external behavior is completely defined by its provided and required interfaces. Because of this, one component can be replaced by another that supports the same protocol.

Components can have attributes and operations and can participate in association and generalization relationships. Components are structured classifiers and can have an internal structure comprising parts and connectors. We introduced structured classifiers in Section 18.12.1, and if you haven't read that yet, we advise you to read it now before proceeding with this section.

Components can represent something that can be instantiated at runtime, such as an EJB (Enterprise JavaBean), or they may represent a purely logical construct, such as a subsystem, that is only instantiated indirectly by virtue of its parts being instantiated.

A component may be manifest by one or more artifacts. An artifact represents something in the physical world, such as a source file. For example, an EJB component might be manifest by a JAR (Java ARchive) file. We discuss artifacts in more detail in Section 24.5.

The component diagram can show components, dependencies between components, and the way in which classifiers are assigned to components. As illustrated in Figure 19.15, a component is drawn as a box with the stereotype «component» and/or a component icon in its top right-hand corner. Components may have provided and required interfaces and ports.

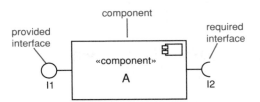

Figure 19.15

A component can have an internal structure. You can show the parts nested inside the component (Figure 19.16) or externally, connected to it by dependency relationships. Both forms are syntactically equivalent, although we think the nested notation is often clearer.

When a component has internal structure it will usually delegate responsibilities defined by its interfaces to one or more of its internal parts. In Figure 19.16, the component A provides the interface I1 and requires the interface I2. It encapsulates two parts of type b and c. It delegates the behavior specified by its provided and required interfaces to b and c respectively.

Interfaces allow you to connect components in a flexible way.

Components may depend on other components. To decouple components you *always* mediate the dependency with an interface. When a component

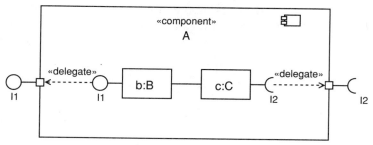

Figure 19.16

requires an interface, you can show this as a dependency between the component and the interface or you can use an assembly connector as illustrated in Figure 19.17.

In Figure 19.17 you can see the following.

- The Party component provides two interfaces of type IParty and IAddress. These interfaces are represented as balls.
- The MailingListManager component requires two interfaces of type IAddress and IPostBox. These are represented as sockets.
- There is an assembly connector between the Party component and the MailingListManager component. This shows that the MailingListManager is communicating with the Party component via the provided IAddress interface.
- In this model the Party component is acting as a façade (see Section 19.12.1) to decouple the MailingListManager component from the details of the Address component.

Components are often shown simply as black boxes with their supplied and required interfaces attached to them. However, you can also have a white-box

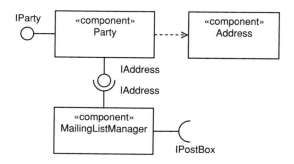

Figure 19.17

view of a component as shown in Figure 19.18. This white-box view exposes the internal details of the component. It can show any provided interfaces, required interfaces, realizations, or associated artifacts.

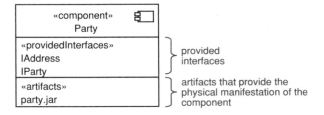

Figure 19.18

19.9 Component stereotypes

Components are possibly the most stereotyped UML element. This is because a component can be used to represent many different types of things. UML 2 provides a small set of standard component stereotypes that are listed in Table 19.2. We look at one of these, «subsystem», in more detail in the next section.

Table 19.2

Stereotype	Semantics
«buildComponent»	A component that defines a set of things for organizational or system-level development purposes
«entity»	A persistent information component representing a business concept
«implementation»	A component definition that has no specification itself – it is an implementation for a separate «specification» to which it has a dependency
«specification»	A classifier that specifies a domain of objects without defining the physical implementation of those objects – for example, a component stereotyped by «specification» only has provided and required interfaces and no realizing classifiers
«process»	A transaction-based component
«service»	A stateless, functional component that computes a value
«subsystem»	A unit of hierarchical decomposition for large systems

If you are using UML profiles in your modeling, these probably define their own component stereotypes.

19.10   Subsystems

> A subsystem is a component that acts as a unit of decomposition for a larger system.

A subsystem is a component that acts as a unit of decomposition for a larger system. Subsystems are drawn as components stereotyped «subsystem».

A subsystem is a logical construct that is used to decompose a large system into manageable chunks. Subsystems themselves *can't* be instantiated at runtime, but their contents can.

From the UP perspective, subsystems are a key structuring concept. Breaking a system down into subsystems factors a large, difficult development problem into many smaller and more manageable subproblems. This is the key to successful system development using UP.

> Use interfaces to hide the implementation details of subsystems.

Interfaces go hand-in-hand with subsystems as shown in Figure 19.19. In this example, the GUI subsystem *only* knows about the CustomerManager, AccountManager, and OrderManager interfaces. It does not know anything about the internals of the implementing BusinessLogic subsystem. This means that you could, in principle, replace the BusinessLogic subsystem with another subsystem entirely, or even with several subsystems, as long as together they provided the same set of interfaces. Similarly, you could replace the GUI subsystem with a different GUI subsystem provided it required the same set of interfaces. Using interfaces in this way decouples subsystems and creates architectural flexibility.

Interfaces connect subsystems to create a system architecture.

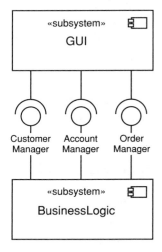

Figure 19.19

19.11   Finding interfaces

As you design a system or part of a system, it is worth examining the design model to try to find some interfaces. This is quite easy to do—proceed as follows.

- Challenge each association – look at each one and ask the question, "Should this association really be to a particular class of objects, or should it be more flexible than this?" If you decide that the association really needs to be more flexible than it would be if it were tied to a particular class, consider using an interface.

- Challenge each message send – look at each one and ask the question, "Should this message send really be to objects of just one class, or should it be more flexible than this?" If it should be more general (i.e., if you can think of cases where the same message could be sent to objects of other classes), consider using an interface.

- Factor out groups of operations that might be reusable elsewhere. For example, if many classes in your system need to be able to print themselves to some output device, think of designing a Print interface.

- Factor out sets of operations that repeat in more than one class.

- Factor out sets of attributes that repeat in more than one class.

- Look for classes that play the same role in the system—the role may indicate a possible interface.

- Look for possibilities for future expansion. Sometimes, with just a little forethought, you can design systems that can be expanded easily in the future. The key question is, "In the future, will other classes need to be added to the system?" If the answer is yes, try to define one or more interfaces that will define the protocol for adding these new classes.

- Look at the dependencies between components – mediate these by assembly connectors where possible.

As you can see, there can be many opportunities for using interfaces. We look at the details of designing with interfaces in the next section.

19.12   Designing with interfaces

When you are designing a system, it is always helpful if things behave as uniformly as possible. Using interfaces, you can design common protocols that might be realized by many classes or components. A good example of this is a system we were working on to provide a common interface to several legacy systems. The problem was that each system had a different communications protocol. We were able to hide this complexity behind a single interface consisting of the operations open(...), read(...), write(...), and close().

Here's another example. If you consider a system that models an organization (a human resources system, for example), there are many classes of things that have a name and address—for example, Person, OrganizationalUnit, Job. All of these classes can play the common role of addressableUnit. It clearly makes sense that all of these classes should have the same interface for handling name and address details. You might therefore define a NameAndAddress interface that they could all realize. Other solutions to this problem may use inheritance, but the interface solution can sometimes be more flexible.

It is worth remembering that classes may have reflexive associations (to themselves) and that there may be roles that are internal to the class. These are also possible candidates for interfaces.

A powerful use of interfaces is to provide the ability to plug things in to systems. One of the ways to make systems flexible and resilient to change is to design the system so that extensions can be plugged in easily. Interfaces are the key to this. If you can design systems around interfaces, then associations and message sends are no longer tied to objects of a particular class but instead are tied to a particular interface. This makes it easier to add new classes to a system as the interfaces define the protocols that the new classes must support in order to plug in seamlessly.

Plug-in algorithms are a good example of software modules that you might want to plug in at will. We were working on a system some time ago that did a big and complex calculation on a large data set. The users wanted to experiment with the calculation algorithm to try to find the optimum strategy. However, the system had not been written taking this into account, and every small change to the algorithm took several man-days as the existing code had to be changed and the system rebuilt. We worked with one of the designers to refactor the system to use an interface to pluggable algorithms. After this work, new algorithms could be tried out in a matter of hours. In fact, we could even switch algorithms while the system was still running.

19.12.1   The Façade pattern

The Façade pattern hides a complex implementation behind a simple interface.

Hiding complex subsystems behind a well-defined, simple interface is known as the Façade pattern. This is documented in [Gamma 1]. This book is a treasure trove of powerful, reusable design patterns that may be used in many different contexts in design models. Gamma has this to say about the Façade pattern: "Structuring a system into subsystems helps reduce complexity. A common design goal is to minimize the communication and dependencies between subsystems. One way to achieve this goal is to introduce a façade object that provides a single, simplified interface to the more general facilities of a subsystem."

The Façade pattern allows information hiding and separation of concerns—you can hide the complex details of the internal workings of a subsystem behind a simple interface. This reduces the complexity of the system and allows you to control and manage coupling between the subsystems.

Interfaces used as a façade can be used to create "seams" in a system. You do this as follows:

- identify cohesive parts of the system;
- package these into a «subsystem»;
- define an interface to that subsystem.

19.12.2 Architecture and the layering pattern

> The layering pattern organizes subsystems into semantically cohesive layers.

The collection of design subsystems and interfaces constitutes the high-level architecture of a system. However, for this architecture to be easy to understand and maintain, you still need to organize the collection of subsystems and interfaces in some coherent way. You can do this by applying an architectural pattern known as layering.

The layering pattern arranges design subsystems and interfaces into layers where the subsystems in each layer are semantically cohesive. The essence of creating a robust layered architecture is to manage the coupling between subsystems by

- introducing new interfaces where needed;
- repackaging classes into new subsystems in a way that reduces the coupling between subsystems.

Dependencies between layers must be managed very carefully as these dependencies represent coupling between layers. Ideally, you want the layers to be as *decoupled* as possible, so try to ensure that

- dependencies go one way;
- all dependencies are mediated by interfaces.

In other words, a subsystem in a layer should require interfaces from the layer below it and provide interfaces to the layer above it wherever possible.

There are many ways of producing layered architectures, and you can have as many layers as make sense. However, the basic pattern is a split into presentation, business logic, and utility layers. As shown in Figure 19.20, it is also quite common to further subdivide the business logic layer. In this case we have two layers—domain and services. The domain layer contains subsystems specific to this particular application, and the services layer contains subsystems that may be reusable in other applications.

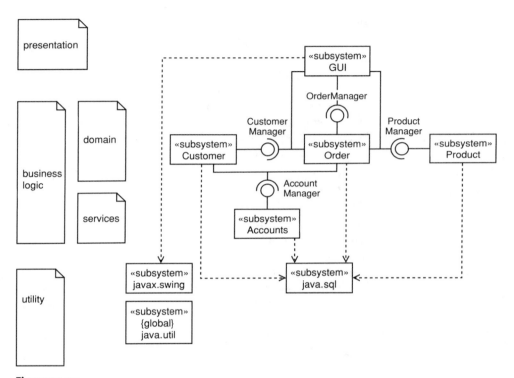

Figure 19.20

Wherever possible, it is best to design to an interface. In Figure 19.20, you can see that the subsystems we have designed ourselves are all connected via interfaces. However, the Java packages are just connected with dependencies, even though each one makes available several interfaces. The reason for this is that while showing your own interfaces is interesting and useful, showing the interfaces made available by standard Java libraries doesn't seem to serve any useful purpose. Notice also that the java.util package, which contains generic components like Strings, is used everywhere and so it is marked with a {global} tag. This tag indicates that the entire public contents of the package are visible everywhere. It is a pragmatic way to indicate that you have chosen *not* to show the dependencies to this package because they don't provide any useful information.

19.13   Advantages and disadvantages of interfaces

Designing to a contract is more flexible than designing to an implementation.

When you design with classes, you are constraining the design to specific implementations. But when you design with interfaces, you are instead designing to contracts that may be realized by many different implementations. Designing to contracts frees the model (and ultimately the system) from implementation dependencies and therefore increases its flexibility and extensibility.

Designing with interfaces allows you to reduce the number of dependencies between classes, subsystems, and components and hence begins to give control over the amount of coupling in a model. In a real sense, coupling is the worst enemy of the object developer, as highly coupled systems are hard to understand, maintain, and evolve. Appropriate use of interfaces can help reduce coupling and separate the model into cohesive subsystems.

Flexibility can lead to complexity – so take care.

However, there are drawbacks to using interfaces. Generally, whenever you make something more flexible, you make it more complex. So when you design with interfaces, you are looking for a trade-off between flexibility and complexity. In principle, you could make every operation of every class an interface—you simply would not be able to understand such a system! There is also often a performance cost to flexibility, but this is usually a minor consideration compared to the increase in complexity.

When you design a system you are trying to capture a very definite set of business semantics in software. Some of these semantics are fluid and change quite rapidly, while others are relatively stable. You need flexibility to help deal with the fluid aspects, but you can simplify systems by dispensing with a certain amount of flexibility for the more stable parts. In a way, this is one of the secrets of good OO analysis and design—identifying the fluid and stable parts of a system and modeling each accordingly.

To be frank, it is more important that a system be correctly modeled than flexibly modeled. Always concentrate on correctly modeling the key business semantics of the system first, and *then* think about flexibility. Remember the KISS rule—keep interfaces sweet and simple!

19.14   What we have learned

Interfaces allow software to be designed to a contract rather than to a specific implementation. You have learned the following.

- The UP activity Design a subsystem is concerned with breaking a system up into subsystems – parts that are as independent as possible.
  — Interactions between subsystems are mediated by interfaces.

- An interface specifies a named set of public features.
  - Interfaces separate specification of functionality from implementation.
  - Interfaces may be attached to classes, subsystems, components, and any other classifier and define the services offered by these.
  - If a classifier inside a subsystem realizes a public interface, the subsystem or component also realizes the public interface.
  - Anything that realizes an interface agrees to abide by the contract defined by the set of operations specified in the interface.
- Interface semantics – the realizing classifier has the following responsibilities for each feature:
  - operation – must have an operation with the same signature and semantics;
  - attribute – must have public operations to set and get the value of the attribute:
    - the realizing classifier is *not* required to have the attribute, but it must behave as though it has;
  - association – must have an association to the target classifier:
    - if an interface specifies an association to another interface, the implementing classifiers of these interfaces must have an association between them;
  - constraint – must support the constraint;
  - stereotype – has the stereotype;
  - tagged value – has the tagged value;
  - protocol – must realize the protocol.
- Designing to an implementation:
  - specific classes are connected;
  - to keep things simple (but rigid), design to an implementation.
- Designing to a contract:
  - a class is connected to an interface that may have many possible realizations;
  - to make things flexible (but possibly more complex), design to a contract.
- Provided interface – an interface provided by a classifier:
  - the classifier realizes the interface;
  - use the "class" style notation when you need to show the operations on the model;
  - use the shorthand "lollipop" style notation when you just want to show the interface without operations.
- Required interface – an interface required by a classifier:
  - the classifier requires another classifier that realizes the interface;
  - show a dependency to a class style interface, a lollipop style interface, or use an assembly connector.

- Assembly connector – joins provided and required interfaces.
- Interface realization vs. inheritance.
  — Interface realization – "realizes a contract specified by".
  — Inheritance – "is a".
  — Both inheritance and interface realization generate polymorphism.
  — Use interfaces to specify the common protocols of classes that should not normally be related by inheritance.
- Port – groups a semantically cohesive set of provided and required interfaces:
  — may have a name, type, and visibility.
- Component – a modular part of a system that encapsulates its contents and whose manifestation is replaceable within its environment:
  — may have attributes and operations;
  — may participate in relationships;
  — may have internal structure;
  — its external behavior is completely defined by its provided and required interfaces;
  — components manifest one or more artifacts.
- Component-based development (CBD) is about constructing software from plug-in parts:
  — you use interfaces to make components "pluggable";
  — by designing to an interface, you allow the possibility of many different realizations by many different components.
- Components can represent:
  — a physical entity (such as an EJB component);
  — a logical entity (such as a subsystem).
- Standard component stereotypes:
  — «buildComponent» – a component that defines a set of things for organizational or system-level development purposes;
  — «entity» – a persistent information component representing a business concept;
  — «implementation» – a component that has no specification itself – it is an implementation for a separate «specification» to which it has a dependency;
  — «specification» – a classifier that specifies a domain of objects without defining the physical implementation of those objects – for example, a component stereotyped by «specification» only has provided and required interfaces and no realizing classifiers;
  — «process» – a transaction-based component;
  — «service» – a stateless, functional component that computes a value;
  — «subsystem» – a unit of hierarchical decomposition for large systems.

- Subsystem – a component that acts as a unit of decomposition for a larger system:
  — a component stereotyped «subsystem»;
  — a logical construct that is used to decompose a large system into manageable chunks;
  — *can't* be instantiated at runtime, but its contents can;
  — breaking a system down into subsystems is a key to successful system development using UP.
  — Subsystems are used to:
    - separate design concerns;
    - represent large-grained components;
    - wrap legacy systems.
  — Use interfaces to hide the implementation details of subsystems:
    - the Façade pattern hides a complex implementation behind a simple interface;
    - the layering pattern organizes subsystems into semantically cohesive layers:
      - dependencies between layers should only go one way;
      - all dependencies between layers should be mediated by an interface;
      - example layers include presentation, business logic, and utility layers.
- Finding interfaces:
  — challenge associations;
  — challenge message sends;
  — factor out groups of reusable operations;
  — factor out groups of repeating operations;
  — factor out groups of repeating attributes;
  — look for classes that play the same role in the system;
  — look for possibilities for future expansion;
  — look for dependencies between components.

chapter 20

Use case realization–design

20.1 Chapter roadmap

In this chapter we look at use case realization–design. This is the process of refining analysis interaction diagrams and class diagrams to show design artifacts. Having already looked in detail at design classes in Chapter 17, we focus here on interaction diagrams. In particular, we discuss the use of inter-action diagrams in design to model central mechanisms. These are the strategic design decisions that you need to make about object persistence, distribution, etc. We also look at using interaction diagrams to capture the high-level interactions within a system by learning how to create subsystem interaction diagrams. In this chapter we cover timing diagrams. These are a new type of diagram introduced in UML 2 that are very useful for modeling hard real-time and embedded systems. Finally, we close the chapter with a real, but simple, example of use case realization–design.

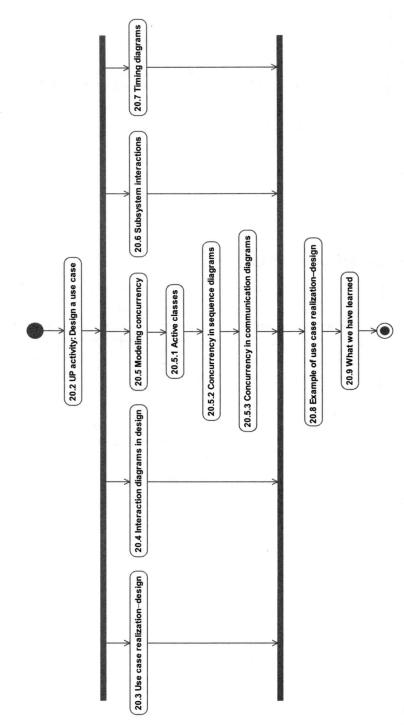

Figure 20.1

20.2   UP activity: Design a use case

The UP activity, Design a use case (Figure 20.2) is about finding the design classes, interfaces, and components that interact to provide the behavior specified by a use case (artifacts modified from the original figure are shown in gray). This is the process of use case realization that we discussed in Chapter 12, but now with the focus on design. This change of focus has several important consequences.

- Use case realizations in design will involve design classes, interfaces, and components rather than analysis classes.

- The process of creating use case realizations in design is likely to uncover new non-functional requirements and new design classes.

- Use case realizations–design help you find what Booch calls central mechanisms [Booch 1]. These are standard ways of solving a particular design problem (such as database access) that are applied *consistently* throughout the system development.

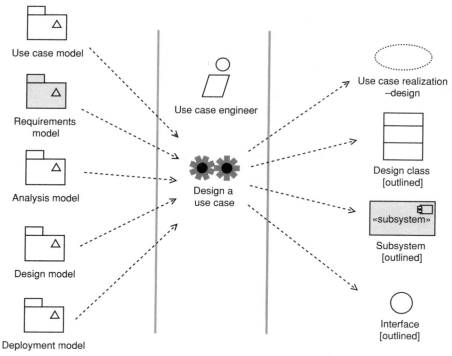

Figure 20.2   Adapted from Figure 9.34 [Jacobson 1] with permission from Addison-Wesley

The following are inputs to Design a use case.

- **Use case model** – see Part 2 of this book (Requirements).
- **Requirements model** – see Part 2 of this book (Requirements).
- **Analysis model** – we covered this in Part 3 of this book (Analysis).
- **Design model** – this is what we are building in this design section of the book. UP shows this artifact as an input to Design a use case to indicate the iterative nature of the process. You refine each artifact as your design activities uncover more and more of the details of the system.
- **Deployment model** – we defer discussion of this to Chapter 24. Again, the deployment model is shown as an input to this design activity to illustrate how the artifacts all evolve together over time.

It's important to realize that design is an iterative process, rather than a sequence of steps. As such, information you discover about one artifact may well affect others. Part of design is keeping all of the artifacts in step.

20.3   Use case realization–design

> "Use case realizations–design" are collaborations of design objects and design classes that realize a use case.

A use case realization–design is a collaboration of design objects and classes that realize a use case. There is a «trace» between an analysis use case realization and a design use case realization. The use case realization–design specifies implementation decisions and realizes the non-functional requirements. It consists of

- design interaction diagrams;
- class diagrams containing the participating design classes.

Your focus for use case realizations in analysis was to capture *what* the system needed to do. In design, you are concerned with *how* the system is going to do it. Thus, you now need to specify implementation details that you simply ignored in the analysis stage. Use case realizations–design are therefore much more detailed and complex than the original analysis use case realizations.

It is important to remember that you only model to help you understand the system you are trying to build. You should limit the amount of work you do in design to that which is useful—this is what is known as strategic design. There is also tactical design, which you can safely leave to the implementation phase. In fact, the only time you design exhaustively is when you intend to generate most of the code from the model. Even then, use case realizations–design rarely play an active role in automatic code generation, and so you only create these as needed to highlight obscure aspects of system behavior.

20.4	**Interaction diagrams in design**

In design you may refine key analysis interaction diagrams or create new ones to illustrate central mechanisms such as object persistence.

Interaction diagrams are a key part of your use case realizations–design. Because it can be easier to show large amounts of information on sequence diagrams, you often focus on these in design, rather than on communication diagrams.

Interaction diagrams in design may be

● a refinement of key analysis interaction diagrams with implementation details added;

● entirely new diagrams constructed to illustrate technical issues that have arisen during design.

In design, you introduce a limited number of central mechanisms such as object persistence, object distribution, transactions, etc., and you often construct example interaction diagrams specifically to illustrate these mechanisms. Interaction diagrams that illustrate central mechanisms often cut across use cases.

To understand the role of sequence diagrams in design, we look at the AddCourse use case we previously discussed in Section 12.9.1. Here is the AddCourse use case again (Figure 20.3).

Use case: AddCourse
ID: 8
Brief description: Add details of a new course to the system.
Primary actors: Registrar
Secondary actors: None.
Preconditions: 1. The Registrar has logged on to the system.
Main flow: 1. The Registrar selects "add course". 2. The Registrar enters the name of the new course. 3. The system creates the new course.
Postconditions: 1. A new course has been added to the system.
Alternative flows: CourseAlreadyExists

Figure 20.3

Figure 20.4 shows the analysis interaction diagram that we created in Section 12.9.1.

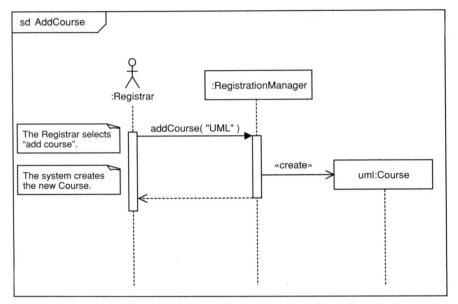

Figure 20.4

Figure 20.5 shows a typical sequence diagram for the AddCourse use case in the early stages of design. You can see that we have added the GUI layer, although this hasn't been modeled very deeply. We have also resolved the high-level operations from the analysis sequence diagram to design-level operations that are specified completely enough to be implemented. For example, object construction is now shown in detail by an explicit constructor operation invocation.

Figure 20.5 also includes a central mechanism: how the Course objects are made persistent. In this case, we have chosen a very simple persistence mechanism—the :RegistrationManager uses the services of a :DBManager to store the Course objects in a database. It is essential that this central mechanism, once defined, should be used *consistently* throughout the rest of the design. We once worked on a large system that had no less than three different persistence mechanisms—clearly, this was two too many!

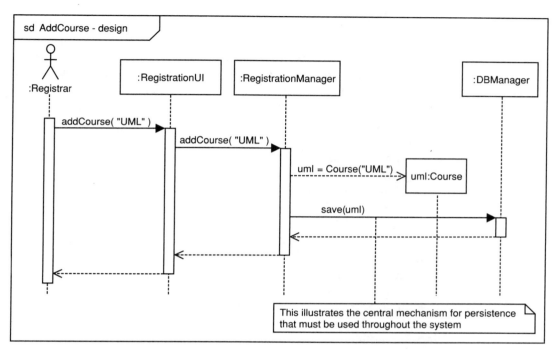

Figure 20.5

20.5   Modeling concurrency

Concurrency is one of the key considerations in design.

Concurrency means that parts of the system execute in parallel. It is one of the key considerations in design.

UML 2 has good support for concurrency:

- active classes (Section 20.5.1);
- forks and joins in activity diagrams (Section 14.8.3);
- the par operator in sequence diagrams (Section 20.5.2);
- sequence number prefixes in communication diagrams (Section 20.5.3);
- multiple traces on timing diagrams (Section 20.7);
- orthogonal composite states in state machines (Section 22.2.2).

In the next few sections we first look at active classes and then concurrency in sequence and communication diagrams.

20.5.1   Active classes

The basic principle for modeling concurrency is that each thread of control or concurrent process is modeled as an *active object*. This is an object that encapsulates its own thread of control. Active objects are instances of *active classes*. Active objects and active classes are drawn as normal classes and objects but with double right and left borders as illustrated in Figure 20.8.

Concurrency tends to be very important for embedded systems, such as the software that operates a photo-processing machine or an automated teller machine. So to investigate concurrency, we consider a very simple embedded system—a security system. This security system monitors a set of sensors that can detect fire or intruders. When a sensor is triggered, the system sounds an alarm. The use case model for the security system is shown in Figure 20.6.

The use case specifications for the system are given in Figure 20.7; we don't consider the use case ActivateFireOnly as we are focusing on the concurrent aspects of the system in this section. Also, these are just very high-level use cases that capture the essence of what the alarm system needs to do. We explore its behavior in more depth in the rest of the section.

Now we need to find the classes. With embedded systems, the hardware on which the system executes can be an excellent source of classes. In fact, it is often the case that the best software architecture is a close match with the physical hardware architecture. In this case, the alarm hardware consists of four components: the control box, the siren, the set of fire sensors, and the set of security sensors. Opening up the control box reveals that there is a controller card for each different type of sensor.

Given the use cases and the information about the physical hardware, you can derive a class diagram for this system as shown in Figure 20.8.

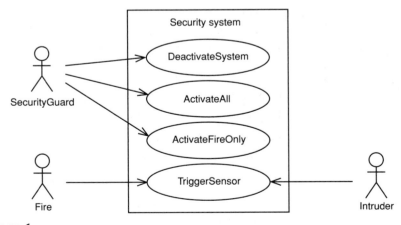

Figure 20.6

Use case: DeactivateSystem
ID: 1
Brief description: Deactivate the system.
Primary actors: SecurityGuard
Secondary actors: None.
Preconditions: 1. The SecurityGuard has the activation key.
Main flow: 1. The SecurityGuard uses the activation key to switch the system off. 2. The system stops monitoring security sensors and fire sensors.
Postconditions: 1. The security system is deactivated. 2. The security system is not monitoring the sensors.
Alternative flows: None.

Use case: ActivateAll
ID: 2
Brief description: Activate the system.
Primary actors: SecurityGuard
Secondary actors: None.
Preconditions: 1. The SecurityGuard has the activation key.
Main flow: 1. The SecurityGuard uses the activation key to switch the system on. 2. The system starts monitoring security sensors and fire sensors. 3. The system sounds the siren to indicate that it is armed.
Postconditions: 1. The security system is activated. 2. The security system is monitoring the sensors.
Alternative flows: None.

Use case: TriggerSensor
ID: 3
Brief description: A sensor is triggered.
Primary actors: Fire Intruder
Secondary actors: None.
Preconditions: 1. The security system is activated.

Main flow:
1. If the Fire actor triggers a FireSensor
    1.1 The Siren sounds a fire alarm.
2. If the Security actor triggers a SecuritySensor
    2.1 The Siren sounds a security alarm.

Postconditions: 1. The Siren sounds.
Alternative flows: None.

Figure 20.7

> Active classes have instances that are active objects.

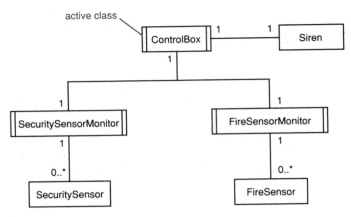

Figure 20.8

We need to use multithreading as the security system must *continuously* monitor the fire and security sensors. The classes ControlBox, SecuritySensorMonitor, and FireSensorMonitor have double right and left borders. This means that they are active classes.

20.5.2   Concurrency in sequence diagrams

Now we have enough information to create a sequence diagram. The sequence diagram for the use case ActivateAll is shown in Figure 20.9. This diagram demonstrates the use of the par, loop, and critical operators.

Here is the walkthrough for Figure 20.9.

1. The :SecurityGuard sends the message activate() to the :ControlBox.

2. The :ControlBox sends the message soundActivatedAlarm() to the :Siren.

3. The :ControlBox spawns two threads of control, represented by the operands of the par operator. Moving down the diagram, we call the first operand of par operand 1 and the second operand of par operand 2.

4. par operand 1:

    4.1. The :ControlBox sends the message monitor() to the :FireSensorMonitor.

    4.2. The :FireSensorMonitor enters a loop polling the :FireSensor. This loop executes once (to set the initial value of the variable fire) and then loops while fire is false.

    4.3. When fire becomes true:

        4.3.1. The :FireSensorMonitor enters a critical section where:

            4.3.1.1. It sends the message fire() to the :ControlBox.

            4.3.1.2. The :ControlBox sends the message soundFireAlarm() to the :Siren.

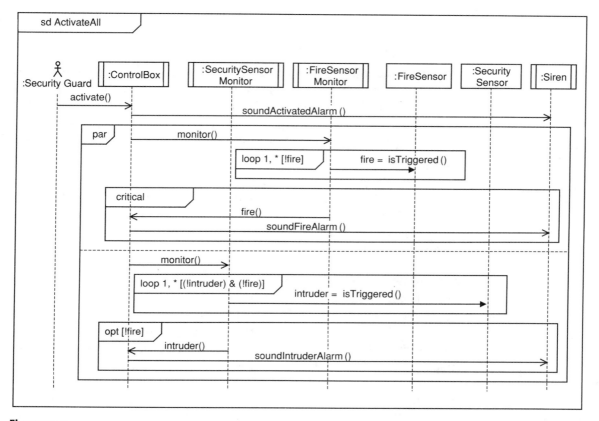

Figure 20.9

5. par operand 1 finishes.
6. par operand 2:
    6.1. The :ControlBox sends the message monitor() to the :SecuritySensorMonitor.
    6.2. The :SecuritySensorMonitor enters a loop polling the :SecuritySensor. This loop executes once (to set the initial value of the variable intruder) and then loops while intruder AND fire are false.
    6.3. When intruder becomes true:
        6.3.1. If fire is false
            6.3.1.1. the :SecuritySensorMonitor sends the message intruder() to the :ControlBox;
            6.3.1.2. the :ControlBox sends the message soundIntruderAlarm() to the :Siren.
7. par operand 2 finishes.
8. The interaction finishes.

There are a few interesting points to note about this interaction.

- Both of the operands of par execute in parallel.

- A critical section represents an atomic behavior that can't be interrupted. This is an important refinement as the triggering of the fire sensor is safety critical and shouldn't be interrupted.

- Both loops have Repeat...Until semantics—they execute once, to set the value of a variable used in their conditions, and then repeat while their conditions are true.

- The fire alarm must always have precedence over the intruder alarm. To achieve this, the loop in par operand 2 is terminated by either a fire() or an intruder() event. This is because we don't want to continue monitoring for intruders when there is a fire! Furthermore, the intruder alarm will only sound if the fire alarm is not already sounding.

Another point about this sequence diagram is that we have shown only a single FireSensor and a single SecuritySensor. This certainly serves to illustrate the behavior, but suppose you wanted to show the system iterating over several SecuritySensors and several FireSensors. To do this, you would have to modify the diagram as shown in Figure 20.10 by adding two more inner loops to traverse the collections of sensors.

Both operands in Figure 20.10 behave the same in terms of looping, so we consider the upper operand that monitors the FireSensors as an example.

You can see that the outer loop remains unchanged. The new inner loop, however, steps over each FireSensor in turn. You can indicate this by using the loop expression:

[for each f in FireSensor]

You can then use the selector [f] to show the FireSensor that the loop has selected as a lifeline on the sequence diagram, so that you can send the message isTriggered() to it. This loop has a break combined fragment that terminates the inner loop and executes its operand when fire is true. You then enter the critical section as before.

It's important to keep sequence diagrams as simple as possible. Your focus in use case realization should be on illustrating how the classes can interact to realize the behavior specified in the use case. In this ActivateAll example, Figure 20.9 is probably sufficient to illustrate the essential behavior of the system, especially if it was supported by some comments. Figure 20.10 might well be too detailed.

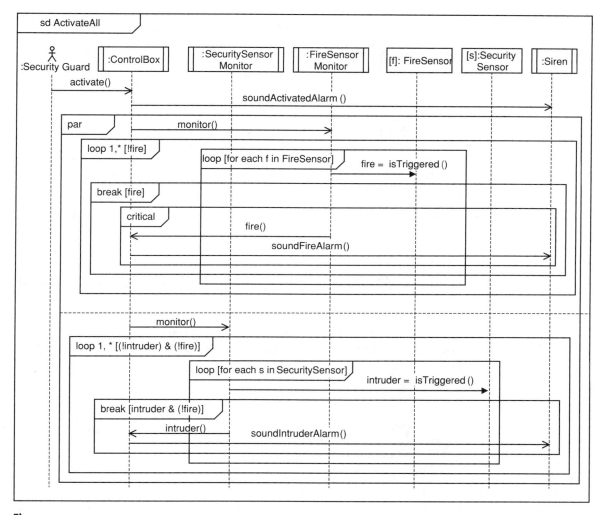

Figure 20.10

20.5.3   Concurrency in communication diagrams

Postfix the
sequence number with
a label to show
different threads of
control.

You show concurrency in communication diagrams by postfixing the sequence number with a label to indicate the thread of control, as shown in Figure 20.11. This communication diagram shows the same interaction that we previously saw as a sequence diagram in Figure 20.9. There are two concurrent threads of control, labeled A and B.

In this example, we assume that there is just one FireSensor instance and one SecuritySensor instance and that the iteration is a polling operation, repeatedly calling the isTriggered() operation of the sensor until it returns true.

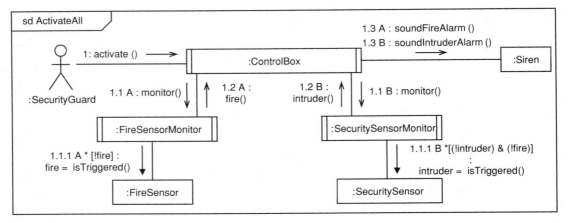

Figure 20.11

Suppose that there were *many* sensors, as we considered for sequence diagrams in Figure 20.10. You then would have to repeatedly traverse the set of sensor instances, polling each one in turn. This requires a nested loop. It is possible to show nested loops on communication diagrams, but we don't know of any easy and neat way to do it! Our advice is that when things get complex, you should use sequence diagrams instead. They have a clearer and more flexible syntax.

20.6   Subsystem interactions

> Subsystem interaction diagrams can show the interactions between parts of the system.

Once you have created a physical architecture of subsystems and interfaces, you may find it useful to model interactions between subsystems because these provide a very useful high-level view of how the architecture realizes use cases without going into the low-level details of individual object interactions.

You treat each subsystem as a black box that simply provides and requires services specified by its public provided and required interfaces. You don't have to worry about the object interactions within the subsystem at all.

Figure 20.12 shows a subsystem called Customer that has a single interface called CustomerManager.

Figure 20.13 is part of a sequence diagram, showing an actor interacting with this subsystem. Notice how we have shown the interface in a box hanging down below the subsystem. Because the interface is a part of the subsystem that can be connected to, it can have its own lifeline and we can show messages going directly to that lifeline.

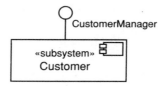

Figure 20.12

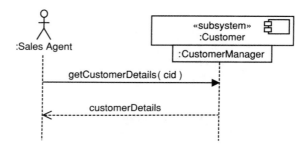

Figure 20.13

20.7   Timing diagrams

One of the areas in which UML 1 was weak was in modeling real-time systems. These are systems in which timing is critical and one event must follow another within a specified time window. We say "time window" rather than "time" because absolute time is *not* accessible to us as developers. Whenever we specify a time in a model, we are really specifying a time plus or minus some error that is determined by external factors such as the accuracy of the system clock. Usually, this isn't a problem except in systems involving very precise time constraints.

> Timing diagrams model timing constraints.

In UML 1, you could express timing constraints on various diagrams, but no single diagram type was devoted explicitly to modeling timing. UML 2 gives real-time modelers the timing diagram. This is a type of interaction diagram that focuses on modeling timing constraints. As such, it is ideal for modeling this aspect of real-time systems. Timing diagrams, similar to UML timing diagrams, have been used successfully in the electronics industry for many years to model the timing constraints of electronic circuits.

The timing diagram is a very simple diagram. Time increases horizontally from left to right, and lifelines and their states (or specific conditions on the lifeline) are shown vertically. Movement between lifeline states and conditions is drawn as a graph. You can see a simple timing diagram for the Siren class in Figure 20.14. This timing diagram illustrates what happens when there is an intruder event and then a fire event. Hopefully, this is a pessimistic scenario, but it's important to model it in order to understand how the intruder and fire detection functions of the alarm system interact.

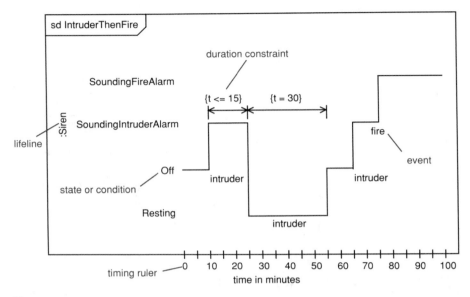

Figure 20.14

Here is a walkthrough for this timing diagram.

t = 0: The :Siren is in the state Off.

t = 10: There is an intruder event, and the :Siren transitions to the state SoundingIntruderAlarm.

t = 25: The intruder alarm can sound for no more than 15 minutes because of local regulations on alarms. The :Siren transitions to the state Resting. It must stay in this state for 30 minutes (again, because of local laws).

t = 35: There is an intruder event but the :Siren is Resting so it can't sound.

t = 55: The :Siren transitions back to the state Off.

t = 65: There is another intruder event. The :Siren transitions from the state Off to the state SoundingIntruderAlarm.

t = 75: There is a fire event. The :Siren transitions from the state SoundingIntruderAlarm to the state SoundingFireAlarm.

t = 100: The interaction finishes, leaving the :Siren in the state SoundingFireAlarm.

You can also draw timing diagrams in a more compact form in which the states are drawn horizontally. Figure 20.15 shows the timing diagram in Figure 20.14 drawn in this way.

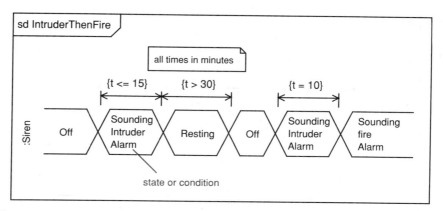

Figure 20.15

With this compact form, the emphasis is usually more on the states and on *relative* time, rather than on any notion of absolute time as modeled by a timing ruler.

You can also use timing diagrams to illustrate timing constraints in interactions between two or more lifelines. Figure 20.16 shows the interaction between the :FireSensorMonitor, :IntruderSensorMonitor, and :Siren lifelines.

There are several interesting points to note about this timing diagram.

You can use timing diagrams to show how an object changes state over time.

- The timing diagram has three compartments, one for each lifeline.
- You can show messages between lifelines on timing diagrams as shown in the figure.
- When triggered, both types of sensor transition to the state Triggered and then back to the state NotTriggered within 1 second (0.016 minutes). This means that both sensors have a quick recovery time—an essential feature.
- The :Siren only responds to intruder events when it is in the state Off. When it is Resting, it ignores intruder events. This is because of local regulations that mandate that intruder alarms should only sound for 15 minutes and then be off for at least half an hour.
- The :Siren *always* responds to fire events even when it is in the state Resting. This is because the fire alarm *must* sound as soon as a fire event happens.

As you can see, timing diagrams provide a useful way to model timing constraints on interactions.

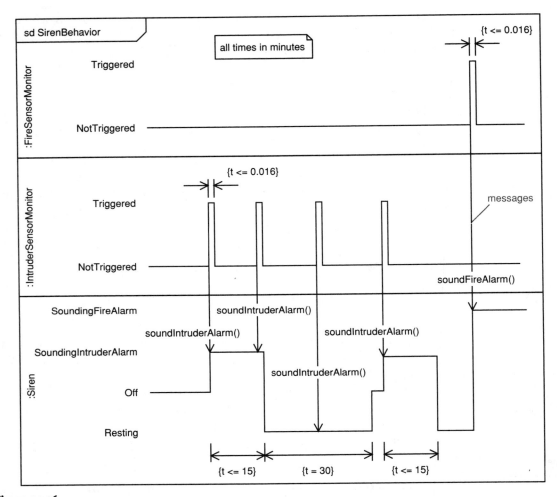

Figure 20.16

20.8   Example of use case realization–design

In this section we take a look at a real example of use case realization–design. The example we use is a simple schema-based use case editor. This is part of the SUMR system that we describe in Appendix 2, and if you haven't already done so, you should read that section first.

As you will have seen from Appendix 2, the application we are going to look at is a simple use case editor that syntax-highlights actor names, use case names, includes, and extends. The use case model for the UseCaseEditor system is shown in Figure 20.17. We developed this system by using the

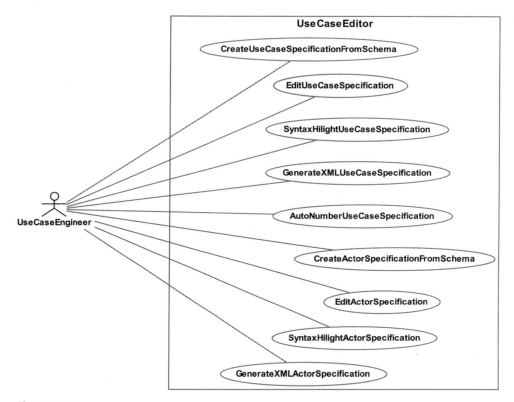

Figure 20.17

MagicDraw UML modeling tool (www.magicdraw.com), so the figures look a bit different from the other figures in this book.

The key use case for this system is probably CreateUseCaseSpecificationFromSchema. This sums up the business benefit of the system—to be able to create (and edit) use case specifications based on preexisting schema. CreateUseCaseSpecificationFromSchema is shown in Figure 20.18.

As the system is very simple, the analysis model wasn't refined to a particularly high degree so that we could very quickly into design. You can see the analysis class diagram in Figure 20.19. It captures our initial ideas about what classes would be needed.

As part of use case realization–analysis, we created the analysis-level sequence diagram shown in Figure 20.20. This diagram illustrates how we intend the system to create a new use case file from an existing schema file.

We came up with the design class model in Figure 20.21. As you can see, there is a big difference between the analysis class diagram and the design class diagram. As we've mentioned, it was such a simple system that we

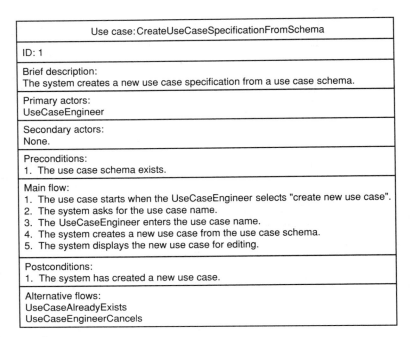

Figure 20.18

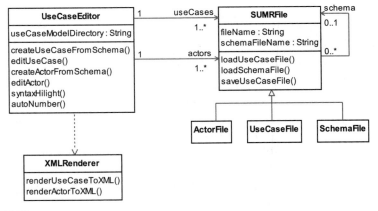

Figure 20.19

moved very quickly into design and did most of the exploratory work in that workflow. If the system had been more complex, we would have spent more time in requirements and analysis.

The use case editor was an exploratory project, and we didn't really understand what would be useful in it until we had completed a few iterations and

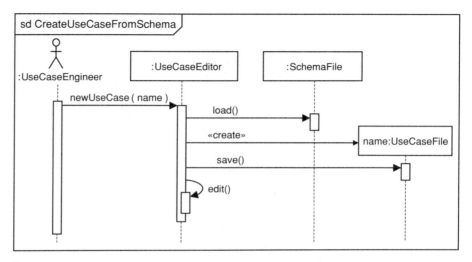

Figure 20.20

had some early executable architectural baselines that we could play with. Also, we didn't try to anticipate the most effective central mechanism for the SUMR files—we evolved that as we built the first iteration of the system.

The use case editor application was developed in Python, and all of the classes prefixed wx come from the wxPython GUI library (www.wxpython .org). This is a powerful, cross-platform GUI library based on wxWidgets (www.wxwidgets.org). These classes have a different naming standard beginning with a lowercase letter rather than the usual uppercase letter. Different naming standards are just a fact of life in software development.

Finally, let's look at a design-level sequence diagram for CreateUseCaseFrom-Schema (Figure 20.22). This sequence diagram is used to illustrate the central mechanism of creating a new use case file from an existing schema file. This is an important diagram as this mechanism must be used consistently throughout the system. You can see that our design works—we have all the right classes and operations available to do the job.

Although we have presented the requirements, analysis, and design artifacts sequentially in this example, you must remember that UP is an iterative process and that sets of these artifacts are actually created in parallel. In particular, the use case model, analysis class diagram, and analysis interaction diagrams will all be worked on together. So will the design class diagram and the design interaction diagrams. It is common to update artifacts created in previous iterations. Remember that each iteration contains some element of each of the workflows, Requirements, Analysis, Design, Implementation, and Test.

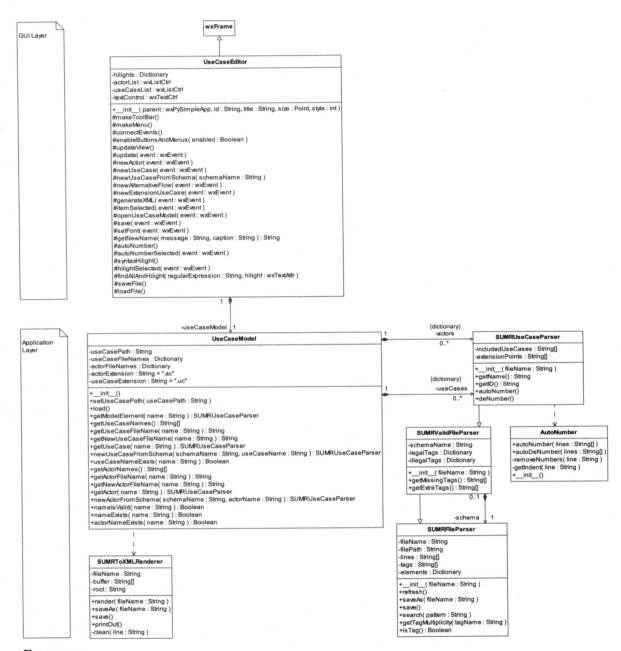

Figure 20.21

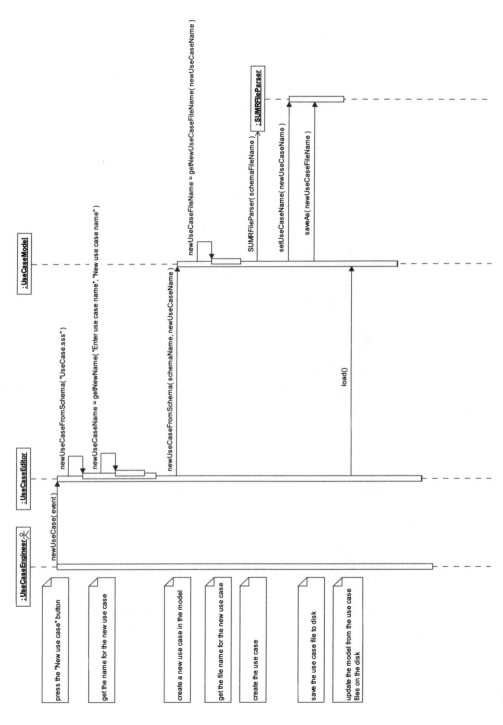

Figure 20.22

20.9   What we have learned

Use case realization in design is really just an extension of use case realization in analysis. You have learned the following.

- The UP activity Design a use case is concerned with finding the design classes, interfaces, and components that interact to provide the behavior specified by a use case.

- Use case realizations–design are collaborations of design objects and classes that realize a use case. They comprise:
  — design interaction diagrams – these are refinements of analysis interaction diagrams;
  — design class diagrams – these are refinements of analysis class diagrams.

- You can use interaction diagrams in design to model central mechanisms such as object persistence; these mechanisms may cut across many use cases.

- Modeling concurrency.
  — Use active classes and objects.
  — Sequence diagrams:
    – par – all operands execute in parallel;
    – critical – the operand executes atomically without interruption.
  — Communication diagrams:
    – postfix the sequence number with a label to indicate the thread of control.
  — Activity diagrams:
    – forks;
    – joins.

- Subsystem interaction diagrams show the interactions between the different parts of the system at a high level:
  — they may contain actors, subsystems, components, and classes;
  — you can show parts of the subsystem (e.g., provided interfaces) in boxes hanging down below the subsystem.

- Timing diagrams – model timing constraints:
  — very useful for modeling hard real-time and embedded systems;
  — time increases horizontally from left to right;
  — lifelines, states, and conditions are placed vertically;
  — transitions between states or conditions are shown as a graph;
  — you can show timing constraints and events;
  — the compact form of the timing diagram emphasizes relative time.

chapter 21

State machines

21.1 Chapter roadmap

In this chapter we discuss state machines. These are an important way of modeling the dynamic behavior of classifiers.

The chapter begins with an introduction to state machines (Section 21.2), a discussion of the two different types of state machines (Section 21.2.1), state machines and classes (Section 21.2.2), and state machine syntax (Section 21.4). It then focuses on the basic components of state machines—states (Section 21.5), transitions (Section 21.6), and events (Section 21.7).

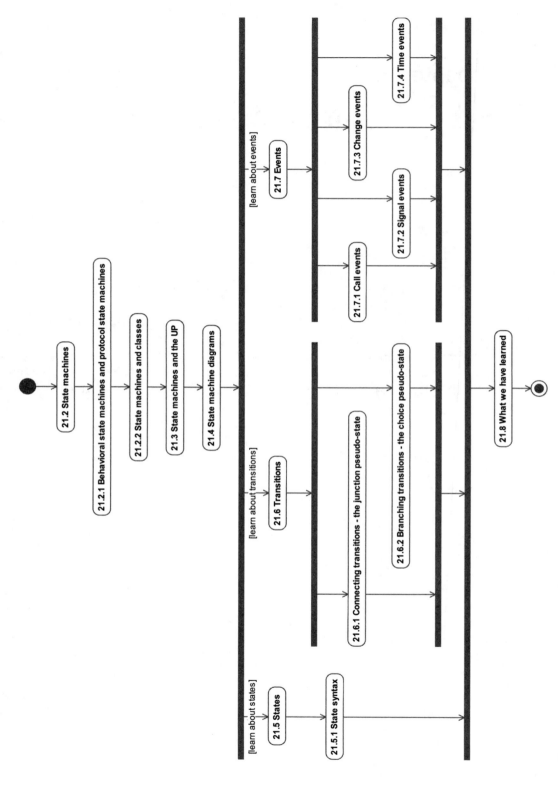

Figure 21.1

21.2 State machines

A state machine models the dynamic behavior of a reactive object.

Activity diagrams and state machine diagrams both model aspects of the dynamic behavior of a system, but they have very different semantics and purposes in modeling. Activity diagrams are based on Petri Nets (see Chapter 14) and tend to be used for modeling business processes in which several objects participate. UML state machines are based on the work of Harel [Harel 1] and tend to be used for modeling the life cycle history of a single reactive object as a finite state machine—a machine that can exist in a finite number of states. The machine makes transitions between these states in response to events in a well-defined way.

The three key elements of state machines are states, events, and transitions:

- state – "a condition or situation during the life of an object during which it satisfies some condition, performs some activity, or waits for some event" [Rumbaugh 1];
- event – "the specification of a noteworthy occurrence that has location in time and space" [Rumbaugh 1];
- transition – the movement from one state to another in response to an event.

We look at states, events, and transitions in much more detail later in this chapter.

A reactive object is an object, in the broad sense of the term, that provides the context for a state machine. Reactive objects—

- respond to external events (i.e., events outside of the object context);
- may generate and respond to internal events;
- have a life cycle modeled as a progression of states, transitions, and events;
- may have current behavior that depends on past behavior.

The real world is full of reactive objects that can be modeled with state machines. In UML modeling, state machines are generally defined in the context of a particular classifier. The state machine then models the behavior common to all instances of that classifier. You can use state machines to model the dynamic behavior of classifiers such as

- classes;
- use cases;
- subsystems;
- entire systems.

21.2.1   Behavioral state machines and protocol state machines

The UML 2 specification tells us that there are two kinds of state machines that share a common syntax:

- behavioral state machines;
- protocol state machines.

Behavioral state machines use states, transitions, and events to define the *behavior* of the context classifier. Behavioral state machines can only be used when the context classifier has a behavior of some sort to be modeled. Some classifiers, for example, interfaces and ports, have no behavior—they simply define a usage protocol. States in behavioral state machines can specify one or more actions that execute when the state is entered, resided in, or exited (see Section 21.5.1).

Protocol state machines use states, transitions, and events to define the *protocol* of the context classifier. This protocol includes the following:

- the conditions under which operations may be called on the classifier and its instances;
- the results of operation calls;
- the ordering of operation calls.

Protocol state machines say nothing about the implementation of this behavior—they only define how the behavior appears to an external entity. Protocol state machines can be used to define the protocol for *all* classifiers, including those that have no implementation. States in protocol state machines *can't* specify actions—this is the job of behavioral state machines.

In practice, modelers rarely distinguish between behavioral and protocol state machines. However, if you want to, you can use the keyword {protocol} after the protocol state machine name.

> Behavioral state machines specify behavior.

> Protocol state machines specify protocol.

21.2.2   State machines and classes

State machines are most commonly used to model the dynamic behavior of classes, and that's what we focus on in the rest of this chapter.

Each class can have a single behavioral state machine that models all the possible states, events, and transitions for all instances of that class.

Each class can also have one or more protocol state machines, although these are more often used with behaviorless classifiers such as interfaces and ports. A class inherits the protocol state machines of its parents.

If a class has more than one state machine, they must be consistent with each other.

The behavioral and protocol state machines for a class should specify the behavior and protocol required by all use cases in which instances of the class participate. Should you find that a use case requires a protocol or behavior that is *not* captured in a state machine, this indicates that the state machines are in some way incomplete.

21.3   State machines and the UP

State machines tend to be used most in the design workflow.

Like activity diagrams, there is no one place where state machines fit into the UP. You can use them in the analysis workflow to model the life cycle of classes that have interesting states such as Order and BankAccount, and you can also use them in the design workflow to model things like concurrency and Java stateful session beans. We have even used them in the requirements workflow when we were trying to understand a complex use case.

As always, the key question is, will creating a state machine for something add value to your model? If creating a state machine helps you understand a complex life cycle or behavior, it is worth doing. Otherwise you shouldn't bother.

You will probably find that you are most likely to use state machines late in the Elaboration phase and early in the Construction phase. This is when you are trying to understand the classes in your system in sufficient detail so that they can be implemented. Sometimes a state machine can be an invaluable aid to this.

From our perspective, the biggest problem with state machines is testing them. The UP test workflow is largely out of scope for this book, but we think it's important to say something about testing state machines as this is one aspect of testing that analysts and designers have to do. When you create a state machine, how do you know it is correct? With most UML modeling tools, you have no option but to perform a manual walkthrough where someone pretends to be the state machine so you can see how it reacts under different circumstances. It's usually best to work in a small group with the state machine owner walking other modelers and domain experts through the machine.

However, the *best* way to create and test state machines is to simulate them. There are several tools available that let you do this, for example, Real-Time Studio from Artisan Software (www.artisansw.com). With simulation, you can execute the state machine to see how it behaves. Some tools also allow you to generate code and test harnesses from state machines. For business modeling, such tools might be overkill, but for real-time embedded systems, where objects may have complex behavior and life cycles, they can be a real boon.

21.4   State machine diagrams

To illustrate state machine diagrams, let us consider a simple real-world example. One of the simplest and most obvious real-world objects that constantly cycles though a state machine is a light bulb. Figure 21.2 shows how you can send events to a light bulb by using a switch. The two events you can send are turnOn (this event models the supply of electric current to the bulb) and turnOff (which cuts off the current).

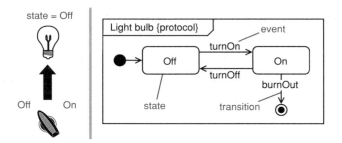

Figure 21.2

A state machine diagram contains exactly one state machine for a single reactive object. In this case, the reactive object is a system comprising the light bulb, the switch, and the electricity supply. The state machine diagram can be drawn in an explicit frame as illustrated in Figure 21.2, or it can exist within implicit frames provided by a modeling tool.

You can prefix the name of the state machine with State Machine if you wish, but this is rarely necessary as state machines have a readily identifiable syntax.

- States are rounded rectangles ("roundtangles"), apart from the initial start state (filled circle) and stop state (bull's eye).
- Transitions indicate possible paths between states and are modeled by an arrow.
- Events are written over the transitions that they trigger.

The basic semantics are also quite simple. When a reactive object in state A receives the event anEvent, it may transition to state B.

Every state machine should have an initial start state (filled circle) that indicates the first state of the sequence and, unless the states cycle endlessly, they should also have a final state (bull's eye) that terminates the sequence of transitions. Typically, you automatically transition from the initial pseudo-state to the first "real" state of the state machine. The initial pseudo-state is just used as a convenient marker for the beginning of the series of state transitions.

In Figure 21.2, when the switch is turned to the "On" position, the event turnOn is sent to the bulb. Now, in state machines, events are considered to be instantaneous. In other words, it takes zero time for the event dispatched from the switch to reach the light bulb. Instantaneous events provide an important simplification to state machine theory that makes it much more tractable. Without instantaneous events we might well have race conditions, where two events race from their source to reach the same reactive object. We would have to model this race condition as some sort of state machine!

The bulb receives the event turnOn and changes state to On in response to the event. This is the crux of state machines—objects may change state on receipt of an event. When the event turnOff is sent to the bulb, it changes state to Off.

> Events cause transitions between states.

At some point, the event burnOut may occur (when the light bulb burns out). This terminates the state machine.

We look at each element of the state machine in detail in the next few sections.

21.5   States

The UML Reference Manual [Rumbaugh 1] defines a state as "a condition or situation during the life of an object during which it satisfies some condition, performs some activity, or waits for some event". The state of an object varies over time, but at any particular point it is determined by

- the object attribute values;
- the relationships it has to other objects;
- the activities it is performing.

> A state is a semantically significant condition of an object.

Over time, objects send messages to one another, and these messages are events that may cause changes in object state. It is important to think quite carefully about what we mean by "state". In the case of the light bulb, we could (if we were quantum physicists) decide that every change to any one of the atoms or subatomic particles in the light bulb constituted a new state. This is perfectly accurate, but it would give us an infinity of states, most of which would be virtually identical.

> Identify the states that make a difference to your system.

However, from the point of view of the user of a light bulb, the only states that make a difference are On, Off, and the final state when the light bulb is burned out. This is the key to successful state modeling—you need to identify the states that *make a difference* to your system.

As another example, consider the simple Color class shown in Figure 21.3.

If we assume that red, green, and blue can each take values 0–255, then based just on the values of these attributes, objects of this class can have 256*256*256 = 16777216 possible states. Now that would be some state machine! However, we must ask ourselves the question: what is the key semantic difference between each of those states? The answer is none. Each of the 16777216 possible states represents a color, and that's all. In fact, the state machine for this class is very boring, as you can model all of the possibilities by a single state.

Color
red : int
green : int
blue : int

Figure 21.3

In summary, there has to be a semantic "difference that makes a difference" between states for you to bother to model them on a state machine. They must add value to your model. You will see examples of state machines that add value throughout this chapter and the next.

21.5.1   State syntax

UML state syntax is summarized in Figure 21.4.

Each state in a behavioral state machine may contain zero or more actions and activities. States in protocol state machines have *no* actions or activities.

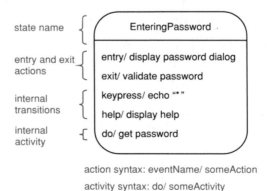

Figure 21.4

<aside>
Actions are instantaneous and uninterruptible.
</aside>

Actions are considered to be instantaneous and uninterruptible, whereas activities take a finite amount of time and can be interrupted. Each action in a state is associated with an internal transition that is triggered by an event. There can be any number of actions and internal transitions within a state.

An internal transition allows you to capture the fact that something worth modeling has happened but that it doesn't cause (or is insufficiently important to warrant modeling as) a transition to a new state. For example, in Figure 21.4, pressing one of the keys on the keyboard is certainly a noteworthy event, but it doesn't cause a transition out of the state Entering-Password. We model this as an internal event, keypress, that causes an internal transition that triggers the action echo "*".

Two special actions—the entry action and the exit action—are associated with the special events entry and exit. These two events have special semantics. The entry event occurs instantaneously and automatically on entry to the state—it is the first thing that happens when the state is entered, and it causes the associated entry action to execute. The exit event is the very last thing that happens instantaneously and automatically on exit from the state, and it causes the associated exit action to execute.

<aside>
Activities take finite time and are interruptible.
</aside>

Activities, on the other hand, take a finite amount of time and may be interrupted by the receipt of an event. The keyword do indicates an activity. Whereas actions always finish because they are atomic, it is possible to interrupt an activity before it has finished processing.

21.6 Transitions

UML transition syntax for behavioral state machines is summarized in Figure 21.5.

<aside>
Transitions show movement between states.
</aside>

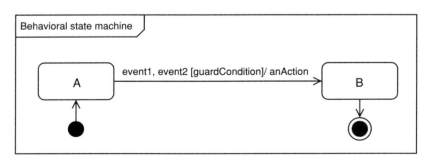

Figure 21.5

Transitions in a behavioral state machine have a simple syntax that may be used for external transitions (shown by an arrow) or internal transitions (nested within a state). Every transition has three optional elements.

1. Zero or more events – these specify external or internal occurrences that can trigger the transition.

2. Zero or one guard condition – this is a Boolean expression that must evaluate to true before the transition can occur. It is placed after the events.

3. Zero or more actions – this is a piece of work associated with the transition, and occurs when the transition fires.

You can read Figure 21.5 as follows. "On (event1 OR event2) if (guardCondition is true) then perform anAction and immediately enter state B."

The action may involve variables in the scope of the state machine. For example:

actionPerformed(actionEvent)/ command = actionEvent.getActionCommand()

In this example, actionPerformed(actionEvent) is an event generated by a button press in a Java GUI. On receipt of this event, we execute an action that stores the name of the button in the variable command.

Transitions in protocol state machines have a slightly different syntax, as illustrated in Figure 21.6.

● There is no action, as we are specifying a protocol rather than an implementation.

● The guard condition is replaced by preconditions and postconditions. Note that the precondition is placed *before* the events and the postcondition after the slash.

In both behavioral and protocol state machines, if a transition has *no* event, it is an *automatic transition*. An automatic transition doesn't wait for an event and fires when its guard condition or precondition is true.

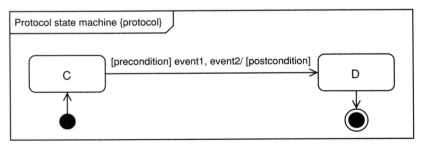

Figure 21.6

21.6.1   Connecting transitions – the junction pseudo-state

Junction
pseudo-states join or
branch transitions.

Transitions can be connected by *junction pseudo-states*. These represent points where transitions merge or branch. They are represented as filled circles that have one or more input transitions and one or more output transitions. The example in Figure 21.7 shows a state machine for the Loan class that we introduced in Section 18.12.2. Loan models the loan of a book from a library. The state machine for Loan has a simple merge junction. This is the most common usage of junction pseudo-states.

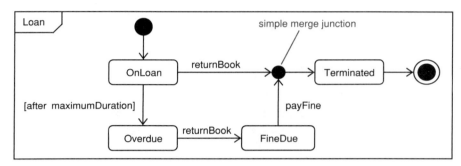

Figure 21.7

A junction pseudo-state may have more than one output transition. If this is the case, each output transition must be protected by a mutually exclusive guard condition so that only one output transition can fire. An example is shown in Figure 21.8, where we have extended the state machine for the Loan class to handle the case in which a Loan may be extended. A business rule is that a borrowed book has to be presented at the library for its Loan to be extended, so the returnBook events are still valid.

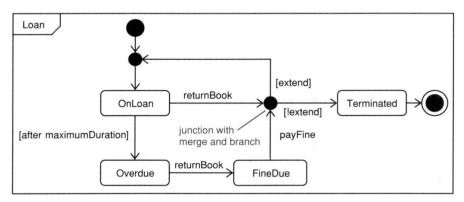

Figure 21.8

21.6.2   Branching transitions – the choice pseudo-state

If you want to show a simple branch *without* a merge, you should use a *choice pseudo-state*, as shown in Figure 21.9.

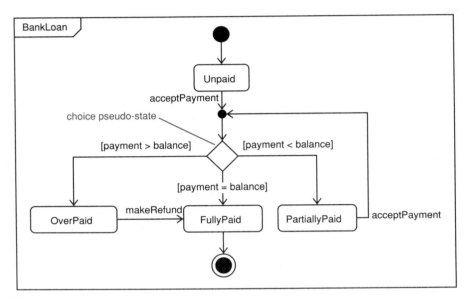

Figure 21.9

> The choice pseudo-state directs the flow through the state machine according to conditions.

The choice pseudo-state allows you to direct the flow through the state machine according to conditions that you specify on its output transitions. For example, Figure 21.9 shows a behavioral state machine for a simple BankLoan class. On receipt of the acceptPayment event, the BankLoan object transitions from the state Unpaid to one of the three states FullyPaid, OverPaid, or PartiallyPaid, depending on the amount of the payment compared to the outstanding balance on the BankLoan.

The conditions on the outgoing transitions of the choice pseudo-state must be mutually exclusive to ensure that only one of them can fire at any time.

21.7   Events

> Events trigger transitions.

UML defines an event as "the specification of a noteworthy occurrence that has location in time and space." Events trigger transitions in state machines.

Events can be shown externally on transitions, as shown in Figure 21.10, or internally within states, as shown in Figure 21.11.

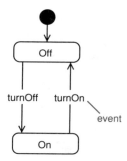

Figure 21.10

There are four types of event, each of which has different semantics:

- call event;
- signal event;
- change event;
- time event.

21.7.1   Call events

> A call event is a request for a specific operation to be invoked.

A call event is a request for a specific operation to be invoked on an instance of the context class.

A call event should have the same signature as an operation of the context class of the state machine. Receipt of a call event is a trigger for the operation to execute. As such, a call event is perhaps the simplest type of event.

The example in Figure 21.11 shows a fragment from the state machine of a SimpleBankAccount class. This class is subject to the following business constraints:

- accounts must always have a balance greater than or equal to zero;
- a withdrawal will be rejected if it would take the balance below zero.

The figure shows internal and external call events. These correspond to operations of the SimpleBankAccount class.

You can specify a sequence of actions for a call event where each action is separated by a semicolon. These actions specify the semantics of the operation, and they can use attributes and operations of the context class. If the operation has a return type, the call event has a return value of that type.

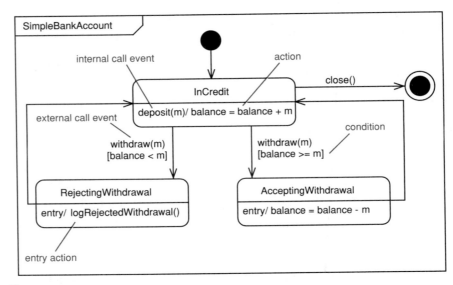

Figure 21.11

21.7.2   Signal events

A signal is a package of information that is sent asynchronously between objects. You model a signal as a stereotyped class that holds the information to be communicated in its attributes, as illustrated in Figure 21.12. A signal usually doesn't have any operations because its sole purpose is to carry information.

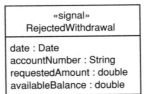

Figure 21.12

In Figure 21.13 we have updated the state machine for SimpleBankAccount so that it sends a signal when a withdrawal is rejected. A signal send is indicated by a convex pentagon with the signal name inside. This is the same syntax as is used in activity diagrams (see Section 15.6 where we discuss signals in more depth).

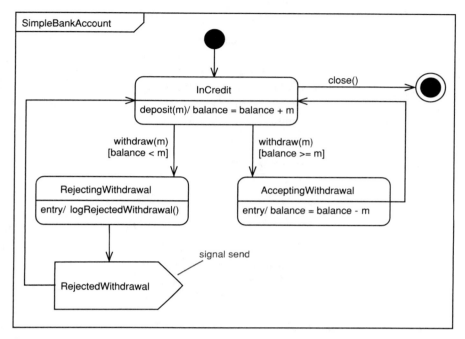

Figure 21.13

A signal receipt is indicated by a concave pentagon, as shown in the state machine fragment in Figure 21.14. It specifies an operation of the context class that accepts the signal as a parameter.

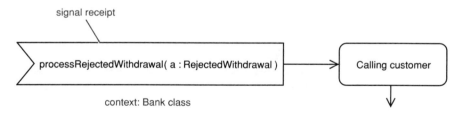

Figure 21.14

You can also show signal receipts on internal or external transitions by using the standard eventName/ action notation discussed in Sections 21.5.1 and 21.6.

Change events

A change event is specified as a Boolean expression, as illustrated in Figure 21.15. The action associated with the event is performed when the value of the Boolean expression transitions from false to true. All values in the Boolean expression must be constants, globals, or attributes or operations of the context class. From the implementation perspective, a change event implies continually testing the Boolean condition while in the state.

> Change events occur when a Boolean expression changes value from false to true.

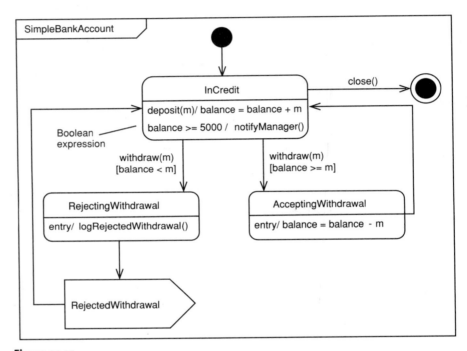

Figure 21.15

In Figure 21.15, we have modified the SimpleBankAccount state machine so that the manager will be notified if the account balance goes greater than or equal to 5000. This notification is so the manager can alert the customer about other investment options.

Change events are *positive edge triggered*. This means they are triggered each time the value of the Boolean expression changes from false to true. The Boolean expression must go back to false and then transition to true again for the change event to be retriggered.

Positive edge triggering is exactly the behavior we want for our Simple-BankAccount. The action notifyManager() will *only* be invoked when the account balance transitions from less than 5000 to 5000 or more. Clearly, if the balance is oscillating rapidly around 5000, the manager will receive multiple notifications. We assume that the manager has some business process in place to handle this.

21.7.4   Time events

> Time events occur in response to time.

Time events are usually indicated by the keywords when and after. The keyword when specifies a *particular* time at which the event is triggered; after specifies a threshold time *after* which the event is triggered. Examples are when(date = 07/10/2005) and after(3 months).

You should always ensure that the units of time (hours, days, months, etc.) are recorded on the diagram for each time event. Any symbols in the expression must be constants, globals, or attributes or operations of the context class.

The example in Figure 21.16 is a fragment from the state machine of a CreditAccount class that has a limited (and somewhat draconian) credit facility. You can see that after a CreditAccount object has been in the state Overdrawn for three months, it transitions to the state Frozen.

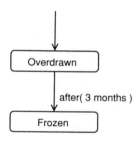

context: CreditAccount class

Figure 21.16

21.8   **What we have learned**

In this chapter you have seen how to construct basic state machines by using states, actions, activities, events, and transitions. You have learned the following.

- State machines are based on the work of Harel.
  - — State machines model the dynamic behavior of a reactive object.
  - — State machine diagrams contain a single state machine for a single reactive object.

- A reactive object provides the context for a state machine.
  — Reactive objects:
    - respond to external events;
    - may generate internal events;
    - have a clear life cycle that can be modeled as a progression of states, transitions, and events;
    - have current behavior that may depend on past behavior.
  — Examples of reactive objects:
    - classes (most common);
    - use cases;
    - subsystems;
    - entire systems.
- There are two types of state machines:
  — behavioral state machines:
    - model the behavior of a context classifier;
    - states in behavioral state machines may contain zero or more actions and activities;
  — protocol state machines:
    - model the protocol of a context classifier;
    - states in protocol state machines have *no* actions or activities.
- Actions – pieces of work that are instantaneous and uninterruptible:
  — may occur within a state, associated with an internal transition;
  — may occur outside a state, associated with an external transition.
- Activities – pieces of work that take a finite time and are interruptible:
  — may occur only within a state.
- State – a semantically significant condition of an object.
  — Object state is determined by:
    - object attribute values;
    - relationships to other objects;
    - activities the object is performing.
  — State syntax:
    - entry action – performed immediately on entry to the state;
    - exit action – performed immediately on exit from the state;
    - internal transitions – these are caused by events that are not significant enough to warrant a transition to a new state:
      - the event is processed by an internal transition within the state;
    - internal activity – a piece of work that takes a finite amount of time and that may be interrupted.

- Transition – a movement between two states.
  — Transition syntax:
    - event – the event that triggers the transition;
    - guard condition – a Boolean expression that must be true before the transition occurs;
    - action – an action that occurs instantaneously with the transition;
    - junction pseudo-state – joins or branches transitions;
    - choice pseudo-state – directs the flow through the state machine according to conditions.
- Event – something of note that occurs to a reactive object. The types of event are:
  — call event:
    - a call for a set of actions to occur;
    - an operation invocation on the object;
  — signal event:
    - the receipt of a signal – a signal is an asynchronous one-way communication between objects;
  — change event:
    - occurs when some Boolean condition changes from false to true (i.e., edge is triggered on the false-to-true transition);
  — time event:
    - keyword after – occurs after a time period;
    - keyword when – occurs when some time condition becomes true.

chapter 22

Advanced state machines

22.1 Chapter roadmap

We begin this chapter with a discussion of composite states. These are states that themselves contain a nested state machine. Section 22.2 introduces the idea of nested state machines, or submachines. We then discuss two types of composite states—the simple composite state (22.2.1) and the orthogonal composite state (22.2.2). In Section 22.3 we look at how we may refer to state machines in separate diagrams by using submachine states.

When you have two or more concurrent submachines, you often need to establish some sort of communication between them. We discuss this in Section 22.4 and introduce a communication strategy that uses attribute values of the context object.

In Section 22.5, we introduce the idea of history, which is about giving a superstate "memory" of its final substate before an outgoing transition. In Sections 22.5.1 and 22.5.2 we discuss the two variants of this, shallow and deep history.

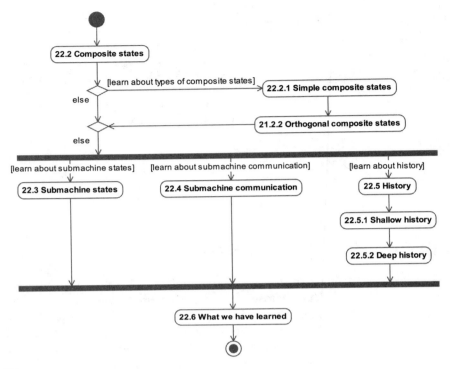

Figure 22.1

22.2   Composite states

Composite states contain one or more nested submachines.

A composite state is a state that contains nested states.

These nested states are organized into one or more state machines called *submachines*. Each submachine exists in its own *region* within the composite state icon. Regions are just areas of the state icon separated by dashed lines. You can see a simple example in Figure 22.2.

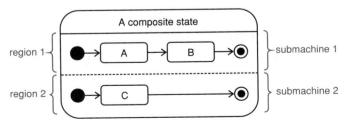

Figure 22.2

Nested substates inherit all of the transitions of their containing superstates.

Nested states inherit all of the transitions of their containing states. This is a very important point. If, for example, the composite state itself has a particular transition, each of the states nested within it *also* has this transition.

The final pseudo-state of a submachine *only applies within that region*. So, for example, in Figure 22.2, if the submachine in region 1 reaches its final state first, that region will terminate, but region 2 will continue to execute. If you wish to stop the execution of the whole composite state, you can use the terminate pseudo-state as shown in Figure 22.3. In this example, the whole composite state stops as soon as the terminate pseudo-state is reached.

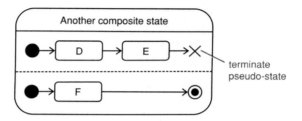

Figure 22.3

Nested states can also be composite states. However, you should generally keep nesting of composite states to a maximum of two or three levels if you can, as any more than this can make the state machine hard to read and understand.

To keep a state machine diagram clear and simple, you sometimes need to hide the details of a composite state. You can indicate that a state is a composite state without explicitly showing its decomposition by adding the *composition icon* to the state. This is an optional adornment, but it gives a very useful indication that a state has a decomposition, so we recommend you always use it. You can see the composition icon in Figure 22.4.

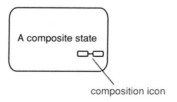

Figure 22.4

There are two types of composite state depending on how many regions they have.

1. Simple composite state – one region only.

2. Orthogonal composite states – two or more regions.

We look at each of these types of composite state in turn in the next two subsections.

Simple composite states

Simple composite
states contain a single
nested state machine.

A simple composite state is a composite state that contains a single region. For example, Figure 22.5 shows the state machine for a class called ISPDialer. This class is responsible for dialing in to an Internet service provider. The state DialingISP is a simple composite state because it only has one region. There are a couple of interesting points about this state machine.

- The transition out of DialingISP triggered by the cancel event is inherited by each of the substates in the DialingISP submachine. This is *very* convenient, as it means that on receipt of the cancel event we will *always* transition from whatever substate we are in to the state NotConnected. Use of super-states and substates in this way can greatly simplify a state machine.

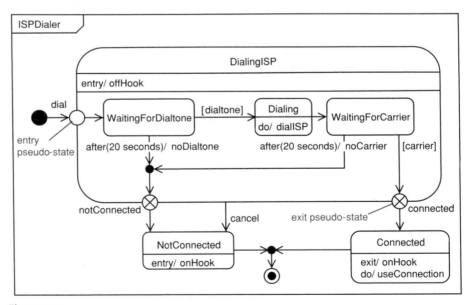

Figure 22.5

- DialingISP has one entry pseudo-state called dial, and two exit pseudo-states called notConnected and connected. An entry pseudo-state is shown as a circle that is usually placed on the border of the composite state (although it may also be placed inside the border), and it indicates a point of entry into the submachine. Similarly, the exit pseudo-state, which is drawn as a circle with a cross in it, indicates an exit from the submachine.

Entry and exit pseudo-states are very useful as they allow you to define different ways of entering and exiting from composite states. They provide connection points to which you connect transitions to/from other states.

Here is a complete walkthrough for the ISPDialer class state machine.

1. We enter the superstate DialingISP via the entry pseudo-state dial and immediately execute the entry action offHook—this puts the modem off-hook.

2. We enter the single region, and the state WaitingForDialtone.

3. We wait in the state WaitingForDialtone for a maximum of 20 seconds.

4. If we don't get a dial tone before 20 seconds has elapsed:
    4.1. we perform the action noDialtone as we transition via the exit pseudo-state notConnected to the state NotConnected;
    4.2. on entry to NotConnected we put the phone back on the hook (onHook action);
    4.3. we transition to the stop state.

5. If we get a dial tone (i.e., the guard condition [dialtone] evaluates to true) within 20 seconds:
    5.1. we transition to the state Dialing where we perform the activity dialISP;
    5.2. as soon as the dialISP activity is finished, we automatically transition to the state WaitingForCarrier;
    5.3. we wait in the state WaitingForCarrier for a maximum of 20 seconds.
    5.4. If we don't get a carrier within 20 seconds:
        5.4.1. we perform the action noCarrier as we transition via the exit pseudo-state notConnected to the state NotConnected;
        5.4.2. on entry to NotConnected we put the phone back on the hook;
        5.4.3. we transition to the stop state.
    5.5. If we get a carrier within 20 seconds:
        5.5.1. we automatically transition from the DialingISP superstate via the exit pseudo-state connected to the Connected state;
        5.5.2. we perform the action useConnection until it is finished;
        5.5.3. on exit from Connected we put the phone back on the hook;
        5.5.4. we transition to the stop state.

6. If at *any point* while we are in the superstate DialingISP we receive the cancel event:

   6.1. we immediately transition to the state NotConnected;

   6.2. on entry to NotConnected we put the phone back on the hook;

   6.3. we transition to the stop state.

22.2.2   Orthogonal composite states

> Orthogonal composite states contain two or more nested submachines that execute concurrently.

Orthogonal composite states contain two or more submachines that execute concurrently.

When you enter the composite state, all of its submachines start executing at once—this is an implicit fork.

There are two ways you can exit from the composite state.

1. Both submachines finish—this is an implicit join.

2. One of the submachines transitions to a state *outside* the superstate, usually via an exit pseudo-state. This does *not* cause a join—there is no synchronization of submachines, and the remaining submachines simply abort.

To investigate concurrent composite states, we need a system that exhibits a degree of concurrency. We model a simple burglar alarm system that consists of a control box, security and fire sensors, and an alarm box. The state machine for the whole system is shown in Figure 22.6.

This state machine captures two essential features of the alarm system.

1. If an intruder sensor is triggered, the alarm box sounds the intruder alarm for 15 minutes before the system resets and goes back into the state Monitoring. This is to comply with zoning laws.

2. If there is a fire while the intruder alarm is sounding, there is an immediate transition from the state SoundingIntruderAlarm to the state SoundingFireAlarm and the fire alarm sounds. This means that the fire alarm always takes precedence over the intruder alarm.

Initializing and Monitoring are composite states. The Initializing composite state is shown expanded in Figure 22.7.

When we enter this state, a fork occurs and two submachines start executing concurrently. In the top submachine, the state InitializingFireSensors runs the initialization process for the fire sensors, and in the bottom submachine, the state InitializingSecuritySensors does the same for the security sensors.

Under normal conditions, we automatically transition from the Initializing superstate when *both* submachines finish. This is a join, and it synchronizes the submachines such that we can't progress unless both the fire sensors *and* the security sensors are initialized. This initialization obviously depends on

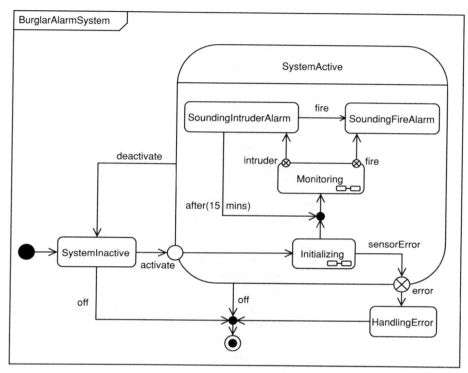

Figure 22.6

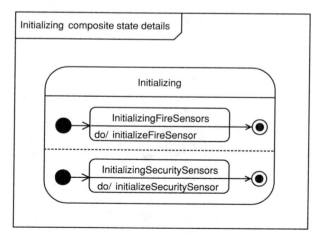

Figure 22.7

the types of sensors being used, but it may, in the simplest case, just be a short "warm up" delay.

There is also a sensorError transition out of the Initializing state (Figure 22.6) that is inherited by both its substates. This allows an immediate exit from Initializing on encountering a sensor error. The Initializing composite state and all its substates also inherit the off transition from their SystemActive superstate. This allows an immediate exit from Initializing (and all other SystemActive substates) on receipt of an off event.

Sometimes you want to start concurrent threads of control, but do *not* need to synchronize them with a join when they complete. This is the case for the Monitoring composite state shown in the state machine diagram in Figure 22.8. This state has some interesting features.

- There is *no* synchronization between the two submachines:
  - on a fire event, we make an explicit transition from MonitoringFireSensors to the fire exit pseudo-state that takes us out of Monitoring. The MonitoringFireSensors submachine terminates but the MonitoringSecuritySensors submachine keeps executing;
  - similarly, on an intruder event, we make an explicit transition from MonitoringSecuritySensors to the intruder exit pseudo-state that takes us out of the Monitoring superstate. The MonitoringSecuritySensors submachine terminates but the MonitoringFireSensors submachine keeps on executing.
- The Monitoring composite state and all its substates inherit the off transition from their SystemActive superstate. You can see this in Figure 22.6. This allows the system to shut down immediately in response to an off event no matter what substate happens to be active.

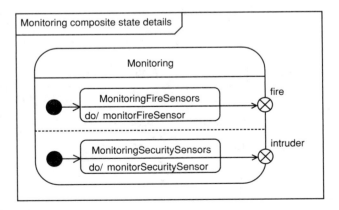

Figure 22.8

From this example, you can see how using concurrent composite states, either with or without synchronization, allows you to model concurrency very effectively.

22.3 Submachine states

A submachine state references another state machine.

A submachine state is a special state that references a state machine recorded in a separate diagram. You can think of it being a bit like a subroutine call from one state machine to another. Submachine states are semantically equivalent to composite states.

You can use submachine states to simplify complex state machines. You partition the state machines into separate diagrams and then, using submachine states, you reference these diagrams from a main diagram.

Submachine states can provide a way to reuse behavior. You define the behavior in one diagram and then reference this diagram whenever you need to. For example, you might have two very similar burglar alarm systems that have some behavior in common. You can define this behavior in its own diagram, and then reference that diagram by using submachine states in the state machines of each burglar alarm system.

Submachine states are named as follows:

state name : name of referenced state machine diagram

Figure 22.9 shows a state machine diagram that describes behavior that we would like to reuse in another diagram. Notice how you can show entry and

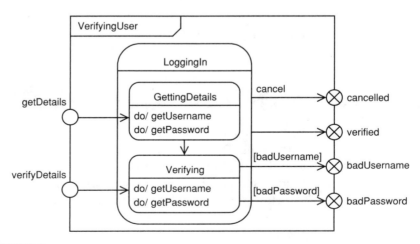

Figure 22.9

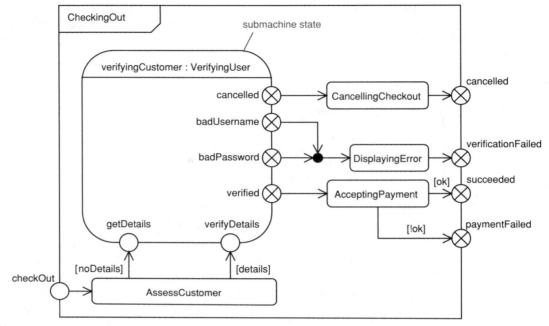

Figure 22.10

exit pseudo-states on the border of the frame. You can also place them inside the border, but we think that putting them *on* the border indicates their function as entry and exit points from the state machine more clearly.

You can reference the VerifyingUser state machine by using a submachine state as shown in Figure 22.10. We have called the submachine state verifying-Customer. When reading this diagram, you have to imagine the contents of the VerifyingUser diagram replacing the submachine state.

22.4   Submachine communication

You have seen in Figure 22.7 how you can use forks and joins to spawn concurrent submachines and then bring them back into synchronization. This is a kind of synchronous communication between the submachines—the concurrent submachines wait for each other until they have *all* finished.

However, very often you need to communicate between submachines but don't want to bring the machines into synchronization to do this. This is called asynchronous communication.

In UML you can achieve asynchronous communication by allowing one submachine to leave "messages" or "flags" as it executes. Other submachines can pick up these flags as and when they are ready.

You create these flags by manipulating attribute values of the state machine's context object. The basic strategy is that one submachine sets attribute values, and other submachines use the attribute values in guard conditions on their transitions.

In the OrderProcessing state shown in Figure 22.11, you can't predict whether a given order will be assembled or paid for first. Some orders may need to wait for new stock to arrive before they can be assembled, and some may be assembled off the shelf. Similarly, some payments might be more or less instantaneous (by credit card, for example) and some might take several working days (by check, for example). However, in this business there is a business rule that creates a logical dependency between the two submachines—you can't deliver an order until it has been assembled *and* paid for.

In the upper submachine of Figure 22.11, when the AcceptingPayment state is finished, we transition to the state PaidFor where we set the value of the attribute paidFor to true. In the lower submachine, when we have finished AssemblingOrder, we can *only* transition to DeliveringOrder when the attribute paidFor is equal to true. We have achieved asynchronous communication between the two submachines by using an attribute as a flag that one submachine sets and the other queries—this is a simple and common mechanism. Finally, both submachines end and synchronize, and we leave the Order-Processing state.

> You can use attribute values to communicate asynchronously between concurrent submachines.

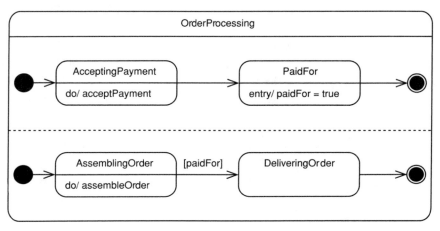

Figure 22.11

22.5   History

You often encounter the following situation when modeling with state machines.

● You are within a substate A of a composite state.

● You transition out of the composite state (and therefore out of substate A).

● You go through one or more external states.

● You transition back into the composite state *but* would like to continue at the substate A where you left off.

How can you achieve this? Clearly, the composite state needs some way of remembering which substate you were in when you left it. This requirement to pick up where you left off is so common that UML includes history pseudo-states specifically to handle it.

With history, you give superstates memory of the last active substate before the superstate was exited. There are two types of history pseudo-state—the shallow and the deep. We consider each of them in turn in the next two sections.

22.5.1   Shallow history

Figure 22.12 shows a state machine for the BrowseCatalog use case in an e-commerce system.

In this example you can transition from the Browsing superstate on three events:

● exit – terminate the state machine and return to whatever you were doing previously (we don't need to consider this in any further detail);

● goToBasket – transition to the composite state DisplayingBasket where the current contents of the shopping basket are displayed;

● goToCheckout – transition to the composite state CheckingOut where the order summarizing the purchases is presented to the customer.

When you return to Browsing from DisplayingBasket or CheckingOut, it would be good to return users to exactly where they were when they left—this is only reasonable.

The shallow history pseudo-state can have many incoming transitions, but only one outgoing transition. The shallow history pseudo-state *remembers* which substate you were in when you left the superstate. If you then transition from an external state back to the history state, the indicator automatically redirects the transition to the last remembered substate (here, DisplayingIndex or DisplayingItem). If this is the first time you have entered the superstate, there will

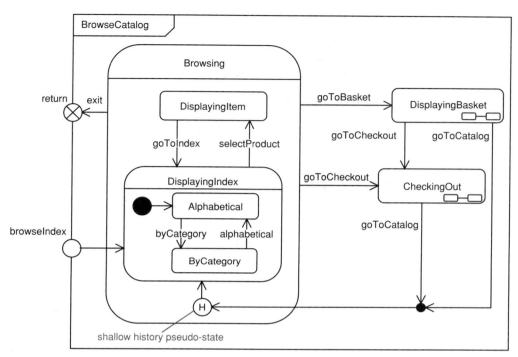

Figure 22.12

be *no* last remembered substate and, in this case, the history state indicator's single outgoing transition fires and you transition to DisplayingIndex.

With history, you give superstates memory of the last active substate before the superstate was exited. With shallow history, you only remember which substate you were in *at the same level* as the history state indicator itself. However, you can see in Figure 22.12 that DisplayingIndex is itself a composite state. Shallow history will not remember the substates within this state—for that you need deep history.

22.5.2   Deep history

> Deep history remembers the last substate you were in at the same level or lower than the deep history pseudo-state.

With deep history, you not only remember which substate you were in at the same level as the history pseudo-state, you remember which sub-substate you were in, to an infinite depth.

In Figure 22.13, we have modified the state machine to use deep history. In this case you will not only return to either DisplayingIndex or DisplayingItem, you will return to the right type of index (Alphabetical or ByCategory). You could model the same thing *without* using deep history, but it would be much more difficult.

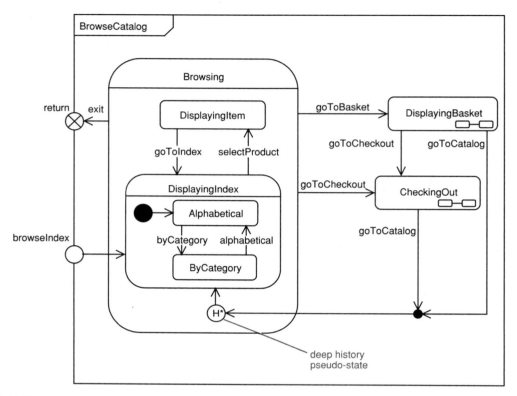

Figure 22.13

Like shallow history, deep history can have many incoming transitions but only a single outgoing transition. The outgoing transition fires if this is the first time you have entered the superstate and there is *no* last remembered substate.

22.6   What we have learned

UML provides a rich state machine syntax that allows you to capture complex behavior in concise state machines. You have learned the following.

- Composite states can contain one or more nested submachines – substates inherit all of the transitions of their superstate.
  — Each submachine exists in its own region.
  — The final pseudo-state only applies within a region.
  — Use the terminate pseudo-state to terminate all regions.

- The sequential composite state contains exactly one nested submachine.
- The concurrent composite state contains two or more nested submachines that execute concurrently.
  - There is a fork on entering the state, and the submachines start their concurrent execution.
  - If all the submachines have a stop state, you can't leave the superstate until all submachines have finished – this is a join.
  - You can leave the superstate without a join if the submachines make explicit transitions to external states.
- A submachine state references another state machine:
  - simplifies complex state machines;
  - reuses state machines.
- Submachine communication:
  - attribute values – one submachine sets the value of an attribute and the other submachines check this value.
- History allows a superstate to remember the last substate before an outgoing transition.
  - Shallow history allows a superstate to remember the last substate at the *same* level as the shallow history pseudo-state before an outgoing transition:
    - on transitioning back into the shallow history pseudo-state, the transition is routed to the last remembered substate;
    - if it is the first entry (no last remembered substate), the single output transition of the shallow history pseudo-state fires.
  - Deep history allows a superstate to remember the last substate at *any* level before an outgoing transition:
    - on transitioning back into the deep history pseudo-state, the transition is routed to the last remembered substate;
    - if it is the first entry (no last remembered substate), the single output transition of the deep history pseudo-state fires.

part 5

Implementation

chapter **23**

The implementation workflow

23.1	Chapter roadmap

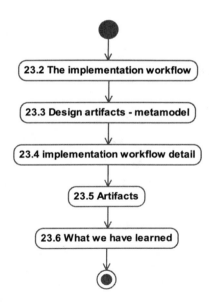

Figure 23.1

There is very little work for the OO analyst/designer in the implementation workflow, so this is the most lightweight part of the book. Nevertheless, implementation does bear some scrutiny as, although the primary activity in the implementation workflow is producing code, you will see that there are still some elements of UML modeling involved.

23.2   The implementation workflow

> The implementation workflow is the main focus of the Construction phase.

The implementation workflow begins in earnest in the Elaboration phase and is the main focus of the Construction phase (Figure 23.2).

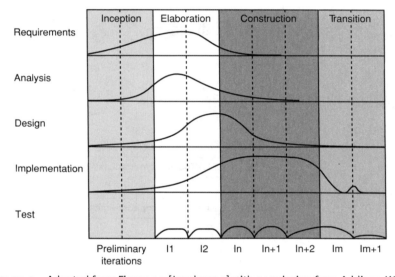

Figure 23.2   Adapted from Figure 1.5 [Jacobson 1] with permission from Addison-Wesley

> Implementation is about transforming a design model into executable code.

Implementation is about transforming a design model into executable code. From the point of view of the analyst/designer, the purpose of implementation is to produce an implementation model if that is required. This model involves the (mostly tactical) allocation of design classes to components. How this is done depends to a great extent on the target programming language.

The main focus of the implementation workflow is to produce executable code. The production of an implementation model may be a by-product of this focus, rather than an explicit modeling activity. In fact, many modeling tools allow you to reverse-engineer an implementation model from source code. This strategy effectively leaves implementation modeling up to the programmers.

However, there are two cases in which an explicit implementation modeling activity, performed by trained OO analyst/designers, might be very important.

- If you intend to generate code directly from the model, you will need to specify details such as source files and components (unless you take the modeling tool defaults).

- If you are doing component-based development (CBD) to reuse components, the allocation of design classes and interfaces to components becomes a strategic issue. You may want to model this first, rather than leave it to the individual programmer.

In this chapter, we look at what's involved in putting together an implementation model.

23.3   Implementation artifacts – metamodel

The relationship between the implementation model and the design model is very simple. The implementation model is really just the implementation view of a design model—that is, it is *part* of the design model. This is shown in Figure 23.3.

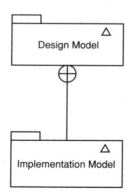

Figure 23.3

The implementation model is the part of the design model that deals with implementation issues. It specifies how the design elements are manifest by artifacts, and how these artifacts are deployed onto nodes. Artifacts represent the specifications of real-world things such as source files, and

> The implementation model is part of the design model.

nodes represent the specifications of hardware or execution environments onto which those things are deployed. The relationship between the design model and implementation model is illustrated in Figure 23.4.

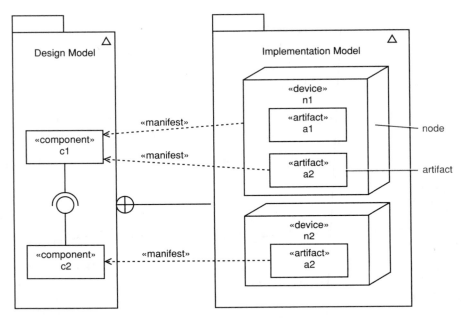

Figure 23.4

The «manifest» relationship between artifacts and components indicates that the artifacts are the physical representations of the components. For example, a component may comprise a class and an interface, and both of these are realized by a single artifact, a file containing source code.

Design components are logical entities that group design elements, but implementation artifacts map to real, physical grouping mechanisms of the target implementation language.

23.4   Implementation workflow detail

As you can see from Figure 23.5, the implementation workflow involves the architect, system integrator, and component engineer. Individual analyst/ designers, or small teams of analyst/designers, may play any of these three

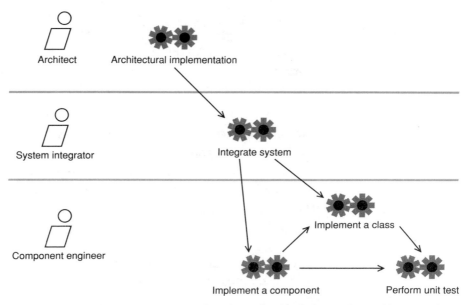

Figure 23.5   Adapted from Figure 10.16 [Jacobson 1] with permission from Addison-Wesley

roles in the implementation workflow. Their focus will be on producing deployment and implementation models (part of architectural implementation). System integration, class implementation, and unit testing are beyond the scope of this book—these are programming activities rather than analysis and design activities. (Note that in Figure 23.5 we have updated the original figure from Implement a subsystem to the more general Implement a component as this is more correct from the UML 2 perspective.)

23.5   Artifacts

The key artifact of the implementation workflow from the point of view of the OO analyst/designer is the implementation model. This model consists of component diagrams to show how artifacts manifest components, and a new type of diagram, the deployment diagram. The deployment diagram models the physical computational nodes on which the software artifacts will be deployed, and the relationships between those nodes. We look at deployment diagrams in detail in Chapter 24.

23.6   What we have learned

Implementation is primarily about creating code. However, the OO analyst/designer may be called on to create an implementation model. You have learned the following.

- The implementation workflow is the main focus of the Construction phase.
- Implementation is about transforming a design model into executable code.
- Implementation modeling is important when:
  — you intend to forward-engineer from the model (generate code);
  — you are doing CBD in order to get reuse.
- The implementation model is part of the design model.
- Artifacts – represent the specifications of real-world things such as source files:
  — components are manifest by artifacts;
  — artifacts are deployed onto nodes.
- Nodes – represent the specifications of hardware or execution environments.

chapter **24**
Deployment

24.1 Chapter roadmap

In this chapter we look at the UP activity Architectural implementation and the way to produce a deployment diagram. This is a diagram that shows how the software you are developing will be deployed over physical hardware and how that hardware is connected. In Section 24.5 we present a simple Java example.

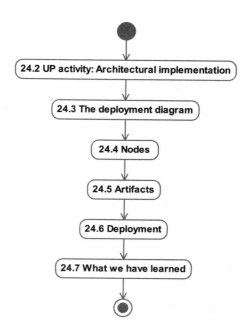

Figure 24.1

24.2   UP activity: Architectural implementation

Architectural implementation is about identifying architecturally significant components and mapping them to physical hardware.

This activity is about identifying architecturally significant components and mapping them to physical hardware—it is about modeling the physical structure and distribution of the system. The key phrase is "architecturally significant". In principle, you could model the physical deployment of the system exhaustively. In practice, this would probably add little value as the exact deployment details of many components will have little architectural importance. The exception to this is if you are generating code from the model. In this case, you might need a more detailed deployment model so that your generator knows where to put its output artifacts and can create the appropriate deployment descriptors and build files.

The UP activity Architectural implementation is shown in Figure 24.2. We have modified this figure from the original in two ways and have identified the changes by graying the affected artifacts.

- In accordance with UML 2 we show a subsystem as a stereotyped component rather than as a stereotyped package.

- We have explicitly shown the artifacts and nodes output from the activity. These were implicit in the original figure.

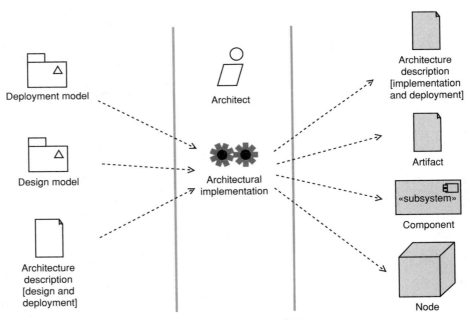

Figure 24.2.   Adapted from Figure 10.17 [Jacobson 1] with permission from Addison-Wesley

From the point of view of the OO analyst/designer, the key activity in Architectural implementation is creating one or more deployment diagrams. The deployment diagram brings components, artifacts, and nodes together to specify the physical architecture of the system. We look at this diagram in detail in the rest of this chapter.

The other activity is updating the architecture description with architecturally important deployment and implementation details.

24.3   The deployment diagram

In UML, deployment is the process of assigning artifacts to nodes or artifact instances to node instances. We look at artifacts and nodes in detail shortly.

The deployment diagram specifies the physical hardware on which the software system will execute and also specifies how the software is deployed on that hardware.

> The deployment diagram maps the software architecture to the hardware architecture.

The deployment diagram maps the software architecture created in design to a physical system architecture that executes it. In distributed systems, it models the distribution of the software across physical nodes.

There are two forms of deployment diagram.

> Descriptor form deployment diagram – artifacts deployed on nodes.

1. Descriptor form – contains nodes, relationships between nodes, and artifacts. A node represents a type of hardware (such as a PC). Similarly, an artifact represents a type of physical software artifact such as a Java JAR file.

> Instance form deployment diagram – artifact instances deployed on node instances.

2. Instance form – contains node instances, relationships between node instances, and artifact instances. A node instance represents a specific, identifiable piece of hardware (such as Jim's PC). An artifact instance represents a specific instance of a type of software, such as the particular copy of FrameMaker (www.adobe.com) used to write this, or a particular JAR file. If you don't know (or don't care about) the details of specific instances, you can use anonymous instances.

Although we're discussing it as an implementation activity, a first-cut deployment diagram is often created in design as part of the process of deciding the final hardware architecture. You might start by creating a descriptor form deployment diagram limited to nodes and the connections between them. You can then refine this into one or more instance form deployment diagrams, showing possible arrangements of anonymous node instances. When you know the details of the hardware at a deployment site, you can create an instance form deployment diagram showing the actual machines at this site, if so required.

The construction of the deployment diagram is therefore a two-step process.

1. In the design workflow, focus mainly on node or node instances and connections.

2. In the implementation workflow, focus on assigning artifact instances to node instances (instance form), or artifacts to nodes (descriptor form).

In the next two sections we look at nodes and artifacts in detail.

24.4   Nodes

> A node represents a type of computational resource.

The UML 2.0 specification [UML2S] states: "A node represents a type of computational resource upon which artifacts can be deployed for execution."
    There are two standard stereotypes for nodes.

- «device» – the node represents a type of physical device such as a PC or a Sun Fire server.

- «execution environment» – the node represents a type of execution environment for software such as an Apache web server or the JBoss EJB (Enterprise JavaBeans) container.

Nodes can be nested in nodes. For example, the descriptor form deployment diagram in shows that zero or more WindowsPCs running the Firefox web browser can be connected to zero or more Apache web servers, each running on a LinuxPC. Notice that by naming the nodes WindowsPC and LinuxPC, we have included both the type of hardware (PC) *and* the operating system—the execution environment for all software running on those devices. This is common practice, as having a separate execution environment node specifically for the operating system clutters the diagram. We show Firefox as an execution environment because it can run plug-in components such as Java applets.

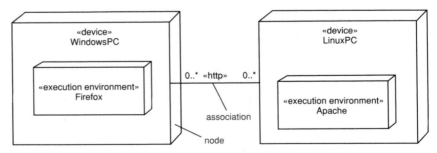

Figure 24.3

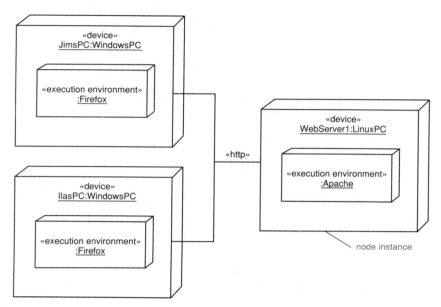

Figure 24.4

An association between nodes represents a communication channel over which information can be passed back and forth. In Figure 24.3 we have stereotyped the association «http» to indicate that it represents an HTTP (HyperText Transport Protocol) connection between the two nodes.

If you want to show specific instances of nodes, you can use the instance form deployment diagram illustrated in Figure 24.4. The figure shows two actual PCs, JimsPC and IlasPC, connected to the Linux machine WebServer1. In the instance form, the node instances represent actual physical devices or actual instances of execution environments running on those devices. We underline the element names to indicate that they represent node instances.

> A node instance represents a specific computational resource.

Descriptor form deployment diagrams are good for modeling a type of physical architecture. Instance form deployment diagrams are good for modeling an actual deployment of that architecture at a particular site.

According to *The UML User Guide* [Booch 2], deployment diagrams are the most stereotyped part of UML. You can assign your own icons to stereotypes, and this allows you to use symbols in the deployment diagram that look as much like the actual hardware as possible. This makes it easy to read the deployment diagram at a glance. Having an extensive collection of clip art can help with this! An example of a fully stereotyped descriptor form deployment diagram is shown in Figure 24.5.

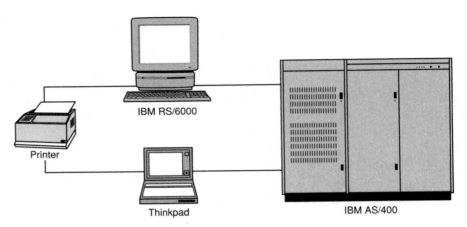

Figure 24.5

24.5   Artifacts

An artifact represents the specification of a concrete, real-world thing such as the source file BankAccount.java. Artifacts are deployed on nodes. Some examples of artifacts are

> An artifact represents the *specification* of a real-world thing such as a file.

- source files;
- executable files;
- scripts;
- database tables;
- documents;
- outputs of the development process, e.g., a UML model.

> An artifact instance represents a specific *instance* of a particular artifact.

An artifact instance represents a specific instance of a particular artifact, for example, a specific copy of BankAccount.java deployed on a particular machine. Artifact instances are deployed on node instances.

> Artifacts can manifest one or more components.

An artifact can provide the physical manifestation for *any* kind of UML element. Typically, they manifest one or more components, as illustrated in Figure 24.6. This figure shows an artifact, librarySystem.jar, that manifests three white-box components, Book, Library, and Ticket. Artifacts are labelled with the stereotype «artifact» and may have an artifact icon placed in their top right-hand corner as shown in the figure. The figure also illustrates that artifacts may depend on other artifacts. In this case, the artifact librarySystem.jar depends on the artifact jdom.jar.

As well as a name, each artifact has a filename in its specification that indicates the physical location of the artifact. For example, this filename could

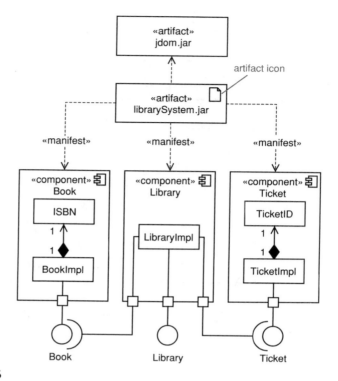

artifact icon

Figure 24.6

specify a URL where the master copy of the artifact is found. Artifact instances have file names that point to the physical location of the instance.

Let's look at the JAR file in Figure 24.6 in more depth. To create this JAR, you perform two steps.

1. Compile the Java source files for the classes Book, ISBN, BookImpl, Library, LibraryImpl, Ticket, TicketID, and TicketImpl.

2. Use the Java jar tool to create a JAR file from these compiled files.

This creates the JAR file shown in Figure 24.7. You can see that this JAR file contains a Java class file for each class and interface in the system. It also contains a directory, META_INF, that contains a file called MANIFEST.MF. This file is generated by the jar tool, and it describes the contents of the JAR. Notice in the figure how you can show dependencies between artifacts and artifacts nested within artifacts.

Although Figure 24.7 is correct from a UML modeling perspective, it is not particularly descriptive, as everything is just an artifact. The .class extension tells you that some of the artifacts represent compiled Java class files,

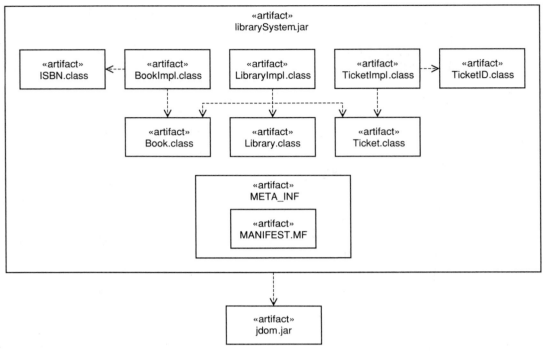

Figure 24.7

but it isn't easy to tell, for example, that META_INF represents a directory. This highlights the need to stereotype artifacts to indicate clearly exactly what each one represents.

UML provides a small number of standard artifact stereotypes that represent different types of files. These are listed in Table 24.1.

Table 24.1

Artifact stereotype	Semantics
«file»	A physical file
«deployment spec»	A specification of deployment details (e.g., web.xml in J2EE)
«document»	A generic file that holds some information
«executable»	An executable program file
«library»	A static or dynamic library such as a dynamic link library (DLL) or Java Archive (JAR) file
«script»	A script that can be executed by an interpreter
«source»	A source file that can be compiled into an executable file

You can expect that various UML profiles will be developed over time for specific software platforms such as J2EE (Java 2 Platform, Enterprise Edition) and Microsoft .NET. These will provide a richer set of artifact (and other) stereotypes. The UML 2.0 specification [UML2S] provides example profiles for J2EE and EJB, Microsoft COM, Microsoft .NET, and CORBA (Common Object Request Broker Architecture).

Table 24.2 shows the sample Java profile.

This profile isn't sufficient for modeling Java applications—it is missing a stereotype for Java class files and for directories. We extend the profile with the two new stereotypes listed in Table 24.3.

In Figure 24.8 we have applied the extended sample Java profile from the UML specification to our model. As you can see, the diagram is much more meaningful when you apply descriptive stereotypes.

Table 24.2

Stereotype	Applies to	Semantics
«EJBEntityBean»	Component	EJB entity bean
«EJBSessionBean»	Component	EJB session bean
«EJBMessageDrivenBean»	Component	EJB message-driven bean
«EJBHome»	Interface	EJB home interface
«EJBRemote»	Interface	EJB remote interface
«EJBCreate»	Operation	EJB create operation
«EJBBusiness»	Operation	An operation that supports the business logic of the EJB remote interface
«EJBSecurityRoleRef»	Association	An association between an EJB and a supplier that provides a reference to a security role
«EJBRoleName»	Actor	The name of a security role
«EJBRoleNameRef»	Actor	A reference to a security role
«JavaSourceFile»	Artifact	A Java source file
«JAR»	Artifact	A Java ARchive file
«EJBQL»	Expression	An expression in the EJB query language

Table 24.3

Stereotype	Applies to	Semantics
«JavaClassFile»	Artifact	A Java class file (a compiled Java source file)
«directory»	Artifact	A directory

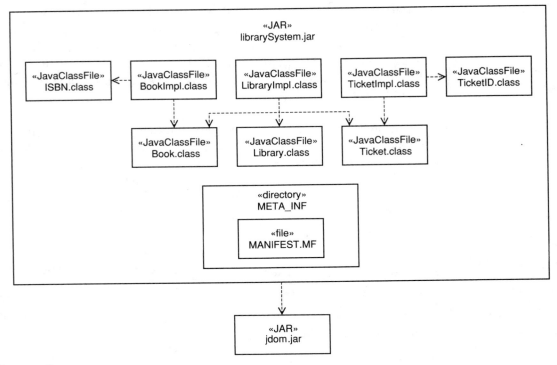

Figure 24.8

24.6   Deployment

A simple instance form deployment diagram is shown in Figure 24.9.

This example is from the Java tutorial (www.java.sun.com). It is a currency converter application. Figure 24.9 shows an Enterprise application ARchive (EAR) file called ConverterApp.ear deployed into a J2EE Server execution environment on a node called server of type WindowsPC. The J2EE Server is an application server from Sun that is shipped as part of J2EE. EAR files are a special type of JAR file that hold J2EE applications. The deployed server application is used by the client application, ConverterClient.jar, which executes on a node called client that is also of type WindowsPC.

You can attach a deployment specification to a deployed artifact as shown in the figure. The deployment specification contains key details about the deployment. In this case, we specify three things:

- EnterpriseBeanClass – this is the class that contains the logic of the bean;

- EnterpriseBeanName – this is the name that clients can use to access the bean;

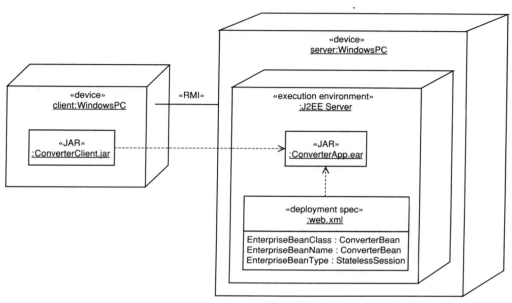

Figure 24.9

- EnterpriseBeanType – this is the type of the bean. In this case, it is a stateless session bean—a bean used for simple transactions that has no state and is not persistent.

There is much more to EJB deployment than this simple example would suggest, and some of these details even depend on the execution environment. However, the purpose of modeling in deployment is to capture the *key* deployment details, and so the deployment descriptor shown may well be sufficient.

24.7   What we have learned

Deployment diagrams allow you to model the distribution of your software system over physical hardware. You have learned the following.

- The UP activity Architectural implementation is about identifying architecturally significant components and mapping them to physical hardware.
- The deployment diagram maps the software architecture to the hardware architecture.
- In the design workflow you can create a "first cut" deployment diagram by identifying nodes or node instances, and relationships – you refine

this as part of the implementation workflow by adding components or component instances.

- The descriptor form deployment diagram may be used to model what types of hardware, software, and connections there will be in the final deployed system.
  — It describes a whole set of possible deployments.
  — It shows:
    - nodes – what types of hardware run the system;
    - relationships – the types of connections between the nodes;
    - components – the types of components deployed on particular nodes.
- The instance form deployment diagram shows a particular deployment of the system over specific, identifiable pieces of hardware.
  — It describes one specific deployment of the system, perhaps at a specific user site.
  — It shows:
    - node instances – specific pieces of hardware;
    - relationship instances – specific relationships between node instances;
    - component instances – specific, identifiable pieces of software deployed on a node instance; for example, a particular copy of Microsoft Office with a unique serial number.
- Node – represents a type of computational resource.
  — «device» – a type of physical device such as a PC or a Sun Fire server.
  — «execution environment» – a type of execution environment for software such as an Apache web server.
- Node instance – represents a specific computational resource.
- Artifact – represents the specification of a real-world thing such as a particular executable file.
  — Artifacts can manifest one or more components.
- Artifact instance – represents a specific instance of a particular artifact, such as a specific copy of a particular executable file deployed on a particular machine.

part 6

Supplementary material

chapter 25

Introduction to OCL

25.1 Chapter roadmap

Originally, we only intended to write a *very* short introduction to OCL, primarily to cover the requirements of UML certification. The more we looked at the existing OCL literature however, the more we felt the need for a simple yet complete description of the language targeted directly at the OO analyst/ designer. This is what we present here. It is based on *Unified Modeling Language: OCL, version 2.0* [OCL1]. Be aware that there might be some small changes to the specification by the time we get to press.

As an OO analyst/designer, you might not be particularly aware of OCL. Hopefully, by the end of this chapter, you will understand what OCL is and will appreciate the possibilities it presents for precise UML modeling.

This is quite a big chapter, so we have only included the main topics in the chapter roadmap.

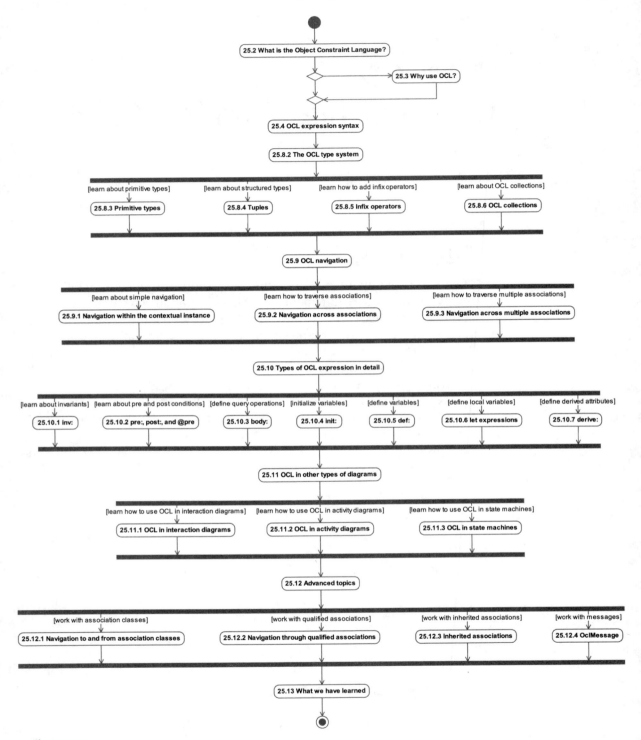

Figure 25.1

25.2   What is the Object Constraint Language (OCL)?

OCL can specify queries, constraints, and query operations.

OCL is a language that allows you to add extra information to a UML model. It is a standard extension to UML that allows you to do the following:

- write queries to access model elements and their values—it is a query language a bit like SQL;

- state constraints on model elements—you can define business rules as constraints on model elements;

- define query operations.

OCL is *not* an action language for UML because OCL expressions have no side effects.

It's vital to understand that you can't specify behavior with OCL—it is *not* an action language for UML. This is because OCL expressions *have no side effects*, so:

- OCL can't change the value of a model element—you can only query values and state conditions on values;

- OCL can't define an operation other than a query operation;

- OCL can only execute query operations that don't change values;

- OCL can't be used to specify business rules dynamically at runtime—it can only be used to specify business rules at modeling time.

You can store OCL expressions in files associated with your UML model. How this is done depends on the particular modeling tool you are using. However, the OCL specification defines an XML-based interchange format so that you can move OCL expressions between tools.

You can also attach OCL expressions directly to UML model elements as notes. This has the advantage that it makes the OCL expressions visible in the model, and the disadvantage that it can clutter the model if there are a lot of expressions.

25.3   Why use OCL?

There are several reasons why you might find OCL useful.

- OCL allows suitably enabled modeling tools to reason about UML models—for example, this might involve checking their consistency.

- OCL allows suitably equipped modeling tools to generate code based on OCL expressions—for example, a tool might generate code to enforce OCL constraints such as operation preconditions and postconditions.

- OCL allows you to be more precise in your modeling—this makes your models less open to misinterpretation.

- OCL is a part of OCUP (OMG Certified UML Professional) Advanced certification—there is only a small amount of OCL in the test, but it *is* there.

There are several reasons why you might *not* find OCL useful.

- OCL is quite hard to read—the syntax is irregular and has lots of odd "shortcut" forms.

- At this time, few modelers know OCL, and even fewer programmers—so you might find that there is no audience for your OCL expressions.

- You might not need the level of precision that OCL offers—for example, if you are creating an informal UML model that will be given to programmers for elaboration, OCL might be overkill.

Our position on OCL is that it is just another tool in your modeling toolbox that can help you create precise UML models. It's useful to know about it so that you can use it where it adds real value.

25.4   OCL expression syntax

OCL is a small language, but it has a surprisingly difficult syntax that is still evolving. In particular, it has syntactic exceptions and shortcuts that can sometimes lead the uninitiated astray. The syntax appears to be mostly C/C++/Java style with some Smalltalk-like elements.

OCL language semantics (which are formally defined) are independent of any concrete syntax. This can allow alternative OCL syntaxes to emerge over time. There is already an SQL-like OCL syntax for business modeling that you can find described in [Warmer 1].

We take a lot of care in this chapter to try to highlight the less intuitive aspects of OCL syntax (and semantics) and make them as clear as we can!

Unlike most mainstream programming languages, OCL is a declarative language. This means that you describe the result you want rather than how to achieve that result. Languages like Java, C#, C++, and most other mainstream languages are procedural—you describe step by step how the result you want is achieved.

In a conventional programming language you create programs that execute to deliver some value to the user.

OCL expressions are attached to UML model elements.

In OCL you write expressions that are attached to elements of a UML model to specify or constrain the model in some way. This is a fundamental point and is perhaps the biggest stumbling block that modelers and programmers face when first encountering OCL. OCL is *not* a programming language, it is a constraint language. The essential point to keep in mind is that in OCL you are specifying queries and conditions, *not* behaviors.

The general form of an OCL expression is illustrated in Figure 25.2.

package context

package <packagePath>

expression context { **context** <contexualInstanceName>:<modelElement>

<expressionType> <expressionName>: } expression
<expressionBody>

<expressionType> <expressionName>: } expression
<expressionBody>

...

endpackage

Figure 25.2

In Figure 25.2 we use **boldface** to indicate an OCL keyword and the color gray to indicate an optional element. The angle brackets (<...>) indicate a placeholder that you must replace with the appropriate thing.

Each OCL expression has a value.

OCL is a typed language, and every OCL expression evaluates to an object of some type. As you can see from Figure 25.2, OCL expressions may be broken down into three parts:

- the package context (optional);
- the expression context (mandatory);
- one or more expressions.

We consider each of these parts in detail in the next few sections. To do this, we use the model in Figure 25.3 to provide a context for our example OCL expressions.

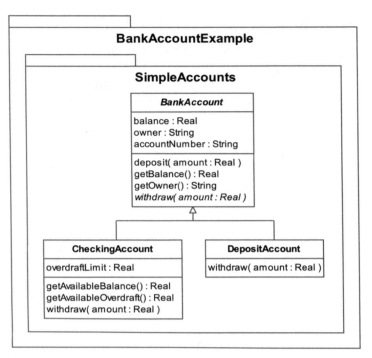

Figure 25.3

25.5   Package context and pathnames

The optional package context allows you to specify a package that defines the namespace for the OCL expression. The package context is subject to the following rules.

● If you *don't* specify a package context, the namespace for the expression defaults to the whole model.
● If you attach an OCL expression directly to a model element, the namespace for the expression defaults to the owning package of the element.

For example, in Figure 25.3, you could specify the package context as

package BankAccountExample::SimpleAccounts

   ...

endpackage

If the elements in your UML model all have unique names, you don't need to use the package context, as you can refer to each element unambiguously by name. However, if elements in *different* packages have the *same* name, you can

- define a package context for each OCL expression that refers to any of the elements OR
- refer to the elements using full pathnames, for example,

BankAccountExample::SimpleAccounts:BankAccount.

The OCL syntax for pathnames is

Package1::Package2:: ... ::PackageN::ElementName

25.6   The expression context

> The expression context indicates the UML model element to which the OCL expression is attached.

The expression context indicates the UML model element to which the OCL expression is attached.

For example, if you wanted to attach an OCL expression to the Checking-Account class in Figure 25.3, you could define the expression context as follows:

```
package BankAccountExample::SimpleAccounts
  context account:CheckingAccount

  ...
endpackage
```

> Write your OCL expressions in terms of the contextual instance.

The expression context defines a *contextual instance* that has an optional name (account) and a mandatory type (CheckingAccount).

Think of a contextual instance as being an exemplar instance of the class that you can use in your OCL expressions.

If you give the contextual instance a name, you can refer to it using this name within the body of the expression. If you *don't* give the contextual instance a name, you can refer to it using the OCL keyword self. We tend to use the keyword.

In the expression above, the contextual instance is an instance of the CheckingAccount class that you can refer to as account or self.

The type of the contextual instance depends on the expression context.

- If the expression context is a classifier, the contextual instance is always an instance of that classifier.
- If the expression context is an operation or an attribute, the contextual instance is generally an instance of the classifier that *owns* the operation or attribute.

When you attach an OCL expression to a model element as a note (Figure 25.4), the expression context is determined by the attachment point of the note, so you don't need to specify it explicitly.

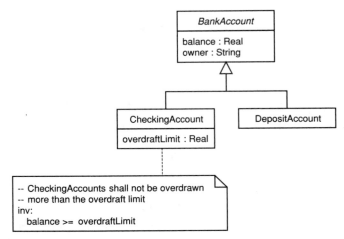

Figure 25.4

25.7   Types of OCL expressions

There are two categories of OCL expressions – those that constrain and those that define.

There are eight different types of OCL expressions, as summarized in Table 25.1. You can see that these expressions split into two categories—those specifying constraints (inv:, pre:, and post:) and those specifying attributes, operation bodies, and local variables (init:, body:, def:, let, and derive:).

You can give an expressionName to the operations that constrain (inv:, pre:, and post:). This allows you to refer to them by name, perhaps to link them to use case specifications or other requirements documents. Good OCL style indicates that you should

- always name constraints (even though the name is optional);
- choose descriptive names that summarize the semantics of the constraint;
- ensure that constraint names are unique within your model;
- use lowerCamelCase for constraint names.

You *can't* give an expression name to the operations that define (init:, body:, def:, let, derive:).

We cover the detailed semantics of the different types of OCL expression in Section 25.10, once we have discussed the expression body and OCL expression syntax.

Table 25.1

Expression type	Syntax	Applies to	Contextual instance	Semantics	Section
Operations that constrain					
invariant	inv:	Classifier	An instance of the classifier	The invariant must be true for all instances of the classifier	25.10.1
precondition	pre:	Operation Behavioral feature	An instance of the classifier that owns the operation	The precondition must be true before the operation executes	25.10.2
postcondition	post:	Operation Behavioral feature	An instance of the classifier that owns the operation	The postcondition must be true after the operation executes The keyword result refers to the result of the operation	25.10.2
Operations that define					
query operation body	body:	Query operation	An instance of the classifier that owns the operation	Defines the body of a query operation	25.10.3
initial value	init:	Attribute Association end	The attribute The association end	Defines the initial value of the attribute or the association end	25.10.4
define	def:	Classifier	An instance of the classifier that owns the operation	Adds variables or helper operations to a context classifier These are used in OCL expressions on the context classifier	25.10.5
let	let	OCL expression	The contextual instance of the OCL expression	Adds local variables to OCL expressions	25.10.6
derived value	derive:	Attribute Association end	The attribute The association end	Defines the derivation rule for the derived attribute or association end	25.10.7

25.8 The expression body

The expression body contains the meat of the OCL expression. You can see a simple example in Figure 25.4.

Over the next few sections, we introduce OCL syntax with a view to being able to construct OCL expression bodies.

25.8.1 Comments, keywords, and precedence rules

Comments are ignored by OCL processors. Use comments liberally to document your OCL expressions to make them more understandable.

A good way to comment an OCL expression is simply to write the expression out in English (or German or whatever your language is). You will see examples of how to do this throughout this chapter.

OCL has two styles for comments:

> Use comments liberally to make OCL expressions more understandable.

– – This is a single line comment. The rest of the line after the two minus signs is ignored.

/* This is a multiple line comment.
Everything between the comment delimiters is ignored. */

We prefer to use the single line comment.

OCL has a very small set of keywords that you *can't* use as names in OCL expressions:

and, attr, context, def, else, endif, endpackage, if, implies, in, inv, let, not, oper, or, package, post, pre, then, xor, body, init, derive.

We cover each of these as the chapter progresses.

OCL operations are subject to precedence rules as illustrated in Figure 25.5.

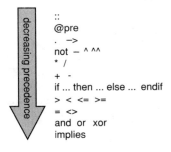

Figure 25.5

In any OCL expression, the operations with the highest precedence are executed first. So, for example,

1 + 2 * 3

evaluates to 7 because * has a higher precedence than +.

Precedence can be overridden by the use of brackets, so

(1 + 2) * 3

evaluates to 9.

It's always good style in *any* language to use brackets rather than rely on precedence rules!

25.8.2 The OCL type system

OCL is a strongly typed language, and you need to understand its type system to be able to write OCL expressions.

All languages come with a set of primitive types, and OCL is no exception. The primitive types are Boolean, Integer, Real, and String—we discuss these in Section 25.8.3. OCL also has a structured type, the Tuple, that we discuss in Section 25.8.4.

As well as the primitive types and Tuples, OCL has an important set of built-in types, summarized below.

● OclAny – the supertype of all types in OCL and the associated UML model;

● OclType – a subclass of OclAny—an enumeration of all types in the associated UML model;

● OclState – a subclass of OclAny—an enumeration of all the states in the associated UML model;

● OclVoid – the "null" type in OCL—it has a single instance called OclUndefined;

● OclMessage – represents a message (see Section 25.12.4).

> OCL primitive types are **Boolean, Integer, String,** and **Real.**

> All classifiers in the UML model are available to OCL expressions.

> **OclAny** is the supertype of all types in OCL.

An unusual, but crucial, aspect of the OCL type system is that *all* of the classifiers in the associated UML model become types in OCL. This means that OCL expressions can refer *directly* to classifiers in the associated model. This is what makes OCL work as a constraint language.

In OCL *every* type is a subtype of OclAny. Primitive types are direct subtypes of OclAny, whereas UML model types are subclasses of OCLType, which itself is a subclass of OclAny. Each type inherits the small set of useful operations summarized in Table 25.2.

Perhaps the most unusual OclAny operation is allInstances(). This is a class scope operation (it applies directly to the class, rather than to any specific instance) and it returns the Set of all instances of that class in existence when

Table 25.2

OclAny operation	Semantics
Comparison operations	
a = b	Returns true if a is the same object as b, otherwise returns false
a <> b	Returns true if a is *not* the same object as b, otherwise returns false
a.oclIsTypeOf(b : OclType) : Boolean	Returns true if a is the same type as b, otherwise returns false
a.oclIsKindOf(b : OclType) : Boolean	Returns true if a is the same type as b, or a subtype of b
a.oclInState(b : OclState) : Boolean	Returns true if a is in the state b, otherwise returns false
a.oclIsUndefined() : Boolean	Returns true if a = OclUndefined
Query operations	
A::allInstances() : Set(A)	This is a class scope operation that returns a Set of all instances of type A
a.oclIsNew() : Boolean	Returns true if a was created by the execution of the operation
	Can only be used in operation postconditions
Conversion operations	
a.oclAsType(SubType) : SubType	Evaluates to a retyped to SubType
	This is a casting operation, and a may only be cast to one of its subtypes or supertypes
	Casting to a supertype allows access to overridden supertype features

the operation is called. No commonly used programming language has this facility built in, so the OCL specification defines allInstances() as an optional compliance point for tools that implement OCL. This means that your OCL tool may not be able to evaluate expressions that use allInstances().

At first it may appear strange that the types you have carefully defined in your UML model each automatically get a new supertype, OclType, when they are referred to in OCL expressions. However, OCL has to do this so that there is a common object protocol (defined by OclAny) that it can use to manipulate types.

25.8.3   Primitive types

The OCL primitive types are Boolean, Integer, Real, and String. These have much the same semantics as they do in any other language (Table 25.3).

Table 25.3

OCL basic type	Semantics
Boolean	Can take the value true or false
Integer	A whole number
Real	A floating point number
String	A sequence of characters String literals are single quoted, e.g., 'Jim'

Because OCL is a modeling language rather than a programming language, the OCL specification places *no limits* on the length of Strings, the size of Integers, and the size and precision of Reals.

25.8.3.1   Boolean

The Boolean type has two values, true and false. It has a set of operations that return Boolean values. The binary operations are summarized in the Table 25.4. This truth table shows the results of the Boolean operations for input values a and b.

Table 25.4

a	b	a = b	a<>b	a.and(b)	a.or(b)	a.xor(b)	a.implies(b)
true	true	true	false	true	true	false	true
true	false	false	true	false	true	true	false
false	true	false	true	false	true	true	true
false	false	true	false	false	false	false	true

All of these operations should be familiar to you from other programming languages, except for implies. This comes from formal logic and consists of a premise, a, and a conclusion, b. The result of the operation is true when the premise and the conclusion have the same value, or when the premise is false and the conclusion is true. It is false when the premise is true and the conclusion is false.

There is also a unary not operator, shown in Table 25.5.

Table 25.5

a	not a
true	false
false	true

Boolean expressions are often used in if...then...else expressions according to the following syntax:

```
if <booleanExpression> then
  <oclExpression1>
  else
  <oclExpression2>
endif
```

25.8.3.2   Integer *and* Real

Integer represents a whole number, and Real represents a floating point number. There are no limits on the length of Integers or on the length or precision of Reals. Integer and Real have the usual set of infix arithmetic operations with the standard semantics:

$=, <>, <, >, <=, >=, +, -, *, /$

They also have the operations described in Table 25.6.

Table 25.6

Syntax	Semantics	Applies to
a.mod(b)	Returns the remainder after a is divided by b e.g., a = 3, b = 2, a.mod(b) returns 1	Integer
a.div(b)	The number of times that b fits completely within a e.g., a = 8, b = 3, a.div(b) returns 2	Integer
a.abs()	Returns positive a e.g., a = (–3), a.abs() returns 3	Integer and Real
a.max(b)	Returns the larger of a and b e.g., a = 2, b = 3, a.max(b) returns b	Integer and Real
a.min(b)	Returns the smaller of a and b e.g., a = 2, b = 3, a.min(b) returns a	Integer and Real

Table 25.6 Continued

Syntax	Semantics	Applies to
a.round()	Returns the Integer closest to a	Real
	If there are two integers equally close, it returns the largest	
	e.g., a = 2.5, a.round() returns 3 rather than 2 a = (−2.5), a.round() returns −2 rather than −3	
a.floor()	Returns the closest Integer less than or equal to a	Real
	e.g., a = 2.5, a.floor() returns 2 a = (−2.5), a.floor() returns −3	

25.8.3.3 String

The OCL String operations (Table 25.7) are again pretty standard—you can expect to find a similar set in just about any language.

Table 25.7

Syntax	Semantics
s1 = s2	Returns true if the character sequence of s1 matches the character sequence of s2, else returns false
s1 <> s2	Returns true if the character sequence of s1 does *not* match the character sequence of s2, else returns false
s1.concat(s2)	Returns a new String that is the concatenation of s1 and s2 e.g., 'Jim'.concat(' Arlow') returns 'Jim Arlow'
s1.size()	Returns the Integer number of characters in s1 e.g., 'Jim'.size() returns 3
s1.toLower()	Returns a new String in lower case e.g., 'Jim'.toLower() returns 'jim'
s1.toUpper()	Returns a new String in upper case e.g., 'Jim'.toUpper() returns 'JIM'
s1.toInteger()	Converts s1 to an Integer value e.g., '2'.toInteger() returns 2
s1.toReal()	Converts s1 to a Real value e.g., '2.5'.toReal() returns 2.5

Continued

Table 25.7   Continued

Syntax	Semantics
s1.substring(start, end)	Returns a new String that is a substring of s1 from the character at position start to the character at position end
	Notes:
	* start and end must be Integers * The first character in s1 is at index 1 * The last character in s1 is at index s1.size()
	e.g., 'Jim Arlow'.substring(5, 9) returns 'Arlow'

> **OCL Strings** are immutable.

OCL Strings are immutable—this means once initialized, they can't be changed. An operation such as s1.concat(s2) always returns a new String.

25.8.4   Tuples

> **Tuples** are structured objects that have one or more named parts.

Tuples are structured objects that have one or more named parts. Tuples are necessary because some OCL operations return multiple objects. Tuple syntax is as follows:

Tuple { partName1:partType1 = value1, partName2:partType2 = value2, ... }

The name and value of each part is mandatory, its type is optional, and the order of the parts is undefined.

Here is a Tuple that represents information about this book:

Tuple { title:String = 'UML 2 and the Unified Process', publisher:String = 'Addison Wesley' }

Tuple parts can be initialized by any valid OCL expression. In this simple example, we have used String literals.

You access the parts of a Tuple by using the dot operator. For example, the following expression returns the value 'Addison Wesley':

Tuple { title:String = 'UML 2 and the Unified Process', publisher:String = 'Addison Wesley' }.publisher

OCL is a strongly typed language, so each Tuple *must* have a type. TupleTypes are anonymous types. They have no name and are *implicitly* defined when you create the Tuple. However, it's possible to *explicitly* define a TupleType type. For example, the TupleType for the Tuple above can be written in OCL as

TupleType { title:String, publisher:String }

You typically only need to explicitly define a TupleType if you want to create a collection (see Section 25.8.6) of the type, for example,

Set(TupleType{ title:String, publisher:String}) - - creates a Set that can hold Tuple objects

25.8.5 Infix operators

As you will have seen in the last few sections, the operations associated with the OCL primitive types are of two forms. There is normal operation call syntax, for example,

a.toUpper()

and then there are infix operators, where the operator is placed *between* its operands, for example,

a < b

Infix operators are a syntactic convenience. Instead of writing a.lessThan(b) you write a < b, which is a bit more readable, especially in complex expressions.

You can also use infix operators with the types from the associated UML model, *provided* you give them operations with the right signature. The class Money shown in Figure 25.6 defines some Boolean and arithmetic infix operations.

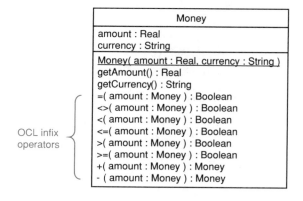

Figure 25.6

So if a and b are both type Money, you can use expressions such as

a < b

However, please note that explicit operation calls such as a.<(b) are *illegal*, according to the OCL specification, even though you might reasonably expect them to be allowed!

25.8.6 OCL collections

OCL provides a fairly comprehensive set of collection types. These can hold other objects including other collections.

OCL collections are immutable. This means collection operations *don't* change the state of the collection. For example, when you call an operation to add or remove an item from a collection, that operation returns a *new* collection, leaving the original collection unchanged.

We have already mentioned OCL collection types in Section 18.10— their semantics are summarized in Table 25.8. Notice how each of the OCL collection types corresponds to a pair of association end properties. The default association end properties are { unordered, unique }.

Table 25.8

OCL collection	Ordered	Unique (no duplicates allowed)	Association end properties
Set	No	Yes	{ unordered, unique } – default
OrderedSet	Yes	Yes	{ ordered, unique }
Bag	No	No	{ unordered, nonunique }
Sequence	Yes	No	{ ordered, nonunique }

OCL collections are actually templates (see Section 17.7) that must be instantiated on a type before they can be used. For example, the OCL expression

Set(Customer)

instantiates the Set templaté on the Customer type. This defines a Set that holds objects of type Customer. You can instantiate OCL collections on any of the available types.

You can specify collection constants by simply enumerating their elements in braces:

OrderedSet{ 'Monday', 'Tuesday', 'Wednesday', 'Thursday', 'Friday' }

This automatically instantiates the collection template on the type of the elements.

Sequences of Integer literals have their own special syntax using an *interval specification*:

<start> ... <end>

This means "all of the Integers between <start> and <end>" where <start> and <end> are OCL expressions that evaluate to Integers. For example,

Sequence{ 1 ... 7} is equivalent to Sequence{ 1, 2, 3, 4, 5, 6, 7 }
Sequence{ 2 ... (3 + 4) } is equivalent to Sequence{ 2, 3, 4, 5, 6, 7 }

Collections can contain other collections, for example,

OrderedSet{ OrderedSet{ 'Monday', 'Tuesday' }, OrderedSet{ 'Wednesday','Thursday', 'Friday' } }

25.8.6.1   *Collection operations*

Collections have an extensive set of operations. These *must* be invoked with a special syntax that uses the arrow operator:

aCollection–>collectionOperation(parameters...)

> Any single object can be treated as a Set containing exactly one element.

This special syntax is necessary because OCL can treat any single object as a Set containing only that object. Therefore, if the object has an operation called, for example, count(), and Set also has an operation called count(), OCL needs some way to distinguish between the two count() operations—the one belonging to the object and the one belonging to the collection. It does this by invoking object operations using the dot operator and invoking collection operations using the arrow operator.

In the next few sections we summarize the semantics of the collection operations. For ease of reference we have organized them into the following categories:

- conversion operations – convert one type of collection into another (see Section 25.8.6.2);

- comparison operations – compare collections (see Section 25.8.6.3);

- query operations – get information about the collection (see Section 25.8.6.4);

- access operations – access elements in the collection (see Section 25.8.6.5);

- selection operations – return a new collection containing a subset or superset of a collection (see Section 25.8.6.6).

In addition, OCL collections have a complete set of iteration operations. These are quite complex and have an unusual syntax, so we discuss them separately in Section 25.8.7.

We have introduced a couple of conventions to make our discussion of collections easier and more compact:

- X(T) – a shortcut notation where X can be Set, OrderedSet, Bag, or Sequence;

- target collection – the object that the operation is called on.

When reading the following sections, remember that the collection types are *template* types. This means that

Set(T) is a Set instantiated on type T.
So X(T) represents a Set, OrderedSet, Bag, or Sequence instantiated on type T.

25.8.6.2   Conversion operations

The conversion operations (Table 25.9) convert a collection of one type into another by returning a new collection of the required type. For example,

Bag{ 'Homer', 'Meg' }–>asOrderedSet()

returns a new Set containing the Strings 'Homer' and 'Meg'.

The constraints of both the source collection and the result collection are honored. In this case, the source collection is unordered, but the result collection is ordered so that the operation establishes an arbitrary order for the result collection.

Table 25.9

Conversion operations	
Collection operation	**Semantics**
X(T)::asSet() : Set(T) X(T)::asOrderedSet() : OrderedSet(T) X(T)::asBag() : Bag(T) X(T)::asSequence() : Sequence(T)	Converts a collection from one type of collection to another
	When a collection is converted to a Set, duplicate elements are discarded
	When a collection is converted to an OrderedSet or a Sequence, the original order (if any) is preserved, else an arbitrary order is established
X(T)::flatten() : X(T2)	Results in a new flattened collection instantiated on T2
	For example, if we have:
	Set{ Sequence{ 'A', 'B' }, Sequence{ 'C', 'D' } }
	the Set is instantiated on a Sequence that is instantiated on String – the result of flattening the Set is therefore a Set of String

25.8.6.3   Comparison operations

The comparison operations (Table 25.10) compare the target collection with a parameter collection of the same type and return a Boolean result. The operations take into account the ordering constraints of the collections.

25.8.6.4   Query operations

The query operations (Table 25.11) allow you to obtain information about the collection.

Table 25.10

Comparison operations	
Collection operation	**Semantics**
X(T)::=(y : X(T)) : Boolean	Set and Bag – returns true if y contains the same elements as the target collection
	OrderedSet and Sequence – returns true if y contains the same elements in the same order as the target collection
X(T)::<>(y : X(T)) : Boolean	Set and Bag – returns true if y does *not* contain the same elements as the target collection
	OrderedSet and Sequence – returns true if y does *not* contain the same elements in the same order as the target collection

Table 25.11

Query operations	
Collection operation	**Semantics**
X(T)::size() : Integer	Returns the number of elements in the target collection
X(T)::sum() : T	Returns the sum of all of the elements in the target collection
	Type T *must* support the + operator
X(T)::count(object : T) : Integer	Returns the number of occurrences of object in the target collection
X(T)::includes(object : T) : Boolean	Returns true if the target collection contains object
X(T)::excludes(object : T) : Boolean	Returns true if the target collection does *not* contain object
X(T)::includesAll(c : Collection(T)) : Boolean	Returns true if the target collection contains everything in c
X(T)::excludesAll(c : Collection(T)) : Boolean	Returns true if the target collection does *not* contain all of the elements in c
X(T)::isEmpty() : Boolean	Returns true if the target collection is empty, else returns false
X(T)::notEmpty() : Boolean	Returns true if the target collection is not empty else, returns false

25.8.6.5   *Access operations*

Only the ordered collections OrderedSet and Sequence allow you to access their elements directly by position in the collection (Table 25.12). To access elements of unordered collections, you have to iterate through the whole collection from the beginning to the end.

Table 25.12

Access operations	
Collection operation	**Semantics**
OrderedSet(T)::first() : T Sequence(T)::first() : T	Returns the first element of the collection
OrderedSet(T)::last() : T Sequence(T)::last() : T	Returns the last element of the collection
OrderedSet::at(i) : T Sequence::at(i) : T	Returns the element at position i
OrderedSet::indexOf(T) : Integer	Returns the index of the parameter object in the OrderedSet

25.8.6.6   Selection operations

The selection operations (Table 25.13) return new collections that are super-sets or subsets of the target collection. We have used Venn diagrams to illustrate the set theoretical operations union, intersection, symmetric difference, and complement.

Table 25.13

Selection operations	
Collection operation	**Semantics**
X(T)::union(y : X(T)) : X(T)	Returns a new collection that is the result of appending y to the target collection – the new collection is always of the same type as the target collection Duplicate elements are removed and an order established as necessary
Set(T)::intersection(y : Set(T)) : Set(T) OrderedSet(T)::intersection(y : OrderedSet(T)) : OrderedSet(T)	Returns a new collection containing elements common to y and the target collection

Table 25.13   Continued

Selection operations	
Collection operation	**Semantics**
Set(T)::symmetricDifference(y : Set(T)) : Set(T) OrderedSet(T)::symmetricDifference(y : OrderedSet(T)) : OrderedSet(T)	Returns a new Set that contains elements that exist in the target collection and y, but not in both
Set(T)::-(y : Set(T)) : Set(T) OrderedSet(T)::-(y : OrderedSet(T)) : OrderedSet(T)	Returns a new Set that contains all elements of the target collection that are *not* also in y In set theory, the return set is the *complement* of a with respect to b
X(T)::product(y : X(T2)) : Set(Tuple(first : T, second : T2))	Returns the Cartesian product of the target collection and y – this is a Set of Tuple{ first=a,second=b } objects where a is a member of the target collection and b is a member of y e.g., Set{ 'a',' b' }–>product(Set{ '1','2' }) returns Set{ Tuple{ first='a', second='1' }, Tuple{ first='a',second='2' }, Tuple{ first='b', second='1' }, Tuple{ first='b',second='2' } }
X(T)::including(object : T) : X(T)	Returns a new collection containing the contents of the target collection plus object If the collection is ordered, object is appended
X(T)::excluding(object : T) : X(T)	Returns a new collection with all copies of object removed

Continued on next page

Table 25.13   Continued

Selection operations	
Collection operation	**Semantics**
Sequence(T)::subSequence(i : Integer, j : Integer) : Sequence(T)	Returns a new Sequence that contains elements from index i to index j of the target collection
OrderedSet::subOrderedSet (i : Integer, j : Integer) : OrderedSet(T)	Returns a new OrderedSet that contains the elements from index i to index j of the target OrderedSet
OrderedSet(T)::append(object : T) : OrderedSet(T) Sequence(T)::append(object : T) : Sequence(T)	Returns a new collection with object added on to the end
OrderedSet(T)::prepend(object : T) : OrderedSet(T) Sequence(T)::prepend(object : T) : Sequence(T)	Returns a new collection with object added on to the beginning
OrderedSet(T)::insertAt(index : Integer, object : T) : OrderedSet(T) Sequence(T)::insertAt(index : Integer, object : T) : Sequence(T)	Returns a new collection with object inserted at the index position

25.8.7   Iteration operations

The iteration operations allow you to loop over the elements in a collection. They have the general form illustrated in Figure 25.7.

aCollection –><iteratorOperation>(<iteratorVariable> :<Type> |
                                   <iteratorExpression>
)

Figure 25.7

Words in angle brackets (<...>) represent placeholders that you must replace with the appropriate things. Words in gray indicate optional parts.

Iterator operations work as follows: The iteratorOperation visits each element of aCollection in turn. The current element is represented by an iteratorVariable. The iteratorExpression is applied to the iteratorVariable to produce a result. Each iteratorOperation handles the result in its own particular way.

The Type of the iteratorVariable is optional as it is always the same type as the elements in aCollection. The iteratorVariable itself is also optional. When each element of the collection is visited, all of its features are *automatically* accessible to the iteratorExpression and can be accessed directly by name. For example, if the element is a *BankAccount* object with an attribute called balance, the iteratorExpression can refer to balance directly.

However, omitting the iteratorVariable can be dangerous, and we think it is bad style. This is because the iteratorExpression first searches its own namespace for any variable it needs and, if it can't find the variable, searches up through enclosing namespaces. If you omit the iteratorVariable, there is a risk that the iteratorExpression might find the wrong thing.

We have divided the iterator operations into Boolean operations (those that return a Boolean value) and selection operations (those that return a selection from the collection). The operations are summarized in Table 25.14.

Table 25.14

Boolean iterator operations	Semantics
X(T)::exists(i : T I iteratorExpression) : Boolean	Returns true if the iteratorExpression evaluates to true for at least one value of i, else returns false
X(T)::forAll(i : T I iteratorExpression) : Boolean	Returns true if the iteratorExpression evaluates to true for all values of i, else returns false
X(T)::forAll(i : T, j : T ..., n : T I iteratorExpression) : Boolean	Returns true if the iteratorExpression evaluates to true for every { i, j ... n } Tuple, else returns false The set of { i, j ... n } pairs is the Cartesian product of the target collection with itself
X(T)::isUnique(i : T I iteratorExpression) : Boolean	Returns true if the iteratorExpression has a unique value for each value of i, else returns false
X(T)::one(i : T I iteratorExpression) : Boolean	Returns true if the iteratorExpression evaluates to true for exactly one value of i, else returns false
Selection iterator operations	**Semantics**
X(T)::any(i : T I iteratorExpression) : T	Returns a random element of the target collection for which iteratorExpression is true
X(T)::collect(i : T I iteratorExpression) : Bag(T)	Returns a Bag containing the results of executing iterator-Expression once for each element in the target collection (See Section 25.9.2 for a shorthand notation for collect(...))
X(T)::collectNested(i : T I iteratorExpression) : Bag(T)	Returns a Bag of collections containing the results of executing iteratorExpression once for each element in the target collection Maintains the nesting of the target collection in the result collection

Continued on next page

Table 25.14 Continued

Selection iterator operations	Semantics
X(T)::select(i : T l iteratorExpression) : X(T)	Returns a collection containing those elements of the target collection for which the iteratorExpression evaluates to true
X(T)::reject(i : T l iteratorExpression) : X(T)	Returns a collection containing those elements of the target collection for which the iteratorExpression evaluates to false
X(T)::sortedBy(i : T l iteratorExpression) : X(T)	Returns a collection containing the elements of the target collection ordered according to the iteratorExpression The iteratorVariable *must* be of a type that has the < operator defined

It's worth taking a closer look at forAll(...). This operation has two forms. The first form has a single iteratorVariable, and the second has many. The second form is shorthand for many nested forAll(...) operations.

For example, consider two nested forAll(...) operations as follows:

c–>forAll(i l c–>forAll(j l iteratorExpression))

You can write this as

c–>forAll(i, j l iteratorExpression)

The effect of both of these forms is to iterate over a set of { i, j } pairs that is the Cartesian product of c with itself. An example will clarify this. Suppose

c = Set{ x, y, z }

The Cartesian product of c with itself is the Set

{ {x,x}, {x,y}, {x,z}, {y,x}, {y,y}, {y,z}, {z,x}, {z,y}, {z,z} }

Then c–>forAll(i, j l iteratorExpression) iterates over each subset in this Set, and i and j are each assigned one of the elements of the subset. You can then use i and j in the iterator expression.

We think the multiple parameter form of forAll(...) is confusing, and you should avoid it.

All of these iteration operations (apart from the multiple parameter forAll(...)) are special cases of the more general iterate operation that we examine in the next section.

25.8.7.1   The iterate operation

You can perform your own custom iterations by using the OCL iterate operation. This has the form shown in Figure 25.8.

```
aCollection –>iterate( <iteratorVariable > : <Type>
                 <resultVariable> : <ResultType > = <initializationExpression> |
                    <iteratorExpression>
                 )
```

Figure 25.8

You can see that as well as the iteratorVariable and its Type (which are *mandatory* in this case), there is a resultVariable that can have a different type. The resultVariable gets its initial value from the initializationExpression and its final value from successive applications of the iteratorExpression.

The iterate operation works as follows. The resultVariable is initialized to some value by the initializationExpression. The iterate operation then executes the iteratorExpression for each member of aCollection in turn, using the iteratorVariable and the current value of the resultVariable. The result of evaluating iteratorExpression becomes the new value of resultVariable that will be used when iteratorExpression executes on the next element of the collection. The value of the iterate(...) operation is the final value of the resultVariable.

It's easy to see from a simple example how the iterate operation works.

```
Bag{ 1, 2, 3, 4, 5 }–>iterate( number : Integer;
                 sum : Integer = 0 |
                 sum + number
             )
```

This expression evaluates to the sum of the numbers in the Bag. In this case, it evaluates to 15. This is exactly equivalent to

```
Bag{ 1, 2, 3, 4, 5 }–>sum()
```

The iterate operation is the most general iterator, and it can be used to simulate all of the others. Here is an example that selects all of the positive numbers from a Set.

```
Set{ –2, –3, 1, 2 }–>iterate( number : Integer;
        positiveNumbers : Set(Integer) = Set{} |       – – initialize to the empty Set
        if number >= 0 then                            – – skip negative numbers
            positiveNumbers–>including( number )  – – append number to the result Set
        else
            positiveNumbers                            – – just return the resultVariable itself
        endif
    )
```

This is exactly equivalent to

Set{ −2, −3, 1, 2 }−>select(number : Integer | number >= 0)

25.9   OCL navigation

> Navigation is the ability to get from a source object to one or more target objects.

Navigation is the process whereby you follow links from a source object to one or more target objects.

Navigation is possibly the most complex and difficult area of OCL. Yet in order to write an OCL expression, you have to know how to navigate from the expression context to other model elements that you need to refer to. This means that you must use OCL as a navigation language.

OCL navigation expressions can refer to any of the following:

- classifiers;
- attributes;
- association ends;
- query operations (these are operations that have the property isQuery set to true).

In the OCL specification [OCL1] these are called *properties*.

In the next section we look at simple navigation within the contextual instance, and then in the following section at navigation across relationships of multiplicity 1 and greater than 1.

25.9.1   Navigation within the contextual instance

Let's look at a simple example of navigation to access features of the contextual instance. Figure 25.9 shows a class A that has a single attribute, a1, and a single operation, op1().

Figure 25.9

Assuming class A is the expression context, you can write the OCL navigation expressions listed in Table 25.15.

Table 25.15

Navigation expression	Semantics
self	The contextual instance – an instance of A
self.a1 a1	The value of attribute a1 of the contextual instance
self.op1() op1()	The result of op1() called on the contextual instance The operation op1() *must* be a query operation

There are several important points to note about this example.

- You access the contextual instance by using the keyword self.
- You access properties of the contextual instance directly or by using self and the dot operator. As a matter of style, we prefer to be explicit and use self and the dot operator.
- The only operations you can access are query operations.

25.9.2 Navigation across associations

Navigation gets a bit more complicated when you navigate across associations. Typically, you can navigate only across associations that are navigable, and you can access only public class features. However, the OCL specification allows an OCL evaluator *optionally* to have the ability to traverse non-navigable associations and access private and protected features. If you are using an OCL evaluator to evaluate OCL expressions, you should check its documentation to see what is supported.

Figure 25.10 shows some navigation expressions across an association between two classes A and B, where the multiplicity at end b is 1.

Example model		Navigation expressions (A is the expression context)	
		Expression	Value
		self	The contextual instance – an instance of A
		self.b	An object of type B
		self.b.b1	The value of attribute B::b1
		self.b.op1()	The result of operation B::op1()

Figure 25.10

Use the dot operator to navigate across associations.

Navigation semantics depend on the multiplicity on the target end of the association.

You navigate across an association end by using the dot operator as if the role name were an attribute of the context class. The navigation expression can return the object (or objects) at the target end, the values of its attributes, and the results of its operations.

Navigation gets more complicated when the multiplicity on the target end of the association is greater than 1. This is because navigation semantics depend on multiplicity.

Figure 25.11 shows some navigation expressions across an association between two classes, C and D, where the multiplicity at end d is many.

Example model		Navigation expressions	
		Expression	Value
		self	The contextual instance – an instance of C
C — d — D		self.d	A Set(D) of objects of type D
c1:String — * — d1:String		self.d.d1	A Bag(String) of the values of attribute D::d1 Shorthand for self.d->collect(d1)
context — op1():String		self.d.op1()	A Bag(String) of the results of operation D::op1() Shorthand for self.d->collect(op1())

Figure 25.11

The navigation expression

self.d

returns a Set(D) of d objects.

This means that the dot operator is overloaded. When the multiplicity on the target end is 1 or 0..1, it returns an object of the same type as the target class. When the multiplicity is greater than 1, it returns a Set instantiated on the target class.

By default, the dot operator returns a Set when multiplicity is > 1.

By default, the dot operator will return a Set of objects when multiplicity is many. However, you can specify the type of collection it returns by using the association end properties listed in Table 25.16.

Table 25.16

OCL collection	Association end properties
Set	{ unordered, unique } – default
OrderedSet	{ ordered, unique }
Bag	{ unordered, nonunique }
Sequence	{ ordered, nonunique }

> Accessing a property of a collection is a shorthand for collect(...).

When you access a property of a collection, for example,

self.d.d1

this is shorthand for

self.d–>collect(d1)

You may remember from Section 25.8.7 that collect(iteratorExpression) returns a Bag containing the results of executing the iteratorExpression for each element in the collection. In this case, it returns the Bag of values of attribute d1 for each D object in the Set(D) obtained by traversing self.d.

Similarly,

self.d.op1()

is shorthand for

self.d–>collect(d.op1())

The result of this expression is a Bag containing the return values of operation op1() applied to each D object in the Set(D) obtained by traversing self.d.

The collect() operation always returns a flattened collection. Should you need to preserve the nesting of the target collection in the returned collection, you must use collectNested().

25.9.3   Navigation across multiple associations

In this section we look at navigation across two or more associations.

In principle, it's possible to navigate across any number of associations. In practice, you minimize the amount of navigation and limit it to two associations at most. This is because long navigation expressions are error-prone and can be difficult to understand. They also make your OCL expressions quite verbose.

Let's look at a simple example of navigation across two associations (see Figure 25.12).

> Navigation beyond a relationship end of multiplicity > 1 returns a Bag.

You can see that navigation beyond the end of an association with multiplicity greater than 1 always results in a Bag. This is because it is equivalent to applying collect(...). For example, the expression

self.k.l.l1

is equivalent to

self.k–>collect(l)–>collect(l1)

In a similar way, you can extend navigation across more than two associations, but we don't recommend this.

Example model						Navigation expressions	
						Expression	Value
						self	The contextual instance – an instance of A
A	b	B	c	C		self.b	An object of type B
a1:String	1	b1:String	1	c1:String		self.b.b1	The value of attribute B::b1
context						self.b.c	An object of type C
						self.b.c.c1	The value of attribute C::c1
						self	The contextual instance – an instance of D
D	e	E	f	F		self.e	An object of type E
d1:String	1	e1:String	*	f1:String		self.e.e1	The value of attribute E::e1
context						self.e.f	A Set(F) of objects of type F
						self.e.f.f1	A Bag(String) of values of attribute F::f1
						self	The contextual instance – an instance of G
G	h	H	i	I		self.h	A Set(H) of objects of type H
g1:String	*	h1:String	1	i1:String		self.h.h1	A Bag(String) of values of attribute H::h1
context						self.h.i	A Bag(I) of objects of type I
						self.h.i.i1	A Bag(String) of values of attribute I::i1
						self	The contextual instance – an instance of J
J	k	K	l	L		self.k	A Set(K) of objects of type K
j1:String	*	k1:String	*	l1:String		self.k.k1	A Bag(String) of values of attribute K::k1
context						self.k.l	A Bag(L) of objects of type L
						self.k.l.l1	A Bag(String) of values of attribute L::l1

Figure 25.12

25.10 Types of OCL expression in detail

We introduced the different types of OCL expressions in Section 25.7. Now that we have covered OCL syntax, we can look at each of them in detail. We use the simple model in Figure 25.13 as an example.

25.10.1 inv:

An invariant is something that must be true for all instances of its context classifier.

Consider the simple bank account model in Figure 25.13. There are four business rules about CheckingAccounts and DepositAccounts.

1. No account shall be overdrawn by more than $1000.

2. CheckingAccounts have an overdraft facility. The account shall not be overdrawn to an amount greater than its overdraft limit.

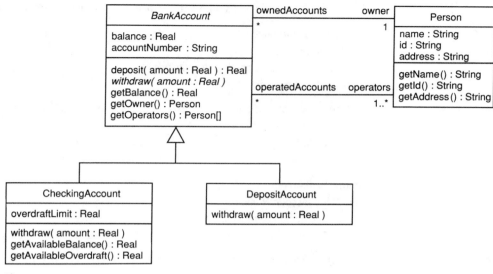

Figure 25.13

3. DepositAccounts shall never be overdrawn.

4. Each accountNumber shall be unique.

We can express the first rule, no account can be overdrawn by more than $1000, as an invariant on the *BankAccount* class because it must be true for all instances of *BankAccount* (i.e., all instances of its subclasses).

```
context BankAccount
  inv balanceValue:
    – – a BankAccount shall have a balance > –1000.0
    self.balance >= (–1000.0)
```

This invariant is inherited by the two subclasses, CheckingAccount and DepositAccount. These subclasses can *strengthen* this invariant but can never *weaken* it. This is to preserve the substitutability principle (see Section 10.2).

> A subclass can strengthen a superclass invariant but can't weaken it.

Rules 1 and 2 may be expressed as invariants on the CheckingAccount class:

```
context CheckingAccount
  inv balanceValue:
    – – a CheckingAccount shall not be overdrawn by more than its overdraft limit
    self.balance >= (–overdraftLimit)
  inv maximumOverdraftLimit:
    – – a CheckingAccount shall not be overdrawn by more than 1000.0
    self.overdraftLimit <= 1000.0
```

Rule 3 may be expressed as an invariant on the DepositAccount class:

context DepositAccount
  inv balanceValue:
    − − DepositAccounts shall have a balance of zero or more
    self.balance >= 0.0

Notice how both of these subclasses have strengthened the BankAccount::balance class invariant by overriding it.

You can express the constraint that each account must have a unique accountNumber as an invariant on the *BankAccount* class:

context BankAccount
  inv uniqueAccountNumber:
    − − each BankAccount shall have a unique accountNumber
    BankAccount::allInstances()−>isUnique(account | account.accountNumber)

In Figure 25.13, you can see that each *BankAccount* has exactly one owner and one or more operators. The owner is the Person who owns the account, and the operators are other People who have the right to withdraw money and access the account details. There is a business constraint that the owner must also be an operator. You can capture this constraint as follows:

context BankAccount
  inv ownerIsOperator:
    − − the owner of the BankAccount shall be one of its operators
    self.operators−>includes(self.owner)

We can write the following constraint on Person:

context Person
  inv ownedAccountsSubsetOfOperatedAccounts:
    − − a Person's ownedAccounts shall be a subset of a Person's operatedAccounts
    self.operatedAccounts−>includesAll(self.ownedAccounts)

When comparing objects of the same type in OCL expressions, you need to be aware that they may be

- identical – each object refers to the same region of memory (they have identical object references);

- equivalent – each object has the same set of attribute values but different object references.

In the OCL expressions above, we are always careful to compare objects on the basis of object identity or equivalence as appropriate. You need to be careful about this. For example, comparing *BankAccount* objects (comparison based on identity) is *not* the same as comparing the accountNumbers of those objects (comparison based on equivalence).

25.10.2   pre:, post:, and @pre

pre: and post: apply to operations.

Preconditions and postconditions apply to operations. Their contextual instance is an instance of the classifier to which the operations belong.

- Preconditions state things that must be true *before* an operation executes.
- Postconditions state things that must be true *after* an operation executes.

Refer to our simple *BankAccount* example in Figure 25.13 and consider the deposit(...) operation that both CheckingAccount and DepositAccount inherit from *BankAccount*. There are two business rules.

1. The amount to be deposited shall be greater than zero.
2. After the operation executes, the amount shall have been added to the balance.

You can express these rules concisely and accurately in preconditions and postconditions on the BankAccount::deposit(...) operation as follows:

```
context BankAccount::deposit( amount : Real ) : Real
  pre amountToDepositGreaterThanZero:
    - - the amount to be deposited shall be greater than zero
    amount > 0


  post depositSucceeded:
    - - the final balance shall be the original balance plus the amount
    self.balance = self.balance@pre + amount
```

The precondition amountToDepositGreaterThanZero must be true before the operation can execute. It ensures that

- deposits of zero amount can't be made;
- deposits of negative amounts can't be made.

The postcondition depositSucceeded must be true after the operation has executed. It states that the original balance (balance@pre) is incremented by amount to give the final balance.

attributeName@pre refers to its value *before* the operation executes.

Notice the use of the @pre keyword. This keyword can be used *only* within postconditions. The balance attribute has one value before the operation executes and another value after the operation executes. The expression balance@pre refers to the value of balance *before* the operation executes. You often find that you need to refer to the original value of something in a postcondition.

For completeness, here are the constraints on the BankAccount::withdraw(...) operation.

```
context BankAccount::withdraw( amount : Real )
  pre amountToWithdrawGreaterThanZero:
    – – the amount to withdraw shall be greater than zero
    amount > 0


  post withdrawalSucceeded:
    – – the final balance is the original balance minus the amount
    self.balance = self.balance@pre – amount
```

Before leaving preconditions and postconditions, we have to consider inheritance. When an operation is redefined by a subclass, it gets the preconditions and postconditions of the operation it redefines. It can only change these conditions as follows.

● The redefined operation may only *weaken* the precondition.

● The redefined operation may only *strengthen* the postcondition.

These constraints ensure that the substitutability principle (Section 10.2) is preserved.

25.10.3 body:

You can use OCL to specify the result of a query operation. All of the getXXX() operations in our simple *BankAccount* model (Figure 25.13) are query operations:

```
BankAccount::getBalance() : Real
BankAccount::getOwner() : Person
BankAccount::getOperators() : Set( Person )
CheckingAccount::getAvailableBalance() : Real
CheckingAccount::getAvailableOverdraft() : Real
```

The OCL expressions for the *BankAccount* query operations are trivial, and in fact you usually wouldn't bother writing them. They are shown below by way of example:

```
context BankAccount::getBalance() : Real
  body:
    self.balance
```

```
context BankAccount::getOwner() : Person
  body:
    self.owner
```

```
context BankAccount::getOperators() : Set(Person)
  body:
    self.operators
```

The CheckingAccount query operations are more interesting:

```
context CheckingAccount::getAvailableBalance() : Real
  body:
    -- you can withdraw an amount up to your overdraft limit
    self.balance + self.overdraftLimit
```

```
context CheckingAccount::getAvailableOverdraft() : Real
  body:
    if self.balance >= o then
      -- the full overdraft facility is available
      self.overdraftLimit
    else
      -- you have used up part of the overdraft facility
      self.balance + self.overdraftLimit
    endif
```

You can see that in these two query operations, OCL specifies how to calculate the result of the operation. The return value of the operation is the result of evaluating the OCL expression.

25.10.4   init:

You can use OCL to set the initial value of attributes. For example:

```
context BankAccount::balance
  init:
    o
```

You typically only use this feature of OCL when initialization is complex. Simple initializations (like the one above) are best placed directly in the attribute compartment of the class.

25.10.5   def:

OCL lets you add attributes and operations to a classifier with the stereotype «OclHelper». They can only be used in OCL expressions. The added attributes def: lets you define variables and helper operations on a classifier for use in other OCL expressions.

are known in OCL as variables, and they are used much like variables in other programming languages. The added operations are called helper operations because they are used to "help out" in OCL expressions.

Use variables and helper operations to simplify OCL expressions.

Let's look at an example. Consider these constraints that we defined earlier:

```
context CheckingAccount::getAvailableBalance() : Real
  body:
    -- you can withdraw an amount to take your account down to your overdraft limit
    balance + overdraftLimit
```

```
context CheckingAccount::getAvailableOverdraft() : Real
  body:
    if balance >= 0 then
      -- the full overdraft facility is available
      overdraftLimit
    else
      -- you have used up part of the overdraft facility
      balance + overdraftLimit
    endif
```

You can see that balance + overdraftLimit occurs in two expressions. It therefore makes sense to define this once as a variable, availableOverdraft, that can be reused by both expressions. You use the def: statement to do this.

```
context CheckingAccount
  def:
    availableBalance = balance + overdraftLimit
```

You can then rewrite the two constraints using this variable:

```
context CheckingAccount::getAvailableBalance() : Real
  body:
    -- you can withdraw an amount to take your account down to your overdraft limit
    availableBalance
```

```
context CheckingAccount::getAvailableOverdraft() : Real
  body:
    if balance >= 0 then
      -- the full overdraft facility is available
      overdraftLimit
    else
      -- you have used up part of the overdraft facility
      availableBalance
    endif
```

You can also define helper operations. For example, a useful helper operation for use in OCL expressions might be one that checks if a withdrawal is possible. You could define this as follows:

```
context CheckingAccount
  def:
    canWithdraw( amount : Real ) : Boolean = ( (availableBalance – amount ) >= 0 )
```

25.10.6   **let** expressions

Whereas def: lets you define variables for use in the scope of the expression context, let allows you to define a variable that is limited to the scope of a particular OCL expression. These variables are like local variables in conventional programming languages, and you use them in pretty much the same way—to capture a calculated value that you need to use more than once in the expression.

The let expression has two parts, let and in.

```
let <variableName>:<variableType> = <letExpression> in
  <usingExpression>
```

The first part assigns the value of <letExpression> to <variableName>. The second part defines <usingExpression>. This is the OCL expression in which the variable is in scope and can be used.

In our simple bank account example, there isn't really anywhere that we *need* to use a let expression. However, for illustration, consider this example in which we have defined a variable called originalBalance, local to the constraint withdrawalSucceeded.

```
context BankAccount::withdraw( amount : Real )
  post withdrawalSucceeded:
    let originalBalance : Real = self.balance@pre in
      – – the final balance is the original balance minus the amount
      self.balance = originalBalance – amount
```

25.10.7   **derive:**

You can use OCL to specify values for derived attributes.

For example, we can refactor our simple bank account example so that the available balance and the available overdraft are expressed as derived attributes, as shown in Figure 25.14.

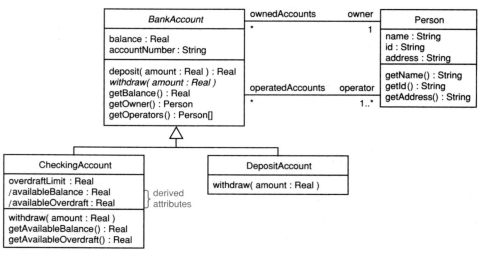

Figure 25.14

The derivation rules for these derived attributes can be expressed as follows:

context CheckingAccount::availableBalance : Real
  derive:
    −− you can withdraw an amount up to your overdraft limit
    balance + overDraftLimit

context CheckingAccount::availableOverdraft : Real
  derive:
    if balance >= 0 then
      −− the full overdraft facility is available
      overdraftLimit
    else
      −− you have used part of the overdraft facility
      overdraftLimit + balance
    endif

This simplifies the definitions of the CheckingAccount::getAvailableBalance() and CheckingAccount::getAvailableOverdraft() operations as follows:

context CheckingAccount::getAvailableBalance() : Real
  body:
    availableBalance

context CheckingAccount::getAvailableOverdraft() : Real
  body:
    availableOverdraft

25.11   OCL in other types of diagrams

Up to now, we have just considered use of OCL in class diagrams. However, you can also apply OCL to other types of diagrams such as the following:

- interaction diagrams (see Chapter 12);
- activity diagrams (see Chapters 14 and 15);
- state machines (see Chapters 21 and 22).

We look at how OCL is used in these types of diagrams over the next few sections.

25.11.1   OCL in interaction diagrams

You use OCL in interaction diagrams to express constraints. It's worth bearing in mind that you *can't* express behavior with OCL, as the language has no side effects.

You can use OCL in an interaction diagram anywhere you need to do the following:

- specify a guard condition;
- specify a selector for a lifeline (see Section 12.6);
- specify message parameters.

Let's look at an example of using OCL in sequence diagrams. Figure 25.15 shows the class diagram for a simple e-mail system.

The EmailAddress class represents an e-mail address. For example, the e-mail address jim@umlandtheunifiedprocess.com would be represented as an object of the EmailAddress class as shown in Figure 25.16. In this case, the operation EmailAddress:getName() returns "Jim", EmailAddress::getDomain() returns "umlandtheunifiedprocess.com", and EmailAddress::getAddress() returns "jim@umland-theunifiedprocess.com". EmailAddress objects are equivalent if their address attributes have the same value.

This system has a white list/black list policy for dealing with unsolicited mail.

- All mail whose fromAddress is in the blackList is deleted.
- All mail whose fromAddress is in the whiteList is filed in the inBox.
- All other mail is filed in the reviewBox.
- The state of the Message changes according to whether it is spam (it is deleted), Legitimate, or Unclassified.

Figure 25.17 shows a sequence diagram for the MailSystem::classifyMessage(m : Message) operation. We present the activity diagram for this operation in the

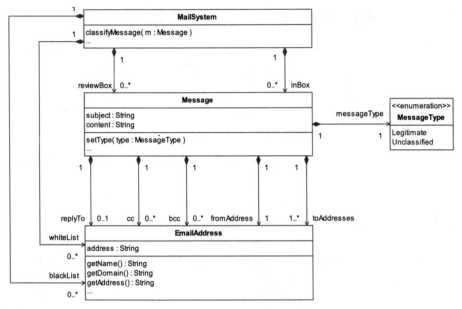

Figure 25.15

Figure 25.16

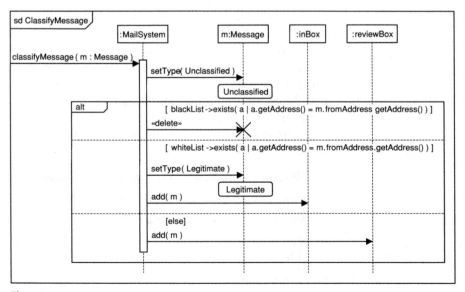

Figure 25.17

next section in Figure 25.18, and you should be able to see how the two diagrams fit together. The sequence diagram specifies what classes and operations realize the behavior described by the activity diagram.

MailSystem is the expression context, and we have used OCL to specify the conditions in the alt combined fragment.

We have also used OCL to specify object state on the diagram (although this is a trivial use of OCL as the OCL and UML syntax for states is the same).

25.11.2   OCL in activity diagrams

You can add activity diagrams to any UML modeling element to specify its behavior. Use OCL in activity diagrams to specify the following:

- call action nodes;
- guard conditions on transitions;
- object nodes;
- object state.

For example, Figure 25.18 shows a very simple activity diagram for the ClassifyMailMessage behavior of the e-mail system that we described in the previous section.

You can see that we have used OCL to specify objects, object state, and conditions.

OCL is about precise modeling, and activity diagrams are, by their very nature, sometimes imprecise. Also, activity diagrams are often shown to non-technical stakeholders. It's therefore questionable how useful OCL is with this type of diagram. For example, the constraints in Figure 25.18 could have been expressed just as clearly in plain English. When you consider using OCL in activity diagrams, always think about the purpose of the diagram and its audience.

25.11.3   OCL in state machines

OCL is used in state machines to specify the following:

- guard conditions;
- conditions on states;

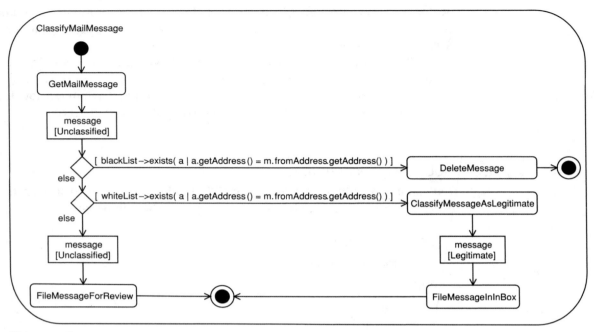

Figure 25.18

- the targets of actions;
- operations;
- parameter values.

The contextual instance is an instance of the classifier that owns the state machine. As an example, consider the CheckingAccountActive state machine for the CheckingAccount class in Figure 25.19.

You can see from the figure that we have used OCL syntax on the diagram in the guard conditions. To make the state machine work, we also need the following constraints, which we have recorded separately to keep the diagram free of clutter.

```
context CheckingAccount::balance
   int:
   o


context CheckingAccount
   inv:
     oclInState( InCredit ) implies ( balance >= o )
```

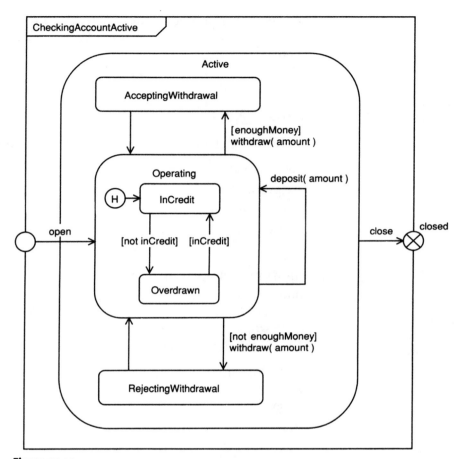

Figure 25.19

inv:
  oclInState(Overdrawn) implies (balance < 0)

def:
  availableBalance = (balance + overdraftLimit)

def:
  enoughMoney = ((availableBalance – amount) >= 0)

def:
  inCredit = (balance >= 0)

Notice how we refer to the InCredit state, using oclInState(InCredit). Alternatively, you could attach the invariant (balance >= 0) directly to the InCredit state as a note.

25.12   Advanced topics

In this section we look at some aspects of OCL that you won't often use:

- navigation to and from association classes;
- navigation through qualified associations;
- inherited associations;
- OCLMessage.

25.12.1   Navigation to and from association classes

> Use the association class name to navigate to an association class.

We discuss association classes in Section 9.4.5. You can navigate *to* an association class by using the association class name. For example, consider Figure 25.20.

You can express the query operation getJobs() as follows:

```
context Person::getJobs() : Set(Job)
  body:
    self.Job
```

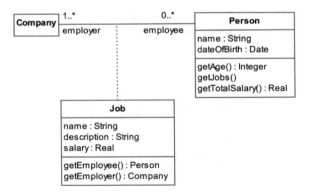

Figure 25.20

The expression self.Job returns the Set of all Job objects associated with a given Person object. You can use this Set in OCL expressions. Suppose a business rule states that a Person can't have two Jobs with the same name. You can express this in OCL as follows:

```
context Person
  inv:
    – – a person can't have the same Job more than once
    self.Job–>isUnique( j : Job | j.name )
```

Suppose the Company operates a wind-down-to-retirement scheme and there is a business rule that a Person over 60 can't have more than one Job. You can express this in OCL as follows:

```
context Person
  inv:
    – – people over 60 can only have one Job
    (self.getAge( ) > 60) implies (self.Job–>count( ) = 1)
```

To get the total salary of a Person, you need to add up the salary for each Job:

```
context Person::getTotalSalary() : Real
  body:
    – – return the total salary for all Jobs
    self.Job.salary–>sum()
```

You can easily navigate *from* an association class by using the rolenames on the relationship as usual. For example, here is the OCL for the getEmployee() and getEmployer() operations of Job.

```
context Job::getEmployee() : Person
  body:
    self.employee
```

```
context Job::getEmployer() : Company
  body:
    self.employer
```

25.12.2   Navigation through qualified associations

To navigate a qualified association, place the qualifiers in square brackets after the rolename.

We discuss qualified associations in Section 9.4.6. To navigate across a qualified association, simply place the qualifier (or a comma-delimited list of qualifiers) in square brackets after the rolename.

Figure 25.21 shows a simple model of a club in which membership can be at a particular level. Suppose there is a business rule that the member ID

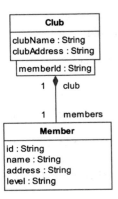

Figure 25.21

of 00001 is always reserved for the club chairman. This can be expressed in OCL as follows:

```
context Club
   inv:
      – – the Chairman always has member id 00001
      self.members['00001'].level = 'Chairman'
```

You can see how we have used the qualified association with a specific value for the qualifier to select a single object from the self.members Set.

25.12.3   Inherited associations

Consider the model in Figure 25.22. This is adapted from [Arlow 1] and shows a model for units of measurement and systems of units.

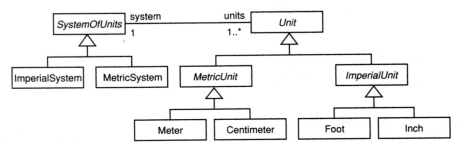

Figure 25.22

There are two different types of *Unit*, *MetricUnits* and *ImperialUnits*. *MetricUnits* belong to the MetricSystem and *ImperialUnits* belong to the ImperialSystem. However, the UML model as it stands *doesn't* say this—in fact, it says that any *Unit* can belong to any *SystemOfUnits*. You can make the model more precise by subclassing the relationship between *SystemOfUnits* and *Unit* as shown in Figure 25.23.

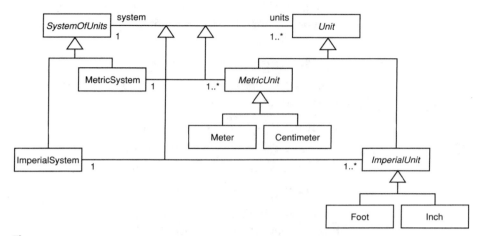

Figure 25.23

This solves the problem but makes the diagram look a bit untidy, and things get rapidly out of hand as the number of *Unit* and *SystemOfUnits* subclasses increases.

A neater way to solve the problem is to define OCL constraints as follows:

```
context MetricUnit
  inv:
    – – belongs to the Metric system
    self.system.oclIsTypeOf( MetricSystem )
```

```
context ImperialUnit
  inv:
    – – belongs to the Imperial system
    self.system.oclIsTypeOf( ImperialSystem )
```

```
context MetricSystem
  inv:
    – – all units must be of kind MetricUnit or one of its subclasses
    self.units–>forAll( unit | unit.oclIsKindOf( MetricUnit ) )
```

```
context ImperialSystem
  inv:
    – – all units must be of kind ImperialUnit or one of its subclasses
    self.units–>forAll( unit | unit.oclIsKindOf( ImperialUnit ) )
```

Notice how we have used the OCL expressions oclIsKindOf(...) and oclIsTypeOf(...).

- oclIsKindOf(...) returns true if the type of the object is the same as the type specified by the parameter *or* one of its subclasses.
- oclIsTypeOf(...) returns true if the type of the object is *exactly* the same as the type specified by the parameter.

25.12.4   OclMessage

OCL message expressions can only be used within postconditions. They allow you to do the following:

OCL message expressions can only be used within postconditions.

- ensure that a message has been sent;
- ensure that a message has returned;
- get the return value of a message;
- return a collection of messages sent to an object.

In OCL every operation call or signal send is an instance of OclMessage. This has the set of operations listed in Table 25.17.

There are also two operators that apply to messages. These are explained in Table 25.18.

Table 25.17

OclMessage operation	Semantics
aMessage.isOperationCall() : Boolean	Returns true if the message represents the calling of an operation
aMessage.isSignalSent() : Boolean	Returns true if the message represents the sending of a signal
aMessage.hasReturned() : Boolean	Returns true if the message was an operation call that returned a value
aMessage.result() : T	Returns the result of the called operation T represents the return type of the operation call

Table 25.18

Message operator	Name	Semantics
anObject^aMessage()	has sent	Returns true if aMessage() was sent to anObject Can only be used in postconditions
anObject^^aMessage()	get messages	Returns the Sequence of aMessage() messages sent to anObject

If the message has parameters, you can use a special syntax with the has sent and get messages operators. This allows you to specify actual parameters or just the types of parameters. The syntax is summarized in Table 25.19.

Table 25.19

has sent with parameters	Semantics
anObject^aMessage(1, 2)	Returns true if aMessage(...) was sent to anObject with parameter values 1 and 2
anObject^aMessage(?:Integer, ?:Integer)	Returns true if aMessage(...) was sent to anObject with parameters of type Integer
get messages with parameters	**Semantics**
anObject^^aMessage(1, 2)	Returns the Sequence of all messages sent to anObject with parameter values 1 and 2
anObject^^aMessage(?:Integer, ?:Integer)	Returns the Sequence of all messages sent to anObject with parameters of type Integer

To investigate messages in OCL, we use the Observer pattern that is fully described in [Gamma 1]. A simple instantiation of this pattern is shown in Figure 25.24. The semantics of the Observer pattern are straightforward—Subject has a set of zero or more Observers. When the Subject changes, its notify() operation is called, and this in turn calls the update() operation of each Observer attached to it. A typical use of this pattern might be to update a screen when an underlying business object changes.

Figure 25.24

The semantics of the Subject operations are summarized in Table 25.20.

Table 25.20

Subject operation	Semantics
attach(o : Observer)	Attaches an Observer object
detach(o : Observer)	Detaches an Observer object
notify()	Calls the update() operation on each Observer – this is called when the Subject changes and wishes to notify the Observers of that change

Let's look at possible postconditions on Subject operations that might involve messages.

According to Table 25.20, a postcondition on Subject::notify() is that the Observer::update() has been called for each of the attached Observers. You can express this in OCL as follows:

```
context Subject::notify()
  post:
    -- each observer shall have been notified by calling update()
    self.observers.forAll( observer | observer^update() )
```

In this postcondition we iterate over the Set of observers and check that each one received an update() message. The ^ operator is the "has sent" operator. It returns true if the specified message was sent by the operation. It can only be used in postconditions.

When the message is synchronous (you know it will return), you can check the message return value:

```
context Subject::notify()
  post:
    -- the return value of update() shall be true for each observer
    self.observers.forAll( observer |
                    observer^update().hasReturned() implies
                    observer^update().result()
                    )
```

25.13   What we have learned

In this introduction to OCL, you have learned the following:

- OCL is a standard extension to UML. It can:
  — specify queries;
  — specify constraints;
  — specify the body of query operations;
  — specify business rules at modeling time.
- OCL is *not* an action language for UML. It can't:
  — change the value of a model element;
  — specify the body of an operation (other than query operations);
  — execute operations (other than query operations);
  — specify business rules dynamically.

- OCL expressions.
  - — Consist of:
    - – a package context (optional) – defines the namespace for the OCL expression;
    - – an expression context (mandatory) – defines the contextual instance for the expression;
    - – one or more expressions.
  - — You can define the expression context explicitly or by putting the OCL expression in a note and attaching it to a model element.
- Contextual instance – an exemplar instance of the expression context:
  - — write OCL expressions in terms of the contextual instance.
- Types of OCL expression.
  - — inv: – invariant:
    - – applies to classifiers;
    - – contextual instance – an instance of the classifier;
    - – the invariant must be true for all instances of the classifier.
  - — pre: – operation precondition:
    - – applies to operations;
    - – contextual instance – an instance of the classifier that owns the operation;
    - – the precondition must be true before the operation executes.
  - — post: – operation postcondition:
    - – applies to operations;
    - – contextual instance – an instance of the classifier that owns the operation;
    - – the postcondition must be true after the operation executes;
    - – the keyword result refers to the result of the operation;
    - – feature@pre returns the value of feature before the operation executed:
      - – can only use @pre in postconditions;
    - – OclMessage can only be used in postconditions.
  - — body: – define a query operation body:
    - – applies to query operations;
    - – contextual instance – an instance of the classifier that owns the operation.
  - — init: – set an initial value:
    - – applies to attributes or association ends;
    - – contextual instance – the attribute or association end.
  - — def: – add attributes and operations to a classifier with the stereotype «OclHelper»:
    - – applies to a classifier;

- contextual instance – an instance of the classifier;
- adds attributes and operations to a classifier with the stereotype «OclHelper»:
  - can only use these in OCL expressions.
- let – define a local variable:
  - applies to an OCL expression;
  - the contextual instance of the OCL expression.
- derive: – define a derived value:
  - applies to attributes or association ends;
  - contextual instance – an instance of the classifier that owns the operation.

- Comments:
  - /* multiple line */
  - – – single line

- Precedence:
  - ::
  - @pre
  - .
  - ->
  - not – ^ ^^
  - * /
  - + –
  - if then else endif
  - > < <= >=
  - = <>
  - and or xor
  - implies

- The OCL type system.
  - OclAny:
    - the supertype of all OCL types and types from the UML model.
  - OclType:
    - OclAny subclass;
    - an enumeration of all types in the associated UML model.
  - OclState:
    - OclAny subclass;
    - an enumeration of all the states in the associated UML model.
  - OclVoid:
    - the "null" type in OCL – it has a single instance called OclUndefined.
  - OclMessage – use to:
    - ensure that a message has been sent;
    - ensure that a message has returned;

- get the return value of a message;
- return a collection of messages sent to an object.
— OCL primitive types:
  - Boolean;
  - Integer;
  - Real;
  - String.
— Tuples – a structured type:
  - Tuple { partName1:partType1 = value1, partName2:partType2 = value2, ... }

● Infix operators – to add these to UML types, simply define an operation with the appropriate signature, e.g., =(parameter) : Boolean.

● Collections:
  — Set – { unordered, unique } (the default)
  — OrderedSet – { ordered, unique }
  — Bag – { unordered, nonunique }
  — Sequence – { ordered, nonunique }

● Collection operations must be invoked with –>.

● Iteration operations:
  — aCollection–><iteratorOperation>(<iteratorVariable>:<Type> | <iteratorExpression>);
  — <iteratorVariable> and <Type> are optional.

● Navigation within the contextual instance:
  — self – accesses the contextual instance;
  — dot operator – accesses features of the contextual instance.

● Navigation across associations:
  — self – accesses the contextual instance;
  — role name – refers to an object or set of objects at the end of the association;
  — dot operator – is overloaded:
    - self.roleName:
      - multiplicity 1 – accesses the object at the end of the association;
      - multiplicity > 1 – accesses the collection at the end of the association;
    - self.roleName.feature:
      - multiplicity 1 – returns the value of the feature;
      - multiplicity > 1 – returns the Bag of values of the feature for all participating objects (shorthand for self.roleName->collect(feature)).

● Navigation across multiple associations, where *any* multiplicity > 1:
  — self.roleName1.roleName2.feature – returns the Bag of all values of the feature for participating objects.

- OCL in interaction diagrams – use to specify:
  - a guard condition;
  - a selector for a lifeline;
  - message parameters.
- OCL in activity diagrams – use to specify:
  - call action nodes;
  - guard conditions on transitions;
  - object nodes;
  - operations;
  - object state.
- OCL in state machines – use to specify:
  - guard conditions;
  - conditions on states;
  - the targets of actions;
  - operations;
  - parameter values.
- Navigation to and from association classes:
  - to – use association class name;
  - from – use role names.
- Navigation through qualified associations:
  - place comma-delimited list of qualifiers in square brackets after the role name.
- Inherited associations:
  - use OCL expressions to constrain the types of participants in inherited associations.

Appendix **1**
Example use case model

A1.1 Introduction

Our experience is that UML models are antagonistic to paper. If you've ever printed out a large UML model, including specifications, you'll know precisely what we mean! UML models are best viewed in a flexible, hypertext medium. At this time, this means either a modeling tool or a website.

Including a complete UML worked example in this book would have made it considerably thicker and more expensive. We would also have been responsible for a lot more dead trees. We have therefore decided to provide the UML worked example for this book on our website (www.umlandtheunifiedprocess .com). We think you will find it much easier to navigate online than on paper.

In the example we walk through the OO analysis and design activities required to create a small web-based e-commerce application. We present a few simplified highlights of the use case model in this appendix to give you a taste of what is available on the site!

A1.2 Use case model

The use case model is for a simple e-commerce system that sells books and CDs. The system is called the ECP (E-Commerce Platform). Figure A1.1 shows the final result of use case modeling.

The use case model will give you a fair idea of what this system does, but please refer to the website for more details and background.

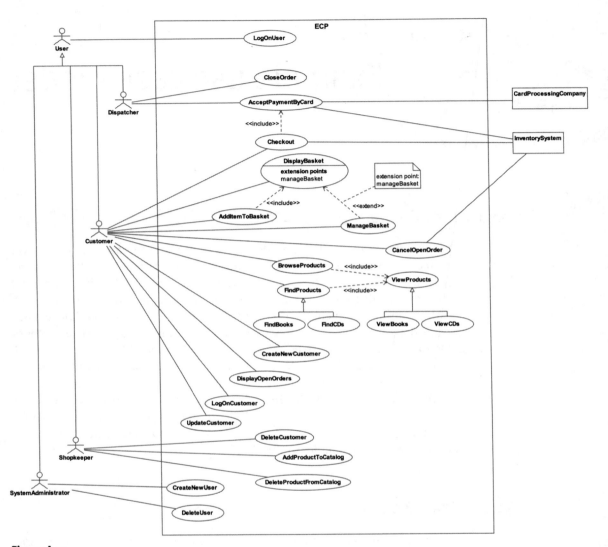

Figure A1.1

A1.3   Example use cases

We look at a subset of the use case model—see Figure A1.2. This subset shows normal use cases, an extending use case, and «include» and «extend» relationships.

The use cases in Figure A1.2 are detailed in Figures A1.3 to A1.6.

In the use case specifications we have included all of the important use case detail but have omitted general document information (such as company branding, author information, version information, and other attributes). These things tend to be company specific, and many companies have standard headers that are applied to all documents.

Although the use case specification may be stored directly in a UML modeling tool, support for it is often quite weak, being limited to plain text. For this reason, many modelers save the use case specification in a richer document format, such as Word or XML, and link to these external documents from the use case model in the modeling tool. See Appendix 2 for some ideas about using XML to record use case specifications.

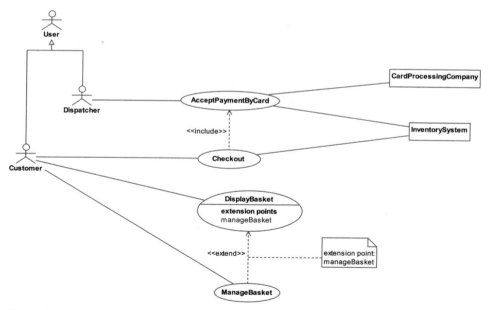

Figure A1.2

Use case: Checkout
ID: 6
Brief description: The Customer checks out. The system creates an order based on the contents of the shopping basket, and the Customer pays the order.
Primary actors: Customer
Secondary actors: InventorySystem
Preconditions: 1. The Customer is logged on to the system.
Main flow: 1. The use case begins when the Customer selects "checkout". 2. The system asks the Inventory actor to provisionally reserve the items in the shopping basket. 3. For each item that is out of stock   3.1 The system informs the Customer that the item is currently unavailable and it is removed from the order. 4. The system presents the final order to the Customer. The order includes an order line for each product that shows the product identifier, the product name, the quantity, the unit price, the total price for that quantity. The order also includes the shipping address and credit card details of the Customer and the total cost of the order including tax and postage and packing. 5. The system asks the Customer to accept or decline the order. 6. The Customer accepts the order. 7. include(AcceptPaymentByCard)
Postconditions: 1. The Customer has accepted the order. 2. The ordered items have been reserved by the Inventory actor.
Alternative flows: None.

Figure A1.3

Use case: AcceptPaymentByCard
ID: 1
Brief description: The Customer makes payment for an order by credit card.
Primary actors: Customer
Secondary actors: CardProcessingCompany InventorySystem Dispatcher
Preconditions: 1. The Customer is logged on to the system. 2. Some inventory items have been provisionally reserved for the Customer.

Main flow:
1. The use case begins when the Customer accepts the order.
2. The system retrieves the Customer's credit card details.
3. The system sends a message to the CardProcessingCompany that
     includes merchant identifier, merchant authentication, name on card,
     number of card, expiry date of card, amount of transaction.
4. The CardProcessingCompany authorizes the transaction.
5. The system notifies the Customer that the card transaction has been
     accepted.
6. The system gives the Customer an order reference number for
     tracking the order.
7. The system tells the InventorySystem to reserve the required items.
8. The system sends the order to the Dispatcher.
9. The system changes the order's state to pending.
10. The system displays an order confirmation that the Customer may
     print out.

Postconditions: 1. The order status has been set to pending. 2. The Customer's credit card has been debited by the appropriate amount. 3. Some inventory items have been reserved to cover the order. 4. The order has been sent to the Dispatcher.
Alternative flows: CreditLimitExceeded BadCard CreditCardPaymentSystemDown

Figure A1.4

Use case: DisplayBasket
ID: 13
Brief description: The system displays the contents of the Customer's shopping basket.
Primary actors: Customer
Secondary actors: None.
Preconditions: None.

Main flow:
 	
1. The Customer selects "display basket".
2. If there are no items in the basket
    2.1 The system tells the Customer that the basket is empty.
    2.2 The use case terminates.
3. For each product in the basket
    3.1 The system displays the product id, quantity, details, unit price, and total
       price.
extension point: manageBasket

Postconditions: None.
Alternative flows: None.

Figure A1.5

Extension use case: ManageBasket
ID: 20
Brief description: The Customer changes the contents of the shopping basket.
Primary actors: Customer
Secondary actors: None.
Preconditions: 1. The system is displaying the shopping basket.

Main flow:
 	
1. While the Customer is updating the basket
    1.1 The Customer selects an item in the basket.
    1.2 If the Customer selects "remove item"
        1.2.1 The system displays the message "Are you sure you want to remove
               the selected item from your basket?".
        1.2.2 The Customer confirms the removal.
        1.2.3 The system removes the selected item from the basket.
    1.3 If the Customer enters a new quantity for the selected item
        1.3.1 The system updates the quantity for the selected item.

Postconditions: None.
Alternative flows: None.

Figure A1.6

Appendix 2

XML and use cases

A2.1 Using XML for use case templates

As you have seen, UML 2 does not define a formal standard for documenting use cases. Modelers either have to use the often rather limited facilities offered by UML modeling tools or define their own approach. The most common approach at the moment seems to be to create the use case model in a modeling tool, then link the use cases and actors to external documents that contain their detailed specifications. These documents are usually created on a word processor. However, a word processor isn't the best tool for this; although it allows you to format and structure the use case and actor specifications, it does not allow you to capture the semantics of that structure.

We believe that structured XML documents are the natural format for use case specifications. XML is a semantic markup language, so it separates the semantic structure of the document from its formatting. Once you have a use case or actor specification captured as an XML document, you can transform it in many different ways by using XSL [Kay 1]. You can render specifications as HTML, PDF, or word processor documents, and you can also query the specifications to extract specific information.

The structure of XML documents may be described with the XML Schema Definition Language (XSL). We present some simple XML schema for actors and use cases on our website. They are available to download and use under the GNU General Public License (see www.gnu.org for details).

Detailed descriptions of XML and XSL are beyond the scope of both this book and our website. However, on the site we provide useful links to XML and XSL learning resources.

Because XML requires special editors and can be complex for stakeholders to use, we have recently devised a simple approach to creating use cases (and other project documents) in XML and other formats. We discuss this briefly in the next section.

A2.2 SUMR

SUMR (pronounced "summer") stands for Simple Use case Markup–Restructured. It is a simple plain text markup language for use cases. SUMR documents can be easily transformed into XML, HTML, and other formats.

SUMR has a number of advantages.

- It is *very* simple—you can learn the markup syntax in about a minute.

- It does not require fancy word processors or editing features—you can create SUMR documents using any text editor that supports plain text and you can enter SUMR text straight into an HTML form field if you need to.

- It is structured—SUMR documents have a schema. You can create your own schema or use the default ones we supply.

- It is free under the GNU copyleft (www.gnu.org/copyleft).

To give you a flavor of what SUMR is all about, Figure A2.1 shows a simple use case tagged up as a SUMR document.

The syntax is simple—anything prefixed and postfixed by a colon (like :this:) is a tag. The body of the tag starts on the next line after the tag and continues until the next blank line.

SUMR is entirely concerned with the structure and semantics of the document, *not* how it is displayed. It allows you to capture relevant information quickly and efficiently, without having to bother about formatting, document templates, or complex tag languages.

Each SUMR document may have a schema defined in the special :schema: tag. A SUMR schema is a SUMR document that defines the tags that can be used in other SUMR documents. Figure A2.2 shows the SUMR schema used by our example use case. As you can see, SUMR schemas can be self-documenting provided they are well written.

Once you have a schema, you can use SUMR tools to do the following:

- transform use cases that accord to the schema into XML;

- generate sample XSL stylesheets to transform the XML into
   — XHTML plus a Cascading Style Sheet (CSS);
   — XML-FO (XML formatting objects).

The SUMR tools generate default stylesheets for you. This is a useful feature as you only have to customize the stylesheets, rather than write them from scratch. It is also a very flexible approach, as the stylesheets give you almost complete control over how the SUMR documents will be rendered.

file AddItemToBasket.uc

```
:schema:
UseCase.sss

:name:
AddItemToBasket

:id:
2

:parents:
1. None

:primaryActors:
1. Customer

:secondaryActors:
1. None

:brief:
1. The Customer adds an item to their shopping basket.

:pre:
1. The Customer is browsing products.

:flow:
1. The Customer selects a product
2. The Customer selects "add item".
3. The system adds the item to the Customer's shopping basket.
4. :inc:DisplayBasket

:post:
1. A product has been added to the Customer's basket.
2. The contents of the basket are displayed.

:alt:
1. None

:req:
1. None
```

Figure A2.1

file UseCase.sss

```
:schema:
UseCase.sss

:name:
Write the name of the use case here. Use case names are in UpperCamelCase with
no spaces.

:id:
Write the unique project identifier for the use case here.

:parents:
Write the names of the parent use cases here.
If this use case has no parents, write None here.

:primaryActors:
Write the names of the primary actors here.
There must be at least one primary actor.

:secondaryActors:
List the names of the secondary actors here.
Secondary actors participate in the use case, they do not start the use case.
If there are no secondary actors, write None here.

:brief:
Write a brief description of your use case here. This description should be no
more than a couple of paragraphs.

:pre:
Write the preconditions here, one on each line.
If the use case has no preconditions, write None here.

:flow:
Write the main flow here.
Each step should be time-ordered and declarative.
:ext:WriteExtensionPointsLikeThis
Note that extension points are NOT numbered.
If you need to show nested steps
 Indent them by one space for each level of indent like this.
Include other use cases like this :inc:AnotherUseCase.
This is the final step.

:post:
Write the postconditions here, one on each line.
If there are no postconditions, write None here.
```

Figure A2.2

```
:alt:
List the names of the alternative flows here, one on each line.
If there are no alternative flows, write None here.

:req:
List any special requirements related to the use case here. These are
typically non-functional requirements.
If there are no special requirements, write None here.
```

Figure A2.2   Continued

Figure A2.3 shows the example use case from Figure A2.1, transformed into XML by one of the SUMR tools.

Once the use case is in XML format, you can use the generated XSL stylesheets to transform it further. The most flexible option is to transform the XML into XML-FO; you can then use Apache FOP (http://xml.apache.org/fop/index.html) to render this into a wide range of other output formats including PDF and PostScript. Figure A2.4 shows the use case rendered as PDF using the default XML-FO stylesheet generated from the schema. The default style isn't much to look at, but you can customize it as much as you like by editing the generated stylesheet that produces it.

Finally, Figure A2.5 shows a simple structured editor for SUMR documents that we include in the toolset. This can validate a use case or actor against its schema, and has syntax highlighting and autonumbering. It is a perfectly serviceable tool for small-to-medium size use case models.

You can get more information about SUMR, and download the tools and example schemas, from our website (www.umlandtheunifiedprocess.com).

We hope you enjoy using this tool set. We value any feedback that you might send us via our website.

file AddItemToBasket.uc

```xml
<?xml version="1.0" encoding="UTF-8"?>
<UseCase.sss>
   <schemaSection>
      <schema>UseCase.sss</schema>
   </schemaSection>
   <nameSection>
      <name>AddItemToBasket</name>
   </nameSection>
   <idSection>
      <id>2</id>
   </idSection>
   <parentsSection>
      <parents>1. None</parents>
   </parentsSection>
   <primaryActorsSection>
      <primaryActors>1. Customer</primaryActors>
   </primaryActorsSection>
   <secondaryActorsSection>
      <secondaryActors>1. None</secondaryActors>
   </secondaryActorsSection>
   <briefSection>
      <brief>1. The Customer adds an item to their shopping basket.</brief>
   </briefSection>
   <preSection>
      <pre>1. The Customer is browsing products.</pre>
   </preSection>
   <flowSection>
      <flow>1. The Customer selects a product</flow>
      <flow>2. The Customer selects "add item".</flow>
      <flow>3. The system adds the item to the Customer's shopping basket.</flow>
      <flow>4. :inc:DisplayBasket</flow>
   </flowSection>
   <postSection>
      <post>1. A product has been added to the Customer's basket.</post>
      <post>2. The contents of the basket are displayed.</post>
   </postSection>
   <altSection>
      <alt>1. None</alt>
   </altSection>
   <reqSection>
      <req>1. None</req>
   </reqSection>
</UseCase.sss>
```

Figure A2.3

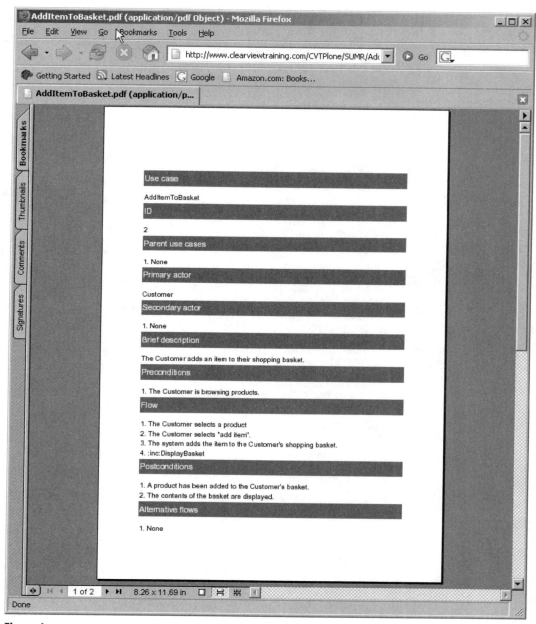

Figure A2.4

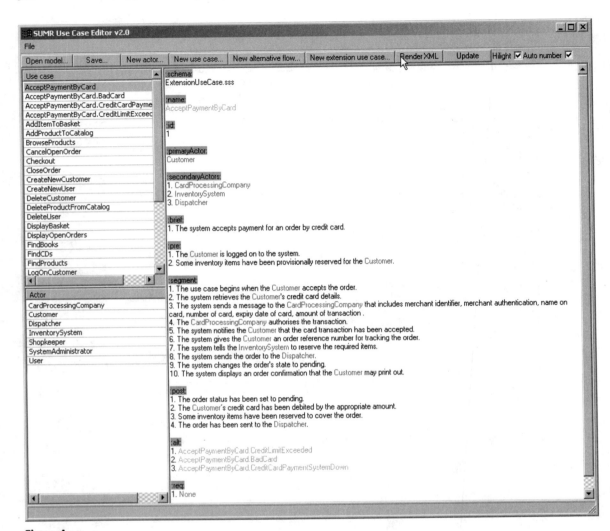

Figure A2.5

Bibliography

[Alexander 1], *Writing Better Requirements*, Ian F. Alexander, Richard Stevens, Ian Alexander, Addison-Wesley, 2002, ISBN 0321131630

[Ambler 1], *The Unified Process Inception Phase*, Scott W. Ambler, Larry L. Constantine, CMP Books, 2000, ISBN 1929629109

[Ambler 2], *The Unified Process Elaboration Phase*, Scott W. Ambler, Larry L. Constantine, Roger Smith, CMP Books, 2000, ISBN 1929629052

[Ambler 3], *The Unified Process Construction Phase*, Scott W. Ambler, Larry L. Constantine, CMP Books, 2000, ISBN 192962901X

[Arlow 1], *Enterprise Patterns and MDA: Building Better Software with Archetype Patterns and UML*, Jim Arlow, Ila Neustadt, Addison-Wesley, 2004, ISBN 032111230X

[Booch 1], *Object Solutions*, Grady Booch, Addison-Wesley, 1995, ISBN 0805305947

[Booch 2], *The Unified Modeling Language User Guide*, Grady Booch, Ivar Jacobson, James Rumbaugh, Addison-Wesley, 1998, ISBN 0201571684

[Chomsky 1], *Syntactic Structures*, Noam Chomsky, Peter Lang Publishing, 1975, ISBN 3110154129

[Frankel 1], *Model Driven Architecture: Applying MDA to Enterprise Computing*, David S. Frankel, John Wiley & Sons, 2003, ISBN 0471319201

[Gamma 1], *Design Patterns*, Erich Gamma, Richard Helm, Ralph Johnson, John Vlissides, Addison-Wesley, 1995, ISBN 0201633612

[Harel 1], *Modeling Reactive Systems with Statecharts: The Statemate Approach*, David Harel, Michal Politi, McGraw Hill, 1998, ISBN 0070262055

[Jacobson 1], *Unified Software Development Process*, Ivar Jacobson, Grady Booch, James Rumbaugh, Addison-Wesley, 1999, ISBN 0201571692

[Kay 1], *XSLT Programmer's Reference*, 2nd Edition, Michael Kay, Wrox Press Inc., 2001, ISBN 1861005067

[Kleppe 1], *MDA Explained: The Model Driven Architecture – Practice and Promise*, Anneke Kleppe, Jos Warmer, Wim Bast, Addison-Wesley, 2001, ISBN 032119442X

[Kroll 1], *The Rational Unified Process Made Easy: A Practitioner's Guide to Rational Unified Process*, Per Kroll, Philippe Kruchten, Grady Booch, Addison-Wesley, 2003, ISBN 0321166094

[Kruchten 1], *The Rational Unified Process, An Introduction*, Philippe Kruchten, Addison-Wesley, 2000, ISBN 0201707101

[Kruchten 2], "The 4+1 View of Architecture", Philippe Kruchten, *IEEE Software*, 12(6) Nov. 1995, pp. 45–50

[Leffingwell 1], *Managing Software Requirements: A Use Case Approach,* 2nd Edition, Dean Leffingwell, Don Widrig, Addison-Wesley, 2003, ISBN 032112247X

[Meyer 1], *Object Oriented Software Construction*, Bertrand Meyer, Prentice Hall, 1997, ISBN 0136291554

[Mellor 1], *Agile MDA*, Stephen J Mellor, *MDA Journal,* June 2004, www.bptrends.com

[OCL1], *Unified Modeling Language: OCL, version 2.0*, www.omg.org

[Pitts 1], *XML Black Book,* 2nd Edition, Natalie Pitts, Coriolis Group, 2000, ISBN 1576107833

[Rumbaugh 1], *The Unified Modeling Language Reference Manual,* 2nd Edition, James Rumbaugh, Ivar Jacobson, Grady Booch, Addison-Wesley, 2004, ISBN 0321245628

[Standish 1], *The CHAOS Report (1994)*, The Standish Group, www.standishgroup.com/sample_research/chaos_1994_1.php

[UML2S], *Unified Modeling Language: Superstructure, version 2.0*, www.omg.org

[Warmer 1], *The Object Constraint Language: Getting Your Models Ready for MDA*, Jos Warmer, Anneke Kleppe, Addison-Wesley, 2003, ISBN 0321179366

Index

Enterprise Patterns and MDA,
Also from Jim Arlow and Ila Neustadt,
Is the Perfect Companion to *UML 2*
and the Unified Process.

Enterprise Patterns and MDA
Jim Arlow and Ila Neustadt
ISBN: 0-321-11230-X

Enterprise Patterns and MDA will help you learn object modeling by example. The book provides a set of reusable UML models (archetype patterns) covering key domains found in virtually every business. It provides the following patterns:

- Party—how to model people and organizations
- PartyRelationship—how to model relationships between people and organizations
- CRM—a simple customer relationship management model
- Product—how to model products and services
- Inventory—how to model inventory of goods or services
- Order—how to model order processing and management
- Quantity—how to model quantities of things
- Money—how to model money and currency
- Rule—how to model business rules

The book also discusses:

- The theory behind archetype patterns
- How to document UML models effectively using Literate Modeling
- How to incorporate archetype patterns in your own systems
- How to use archetype patterns with MDA